UNEMPLOYED ST

G000128657

H

UNEMPLOYED STRUGGLES
1919-1936

My Life and Struggles
Amongst the Unemployed

WAL HANNINGTON

With a new Introduction by
Will Paynter

With forty-two Illustrations

LAWRENCE AND WISHART LIMITED

CONTENTS

INTRODUCTION
TO THE 1977 REPRINT

by WILL PAYNTER
General Secretary of the National Union of Mineworkers,
1959–1968

As one who was active in the unemployed workers' movement between 1931 and 1939, I welcome this new edition of *Unemployed Struggles*, and congratulate the publishers on their enterprise. Unemployment has again become a serious social problem and it is important that the Labour and Trade Union movement of today should be aware of the struggles waged on the same issue in the recent past. No-one is better qualified than Wal Hannington to place on record the turbulent history of the inter-war years. His name during the period was synonymous with unemployed struggles. His book, in my view, is the most authoritative document on unemployment and the fight waged against it covering the two decades from 1919 to 1939. In the immediate post-war years he suffered periods of unemployment himself and from 1920 onwards he was the outstanding and acknowledged leader, organiser and inspiration of the unemployed throughout Great Britain. Through his efforts the National Unemployed Workers Movement was formed, which was the main, and in many places the only, organisation of the unemployed, agitating and organising campaigns in support of the demand for work or full maintenance, as well as giving service in advising and representing the unemployed at the Labour Exchanges, the Courts of Referees and before Commissioners.

Walter Hannington was born on 17th June 1896, in Randall Street, Camden Town, into a large family of brothers and sisters. His father was a bricklayer, but Wal did not follow into his father's trade. From the age of fourteen he served his apprenticeship as a tool-maker and was highly skilled in this craft. He married in 1917, his wife, Winnie, standing by him through the hard times of persecution and imprisonment, into the somewhat better times of later years. There was one daughter of the marriage which had endured for almost fifty years when he tragically died from a heart attack in November 1966. During World War I, he was engaged on highly important work as a tool-maker and for this reason was exempted from military service. He was an active member of the Trade Union and of the early Socialist movement right from his teens, and later became a lifelong member of the Communist Party.

In the Introduction to the original edition, Tom Mann wrote, 'unemployment is a condemnation of society; there is no national necessity for anyone to be short of life's essentials.' The unemployed were then short of life's essentials just as they are today, and now as then are compelled to fight for work or full maintenance. The difference, however, is that today the Trade Unions as a whole lead and support the demand, so that employed and unemployed are united in common cause.

Throughout the inter-war years unemployment did not fall below the million mark, the figure that now causes general concern, the difference being its relation to the total insured population. Today the insured population is around ten million more than then. Very frequently, and for long periods, the numbers rose to above two million, and within this number there was a hard core of unemployed in the older industrial communities. In fact the areas of heavy unemployment now are the same; they were called 'distressed areas' then but now they are 'development regions', new words to cover a continuous condition. The reason for the condition is the same too, the contraction of the older industries and the failure to anticipate and plan to meet the social consequences. Unemployment is degrading and demoralising. It is not only a denial of the right to work, it is a denial of the right to human dignity and self-respect. I can recall my first visits to the desolate and distressed areas at the head of the mining valleys of Monmouthshire and Glamorganshire and being apalled at the visual evidence of dereliction and misery. And my standards of judgement were far from high, being unemployed myself and used to the grim prospect of the Rhondda valleys. The scene was of chronic poverty and human degradation in a setting of slum housing, drab terraced streets that had been hurriedly thrown up on the mountain slopes to house those who generations before had provided the labour for the old blast furnaces and early pits. In this environment, shabbily dressed men and boys were idling on street corners or sitting on convenient dry walls; men who when employed washed and shaved and dressed neatly before coming to the streets, but now unshaven, in mufflers and untidy, a miserable testimonial to the demoralising effect of being out of work. They were scenes not unique to South Wales, but common throughout the distressed areas of the country.

Unemployment benefit was barely enough for a minimum level of subsistence. Twenty-six shillings a week for man and wife with a few shillings extra for each child, and this reduced in 1931 by ten per cent. My father and I were both unemployed when the Means Test was introduced later that year and the total benefit we received to support a family of three adults was 27/6d. a week, because of a rent concession to my father for reading a water meter under the front room floor each morning! Even accepting the higher value of money then, this was acute poverty and was the common lot of all unemployed. It will be said that the unemployed today are treated more generously and this may be so, but in relation to modern wealth production and the capacity of society to produce 'life's essentials', there is little relative improvement.

The Regulations governing the payment of benefit were applied with severity. The 'not genuinely seeking work' condition was used to badger men to tramp the region looking for that which did not exist, vacant jobs. Local leaders of the N.U.W.M. were expert in providing advice and the physical details of managers of the main factories and pits. The effect of the 'means test' affected not only the amount of benefit but placed a levy on the earnings of employed members of a family. The employed member had to contribute to the upkeep of the unemployed member, in the calculation of the families' 'means' and their 'needs'.

In the pages of the book the struggles against these measures is vividly told. Leaders of the unemployed movement were harrassed and persecuted by the police, in fact it is safe to say that most local and national leaders saw the inside of a police court and a prison cell, and this is certainly true in the case of Wal Hannington. Demonstrations and Hunger Marches were met with violence far greater than anything seen in recent years. Hunger marchers when they reached London were virtually marching within a police box, with a policeman alongside each rank and in front and behind the column. But the response from the towns and villages through which the Marchers passed was tremendous, thousands lining the streets, the reception committees having worked for weeks previously to accommodate and feed the marching men. I know of no greater thrill than to march past the Marble Arch into Hyde Park, through a sea of cheering people, a narrow lane being kept by a long line of policemen with linked arms, through which we marched like a company of well disciplined soldiers in a Workers Army.

The last Hunger March took place after *Unemployed Struggles* was written, and as with all previous marches Wal Hannington was the national leader. Contingents came from all parts of the country, arriving in London around 7th November 1936. The aim was to bring pressure on Parliament, to abolish the 'means test' and for work for the unemployed. The build-up to this final March saw the biggest mobilisation of people on the streets for many generations. I recall a demonstration in the Rhondda on Sunday, 26th July, when the press estimate was a hundred thousand marching men, women and children. The chapels and churches closed their services to take part. Similar demonstrations were taking place all over the country. It was a period of unity of the left. Aneurin Bevan, Harry Pollitt, Stafford Cripps, and others were campaigning in a Popular Front movement. In South Wales the co-ordinating committee for the campaign and the March included Labour, Communist, Union and church representatives, and the end result was the biggest march ever. There was little difficulty with the police and the reception by Parliament was far less hostile. During a similar march in 1932, getting to Parliament involved a running fight with the police in London streets; the earlier Hyde Park meeting was surrounded by bitter fights with the police. I was arrested and gaoled until bailed out by Wal Hannington in the early hours of the following morning. But on this occasion, supported by a united and broadly-based movement, the reception was different. On this occasion not only did marchers lobby Parliament, but the National leaders were for the first time allowed to put their own case directly to the Minister of Labour and his staff. One of the results was a new set of Regulations for the Assistance Boards, which alleviated but did not remove real hardship.

The lessons to be learned from this March and the struggles recorded in this book are clear. They are: one, that unemployment is a scourge to be fought and eliminated; two, that action must involve the unity of employed and unemployed; three, that the Trade Unions must initiate and maintain pressure for work or full maintenance; and four, that unity of the left in the Labour and Trade Union movement is the guarantee of success.

The Second World War brought a period of full employment, and Wal Hannington returned to his trade as a tool-maker. An active member of the Amalgamated Engineering Union, it was not long before he was elected to full-time Union Office in the London district, work at which he continued until retirement.

INTRODUCTION
By TOM MANN

AS one who has been closely identified with the unemployed movement for many years, I gladly welcome this book by Wal Hannington. I am confident it will be appreciated by all who have been associated with the movement, as well as by those who read it in order to understand the nature and the effects of the struggle put up by the workless on their own behalf.

To say the author is to be congratulated upon the astonishing amount of information he supplies, and the vivid way in which it is presented, is altogether inadequate. His detailed account of each of the many struggles brings out admirably the courage and capacity displayed by leaders and rank and file; and their remarkable tact, resourcefulness, and expert organizing ability.

Naturally, my mind goes back to earlier struggles among the unemployed in the eighties of last century. I have a vivid recollection of the agitation in the year 1886, exactly fifty years ago. The unemployed were active in that year of depression, and the Social Democratic Federation, to which I belonged, helped in organizing many demonstrations in London and the provinces.

In October, 1886, many meetings were held. The unemployed were demanding assistance, and in order to bring the matter before the public and the authorities it was decided to organise a march of unemployed on 9th November, and it was arranged that the unemployed should follow the Lord Mayor's procession. Sir Charles Warren, chief superintendent of the metropolitan police, having seen the handbills of the S.D.F. calling on the unemployed to march, issued posters in prominent places forbidding any march on the route of the Lord Mayor's procession. The committee in charge issued in reply bills stating "as Trafalgar Square is not on the line of route we call on you to attend in your thousands in Trafalgar Square on Lord Mayor's Day."

The superintendent thereupon issued more large posters again forbidding marchers to follow the Mayor's procession, and adding in large type "NOR IN TRAFALGAR SQUARE." The excitement was great and crowds were exceptional as the time for the official procession drew nigh; police were stationed around the Square two deep on the National Gallery side.

The men's committee had decided to appoint some of their number (including John—afterwards Colonel—Ward) to attempt to get through the police cordon, while others (including myself) were in readiness to break through into the Square and make for the plinth of Nelson's Column, as speakers. The attempt to get through resulted in Ward's arrest, but gave the chance for others of us to get through the police ranks and on to the plinth, while thousands swarmed into the Square and held a very successful demonstration. I have been in close relationship with the unemployed agitation ever since.

The following year, 1887, I was living in Newcastle-on-Tyne, where the percentage of unemployed was exceptionally high. After holding many meetings of workless and formulating a programme of demands on the local town council, we arranged to attend the cathedral church of St. Nicholas in an orderly way, but in large numbers. We had been learning a suitable song for marching, to the tune of "Onward, Christian Soldiers!" written by a Socialist parson.

On the Sunday morning I was addressing a large meeting of unemployed prior to marching to church, when I saw the chief superintendent of police and the mayor (Sir Benjamin Brown) come along and stand listening. Ignoring their presence I proceeded to arrange the procession for starting, when the mayor approached, saying, "Are you going to church?" I replied, "Yes, Mr. Mayor," and he inquired, "May I come with you?" "With pleasure, Mr. Mayor." The mayor walked by my side into church and sat through the service with the unemployed.

No disorder took place, and the same week at the town council meeting the mayor heartily supported some of the proposals we had made for the council's consideration. One of these, which was adopted, was the planting of trees around the Town Moor to give work for some and to beautify the town.

Since that time the dole has come into being, with fluctuations in amounts and conditions, and the National Unemployed Workers' Movement has been formed, has developed, and has been continuously active. This book of Wal Hannington shows how essential it has been and will continue to be until the trade union and labour forces show a disposition and determination to take up the matter of unemployment and its solution as a vital part of their work.

It is a lamentable fact that many of the employed are utterly indifferent to the hardships of those not in work; this I believe, is less true than it was, and will become rapidly less so, at least amongst the more intelligent. As workers, we still have much to learn, and the rapidly changing conditions of the capitalist system must stimulate thought and action in learning how to change effectively the basis of society. Unemployment is a condemnation of society; there is no natural necessity for anybody to be short of life's essentials. Therefore, whilst we must deal with the most urgent things first, and take action to remove the human suffering arising from the shortage of necessities (demanding and getting at least the scale drafted by the N.U.W.M.) yet no one who thinks the subject out will rest until the whole system is changed to one of genuine co-operation.

Given co-operative ownership of the means of life, together with the co-operative control of all industry on a basis of social justice, which forbids exploitation, there will be no unemployment and no worry about poverty, which will be entirely abolished.

Meanwhile action of a practical character calculated to overcome the obstacles to advance is called for, and Comrade Wally Hannington has for a good many years been keen to sense the hardships of the unemployed and their dependents. Having himself had many considerable spells of unemployment, he has known by actual deprivation of life's essentials what suffering of this nature means. And he has ever been amongst the first to combat these bad conditions even though in doing so he added seriously to his chances against getting and keeping a job. I personally pay my deepest respects to him for the readiness he has ever shown to head a deputation, to help in organizing and leading a march, and for the kindly comradeship he shows under all circumstances.

Space will not admit of comment on the many times Wal has been in prison for standing up for his class. To read of the intensely interesting struggles that have led to these incarcerations is to be brought into direct contact with the struggles for bread in this day of capitalist civilization. Underlying all this activity is the continuous battling for the standard established by the unions. As far back as 1921 the London District Council of the unemployed declared: "We wish to state most emphatically that in no circumstances will we allow ourselves as unemployed to be used as instruments for blacklegging against the miners or any section of the workers who may strike in sympathy." To this principle they have always been loyal.

The author does not omit to mention and pay tribute to the fine qualities of his colleagues. To one of these I desire to raise my hat in reverence—John McLean of Glasgow—a splendid man and fearless fighter, who literally died for the cause; and another fine Scotsman, yet vigorously active—Harry McShane—a courageous fighter and loyal comrade; with big Peter Kerrigan and a hundred others from the North.

Hannington shows full appreciation of the good work of George Lansbury on many occasions, particularly when he was in charge of the *Daily Herald*. Other stalwarts dealt with include Arthur Horner, now president of the South Wales Miners' Federation, Tom Dingley of Coventry, and Bob Lovell of the A.E.U.—each of whom has rendered great service in the years of agitation.

At the time of writing—September, 1936—another hunger march is being organized on a national scale to resist the operation of Part II of the 1934 Unemployment Act. Let those who wonder whether these marches are of value try and realize the policy pursued by the ruling class in dealing with the unemployed. Until recently the boards of guardians were primarily responsible for administering public relief; and later these duties devolved on the town councils. These bodies being publicly elected, the electors had some choice in the persons elected on a democratic basis, but by the Act of 1934 the administration of assistance is no longer in the hands of a democratically elected body, but of a Minister and Boards not amenable to popular election. In short, all semblance of democracy is taken away and the principle of fascist dictatorship substituted.

The Minister of Labour—Sir Henry Betterton—was made a peer and given a salary of £5,000 a year (roughly £100 a week), with an assistant at £60 a week and a secretary at £35 a week.

The purpose of these changes from democratic to bureaucratic administration is that such experts shall supervise the cutting down of the paltry few shillings received by the unemployed—many of whom do not receive as much in a year as these administrators receive in a week.

Present day society rests upon investments, which means living at the expense of the workers. This is counted as moral, it is approved by religion, endorsed by those who speak of righteousness, of holiness, and yet who help to perpetuate a system based upon legalized ROBBERY. It was to this kind of exploitation that Ruskin referred when he said, "But Occult Theft—theft which hides itself from itself even, and is legal, respectable and cowardly—corrupts the body and soul of man to the last fibre of them." (See *Fors Clavigera, Letters to Workmen*, by John Ruskin, Letter VII.)

The reader will do well to give careful attention to the case of the arrest and imprisonment of Sid Elias for having written a letter addressed to Wal Hannington, but which the latter did not receive through absence from the office. Much use was made of this letter by the police in the trial and a great bogey was made of it by some of the capitalist papers, though it was an ordinary letter dealing with practical details of the march then being organised. Wal Hannington's account of his imprisonment about the same time, on the charge of "attempting to cause disaffection amongst the metropolitan police," will be read with keen interest.

Another point of special note is the arrest and imprisonment of Emrys Llewellyn, at that time the secretary of the N.U.W.M., and of myself—which was not for any offence committed. Sir Chartres Biron, the magistrate at Bow Street, said to us in the dock, "You are not charged with having committed any offence; it is a precautionary measure." When the magistrate called upon us to give an undertaking to keep the peace, I said, "I am not conscious of having broken the peace," and the magistrate replied, "You are not charged with having broken the peace." We both declined to give any undertaking and were each sentenced to two months inside and served it at Brixton Prison.

It is with admiration and pride that one reads this complete account of the doings of the unemployed in Scotland; the workless there are certainly not spineless, nor do they go about in fear and trembling of the authorities; over and over again they have not only demonstrated and marched longer than any other sections to reach London, but have been a splendid stimulus to the workers in or out of work.

Similarly from the mountains and valleys of Wales the victims of a played-out system, many of them compulsorily idle for many consecutive years, have refused to be driven like sheep. They have pluckily faced the situation—and the tramp of the marchers, the fine mass singing of the crowds, and the shouting of the slogans have carried over the hills and spurred them on to noble endeavour.

It is an outrage that time and energy should have to be spent in such fashion, but it would be a hundred times worse if, the necessity being as it is, there was an absence of courage and capacity to organize and face the situation.

We must never forget that whilst the capitalist class remains dominant, on our side as workers there must be pluck and militancy, not quiescence and cowardice. I urge that no time be lost in preparing, on a far larger scale than ever, to show our complete dissatisfaction with a system that enforces worklessness on us and makes possible the disgusting patronage of the plutocracy; if they cannot or will not solve the problem then it is time for the workers to face up to the situation and usher in the better conditions.

Are we to tolerate such a system for ever—class domination so plain tha little thought is necessary to realize its slavish character? I declare for myself that, whilst I realize the special urgency of action now, to relieve the sufferings of the workless and their dependents, I urge that no man can be satisfied until the management of all industry shall be in the hands of the entire community on a basis of social justice free from all exploitation.

This work of Wal Hannington gives a most vivid insight into the daily struggles carried on, showing clearly the results of these struggles and their necessity. The writer has rendered a great service by its production.

October, 1936.   TOM MANN.

Chapter I

THE PRELUDE IN THE WORKSHOPS

PEACE came at last! At eleven o'clock on the morning of 11th November, 1918, the maroons boomed forth the arrival of the armistice. The factory sirens took up the signal and shrieked the glad news. Workers in the factories heralded the peace by beating on the benches with hammers, spanners or other tools of their trade. The union jacks were brought out in their thousands. They were being hoisted on the flag-masts of all buildings and draped from the windows of factories and homes.

The four years of slaughter and suffering had at last come to an end, and the end was the signal for an outburst of joy and patriotic enthusiasm. Were we not the victors in the war? Then bring out your national flags! Give colour to the celebrations of victory and peace!

I was working at the time in a North London engineering firm, and was the elected shop steward on behalf of the men. We had made it a strong trade-union shop. Amongst the fitters and turners were several ardent socialists including myself. We were members of the British Socialist Party and had devoted almost every moment of our spare time, including meal-times in the factory, to an intensive study of Marxian literature. We were also eagerly studying every scrap of available information about the Russian Bolshevik revolution.

We understood the cause of the war. We knew that it was a war in the interests of capitalism, and that the workers of all countries would be the losers unless they followed the example of their Russian fellow-workers by ending the system of capitalism which inevitably created national and international economic conflict and led to war.

We firmly believed that lasting peace could only be secured when the working class had conquered political and economic power and when the world became a federation of socialist republics. Also we knew that nothing had done more to bring an end to the war than the 1917 Russian revolution and the 1918 German revolution—the latter overthrowing the military mon-

1

archy but unfortunately halting half-way by not ending the system of capitalist exploitation.

So when the jubilant clamour arose which announced the armistice, the workers in our factory were as keen as anybody else in expressing their joy and relief. But it was not expressed in a narrow patriotic sense, but in the spirit of international working-class solidarity against the capitalist war-mongers. Working-class slogans were shouted and cheered as the operators shut down their machines, and the men on the benches laid down their files and beat-in the armistice with their hammers.

The newspapers had announced the previous day the arrangements for the armistice, and one of the workers had come to work prepared for the occasion. So a few minutes after 11 o'clock, this worker and I, whose plans had been made known to the other workers and had received their approval, quietly slipped out of our shop and, making our way to the roof of the building, ran up the red flag—the flag of the international working class.

There it floated proudly in the breeze as though hurling defiance at the flags of British capitalism which were being unfurled in their thousands over the city.

The management were blissfully ignorant of what had happened and they were only made aware of it when during the afternoon a crowd of "patriots" began to gather outside the factory. But we had finished work for the day at twelve noon and so the management had to nurse their anger until next morning.

Inquiries were carefully made in an effort to discover who had committed this shameful outrage. But nobody squeaked. Working-class loyalty prevailed. But although the management could extract no incriminating statement from any employee, they nevertheless had a shrewd suspicion, and one of the bosses was heard to remark: "It was that damned shop steward Hannington who organised it."

I should undoubtedly have been sacked on the grounds of suspicion, but for two things—one, that my discharge would have caused a strike, and, second, that I was a highly skilled toolmaker whose services at that time were not easy to replace.

After a time the affair blew over and was seldom referred to. But in 1919 when trade began to slacken and discharging commenced I was amongst the first batch who got sacked.

There was, however, still a demand for skilled workers in my trade and after a short period of unemployment I again found work as a tool-turner in a firm called the Blick in West London.

But after a few months' steady employment this firm completely closed down and I again became unemployed. A number of other jobs followed but were of short duration either because of my trade-union activities in the shop or because of declining trade.

In October 1919 I was going through one of my spells of unemployment when I received a message from Bob Lovell, a fellow-tradesman who knew of my activities in the union and workshop, and who had recently started work at the famous Slough Transport Depot, a government establishment. His message asked me to meet him next meeting night at the Cricklewood branch of the Toolmakers' Society. I kept the appointment and he then told me that he wanted me to apply for a job at the Slough Depot, where over 5,000 were employed, and where he was already carrying on a fight against a reactionary shop stewards' committee. He stated that there were many grievances amongst the workers, but many of the shop stewards were passive and under the domination of the chairman of the works committee, who appeared to be acting more as a representative of the management than of the men.

He said they were wanting more men at the depot and he wanted me to get a job there in order to strengthen the fight for a militant shop stewards' organisation. He had also written to Tom Dingley of Coventry, who was on the National Committee of the Shop Stewards' and Workers' Committee Movement, urging him also to come down for a job.

I was keen to take on the job and the activity, and next morning I got started in the engine-fitting shop. Dingley followed next day in the tool-room. So we were both in, and soon got down to business. We arranged for talks with groups of militant trade unionists in the dinner-hours. We planned our propaganda and lines of agitation. Both Dingley and I were platform speakers and we began a series of dinner-hour lectures at the works, on various subjects relating to trade-union activity and the working-class movement.

The attendances at the meetings grew day by day until they reached the size of mass meetings. We quickly gathered a tremendous support around us and launched our campaign against the weakness of the shop stewards' committee, particularly the reactionary role of the chairman. In less than a month we had caused important changes in the works committee and both Dingley and I were elected as shop stewards in our respective departments.

We succeeded in getting regular weekly meetings of the works committee (shop stewards from every department throughout the works) and we led a fight for a militant policy in respect to numerous grievances which prevailed in a number of departments. So keen did the struggle on policy become that it ultimately took the form of open mass meetings amongst the men, with both sides, the right-wing and the left-wing representatives, stating their case and fighting for support. For over a week this battle of mass meetings raged throughout the various departments. The left wing, which Dingley and I were leading, were fighting not only for action against the management for improved conditions, but also for our works committee to become part of the National Shop Stewards' and Workers' Committee Movement.

As the campaign developed it was clear that the left wing were gaining ground rapidly. Then came the final round of meetings at which the men were to vote for the policy which they supported. The results were a crushing defeat for the right wing. New elections of shop stewards resulted in the militants sweeping the board.

Tom Dingley became convener of the works committee, I became chairman, and Bob Lovell secretary. The management had, of course, been following the course of the battle, and there is no doubt they were seriously alarmed when "the reds," as we were called, won the day.

They had good cause for their alarm, for we were not long in letting them know what a militant works committee meant. Deputations met the management in several departments to demand the remedying of various grievances about conditions of employment. Negotiations failed to bring results, but when the works committee called for strike action from over 5,000 men and every shop struck solid the management soon came down to satisfactory terms.

The first big battle had resulted in victory for the militant policy, and many who had wavered between the left and the right line now became firm supporters of the left. From then onward, whenever grievances arose, if the shop stewards could not settle the trouble by negotiation they had no difficulty in getting strike action in the department affected, with the threat of a works stoppage if the management did not come to terms within a fixed time. The departmental actions invariably won, and it only became necessary on one occasion in the next six months to resort to a complete stoppage.

This arose over the question of rates of pay on certain classes of work. The works were a government concern and the management at Slough said they had no power to negotiate a settlement because they were acting under orders from Whitehall.

The works were situated about twenty miles from London, several miles from any big town, and stood on a mile and a quarter square of ground in the open country on the outskirts of the town of Slough which at that time was not much more than a large village. Most of the workers lived long distances from the works and travelled daily by special trains which ran into a railway siding in the works. They came chiefly from London, Reading, Staines, Guildford and Windsor. From London three special trains ran from Paddington every morning, and returned with the same workers at night.

Accordingly, when strikes took place in the Slough Depot, they were all stay-in strikes. If they were not settled before leaving-off time in the evening the strikers caught their trains as usual back to their homes and returned next morning to the works, entered it in the usual way, but did no work. The men would have "sing-songs," play cards, read books and chat together while waiting for the shop stewards to report the results of their negotiations.

The complete stoppage over wage rates continued into the third day, when the management called in the leaders of the works committee and informed us that the "people in Whitehall" wanted to meet us that afternoon at the Admiralty building to discuss the dispute.

A meeting of the works committee, consisting of about seventy shop stewards, was immediately convened, and a deputation of seven, including the officers of the committee, was elected. To the sound of cheers from the workers we departed to Whitehall to do battle with the "brass hats".

We were received in a well-furnished room by a group of very efficient men. But not all the efficiency was on their side of the table. Before the interview finished they realised that they were dealing with a group of workers' representatives who knew how to state a case and knew how to fight on the finest points. At the end of an hour and a half we came to terms. We had to concede one or two small points, but in the main it was a complete victory. We hastened from the conference room and rushed back to the Slough Depot, arriving there about an hour before the time of departure. A tremendous mass meeting was called in the chassis shop and from a lorry used as a platform we reported our negotiations in Whitehall. The terms of settlement were unanimously endorsed by the men, and that night as an expression of their solidarity they formed up in marching formation and marched in a body to the railway siding and the depot exits. Next morning work was resumed.

News of the events at Slough had spread far and wide. It was a topic of conversation in many trade-union branches and workers' clubs. In the House of Commons a Conservative member one day rose to ask: "What does the Government intend to do about the existence of the Soviets which have been created in the Slough Government Motor Transport Depot?" The answer was: "We are carefully watching the situation."

The depot was handling all the old army lorries that were being returned from the battle-fields, and it was known of course that sooner or later the depot would either be closed or radically changed. It was commonly spoken of as a "white elephant." Politicians argued that it was not a paying concern and agitation in the government circles was directed towards closing it down or selling it to a private concern.

The blow came in April, 1920. Notices were posted up informing the employees that on April 30th the works would close down and that all employees were under a week's notice. We learnt that the works were to be sold to private enterprise and the managers put the story into circulation that certain men would be asked to continue their service with the new company, if their conduct had proved satisfactory.

There were not many men caught by this trick. The bulk of them saw through the move and were not inclined to stick at their job during the week that they were under notice. It was a week of intense activity for the shop stewards, who took advantage of every opportunity to hold meetings of the men and to spread working-class propaganda. The organ of the National Shop Stewards' and Workers' Committee Movement, *Solidarity*, had a big sale in the works, as well as thousands of pamphlets dealing with the working-class movement.

One afternoon the shop stewards were surprised to learn that at the two main exits small huts were being rapidly erected and that a force of police had been brought into the works. We gathered that that evening as the men left a personal search was to be carried out by the police and works officials to ascertain whether the men were taking out property which did not belong to them. The shop stewards and the men indignantly resented this move and its inference, and it was decided to resist any search.

Wide roads ran through the works, and all the employees assembled in marching formation, twelve abreast, to march out. When we reached the main exit a cordon of police stood across our path, but the workers marched on, and as the dense column of marchers came almost breast to breast with the police the cordon sagged and gave way, and with mighty cheers the workers marched out of the gates. A little scuffling took place when the police tried to recover their lost position, but they were hopelessly out-numbered and the temper of the men was such that they ulti-mately gave it up as a bad job. The organised march out from the works was carried out each evening up to the last day.

As the depot had received the name of "white elephant," the works committee decided to make a fitting end to the "elephant" by organising a mock funeral for the day on which the employ-ment terminated. The carpenters, body-builders and upholsterers agreed to make a huge white elephant. There were to be a clergyman and choir boys in their surplices, the workers were to be the mourners, and pall-bearers were appointed to carry the body of the elephant. The funeral was to start at 9 o'clock in the morning on the last day of employment. Before leaving the works the night previous we saw the elephant completed. It was a splendid piece of work—real craftsmanship had been put into it. It almost seemed a pity to have to bury such a fine specimen. It was carefully covered with a tarpaulin in the body-building department to await the return of the workers next morning. But next day, when we arrived in the works, to our horror and dismay we found that the elephant had disappeared!

The police who had been brought into the works, in conjunc-tion with the management, had evidently decided to put a stop to the mock funeral by a premature cremation! We were not sure that that was the end of the elephant, for no traces of its end were left; it had simply disappeared.

The choir boys were all dressed up in their surplices, the clergyman was ready with his bible, the pall-bearers were bracing themselves for their strenuous task, and the jazz band with its instruments were ready to play the Dead March in *Saul*—but the body had vanished!

We were determined not to be beaten and we decided that another elephant should be quickly constructed. The start of the funeral was postponed until 11.30. The new elephant appeared on time, and the funeral with its 5,000 mourners moved slowly down the roads of the works towards the big space in front of the main offices. The clergyman mounted a dais, the choir boys with their candlesticks gathered at his feet, and the congregation formed a huge semi-circle. The grave-diggers were ordered to dig the grave; it measured twelve feet long by twelve feet wide. The clergyman read the funeral oration—it was an oration over the body of capitalism, ending with a call for the workers of the world to unite to end the system which had created the "white elephant."

The assembled mass of workers were then solemnly called upon to uncover. They had caught the spirit of the thing and they all obeyed. Then just as the elephant was being lowered into the grave the clergyman noticed that the managers and foremen and other members of the staff who were assembled on the big flat roof of the offices were looking down on the scene and had not removed their hats.

He stopped the ceremony and pointed to the roof of the building. A shout went up from the mourners demanding that "respect" be shown by the managers and foremen as well as by the men. The crowd began to move towards the offices; quickly the group on top of the building removed their headgear, and the ceremonies were continued. The grave-diggers shovelled the earth into the grave and the great mock funeral ended by all singing the "Red Flag"—the workers' battle-hymn. The rest of the day was spent in improvised concerts and general merry-making. The numerous red flags which had been used in the funeral were jealously guarded and carried home as souvenirs.

Many small flags hung from the windows of the trains as they steamed for the last time out of the Slough Depot. On the door of the carriage in which I was sitting with other shop stewards, one of the wags just before the train departed, had chalked in big letters: "Slough Soviet makes its last journey."

Next day was May Day. The banners which were carried in the Slough funeral were brought to the Thames Embankment and the Slough workers gathered behind their banner and marched with the rest of the workers to Hyde Park.

After the closing of Slough Depot, I found extreme difficulty in obtaining employment. It is a common belief among engineering workers that the Engineering Employers' Federation have a black list of militant workers which they circulate to their members. I had what appeared to be evidence of this when on more than one occasion, after interviewing a foreman for a job and being told to start next morning, I found on arriving at the firm that for some unexplained reason there was either no job, that the whole thing had been a mistake, or that somebody else had been started.

I well remember on one occasion going in search of work with a fellow trade-unionist by the name of Berridge. We went to a big firm at Hendon, having heard that turners were being taken on at this firm. They had their own labour-recruiting office with a labour superintendent who carried out all enquiries before men were started. Applicants had to fill in a long questionnaire, stating their former places of employment, their qualifications, rates of wages, age, and a host of other matters. The form was filled up in an outer office and then passed through a sliding-window to the inner office, and the applicants in turn would then be called in by the labour superintendent. I was called in first. The superintendent greeted me with a smirky grin on his face. He said, "I see you are applying for a job as a turner?" I answered "Yes," and he replied that he was sorry but the firm were not needing turners now. I bade him good day and left.

The next to go in was Berridge. I waited outside the firm for nearly a quarter of an hour. I wondered why he was so long because I knew he also had applied for a job as a turner. When he came out, to my surprise, he told me that he was starting next morning as a turner. It was pretty clear proof that I was on the black list.

My unemployment continued for some time, until one day a member of my trade union, who was a foreman in a factory at Hendon, asked me if I would like to start with him as a fitter. I said I was anxious to do so because I was beginning to experience domestic difficulties through unemployment. He gave me a start and I decided that I would lie quiet until I had recovered a bit from unemployment. But the first week that I was in the shop I was being pressed by the men to take on the position of shop steward. I succeeded, however, in convincing them that it would be unwise at such an early stage before I had got my footing in the firm. Several weeks went by, and one day the fitter's mate who was working with me called my attention to a notice that was being posted up in the works announcing that a speaker from the Economic League would be coming to address the employees at a dinner-hour meeting on the question of the "importance of increased production."

At this period the big campaign for increased production was under weigh. Several national trade-union leaders were associated with the campaign. Huge posters with their photographs adorned the hoardings in the streets, with such slogans as "The gate to more is to produce more." As a socialist I knew that under capitalism this was all bunk, and when the announcement was made that a lecture was to be given on the subject to the employees at the firm where I was working, I was indignant. My mate asked me if I was going to the meeting. I said "No." I felt sure that if I did go I should not be able to sit quietly and listen to the lecture without challenging the speaker, I could ill afford to again become unemployed, I was already feeling the pinch of poverty, but, try as I would to keep away from the meeting, when the time came I found myself moving towards the meeting-place with the rest.

I said to myself, "Keep quiet; be a listener." I succeeded in doing so until towards the end of the lecture when, to my astonishment, the speaker said: "Even Lenin, the Bolshevik leader in Russia, is urging the workers to increase production!" This was more than I could bear, I jumped to my feet and pointed out that to urge increased production in a state where the workers are in power is an entirely different thing from urging increased production under capitalism. I demanded a debate with the speaker; the crowd supported the challenge; and there and then arrangements were made for the debate to take place a fortnight later.

When the day arrived, the whole of the workers, about one thousand in all, were keen to hear the "fireworks" as they called it. I had little difficulty in riddling the case of my opponent, so much so that the workers would not listen to his last reply, and somebody jumped on to the platform and struck up the "Red Flag" on the piano. The crowd took it up lustily. The speaker then approached me and whilst the crowd was buzzing with excitement and discussing the pros and cons of the case in small groups he congratulated me upon the way in which I had put my case, and then said that at one time he had been a socialist, but had found that what he was doing now paid him much better. He threw out the suggestion that I could also become a lecturer for his organisation with a salary of £8 per week plus organisational expenses, and that if I cared to consider it he would put in a word for me.

I listened with boiling indignation, then turned to the crowd and shouted for order, and announced to the workers the infamous suggestion which had been made to me by this person to "sell out." They stormed round the platform and it was only with extreme difficulty that my antagonist succeeded in reaching the gates of the works safely.

The debate was the talk of the works, but a fortnight later, on pay day, I found in my pay envelope a little notice to the effect that owing to the reduction of staff my services were no longer required. In order not to make my discharge too openly evident of victimisation the management had handed discharges to a number of other workers also, but I later learnt that several of these workers were sent for the following week and re-started.

From that time I began a long period of unemployment. Like thousands of others I found, try as I would, it was impossible to obtain work, for we had entered the period of post-war trade depression, with a constant army of unemployed exceeding in numbers anything that had ever been known before in the history of this country. From that time to the present my political life and activity have been centred around the economic problem of unemployment.

It has been a period of intense and exciting struggle, the outstanding events of which this book seeks to record as part of the great history of the British working class.

Chapter II

UNEMPLOYMENT

COMPULSORY insurance against unemployment was introduced in this country for certain sections of the industrial
workers by the National Insurance Act of 1911. The trades
covered by the Act at that time were limited to building construction works, ship-building, mechanical engineering, ironfounding,
construction of vehicles, and sand-milling, embracing in all about
two and a half million workers. In 1916 the government, no
doubt anticipating unemployment following the war, extended
the scheme to include all munition workers. This brought the
total number of insured workers at the end of 1916 up to nearly
four million. In 1920 the government was again compelled to
widen the basis of insurance by an Act which repealed the 1911
and 1916 Acts and embraced all manual workers with certain
exceptions and non-manual workers earning not more than
£250 a year. This brought the total number of insured persons
up to approximately twelve million.

From the end of 1919 unemployment had been rapidly rising
until in the autumn of 1920 it reached nearly two million. The
majority of these were men recently demobilised from the armed
forces and those who had been connected with the war industries.

Masses of ex-service men who had suffered the horrors of four
years of war were now to taste the bitter fruits of peace in the
form of unemployment and poverty in their homes. Lloyd
George was still the prime minister. During the war he had
coined many tricky phrases which had been popularised as slogans
to induce a war-weary nation to continue its sacrifices. The
soldiers dying on the battlefields had been told that their sacrifices
were not in vain, that they were "fighting for democracy" that
they were "building a new heaven and a new earth," that they
were making "a land fit for heroes to live in," that it would be
a "land flowing with milk and honey."

These phrases lingered on long after the war, but the events
were belying the promises. They rang like bitter mockery in the
ears of the men who had come from the bloody battlefields only

12

to be cast on to the industrial scrap-heap of capitalism and to see increasing privation for themselves and their families.

The disillusionment produced an angry mood amongst the workers which was expressed in protest meetings and other activities all over the country. The Lloyd George government became alarmed; in the rush of demobilisation many men had gone home with their war kit, including their weapons; many still possessed their rifles. The government called for the return of these weapons and, when the response was not up to expectations, they made a special monetary offer of £1 to every man who returned his rifle.

The government had anticipated mass unemployment following the war, and on 25th November, 1918, parliament, realising that there would be anger and resentment unless some provision was made, passed a Bill to pay a "donation" benefit to all unemployed, ex-servicemen and civilians, insured and non-insured, amounting to 29s. a week to men and 25s. to women, plus 6s. for the first dependent child and 3s. for each additional child. This ceased for civilian workers in November 1919, and for ex-service men and women in March 1921.

The threat from the workless also compelled the government to pass a new Unemployment Insurance Act in December 1919, to raise the benefit scales to 11s. a week for all men and women over 18 years of age and 5s. 6d. a week for those unemployed between the ages of 16 and 18. Formerly, from 1911, the benefit scale had stood at only 7s. to insured workers over 18 years of age.

But as the unemployment figures mounted higher so the agitation amongst the unemployed increased. The approach of winter in 1920 saw the first definite forms of organisation amongst the unemployed in many parts of the country. These organisations were of a local character and mostly used the title of "Local Unemployed Ex-service Men's Organisation." In the main they had no clear working-class policy and they appeared to be formed purely for charity-mongering purposes. Demonstrations were organised to march the streets for the sole purpose of begging charity as a means of relieving distress.

In London it was not an uncommon sight to see two separate demonstrations of workless marching past each other in Oxford Street or other parts of the West End, and expressing actual rivalry and opposition, one to another, in scrambling to collect money from the well-to-do shoppers. To take collections on the streets it was necessary to obtain police permits. The police, however, readily granted such permits. They saw the political importance of doing so in more ways than one. They realised that such charity-mongering methods were a safe outlet for the discontent of the unemployed, and were an effective means of keeping the unemployed divided amongst themselves and diverting their attention from the real problem of making the authorities face up to the task of providing adequately for them.

But during the years 1918 to 1920 socialist propaganda had been rapidly winning support amongst the workers. Credit for this was due not only to the revolutionary political parties of the time, particularly the Socialist Labour Party and the British Socialist Party, but also to the National Shop Stewards' and Workers' Committee Movement. This movement played a tremendous part in leading the struggle of the British working class during and immediately following the war. It constituted the recognised leadership of the workers, particularly those connected with the war industries. It initiated and led all their struggles.

This was so because in February 1915, the government, of which Mr. Asquith was prime minister, succeeded in calling a conference of the principal trade-union leaders at which an agreement was made to "call a truce in the class struggle during the war." The trade-union leaders pledged themselves to "fully co-operate with the government for the successful prosecution of the war." By this agreement—known as the Treasury agreement, because the conference was held at the Treasury department—the official trade-union movement found itself bound hand and foot to the war machine and committed to a policy of no strike action for the war period. It was a shameful betrayal of working-class principles and caused wide resentment amongst class-conscious workers. Throughout the war the official leaders of the trade-unions—with one or two honourable exceptions—dropped completely out of the picture so far as giving any leadership in industrial struggles was concerned. On the contrary, they loyally abided by their agreements with the capitalist class and the war government, and used their positions in the trade-unions when disputes broke out to urge the workers to return to work.

In such conditions it was almost inevitable that a rank-and-file movement based upon factory committees should arise. In Scotland, the Clyde Workers' Committee was already a powerful force leading strike action, so much so that Lloyd George, then Minister of Munitions, was compelled to negotiate with it when he visited Glasgow in February, 1915.

After the Treasury conference the workshop committee move-ment was developed in all the chief centres of the war industries, under the name of the National Shop Stewards' and Workers' Committee Movement.   A similar rank-and-file movement developed amongst the miners of South Wales. The movement was not anti-trade-union. It was not set up as an alternative to trade-unionism; on the contrary it became the main driving force for trade-union recruitment in the factories. It became the recognised rank-and-file leadership of the workers in the trade-union branches and at the point of production. It led many successful strikes and became so powerful that in spite of the Treasury agreement the employers were compelled to recognise it and negotiate terms and conditions of employment with it.

Many of the leading militants amongst the shop stewards be-came marked men by the employers and were amongst the first to be sacked when unemployment became widespread. By 1920 there were many who had been active shop stewards and now found themselves in the ranks of the unemployed and recognised the need for organisation of the unemployed, not on charitable lines, but on the basis of a militant working-class policy.

These men could see the futility of the purely local unemployed organisations that had no objective beyond marching the streets begging for charity. Many active trade unionists, themselves unemployed, spurned the idea of association with such bodies, but the ex-shop stewards, especially those who had a socialist understanding, realised that these embryonic unemployed organisa-tions—which, after all, had arisen out of the discontent of the unemployed masses—could be developed on proper working-class lines with a clear policy and could become a mighty force for improvement in the conditions of the unemployed and for protection of working-class standards in general. All they needed was proper guidance and leadership.

There was no organised entry of the ex-shop stewards and militants into these organisations; rather they sought individually an avenue for continuing their activities from the workshop into the field of unemployment because, by their experience, their minds had been trained to think always in terms of organisation wherever the workers had grievances in common with each other.

I joined the local unemployed organisation in St. Pancras, and began the agitation for calling a conference of delegates from similar organisations throughout the London boroughs. At first there was strong opposition to such a proposal by those who lacked any conception of the purpose of organisation beyond that of begging for charity. Many of these had joined the army at an early age, had fought in the war, were demobilised into unemployment, and had therefore had very little connection with industry. They had not had any experience or knowledge of organisation and consequently were not immediately susceptible to the line of policy which I was advocating.

But an event occurred which quickly awakened them and quickened their understanding of their class position. In October 1920, a number of London mayors, led by Mr. George Lansbury, demanded an interview with the prime minister, Mr. Lloyd George, to discuss the alarming increase in unemployment in their boroughs. Demonstrations of the workless marched from all parts of London to give support to the mayors' deputation. They converged on the Thames Embankment in their tens of thousands, and when the mayors proceeded to Downing Street the demonstrators marched along Bridge Street into Whitehall. I was marching at the head of the North London section, which was halted by order of the police at the corner of Downing Street. Other contingents poured in until Whitehall was a dense mass of unemployed workers, many of them wearing their war decorations. The crowd was quite orderly and whilst they were awaiting the return of the mayors there was cheering and singing. Then suddenly mounted and foot police began to charge into the crowd in an effort to clear Whitehall. The density of the crowds behind made it impossible to retreat and we were compelled to fight back at the police or simply stand still and be clubbed down.

A roar of anger rose from the workless as they swayed backwards and forwards, whilst those in the front were struck down by the police. Then as the unemployed began to fight back the police were forced to give ground. With a great rush the unemployed swept forward up Whitehall, breaking through the police formation and scattering them on all sides. But before the demonstrators could reach Trafalgar Square, fresh reinforcements of police were rushed to the top of Whitehall where they commenced batoning the workers down as they tried to escape. The police who wanted to clear Whitehall were now preventing it from being cleared. Dozens of men lay in the roads and on the side-walks groaning with pain as the blood gushed out from wounds inflicted by police batons.

In the midst of the fighting a mounted policeman on a white horse was brought down, and instantly one of the demonstrators, probably an ex-cavalry man—jumped on to the horse's back and began riding down Whitehall. For a second all eyes turned to

the man on the white horse, then the other mounted police began
to charge at him, so he spurred his horse to the gallop, charged
through the police ranks with thousands of workless following.
This unknown hero on the white horse succeeded in getting right
into Downing Street before he was clubbed down.

Eventually the police got control of the situation and the unemployed dispersed to their homes. The mayors had not been
received by Mr. Lloyd George. He apparently was not interested
in hearing about the plight of the workless and had conveniently
left London.

This brutal attack upon the workless in Whitehall caused a
wave of bitter feeling to sweep throughout London and the
provinces. It was the first episode of its kind since the war ended.
It came as a shock to many who hesitated to believe that such
treatment would be meted out to men who had only recently
returned from the battlefields after four years of warfare in which
they had been made to believe that "their grateful country would
never forget them." The "comradeship of the trenches" was
over. Ex-soldiers in blue uniforms were now ready to club down
ex-soldiers in rags at the bidding of the only class which had
profited by the war.

The Whitehall baton charge, however, had the effect of sharply
awakening masses of the unemployed to a clearer understanding
of their class position and making them realise that they would
receive no redress for their plight as unemployed by quietly
looking to a capitalist government for sympathy.

The urge for unity, for organisation with a militant policy,
rapidly gained strength. Everywhere the unemployed spoke in
bitter terms of their conditions and of the treatment which they
had received in Whitehall. "We've got to stand together,"
"We've got to stop begging and start fighting"—these and other
similar remarks were to be heard in all labour-exchange queues
and wherever the unemployed gathered in groups on street
corners.

I raised a discussion in the St. Pancras unemployed organisation
urging the building of an All-London Council of Unemployed,
which would link up the local organisations for joint activities
under a central leadership.

The proposal now received enthusiastic support, and St. Pancras
made itself responsible for convening the inaugural meeting. I
visited all the labour exchanges in London, made contact with
the local unemployed organisations, and received their support.
The conference was held at the end of October 1920, in the

Bookbinders' Hall, John Street, Clerkenwell. Delegates came from twelve London unemployed organisations, and a London District Council of unemployed was established. I was elected London organiser for the council, Percy Haye secretary, and Jack Holt chairman. Both Haye and Holt, like myself, were engineers, and had been active in the shop stewards' movement.

We quickly set about our task and within a few weeks we had the whole of London organised under the London District Council, with delegates from thirty-one London boroughs, meeting twice weekly.

Keen discussions took place in the council on the questions of policy, lines of activity and programme of demands. Those of us who fought for a line of militant activity—for ending the collecting-box methods and for directing the dissatisfaction of the masses into a fight against the national and local government authorities—won the council to our point of view. We then began to shake London with a series of huge demonstrations, under the slogan of "Work or Full Maintenance."

Under the Poor Law Relief Regulation Order of 1911 it was illegal for the local poor law authorities (the board of guardians) to provide outdoor relief to able-bodied persons except in very exceptional circumstances and only on condition that the applicant for relief was set to work by the guardians on task work, and that one-half at least of the relief given should be in kind. In spite of this, we raised the slogan: "Go to the Guardians," and in a very short time in every locality throughout London huge demonstrations of unemployed were marching to the guardians' offices demanding outdoor relief.

Many exciting scenes occurred at these demonstrations. Deputations from the unemployed, after being admitted to the board room, would refuse to leave until the guardians agreed to relieve the distress. Over and over again the police were called in to remove such deputations and frequent clashes occurred.

The agitation for poor law relief became so strong that the guardians were compelled to grant relief to all applicants irrespective of the law, and the government itself appeared helpless to prevent this. The demand that the government must be held responsible for maintaining the unemployed had caught on with a vengeance, and the masses of the unemployed swept into action everywhere to compel this demand.

Simultaneously with this agitation we raised the demand for suitable meeting-places for the unemployed. The borough councils were asked to provide premises, and many did so. Where they were reluctant to make such provision the unemployed took matters into their own hands and seized town halls, public libraries, baths and other such buildings. Sometimes the local council authorities accepted this *fait accompli* and allowed the unemployed to hold the halls that they had seized. In other cases they negotiated with the organisation about alternative and more suitable premises, but sometimes they decided to call in the police to eject the unemployed forcibly. Some bitter fights took place when this happened.

I well remember the seizure of the old Islington library in Essex Road. After taking possession of the library, the unemployed barricaded themselves in and had a constant guard night and day against being evicted. The Islington Borough Council discussed the question and at first decided not to use force but to drive the unemployed out by cutting off the light and water supplies. But this did not prove effective; lamps and candles were used at night-time and food and water were brought in from outside. Whenever anybody left the hall, or wanted to enter it, a strong body of men stood at the door ready to defend the hall if any attempt was made to rush it by the police. This went on for several weeks. The police had been steadily withdrawn and there were no signs of any attempt on the part of the authorities to retake the hall from the unemployed.

The protection of the hall therefore gradually slackened, and it became comparatively easy to walk into the hall at any time, whereas formerly admission could only be obtained by password. One morning, at 5.30 a.m., when nobody was expecting anything to happen, about a hundred policemen were mobilised and rushed to the hall, forced an entry, easily overcoming the small guard on the door, and with drawn truncheons drove the unemployed from the premises.

The London District Council decided to mobilise the support from other boroughs to assist Islington to recover their hall, or to obtain another. From all parts of London contingents of unemployed, many thousands strong, marched into Islington. The plan was that we should seize the Town Hall in Upper Street. A raiding party of about eighty picked men were to travel in groups by tram and bus to a spot immediately in the vicinity of the Town Hall and at a given time rush in and take possession, close the doors and barricade themselves in. The large body of demonstrators were to be marching in the vicinity of the hall when this happened and after the hall had been taken by the raiding party the demonstrators were to march on to the hall to protect it from outside in case the police were mobilised to force an entry.

The plans, however, failed. There had been some leakage of information and it was afterwards clear that the police had knowledge what the plans were, for before the raiding party got near the Town Hall a large force of police were mobilised both outside and inside, and, as the raiding party approached the hall, the police opened the attack. Those in charge of the raiding party had in fact made a serious mistake in the time, and they arrived at the hall half-an-hour earlier than had been fixed. The result was that they were badly beaten up and sixteen were arrested, whilst the demonstrators were over a mile away from the hall.

I was leading the demonstration, and a messenger came to me while we were marching and informed me what had happened. The whole plan had misfired and it was certain that if the demonstrators now went on to the Town Hall it would mean a heavy battle with the police. With this knowledge we nevertheless decided to go on. The police allowed us to come level with the Town Hall in Upper Street; then suddenly a mounted policeman rode straight at me as the leader of the demonstration and struck me down. In a few seconds thousands of men were fighting in the main thoroughfare of Islington. Ordinary pedestrians got mixed up with the demonstrators. The police were merciless in their attack—men, women and children were batoned to the ground.

I had a small bodyguard with me and fortunately when I was struck down they fought like tigers to protect me against further assault and ultimately succeeded in dragging me away from the police into a side street. Several of the men who had been arrested received sentences of imprisonment, and others were fined. The movement raised money for the fines and gave sustenance to the families of those in gaol.

Throughout the country unemployment was still rapidly increasing and the fighting spirit of the unemployed was developing everywhere. In the face of this tremendous upsurge the government was again compelled to revise the unemployment insurance scheme, and in November 1920 another Act was passed which raised the benefit scales to 15s. for a male adult and 12s. for an adult female. This was an increase of 4s. and 1s. respectively. Still no special provision was made for the wife and children of an unemployed worker. Even with this increase the unemployed were still much worse off, taking into consideration the cost of living, than in 1913. The cost-of-living index figure stood at

276 as against 100 for 1913, whilst the benefit scales for an adult male worker had been increased by only a little over 200.

In the "Go to the Guardians" agitation we therefore not only established the principle of outdoor poor law relief to able-bodied persons, but we also succeeded in compelling the authorities to grant substantial supplementary relief over and above that received at the labour exchanges. The capitalist press began to collect information about the amounts received by unemployed families and ran scare headlines about the "luxury of the unemployed at the expense of the ratepayers." They described this "generosity" as "a grave danger to the nation" and as "placing a premium on idleness." But agitation was too strong to be stemmed by such propaganda. The slogan of "Work or Full Maintenance" became the popular battle-cry of the unemployed and in fighting for it we certainly revolutionised the whole system of poor law relief.

In the autumn of 1920 the Lloyd George government attempted to declare open war against Soviet Russia. There had already been armed intervention on the part of British and other Imperialist troops, and Winston Churchill, who was Chancellor of the Exchequer, boasted of having spent one hundred million pounds on subsidising the counter-revolutionary forces of Denikin, Koltchak, Mannerheim and Yudenitch in an effort to destroy the new workers' republic.

In April 1920, Poland had declared war against Soviet Russia, but by July 1920, the Russian Red Army had delivered a smashing defeat upon the invading forces from Poland. The London dockers on 10th May refused to load the vessel known as the *Jolly George* with munitions for Poland and the spark of revolt against the anti-soviet policy of Lloyd George and his government leapt into flame and swept the country. Councils of action were formed everywhere by the workers when Lloyd George on 4th August attempted to commit Britain openly to a war in support of the defeated Polish forces.

At a joint meeting on 9th August the Labour Party and the Trades Union Congress established a National Council of Action. This was followed by a joint national conference on 13th August which delivered an ultimatum to the government, to the effect that, unless they immediately stopped their war plans, general strike action would be organised. Lloyd George found himself in a very difficult position; the men in the army were war-weary; there had been threats of mutiny in a number of regiments immediately after the war, when they were not being demobilised quickly enough; there had been the policemen's national strike in 1919; and now, with the increasing agitation of the unemployed, Lloyd George no doubt realised that he was not in a position to fight against the ultimatum of the Council of Action. The government was compelled to bow before the storm and drop its war plans against the Soviet Union. It was a great victory for international working-class solidarity.

The government, however, would not recognise the Soviet government or establish normal trading relationship with it. The London District Council of the Unemployed discussed the question of trade with Russia. We realised that the Soviet government was anxious to get down to the task of reconstruction and that, if proper facilities were provided, especially trade credits, many unemployed workers, particularly those connected with the metal trades, could be found employment working on orders for Soviet Russia. We therefore advanced the following demand: *"That as a means of finding employment for the unemployed in the trades with which they are associated, the London District Council of Unemployed calls for the re-establishment of trade with Russia and the recognition of the Soviet government."* We popularised this demand and won very extensive support for it amongst the unemployed masses.

From the first moment of serious organisation amongst the unemployed we had in mind the need for maintaining the closest possible relationship with the trade union and labour movement. We were most anxious to avoid the creation of a movement which would be separate and apart from the general working-class movement. In London we had now succeeded in heading the agitation of the unemployed into the channels of a real working-class policy.

The London District Council of the Unemployed decided to approach the joint secretaries of the National Council of Action to urge that their industrial power should be utilised for strengthening the fight of the unemployed for work or full maintenance and for trade with the Soviet Union. Arrangements were made for a deputation from our movement to meet the Parliamentary Committee of the Labour Party at the House of Commons. This took place on 22nd December, 1920. Mr. J. H. Thomas was in the chair.

We vigorously stated our case for joint action of the unemployed and employed against the government on the questions of unemployment and trade with Russia. An interesting incident occurred when in the course of our statement we used the phrase "that we demand that the Labour Party take action on this question." Mr. Thomas promptly remarked that this language was rather too strong and suggested that we should "implore the Labour Party," not make demands on it.

However, the interview was a friendly one. During the evening the House of Commons was to debate the question of trade with Russia and we therefore drafted a short resolution stating the attitude of the unemployed on this question. The Parliamentary Committee of the Labour Party accepted this resolution and it was later read out in the House during the debate, as expressing the feeling of the unemployed on this matter.

After we had stated our case to the Parliamentary Committee, we still urged that our deputation should meet the National Council of Action, and as this body was meeting next morning at 32 Eccleston Square, the offices of the Trades Union Congress, arrangements were made for our deputation to attend. The outcome of this was a recommendation to the executive of the Labour Party that at the conference which was to be held a few days later at the Central Hall, Westminster, to hear the report of the Labour Commission on Ireland, they should devote the afternoon session to a discussion on the problem of unemployment.

The conference received speakers from our movement, discussed the question of unemployment, and decided that a joint meeting of the Executive of the Labour Party, the Parliamentary Committee, and the Trades Union Congress should meet and set up a sub-committee for the purpose of drawing up specific demands in relation to the unemployed. This joint meeting was to be held in the beginning of January 1921, at the Central Hall, Westminster. The London Unemployed Council decided to send a deputation and hurriedly organised a demonstration to pledge support to the committee. About ten thousand unemployed marched to Eccleston Square where we were informed that if our deputation went along to the Central Hall, they would be received by the Joint Committee. The result of this meeting was that the Joint Committee decided to convene a National Labour Conference of delegates from all working-class organisations to be held at the Kingsway Hall, London, on 27th January, 1921.

When this conference assembled it was clear from the outset that there was an overwhelming feeling for strong action against the government on the question of unemployment. But J. H. Thomas, Arthur Henderson and J. R. Clynes played a leading part in steering the conference away from a policy of militant action. J. H. Thomas in particular fought for limiting the agitation to purely parliamentary action, but the mood of the delegates was such that the platform were compelled to accept a resolution calling upon the executive councils of all trade unions affiliated to the Labour Party and the T.U.C. to test the feeling of their membership on the issue of direct action against the government on its failure in respect to unemployment, and that the conference should stand adjourned and re-assemble in the same hall on 23rd February. The conference therefore adjourned at one o'clock after a three hours' sitting.

During the conference the London District Council of the unemployed had asked that a deputation should be received to speak. This was rejected by those in charge, but it created a storm of protest from the delegates that lasted for fully fifteen minutes. Before the adjournment a resolution was passed calling upon the Labour members in the House of Commons to commence an immediate intensive agitation for the following scale of demands: 40s. per week for a married man and 25s. per week for a single adult unemployed worker.

When the conference re-assembled on 23rd February, the right-wing section of the leadership, headed by J. H. Thomas, had carefully prepared to avoid anything in the nature of drastic action being decided upon by the delegates. Many of the delegates had come prepared to vote for twenty-four hour strike action to compel the government to face up to the question of unemployment. The platform refused to allow the delegates to discuss anything other than the official resolution which they had put forward. This resolution contained no proposals for action; it simply condemned the failure of the government on unemployment and referred to the five parliamentary by-elections which at that moment were in progress, urging that the best way in which the workers could express their opposition to the Lloyd George government on its failure in respect to unemployment was to work for the return of the Labour candidates in these by-elections.

This resolution caused an uproar in the conference from start to finish. J. H. Thomas did his utmost to prove to the delegates the importance of confining their action to purely parliamentary debates. From all over the hall delegates claimed the right to move their resolutions, but the platform persistently refused to allow this. At the end of two hours the delegates were compelled by the platform to vote either for, or against, the official resolution. Amidst a tumult of protest from all over the hall the vote was taken and the platform declared that the resolution was carried. The conference then closed.

Half an hour after the hall had emptied, ten thousand London unemployed who had mobilised at Hyde Park marched to the Congress Hall to pledge their solidarity with the employed workers in the fight against unemployment.

Many efforts were made by our London District Council to get the Labour Party executive and the Trades Union Congress to interest themselves in the organisation of the unemployed, but our efforts were of no avail, and we were compelled therefore to continue our work of building an independent unemployed movement.

We felt that organisation of the unemployed was not only necessary for their own protection but was also necessary from the standpoint of preventing the employing class from using the unemployed to undermine the established trade-union standards and conditions. The records of industrial history bear out the fact that the employers always regard the existence of a large army of unemployed as providing the most convenient time for attacking the wages of the employed workers.

In our propaganda amongst the unemployed we therefore laid emphasis upon the need for them to be on their guard against efforts by the employing class to use them as cheap labour or as a blacklegging force during any industrial dispute. We had not long, however, to wait before the ruling class opened their attack on the wage standards by the lock-out of the miners in April 1921. Our London District Council made its attitude to the industrial struggles of the workers clear in the following resolution which was passed on 4th April, 1921, in respect to this lock-out:—

"This London District Council, representing the unemployed in London and Greater London, wish to state most emphatically that in no circumstances will we allow ourselves as unemployed to be used as instruments for blacklegging against the miners or any section of the workers who may strike in sympathy. Further we wish to extend fraternal greetings and congratulations to the miners on the splendid stand which they are making on behalf of the whole of the workers throughout the country to maintain a reasonable standard of existence."

It was in this spirit of working-class solidarity that we were building the organisation of the unemployed. We were urging the employed workers to stand firm everywhere against any attempt to lower their conditions and we were assuring them of the support of the unemployed in such a fight. At the same time we were warning the unemployed to be very careful to inquire into all offers of work to make sure that they were not being used to undercut established rates and conditions.

Early in March 1921 we received information that at the Central Aircraft Factory in Kilburn the employees had accepted reduced rates of pay and that a certain amount of overtime was being worked. The matter was discussed by the Willesden unemployed organisation and it was felt that protest should be made against this. If the unemployed were standing firm against taking work at reduced rates of pay, we felt that the men in the shop should also respond, and on the question of overtime we claimed that when so many workers were unemployed all overtime should be stopped. We were in touch with some of the employees who gave us us a plan of the lay-out of the factory and we decided that we would carry out a raid on this factory on 11th March.

Thirty trustworthy unemployed men were got together and the plan was discussed with them. It was decided that they should assemble at a given point near to the factory entrance, and in order to avoid arousing suspicion several of them should be carrying football togs so that if there were any policemen about they would be disarmed by the belief that we were a group of football enthusiasts gathering for a match.

There were very few people to be seen near this factory, and at a given signal, the "footballers" made straight for the entrance. Once inside the factory many of us were quite at home in the surroundings. As engineers we were accustomed to machines and lost no time in finding the power-motors and shutting them off. Of course everybody in the factory was taken by surprise. We put men on to guard every exit to prevent anybody being sent out for the police and we took charge of the telephones. After stopping the machinery I jumped on to the bench and called the workers around me for a meeting.

I spoke briefly on the question of unemployment, the need for all overtime being stopped, and urged the workers to realise that we, the organised unemployed, would be with them in any fight to prevent any reduction in their wage-rates. Whilst I was speaking, the manager came up, listened for a time to what I had to say, and then demanded that he also put his side of the case. Then a very laughable thing happened. One of the raiders came to me quietly and whispered that the police were outside; by some means which we never discovered—probably an oversight in regard to a telephone line—the police had been sent for and informed of what was happening in the factory.

But by the time the police entered the machine-shop I had

finished speaking and the manager was now up on the bench haranguing the workers. A burly sergeant of the police marched in at the head of a dozen constables and to the amusement of the workers and the raiders, without waiting to grasp the actual situation, he rushed at the manager evidently taking him for the leader of the raid, and began to drag him down from the bench. He in fact succeeded in doing so before the manager—in a state of utter confusion—could acquaint the sergeant with the fact that he was the manager.

The whole incident became a huge joke, the manager and the sergeant looked in a condition of utter bewilderment, whilst the crowd of workers and raiders roared with laughter. The manager then agreed to negotiate with a small committee from the raiders if the remainder immediately left the premises. The raiders departed, but the police remained inside, and our deputation of three then adjourned to the manager's office to discuss the question with him.

Of course, he hotly protested against our tactics but finally gave an undertaking that all overtime would be stopped in the factory as from the next week-end. We later learnt that he kept his word.

A fortnight later we followed up with another factory invasion at the J.A.P. Motor Works at Tottenham, where, after holding a meeting inside the works, the raiders departed before the police could arrive. Later on the tactic of raiding factories was developed and very satisfactory results were achieved. This point is dealt with in subsequent chapters.

Chapter III

STRUGGLE

THE years 1921 and 1922 saw many stormy scenes amongst the unemployed in all parts of the country. The special post-war donation benefit of 29s. a week plus children's allowances came to an end in March 1921, and the great mass of ex-service men who had formerly benefited under this scheme now found the benefit scales for themselves and families savagely cut. No doubt thinking to divide the unemployed against themselves the government raised the unemployment insurance benefit scales from 15s. to 20s. for men and from 12s. to 16s. for women.

By May 1921 the number registered as wholly unemployed at the labour exchanges, excluding those on poor law relief, reached 2,126,800. In addition to these there were 1,194,200 registered as short-time workers, many of them working only about two days a week.

The press contained daily reports of activities of the unemployed in all parts of the country, and the London District Council of the unemployed at the end of February 1921 decided to make an effort to secure national co-ordination of the struggles of the unemployed by calling for a national conference which would create a national organisation.

The *Daily Herald* at that time was in the charge of Mr. George Lansbury, who by publicity in his paper gave us encouragement in our work. Through the *Daily Herald* we made the call for a national conference. Many organisations answered this call, and on 15th April, 1921, the first national conference of the unemployed met at the International Socialist Club, City Road, Hoxton.

At this conference the basis of the National Unemployed Workers' Movement was laid down. All delegates appreciated the need for such a movement. They recognised that unemployment was more than a local question and that national and district machinery was necessary to co-ordinate and lead the struggles of the unemployed.

The principle of "Work or Full Maintenance at Trade-Union

28

Rates of Wages" was taken as a main plank in the platform of the National Movement. It was decided to establish a national headquarters and elect national officials. Percy Haye was elected national secretary; Jack Holt chairman; and I became national organiser.

Although the rates of benefit at the labour exchange had now been made uniform for all unemployed workers, there was great variation in the scales of relief that were being paid in different parts of the country. The national conference laid down the following demands:

36s. for man and wife; 5s. for each child up to 16 years of age; rent up to 15s. a week, plus one cwt. of coal or its equivalent in gas. 30s. for single persons 18 years and over; 15s. for single persons between 16 and 18.

At the end of this first national conference of the unemployed, the delegates returned to their respective localities to intensify their activities and to build up a powerful National Movement.

There is no organisation in Britain which has crammed so much intense and persistent agitation into the period from 1921 to 1936 as the National Unemployed Workers' Movement. It has been fifteen years of continuous battle against poverty and against the repeated attempts of the national and local government authorities to worsen the conditions of millions of the working class. Bad as the conditions of the unemployed are to-day, there can be no question that they would have been infinitely worse had it not been for the persistent struggles organised and led by the National Unemployed Workers' Movement over this period.

Just as the creation of the London District Council made a sharp turn in the character of the struggles of the London unemployed, so now, following the first national conference in 1921, we witnessed the growth of a much clearer perspective and class-conscious struggle throughout the country.

We were still pressing, however, for the trade-union and labour movement to take over the responsibility for organising and leading the work amongst the unemployed, and towards this end the London District Council organised a march of 200 London unemployed to the Labour Party conference at Brighton in June 1921. The Labour Party executive gave us permission to speak in the conference and during this session all the unemployed marchers were accommodated at the back of the hall.

On 30th June, 1921, the government again revised the unemployment benefit rates, this time reducing them to the levels which prevailed before March of the same year, namely 15s. for men and 12s. for women. This gave rise to a wave of mass demonstrations of the unemployed everywhere. In London a huge demonstration took place on 11th July, 1921, to demand that a deputation be received by Dr. MacNamara who was at that time Minister of Labour. Contingents from all over London, headed by their improvised bands and banners, marched to Hyde Park, where they joined as a single demonstration for a march through the West End of London.

The police had already informed us that, as the House of Commons was in session, the metropolitan police by-laws prohibited the demonstration within a radius of a mile of the House. The march through the West End of London, however, came very close to the mile limit, in fact transgressed it at many points. Tens of thousands of hungry and ragged unemployed marching through the West End shopping centre created no small amount of alarm amongst the well-to-do class. The deputation left the demonstration at the corner of Tottenham Court Road and Oxford Street and proceeded to the Ministry of Labour. They were shown into the board room and received by the Minister and other officials. I stated the case against the cuts in the benefit scales, but the chief argument of Dr. MacNamara was that the unemployment insurance fund was already in a state of insolvency and that he had had to borrow £16,000,000 in order to meet the expenditure. He promised, however, carefully to consider all the points of our case and to extend inquiries into the operation of the insurance scheme with a view to modifying the hardships which we claimed were being inflicted upon the unemployed.

The deputation proceeded to Hyde Park where the unemployed at a fixed time had returned to await the result of the interview. The report was given, but there was no cause for any feeling of satisfaction at the results of the meeting with the Minister of Labour and the demonstrators pledged themselves to follow up with increased agitation in all the localities.

The demonstration passed off without any conflict with the police, although several times during the march through the West End it had come very near to this. The results of this interview with the Minister of Labour were made known throughout the country and the unemployed prepared big demonstrations of protest to demand the restoration of the cut in the benefit scales.

Meanwhile demands for poor law relief were overwhelming

many of the boards of guardians. Their expenditure was surpassing anything that they had expected, and in many places they resorted to efforts to cut down both the amounts of relief and the number of recipients. This led to many demonstrations and struggles. During July, 1921, the Wandsworth board of guardians decided to discourage applicants for relief by offering many of them tickets for the workhouse and announcing that there was to be a heavy reduction in the number of able-bodied persons who would be allowed outdoor relief. The guardians no doubt expected that this would in itself be sufficient to reduce the number of applicants.

The unemployed reported to the Battersea and Wandsworth organisation and the whole question was discussed in the committee. It was decided that the unemployed should be advised not only to take the tickets for the workhouse, but to make application for them, and that they should enter the workhouse *en masse*. The local authorities were taken by surprise at this move, and approximately 200 applicants obtained workhouse tickets for themselves and their families, numbering about 700 in all. Arrangements were made by the unemployed committee for them to assemble at Clapham Junction, and headed by a bagpipe band they marched to Wandsworth workhouse, many marching with their children toddling at the side and others carrying babes in arms. On reaching the workhouse gates it was clear that the workhouse authorities were in a dilemma, but as the applicants all had tickets for admission to the workhouse nothing could be done, but admit them. The authorities little knew what they were in for.

The workhouse held 900 inmates and there were already 700. The workhouse master and his staff were almost frantic. How to sleep and feed this army of men, women, and children was certainly a problem. There were not sufficient beds for the new arrivals, nor was there even space. Two big wards had to be cleared out in which the women, children and babies slept on mattresses on the floor. For the men, numbering 200, there was not a foot of space available. But it was July and the weather was very warm, so with blankets supplied by the workhouse the men slept on the lawn.

The workhouse master and his staff were made to realise that the new arrivals could not be ordered about and bullied like ordinary inmates. They had organisation amongst them, and on every grievance as it arose the committee met and sent a deputation to demand meetings with the workhouse master.

Strong complaints were made about the quality of the food and after a number of scenes improvements were conceded, although it was apparent that the workhouse master was not anxious to make conditions too easy lest it be an encouragement for the new arrivals to stay.

Next morning, when breakfast was served, the committee called for the singing of the "Red Flag" and to the surprise and horror of the officials the men, women and children lustily sang the workers' battle-hymn.

The organised march into the workhouse had aroused the attention of the residents in Wandsworth and the surrounding boroughs, and on the second night a demonstration of many thousands marched to the workhouse entrance to express their support for the men, women and children inside. When they arrived at the workhouse cheers and counter-cheers rang out from the demonstrators and the inmates. A large force of police were present, many inside the grounds, and the inmates were kept back from the main gates. From the wall of the workhouse speeches were delivered to the demonstrators outside. Then, to the amazement and jubilation of the demonstrators, about 9 o'clock, just as it was getting dusk, we saw the red flag run up on a flagmast over the workhouse. The demonstration did not depart until almost 11 o'clock at night.

Every inducement was given to the workers inside to depart from the workhouse; a few did so, but the main body held firm and declared that they would not leave until the board of guardians decided to grant outdoor relief. The demonstrations outside the workhouse were a nightly occurrence, and, after one of these demonstrations, two other members of the London District Council and I decided that we would try to get into the workhouse to make contact with our comrades inside and to give advice and information about the progress of the fight.

It was, of course, not possible for us to gain entry to the work-house by application at the main gate. Some surreptitious method had to be found. We discovered that on one side of the work-house the gardens of ordinary houses backed on to the work-house wall, and some time after midnight my two colleagues and I climbed over a fence into a garden, where fortunately we found a pair of steps, which, placed on top of a fowl-house, enabled us to reach the top of the workhouse wall. At this time police were constantly in the grounds of the workhouse, and just as we dropped from the high wall, two policemen who were on patrol heard the noise and discovered us. We explained that we were some of the inmates and had been out to get cigarettes. After an investigation, however, the police remained unsatisfied and decided to interrogate us again next morning. When we reached the lawn where the workers were sleeping, a few of them were awake and they were naturally surprised to see us. During the night we had a talk with the committee and just before breakfast the police began making inquiries for us again. We succeeded however in evading them, and departed by the same way that we had entered.

By 27th July the local authorities in Wandsworth were beaten. The guardians gave an undertaking that they would restore the former position of outdoor relief to able-bodied applicants. The fight having been won, the order was given for the workers inside to depart with an organised victorious march out.

Similar movements were proceeding elsewhere. On 12th August ten thousand Sheffield unemployed marched to the town hall to demand a meeting with the lord mayor. They were headed by a banner inscribed with the sign of the skull and crossbones over the words "Death is better than Starvation!" Before the demonstration started, the police warned the leaders that there would be trouble if the demonstration did not keep away from the front of the town hall. Before reaching the town hall the demonstrators halted on a piece of waste land where a short meeting was held and a deputation of six from amongst their ranks were elected as their representatives. The following resolution was passed to be placed before the lord mayor:

" That we protest emphatically against the twenty-five per cent reduction in state unemployment benefit, that we demand that the hours of task workers be decreased to two days per week, and that all single men thrown off relief work be immediately reinstated in full benefit at the labour exchange, without any waiting period."

The demonstration reformed its ranks and, despite police opposition, marched to the town hall. From the steps of the town hall speakers addressed the crowd whilst the deputation entered and inquired for the lord mayor. They were informed that he was absent but that they would be met by the deputy mayor. The deputation pressed for the attendance of the lord mayor and for representatives from the board of guardians. The representatives from the board of guardians were telephoned for, but the deputy mayor refused to take any steps to get in touch with the lord mayor. Whilst the deputation was inside the town hall the demonstrators outside passed the time in an orderly way by singing and cheering. All traffic in the front of the town hall was blocked and the police were becoming more and more aggressive in an effort to clear the streets.

At 4 o'clock in the afternoon the deputy mayor agreed that he, along with representatives from the board of guardians, would meet the deputation to discuss their case at 6.30 p.m. A request was made that the leaders of the demonstrators should lead the unemployed away from the town hall. This request was refused. At 6.30 the deputation again entered the town hall, but this time the deputy chief constable was inside and the deputation were informed that no interview would be allowed until the crowd had been moved from the main entrance. In an effort to avoid trouble the leaders of the demonstration urged the men to move into a side street, which they did. But the interview was abortive. By 7.45 p.m. most of the crowd had moved back to the main entrance. Every available policeman had been brought to the scene and the chief constable was now in attendance and threatened the arrest of the leaders unless the streets were quickly cleared.

The *Sheffield Daily Telegraph* in its evening edition made some scathing remarks about the demonstration. This incited the unemployed and when the deputation left the town hall it was decided to march to the offices of the *Sheffield Telegraph* and to demand that an apology be published in the paper next day. The editor refused to meet representatives from the unemployed and this gave rise to angry threats which were shouted in the crowd. But just as the demonstration was about to march away, the police drew their truncheons and began to charge into the unemployed.

A battle ensued and eleven demonstrators were arrested. Several days later when these workers were brought into the court, another demonstration took place outside the police court, and another baton charge was made, this time seven arrests taking place. Several men were imprisoned and others fined.

In Bristol, after a series of big demonstrations, the guardians received a deputation from the unemployed and offered a scale of 25s. per week for man and wife and 5s. for each child, 15s. for a single man and 12s. 6d. for a single girl. These terms were reported at a demonstration and accepted, and during the first week five thousand unemployed people had their scales increased to these amounts. But there were certain grievances about the administration and on 6th September five thousand unemployed marched to the guardians' offices in Peter Street. A deputation of ten went forward to ask for an interview. The guardians were in session but they refused to meet a deputation consisting of more than four. This was reported to the crowd and after a meeting it was decided that a further demonstration should be organised for the next day, 7th September.

Six thousand workers marched from the Ropewalk, a favourite meeting spot in Bristol, to Eastville Park, and from there to the guardians' offices. The inspector of police intercepted the deputation at the entrance and informed them that only four would be allowed inside. When this was announced to the demonstrators they shouted their disapproval and immediately the police drew batons and a battle ensued. As the crowd rushed through Bridge Street, a big shopping centre, fifty large panes of glass were broken. These events alarmed the local authorities and the next day the lord mayor sent for the deputation in an effort to allay the anger which was prevalent amongst the workers. The meeting with the lord mayor resulted in the full deputation being allowed to state their case at the next meeting of the city council.

Under the pressure of our agitations, the scales of relief administered by the boards of guardians were being raised almost every week. The capitalist press were calling attention to what they described as the "extravagant" scales. Poplar Borough Council, which had an overwhelming Labour majority and which sided openly with the guardians, was particularly singled out for attack. The council and the guardians denied that their scales were extravagant and claimed that they were only doing their duty in endeavouring to relieve adequately the distress in their locality. The borough council, in fact, took the offensive, and as a protest against the failure of the government to come to the aid of the poorer localities they refused to pay sums of money which were required from their Council by the London County Council and other authorities in respect of services administered by them.

This became the subject of legal proceedings, but the Poplar councillors stood firm. The court ultimately ordered the arrest of the Poplar councillors on 1st September, 1921. The women councillors were put in Holloway gaol, and the men, headed by George Lansbury, in Brixton. They remained in prison for six weeks, until the government rushed through a temporary Act whereby, through the agency of the Metropolitan Common Poor Law Fund, the burden of relief was more evenly distributed between the richer and poorer districts throughout London.

The courageous stand of these councillors aroused the admiration of the whole working class, and great demonstrations from the East End of London to Brixton and Holloway gaols were almost a nightly occurrence.

On 4th October, 1921, a demonstration of forty thousand unemployed took place under the auspices of the London District Council of Unemployed. The object was to demand work or full maintenance, the immediate restoration of the cuts in the benefit scales, and the release of the Poplar councillors. The London District Committee had decided that the demonstration should march to Trafalgar Square. The police warned us that this would not be permitted, since no demonstrations could be held in the square on a week-day. We did not forget, however, that during the war such police regulations had been waived and that Horatio Bottomley and others had held big recruiting meetings during a week-day on this favourite London meeting-place. Therefore, in spite of the police warning, we decided that if possible we would march to the square.

The police, however, had decided to resist this and had mobilised a huge force from all over London and the home counties.   When the great procession began marching from the Embankment, headed by the bands and banners of the movement, we turned up Savoy Street, a small side street leading to the corner of the Strand and Aldwych. The police had apparently anticipated our move and by the time the head of the demonstration reached the Strand we found that all vehicles had been stopped at the Aldwych end of the Strand and packed into a solid block which made it impossible for anybody or anything to pass. The great mass of demonstrators were still on the Embankment and we realised that if trouble started at this point the situation was a most favourable one for the police.

We therefore had no other option but to march into Kingsway, through Covent Garden, and on towards Piccadilly. We found that every turning leading towards the square had been blocked by the police, and ultimately the demonstration proceeded to Hyde Park, via Hyde Park corner. Huge meetings were held in the Park, and amongst the demonstrators there was an insistent demand that we should carry out our objective and go to Trafalgar Square. I called together the members of the London District Council and had a hurried discussion with them in the Park; in view of the feeling of the unemployed we decided to make another effort to get to the square.

By this time it was getting dark. We informed the leaders of the various contingents what the plan was to be—to march along

Oxford Street to Tottenham Court Road, then all banners were to be furled, the bands were to drop out, and the demonstrators were to make their way to the square as individuals by every possible route. When the demonstration reached the corner of Charing Cross Road the plan was carried out, much to the consternation of the police. When they saw the demonstrators breaking the ranks they were puzzled, and did not know how to act. Within a few minutes Charing Cross Road was one seething mass of unemployed swarming towards the square and stretching right across the road, holding up all traffic.

I had previously arranged with a small group of comrades that we would endeavour to reach the plinth in the square and raise the red flag. But at the bottom of Charing Cross Road we were met by a huge force of police and a terrific battle took place. Some of the members of the committee and I, however, succeeded in breaking through by taking the turning at the side of St. Martin's Church, cutting into the Strand and then along to the square. We climbed on to the base of the plinth and hoisted a big red flag. By this time, fighting had broken out on other sides of the square as the demonstrators attempted to break through, and as we raised the red flag on the plinth a tremendous roar of cheers went up from the unemployed, and with a final effort they broke through in their thousands and stormed into the square. But before they could reach the plinth a force of police had been sent to attack us.

With batons drawn they rushed across the base of the plinth and drove us down, but they did not succeed in capturing the red flag. From that moment onward the square itself and the streets surrounding it were one mass of struggling men. The police were merciless in their attack and very severe injuries were inflicted. In fifteen minutes they had got the upper hand of the unemployed and the streets were cleared. We later learnt that many well-to-do people in the vicinity of the square took a stand on the steps of St. Martin's Church to watch the fracas, thinking that they would be safe, but in the melee the police had no time to distinguish between the well-dressed and the ragged, and, like the unemployed, many of these well-to-do sightseers felt the weight of a policeman's truncheon.

At this period stormy scenes were taking place also in many provincial towns. In Liverpool, demonstrations were almost a daily occurrence, with thousands of unemployed marching through the main streets. One day as many as twenty-five thousand Liverpool unemployed assembled in the big square de the Liverpool Art Gallery. The entrance of this gallery long flight of wide, stone steps. The Unemployed Com- had decided that on this day crowds of unemployed should pack into the gallery as a protest against their conditions. It was thought that even if the police were brought into this building they would refrain from any attack because of the damage that would be done to the valuable art treasures.

From amongst the great mass of unemployed assembled in the square, the committee emerged and led the way up the high steps to the entrance. A batch of one hundred and fifty unemployed followed, but before they reached the top of the steps a strong force of police, who had already been in hiding inside the building, rushed out with truncheons drawn and commenced to club down the unemployed. The vast crowd that was gathered in the square rushed up the steps to protect their representatives, whereupon mounted and foot police who had been mobilised in big numbers charged across the square and up the steps, battering down everybody who came in their way.

All the members of the local Unemployed Committee were arrested that night and thrown into gaol. When they appeared in court many of them had their heads swathed in bandages, and according to the press reports strong comment was made by the recorder in the court about the excessive force used by the police in dispersing the demonstrators. All the men on trial were discharged with the exception of two, who were bound over.

Shortly following this struggle the Liverpool guardians conceded increased scales of relief and assured the Unemployed Committee that action would be taken against any relieving officer who refused relief in needy cases. Concessions were also made in respect of rent allowances.

Then came news of the struggle in Leicester. The unemployed had marched to the guardians' offices and a baton charge had taken place. Two leaders of the Unemployed Committee, Jennett and Ley, and nine others were arrested; Jennett and Ley were sentenced to one month's imprisonment each.

On 15th October a big demonstration of unemployed in Cardiff marched to the guardians' offices. The board received the deputation, and the chairman, Archdeacon Buckley, in opening the interview remarked that in "recent years there had been a great change in the character of 'Mr. Bumble' who formerly was not a popular character, and to-day they had on the boards of guardians persons actuated by christian motives and I would not be a christian if I had no sympathetic ideas." He thought that all cases brought before them "should be treated in the spirit of sympathy and of helping our fellow-men."

He said he "knew we were face to face with a gigantic problem which the statesmen of the day had been unable to solve." He said that he supposed that "one solution to the problem was work, and another cheaper food." He said he was "glad that the eight-penny loaf was in sight."

The deputation in stating their case urged that the national scale of the Unemployed Movement should be paid. They gave instances of the terrible poverty prevalent in the Cardiff area. One of the spokesmen, Mr. Price, said: "Last night 187 unemployed workers slept out on timber floats and about 140 in corporation dust-carts. Many of these had been turned out of their lodgings because they could not pay. We find the present scale of relief insufficient and would challenge any one of you on the guardians to come to our homes and live on the maintenance we get. We have been experiencing hunger and suffering too long."

After the deputation withdrew, the guardians made the following decisions:—

1. That the various relief committees be asked to administer the present scale of relief with greater liberality.

2. That in the case of single men over 18 years of age the maximum allowance shall be increased to 17s. a week, of which up to 7s. may be given in cash.

3. That in the case of single men between the ages of 16 and 18 the relief be increased to 10s. a week.

4. That for men on part-time employment half their earnings up to 15s. should not be taken into account in assessing their relief scale.

5. In the case of married families the maximum amount of relief to be £2 10s. 0d. per week where there were dependent children and 25s. for a married couple without children.

Throughout the textile areas of Lancashire the demand for work or full maintenance was gathering strength. Everywhere demonstrations were taking place to demand from the guardians the national scale of the Unemployed Movement. Particularly big demonstrations took place in Manchester, Wigan, Ashton-under-Lyme, Warrington, St. Helens and Altrincham.

Throughout Scotland tremendous demonstrations were also taking place. In Glasgow the late John McLean, who became famous on the Clyde for his courageous stand during the war, was now, along with Harry McShane, rousing the unemployed to action. They led great demonstrations through the central thoroughfares. Glasgow Green was a scene of many stormy battles. In Scotland, as in England, the parish councils were compelled to break through the old conditions governing poor law relief and to grant relief on a less parsimonious scale.

During 1921 John McLean was twice sent to prison for his activities, the second occasion for a speech delivered to the unemployed in which he urged them not to allow themselves quietly to die of starvation. For this speech he was sentenced to twelve months' imprisonment. From the moment he was thrown into gaol the burden of the leadership of the struggle fell upon Harry McShane. He proved worthy of the trust reposed in him and became the stormy petrel of the struggles of the unemployed all over Scotland.

In some parts of Scotland during the latter end of 1921 the struggles of the unemployed took on a very fierce character. Riots broke out in many towns and much damage was done before the authorities would make concessions. In Dundee a public building was burnt to the ground. The Scottish Movement linked up with the national organisation during 1921 and took up the fight for the national scale of demands and the slogan of work or full maintenance.

Immediately following the big Trafalgar Square battle of 4th October, the National Administrative Council of the National Unemployed Workers' Movement decided to ask for an interview with Mr. Lloyd George, the Prime Minister, on 13th October. Representatives from various parts of the country were called to London and arrangements were made for a big demonstration in support of this deputation. Although our letter, asking for the interview, was dated 6th October, we received no acknowledgement or reply until the morning of 13th October, when the following letter was received.

To the Secretary of the   10 Downing Street,
    National Unemployed   London, S.W.1
    Workers' Movement.   October 12th, 1921.
Dear Sir,

I am desired by the Prime Minister to acknowledge receipt of your letter of the 6th instant, in which you ask him to receive a deputation from your Council on the 13th October.

The Prime Minister desires me to assure you that the problem of unemployment is receiving the constant and unremitting attention of the Cabinet, and, further, that he is in touch with the representatives of organised Labour upon the whole subject, and had their views placed before him fully at a Conference yesterday. It is the Prime Minister's intention to make a statement on the whole problem directly Parliament meets on Tuesday.

As regards your request that he should receive a deputation from your body on Thursday, the Prime Minister regrets that it is impossible for him to do so.

Yours faithfully,

(*Signed*) A. J. SYLVESTER.

By the time that this letter was received it was too late to cancel the demonstration, and the national representatives were already in London. We therefore went on with the demonstration and the deputation proceeded to 10 Downing Street. There they were informed that the Prime Minister was not at home and it was suggested that the ministers in charge of the Ministry of Labour and the Ministry of Health should receive the deputation.

A good deal of delay took place whilst officials at 10 Downing Street held hurried consultation. Meanwhile a huge demonstration of the unemployed was marching through the West End. The authorities at Downing Street were undoubtedly aware of this and they were somewhat anxious to facilitate an interview. Ultimately it was arranged that the deputation should proceed to the Ministry of Health in Whitehall. They were received by the following ministers and officials: Sir Alfred Mond (Minister of Health and chairman of the Government Unemployment Committee), Dr. MacNamara (Minister of Labour), Sir A. S. T. Griffiths-Boscawen (Minister of Agriculture), Mr. Short (Home Secretary), Sir P. Lloyd-Graeme (Director of Overseas Trade), Mr. Haworth (Assistant Secretary to the Cabinet), Mr. Wicks (Secretary of the Cabinet Unemployment Committee).

I was in charge of the deputation, and each representative stated his case in respect to the conditions in his area. We pressed for the provision of work schemes at trade-union rates and raised the demand for full maintenance and for our national scale. We strongly condemned the granting of relief on loan and pressed for the provision of free milk for the children of the unemployed and to expectant mothers. To Dr. MacNamara in particular we protested against the number of unemployed who had been struck off the "live" register of the labour exchanges (numbering hundreds of thousands) for whom no adequate alternative provision was being made. Sir Alfred Mond, in concluding the interview said: "I do not think there is anyone who fails to realise

the economic position which we are in to-day. It is terrible that
men and women who all their lives have been in work should now
find themselves suffering unemployment. The Cabinet Committee
are deeply considering the situation and we shall make every
endeavour to replace everyone in useful industry—there is no
avenue which up to the present has not been explored. Part of
our schemes for remedying the evil of unemployment are already
beginning to operate with the local authorities. The boards of
guardians are doing all they possibly can and have laid down
scales of considerable relief." Finally, on being asked to give a
definite reply to our demands, Sir Alfred Mond said he was
unable to do this, but wished to assure us that he was fully
sympathetic to our claims and that a statement would be made in
the House of Commons when it re-opened on Tuesday.

When the deputation departed from the Ministry of Health to
proceed to Hyde Park to give a report of their interview, they
discovered that the demonstration had been broken up by the
police. The demonstrators had reached Cambridge Circus, when
the police had stopped them, claiming that they were within the
mile limit of the House of Commons. An altercation had occurred,
and although the leaders of the demonstration had explained that
they were going through to Hyde Park the police had drawn
their truncheons and a fierce battle had been fought.

The wave of demonstrations and deputations to the authorities
nationally and locally was by now producing results. When
Parliament re-assembled on 18th October, following our interview
with ministers, an announcement was made that the unemployment insurance scales were to be revised and that as from 10th
November, 1921, dependants' allowances would be paid. This
was in fact the introduction of the dependants' allowances which
have continued with improvements up to the present time. This
concession in November 1921 allowed 5s. for the wife of an
unemployed claimant and 1s. for each child. In the following
January, the Ministry of Health, under Sir Alfred Mond, laid
down a scale of poor relief for the metropolitan area. The scale
was as follows:

For man and wife or two adults living together	25s.
For children under 16:	
First child	6s.
Second or third child	5s.
Fourth or any subsequent child	4s.
For an adult living with parents or relatives	10s.
For an adult not so living	15s.

Fuel up to 1 cwt. a week in winter (November 1st to March 31st) or $\frac{1}{2}$ cwt. in summer (April 1st to October 31st) or its equivalent in money (not exceeding 3s. in winter and 1s. 6d. in summer), to be granted in addition to the above amounts.

This was a big advance on any poor law scales previously sanctioned, but in some cases it still fell short of the amount which the unemployed had succeeded in securing from the boards of guardians through their agitation.

Towards the end of November 1921 the second national conference of the unemployed movement was held in the Gorton Town Hall (Manchester). The conference assembled on 21st November and continued in session for three days. It was a truly representative conference of all parts of Great Britain. To the first conference Scotland had not sent delegates, but this time they were well represented.

21st November was a Saturday, and as most of the delegates were signing at the labour exchange it was necessary for them to travel by night trains on Friday night. Send-off demonstrations were organised in all the big centres. The holding of the second national conference was made an important occasion by the unemployed everywhere.

There were many delegates present from various local unemployed associations which were not yet attached to the national movement. Some of them had rather conservative views, but before the end of the conference the militants had won the support of all delegates and the national movement was consolidated by the adherence of those who had previously been outside its ranks.

The form and structure of organisation was debated in the conference and ultimately unanimous agreement was reached. The organisation was to be built as follows: branches of the movement should be open to all unemployed workers who wished to co-operate in the fight against unemployment and for an improvement in their conditions. District councils, consisting of delegates from all the branches in a given district, should meet regularly to plan the activities of the movement on a district basis. A national administrative council, consisting of delegates from all the district councils throughout Great Britain, should be the governing body of the movement and should meet quarterly, or more often if necessary, to review the work of the movement nationally and to give direction on a national basis to its struggles. There should be a head office in London with national officials elected at each national conference. The officials who had been elected at the first conference were re-elected at this conference.

The finances of the movement should be derived by a system of membership contributions of 1d. per week. From these contributions of the membership the machinery of the movement locally, district, and nationally, should be maintained. A system of contribution stamps was introduced. These were to be supplied by headquarters to the district councils at a rate which would give income to headquarters; the district councils in turn would supply the branches in their district with stamps at a rate that would finance the machinery of the district council. This briefly was the form of organisation laid down in this national conference and which has continued to the present time.

Amongst the demands laid down as a programme by this national conference was, first, endorsement of the national scale of relief previously advanced by the movement and:

(a) Provision of work at rates and conditions not below the minimum laid down by the respective trade unions, or, alternatively, full maintenance of the unemployed at trade-union rates, where these rates were not below our demands from the guardians;

(b) Extra relief grants to expectant mothers; milk, etc.;

(c) The provision of three meals a day, week-ends and holidays included, to children of unemployed parents;

(d) No distraint for rent or rates on the goods of an unemployed person;

(e) The preservation of civic rights to a citizen on acceptance of relief because of unemployment;

(f) The abolition of "test" or "task" work for those in receipt of relief through unemployment;

(g) The free unconditional provision of halls to enable the unemployed to meet;

(h) The use of the public parks and recreation grounds for public meetings;

(i) Relief granted to unemployed persons to be a charge on the national exchequer and not on the local rates, and to be administered through the trade unions;

(j) Representation of the unemployed organisation on all employment exchange committees;

(k) The abolition of all overtime in order to prevent unnecessary unemployment.

During the conference emphasis had been laid upon the necessity for the closest possible relationship between the organised unemployed and the labour and trade-union movement.

All branches of the movement were instructed to apply for affiliation to their local trades councils. The conference laid emphasis upon the need for the unemployed playing their part in industrial disputes to prevent the employers from recruiting blackleg labour from amongst their ranks.

This second national conference terminated with the singing of the "Red Flag" and "Auld Lang Syne," and cheers rang through the hall for solidarity of the unemployed in the fight against starvation.

Arrangements had been made by the Manchester unemployed for a big demonstration on the evening that the conference terminated and all the delegates marched from the conference to Stevenson Square to participate. At the end of the meeting the demonstrators decided to march to the various railway stations to give a send-off to the departing delegates. Scenes of enthusiasm took place at the stations and there was a real feeling of strength and organisation amongst the unemployed.

The period following the national conference was marked by the organising of big demonstrations in all parts of the country. In addition we saw the development of our tactics in respect to raids on factories, raids on guardians' offices, the fight against low rates of wages on relief jobs, strike solidarity with workers in dispute and bitter struggles against evictions.

Let me first deal with a number of factory raids which took place during the last two months of 1921.

In St. Pancras a small engineering firm was working regular overtime. The rates of wages paid in the firm were extremely low. The St. Pancras branch of the movement decided to carry out a raid upon this firm. A small picked body of unemployed entered the works, the machinery was stopped, and the workers were called together for a meeting. An appeal was made to the workers to make a fight against their low wages and to stop overtime, and a pledge was given that the organised unemployed would help them in the fight. The manager would give no promise to remedy the conditions and when the raiders left they threatened that unless overtime was stopped they would march several thousand of the unemployed to the factory.

We were later informed that the management had granted an increase of 3s. per week and although overtime was not completely stopped it was considerably reduced.

Following this the Islington branch at the end of October learned that at a works in that area overtime was being worked up to as much as twenty-five hours a week by some workers. This firm was also raided. The manager was in the shop at the time and as soon as he saw what was happening he rushed to his office to telephone for the police, only to find that we had taken the precaution of putting two strong men at the phone to prevent it being used. He had to listen while we addressed the employees on the evils of overtime. After an hour the raiders departed, after warning the management that further raids would follow unless overtime ceased. A dozen or so other raids took place at small factories.

The success of these raids on the smaller firms encouraged us to tackle the big factories. The first big firm to be tackled was one at Edmonton, where approximately 1,500 men and women were employed. The raid took place on 15th December, 1921. It was carefully prepared, all the necessary details concerning the plan of the building being ascertained beforehand. A much larger body of raiders was needed to carry out this job. We used about 150, and great care had to be taken in mobilising them near the works in order not to arouse suspicion. I was in charge of the raiding party, and at 4.15 p.m. I gave the signal for all raiders to rush the main entrance of the firm, enter, and close the gates behind them. The commissionaires on the gates were taken unawares and with the first inrush they attempted to slam the gates to, but the raiders tackled them while the rest of their colleagues entered.

Once inside, the gates were firmly shut and the telephone exchange near the entrance was captured by a group detailed for this task, but subsequent events proved that we had still left a loophole for communication with the police. The bulk of the raiders proceeded to the main workshops. We selected a shop where there were millions of finished fragile articles and where considerable damage would have been done if the police had been brought in and caused trouble.

The news of the raid spread rapidly through the works and the workers gathered in large numbers to hear what we had to say. Many expressed warm sympathy for our stand against overtime. After the meeting had been in progress half an hour we received a message asking us to send a deputation to the main office to interview the responsible officials of the firm. The deputation was courteously received by the management who stated that they were very desirous of getting on with the interview as quickly as possible in order to facilitate the withdrawal of the unemployed from the factory. Whilst the interview was proceeding a knock came at the door and we were informed that about 200 police had been brought into the factory. They were, however, not interfering with the men but were just standing about awaiting orders from the management. After a further quarter of an hour's discussion with the management, the principal of the firm and another manager decided to sign the following agreement which we put to them:

1. That all overtime should cease at Christmas.
2. That in the event of the management contemplating the working of overtime at some future date, before putting it into operation they should first explore all channels to find suitable workers by applying to the local labour exchange, local trade-union branches and the local unemployed organisation.

The main argument of the management had been that they had to work overtime because they were unable to obtain suitable workers. We, of course, had strongly disputed this, but the agreement which they gave us met with our approval and when the results of our interview were reported to the men in the shop it was accepted without dissent. We then asked the manager if the workers would be paid for the time which they had been stopped working by the raid. We received a promise that they would be paid and then the raiders formed up four abreast and marched out of the works, singing the "Red Flag" and the "International." As they came out they were cheered by a big crowd who had heard of the raid and had gathered outside.

On 21st December, 1921, the Walthamstow unemployed held a mass meeting in the public baths. I was present and addressed the meeting. When I had finished speaking, Dick Ellis, who was the local organiser of the unemployed, gave his report as branch organiser. In the course of this he laid emphasis on the fact that systematic overtime was being worked at a big engineering firm in Walthamstow. The branch had previously discussed this question and he reported that for three weeks unemployed pickets had stood at the gates of this factory to meet the workers as they went in and came out, to persuade them against continuing overtime. The picketing, however, had produced no results. When Ellis finished his report a resolution was moved from the body of the hall and carried with acclamation, that a raid should be carried out on the factory in question. I immediately gave this my support, but pointed out that as the matter had now been raised in open meeting it would be necessary for the raid to be carried out immediately to avoid the police taking precautions to prevent it.

We thereupon decided to carry out the raid that dinner-hour, and as the hooter sounded for the men to return to work, four hundred unemployed rushed the gates. We had had no time to plan the seizure of the telephones and the holding of exits; we had to take our chance. Once inside the grounds we proceeded to the machine-shop. The motors had just been started up, but we shut them off and called the employees around us for a mass meeting. We knew, of course, that the police would shortly be on the scene so our speeches were short and to the point, but before I could finish speaking news came through that a large force of police were coming in at the main gate, including mounted police. Most of the employees had by this time taken off their jackets and were ready for work at their machines. I therefore called upon all the raiders to remove their coats so that when the police entered the machine-shop they would not be able to distinguish raiders from employees. We felt fairly safe whilst we were in the machine-shop. We knew that it would be extremly difficult for the police to make a baton charge on such ground. We were on ground that we were accustomed to; the police would be on strange ground, amongst machinery.

The police arrived but took no action, awaiting instructions from the management. I then led a small deputation to the manager's office. He told us that he would not discuss anything until we had removed the raiders from the premises. We hesitated to accept this condition; we wondered whether the management intended to play any dirty tricks, such as arresting the deputation after the men had left, or attacking the men as they went out. We were assured that the management would instruct the police to allow the men to leave unmolested, and we therefore returned to the shop, held a short meeting, and instructed the raiders to depart. They put on their coats and carried out the instruction.

On returning to the management the first question that was put to the deputation was, "What have you got to say about this disgraceful and riotous behaviour?" I replied that this was not what we had come to talk about and that if there was any disgraceful behaviour it was certainly on the part of the management of the firm, who were responsible for working overtime whilst millions of men, women and children were suffering hunger as the result of unemployment. After this exchange of opinions we proceeded to discuss the question of overtime. The management endeavoured to justify the overtime and claimed that it was only being worked on emergency jobs. In reply to this we were able to point out that a number of men in various departments had recently been discharged from the firm on the grounds of reducing the staff, and that certain machines were standing idle whilst others were working overtime.

After half an hour with the management, they refused to give an undertaking that all overtime would cease, but they gave us an assurance that no overtime would be worked in future on ordinary production work unless they found it impossible to get suitable workers. The deputation withdrew and addressed a huge mass meeting outside the works, where they reported the results of their interview.

We later learnt that as the raiders were leaving the works the officious attitude of certain of the police officers had almost caused a conflict, but the unemployed took up a stand on a large iron-scrap heap and were therefore in a strong position to protect themselves in the event of a baton charge. This stand apparently resulted in the police being more cautious and the raiders were able to leave in peace.

This raid on this big works created a sensation throughout London, particularly in the engineering trade. It became the topic of discussion in many engineering branches. It no doubt did much to stimulate the opposition that already existed in the union against systematic overtime, so that when a ballot of the Amalgamated Engineering Union membership took place on the question whether the union should make an agreement for overtime with the Employers' Federation, there was a very large majority against. The practice of factory raids caught on in many localities throughout London, with varying results —sometimes successful, sometimes otherwise.

Important success was achieved by another raid in the Islington area, on 18th January, 1922. This was not a raid over the question of overtime but was an action carried out against the system of piece-work which we learnt was in operation in the firm and by which, we were informed, the rate of wage laid down by the Board of Trade was being evaded. The unemployed took an interest in such a question because our movement was constantly agitating for solidarity with the employed workers in their struggles, and against unemployed taking jobs below trade-union rates.

The raiding party walked into the factory by the main gate, which they then closed and locked behind them. Two men went to the telephones and the machines were stopped. While one of the raiders was addressing the employees, a deputation met the

management, who denied that the employees wanted time work.
The manager was thereupon asked to come out to the meeting.
He did so, and the question was put to the employees, who with
one voice shouted for time work. The manager appeared to be
much surprised. After over an hour's discussion, in which we quoted
the names of three employees of whom we knew, who did not
receive the proper rate of pay, the manager made the following
agreement:

I do hereby agree to pay to the employees in question 5s.,
3s. 10½d. and 2s. 7½d. respectively, being back pay due to them.
I also agree that the principle of time work will be applied
in this factory for a period of one month as a trial, from this
date.
Also that the girls will not be stopped for time lost by this
raid carried out by the unemployed.

This agreement was read out to the raiders and the employees.
It was accepted and the raiders therefore left the premises.

In the days immediately preceding Christmas 1921, several
big demonstrations of unemployed marched through the West
End of London. They were now different demonstrations from
those that had taken place a year previously. The collecting-box
practice had been ended and the unemployed marched not as
beggars, appealing for alms in a servile manner, but as spirited
class-conscious men and women, demanding justice from the
government for their grievances as unemployed. The well-to-do
shoppers in Oxford Street and Regent Street looked in vain for
collecting-boxes in which to drop small contributions for charity.
They heard instead the singing of workers' battle-songs, particularly the "International" and the "Red Flag," and they saw
on the banners and placards carried by the demonstrators
militant slogans such as "We demand full maintenance," "Grant
our National Scale of Relief," "The Poverty of the Workers must
be ended," "Down with the Lloyd George Government" and so
on.

On the last night of the old year the London District Council
decided to organise a London demonstration of the unemployed
to St. Paul's cathedral. The North London section before proceeding to the city held a demonstration outside Pentonville
Prison where Ex-Inspector John Syme and a number of Irish
republican prisoners were incarcerated. This section was led by
an Irish pipe band, and for a whole hour the demonstration

marched and held meetings around the gaol. At 10.30 p.m. they formed up for the march to St. Paul's and before midnight they were met by other contingents with bands and banners from all parts of London.

The regular crowd of New Year revellers which gathers outside St. Paul's at midnight were of course astounded when they saw this invasion by the unemployed. Many of them, wanting their last year's deed to be a contribution to the unemployed, were surprised when they saw no collecting-boxes, and they asked for the collectors, but the demonstrators answered by saying, "We don't want charity! If you want to help the unemployed in the New Year help them in the fight against the government for work or full maintenance." After midnight struck and our bands had played "Auld Lang Syne" and the "Red Flag" the demonstrators formed up for a march through the West End. Crowds of people who had come to celebrate the ringing in of the New Year joined with the unemployed in this march. It was a tremendous mass of people that swept down Ludgate Hill and up Fleet Street into the Strand. Their numbers swelled as they proceeded, others on the sidewalks joining in with the procession. The police were perplexed and appeared powerless. There was such a mix-up of demonstrators and revellers that the police were helpless. They did not want to make a baton charge within the first few minutes of the New Year, so the demonstrators marched through all the main streets of the West End, and at 2 a.m. in the morning in Oxford Street the contingents separated and headed for their respective localities.

The demonstration augured well for the spirit of struggle in the New Year, and the events that followed in the next twelve months fulfilled this augury.

The struggle between the unemployed and the guardians was gaining momentum—and early in the New Year of 1922 there was a series of raids on the guardians who had hitherto been discourteous to deputations of the unemployed, or had refused to meet them. On 10th January, I led a deputation to the Southend board of guardians who were meeting at the workhouse in Rochford. We had informed the board that we would be there at 10.30 a.m., and we were prompt to time, but we were kept waiting in the grounds until one o'clock, without any indication of what the board intended to do about receiving the deputation.

We realised that we might be standing there all day for all they cared, so at one o'clock we took the liberty of proceeding, without invitation, to the board room. We arrived to find the board adjourned for lunch, and the chairman asked us to come back at 2.30. We agreed to do so, and being hungry and cold and having little money amongst us, we demanded from the workhouse master a bread and cheese dinner. This was granted. We left the work-house grounds, but on returning at 2.30 we found the gates shut against us. The gatekeeper stated that he had been instructed to keep us out. Our indignation at this piece of trickery can well be imagined. We were not in the frame of mind to walk quietly away, so we decided to climb over the high gates, and over the top we went.

We made straight for the board room and without ceremony entered, to the amazement of the board and particularly of the chairman, who thought that he had outwitted us. One of the members of the board was Mr. H. H. Elvin, general secretary of the National Union of Clerks, and he moved that the deputation be heard. Other members of the board could see that we were determined to get a hearing, and thinking that this would be the easiest way out of the difficulty they supported Mr. Elvin's motion.

When we had stated our case for increased scales of relief for the unemployed, the chairman asked us to depart, informing us that they would discuss the matter and their opinions would be forwarded to us if we left our addresses. We replied that we wanted an answer that day, that there was terrible suffer-ing amongst the unemployed in the Southend area, and the matter was so urgent that it could not wait. We knew many cases where persons in desperate need had been refused relief. The chairman said we must go; we replied, "We shall wait here for your answer to our demands." When the chairman saw that we were adamant he instructed the workhouse master, who was present in the room, to send for the police, but before the master could get to the door two members of the deputation took up position at the door and refused to allow him to leave. A scuffle ensued, the workhouse master and the members of the deputation falling to the floor. Several members of the board went to the assistance of the master, and we went to the assistance of our comrades, so that in the space of a few seconds the whole room was in an uproar, with a struggling group of unemployed and guardians turning over tables, chairs and everything that got in the way of the fight. A member of the board had, however, succeeded in getting out, and the police later arrived after the fight had ended with the workhouse master suffering a rather severe injury to his leg.

The chairman of the board ordered the police to arrest the deputation immediately, but Mr. Elvin vigorously protested against this, and several other members of the board were very hesitant in supporting this order. Ultimately the deputation were allowed to leave quietly on the understanding that summonses would be issued, but apparently the guardians thought better of it and no prosecutions took place.

The Greenwich and Deptford unemployed organised a deputation on 18th January, 1922, to the guardians' offices with the intention of compelling the board to grant one hundredweight of coal to those who were on relief. This coal allowance had been promised three weeks previously but had not been actually provided. The deputation, numbering twenty, were received by the board. Trouble started as soon as the deputation began to state their case—members of the board continually interrupting them and trying to tie them down to the discussion of only one item.

As the board would not listen quietly to their case the deputation decided on direct action. The doors were fastened and windows were guarded, and for an hour and a half the business of the board was held up whilst threats were hurled at the unemployed by the chairman for their unconstitutional action. Ultimately the police, who had been repeatedly rattling the door, forced it open, but, strange to say, when the police entered the chairman asked them to withdraw. He then opened the meeting of the board, whilst the unemployed stood round the room. Within the space of two minutes he took a vote on the question of the coal allowance, deciding that it should be granted from that afternoon onwards and promising to call a special meeting to deal with the other points that the deputation had raised.

In contrast to the bitter struggles which were being conducted between the guardians and the unemployed in different parts of the country, in Poplar a friendly feeling existed between the guardians and the unemployed. On 25th January, 1922, a demonstration of 15,000 unemployed marched to the Poplar guardians' offices. It was in no sense a hostile demonstration. On the contrary it was a demonstration of support of the guardians who had come under the fire of the reactionaries from all quarters because of the scales which were being paid in Poplar.

The deputation was received by the guardians and urged the adoption of the National Unemployed Workers' Movement national scale of relief. Charlie Sumner was the Labour mayor of Poplar, and after the deputation had stated their case he expressed the opinion that the scale which had been put forward was in fact too modest, taking into consideration the cost of living. The board thereupon decided to increase its scale of relief even beyond the unemployed's demands and they laid down the following scale:

Man and wife, £2 a week.
Each child, up to 16 years of age, 6s. a week.
Rent up to 15s. a week, plus one hundredweight of coal, or its equivalent in gas.
Single person 18 years and over, £1 10s. 0d. a week, plus coal and gas allowance.
Single person, 16 to 18, 15s. a week.
No deductions from these amounts except for monies received at the labour exchange.

The adoption of this new scale by Poplar almost sent the capitalist press editors mad. They screamed and raved about it in almost every edition of their papers and they coined the phrase "Poplarism," which was subsequently used by the reactionaries in municipal and parliamentary election campaigns.

In Camberwell at the end of January 1922, the unemployed learnt that the board of guardians were about to stop the supply of milk for the babies of unemployed parents, so on 1st February a body of Camberwell women, members of the unemployed movement, proceeded to the House of Commons, many of them carrying babies in arms. They carried placards protesting against this injustice. They went to the House of Commons because it had been reported that this economy at the expense of the babies was an instruction from the Ministry of Health. On the placards with which they paraded outside the House of Commons were such inscriptions as the following: "Honour the dead fathers by saving the living"; "Milk is life to a baby—don't take our babies' lives"; "Whilst rich babies are fed, ours are dying for lack of food"; "Our babies' bottles are empty in a land of plenty."

A telegram had been sent by the women to the Minister of Health, Sir Alfred Mond, informing him that they would be at the Ministry of Health at noon, so as Big Ben struck his first boom, the women stopped their poster parade and proceeded to the Ministry of Health in Whitehall. They entered and were told that the Minister of Health could not receive them, but that his secretary, Mr. Stuchbury, would hear what they had to say, along with Dr. Janet Campbell, an official of the Ministry. The women demanded a written guarantee that the milk allowance to mothers and babies in Camberwell would not be touched. This was refused, and the women pointed out that this refusal was tantamount to an admission that the milk was to be taken away. The minister's secretary stated that Sir Alfred Mond had no power to give the guarantee such as the women were demanding, that the matter rested with the board of guardians, and that he would take the matter up with them. The women thereupon insisted that they should at least have a written guarantee that they could come back to the ministry for a meeting in the event of their not being satisfied in the locality. After a good deal of argument the following statement was given:

> Ministry of Health,
> Whitehall.
> February 1st, 1922.

To Mrs. Cole.

In reply to your request that I should see your deputation again if you desire it, I shall be prepared to do so if, after the enquiries which we will make into your complaint, you still desire to come here.

> Yours faithfully,
> H. O. STUCHBURY.

On 28th February a letter was sent from the Ministry of Health to the women as follows:

> Ministry of Health,
> Whitehall, S.W.1.
> February 28th, 1922.

Madam,

I am directed by the Minister of Health to advert to the interview which your deputation had with his officers on the 1st instant, with reference to the supplies of milk to expectant and nursing mothers and children in the Borough of Camberwell.

The Minister has caused enquiries to be made into the matter referred to by the deputation. He is informed that the Camberwell Guardians have now decided that the cost of milk supplied by the Borough Council shall not be taken into account as part of the income of applicants for outdoor relief.

> I am,
> Your obedient servant,
> H. O. STUCHBURY.

Some boards of guardians had persistently refused to meet deputations from the unemployed. Woolwich was such a case. On 2nd February, 1922, the Woolwich branch of the unemployed movement decided to break down this arrogant attitude of the guardians. A strong deputation proceeded to the workhouse where the guardians were meeting, and as police were standing at the main entrance the deputation proceeded to a back entrance.

They gained admission without any interference and made for the board room. When they unceremoniously entered and stated who they were, the chairman of the board immediately declared the meeting closed. Instantly the members of the deputation, who had planned their course of action beforehand, took up positions at the doors and windows and prevented anybody from leaving. The spokesman of the deputation then appealed to the chairman to re-open the business and to put the deputation down as the last item on the agenda. This was refused. The deputation locked the doors and informed the board that they would remain until they got satisfaction. Deadlock continued for about three-quarters of an hour; then some of the workhouse officials who had been trying to enter the board room apparently realised that something was wrong and fetched the police. The doors were locked from the inside. The police demanded admission but the unemployed held firm. After a time the police proceeded to batter in one of the doors. As they broke through one of the unemployed deputation who was guarding that door was severely injured. The guardians had gathered themselves together in the centre of the horseshoe formed by the tables at which they sat. When the police entered they therefore had a clear field to deal with the deputation. They came in with batons drawn and used them freely upon the heads and shoulders of the unemployed, and drove them from the building.

The evening press, of course, reported: "Riotous behaviour by the unemployed in Woolwich."

Similar actions against boards of guardians became a common feature in the activities of the unemployed in many parts of the country. On the same day as the raid took place on the board at Woolwich, a big demonstration of unemployed took place in Cumberland. Contingents of unemployed men and women marched in heavy rain from Barrow-in-Furness, Dalton, Pennington and Ravenstown. They converged on Ulverston workhouse, where the Ulverston and District board of guardians was meeting. The men from Dalton and Ravenstown had to march six miles, but in spite of shabby clothing and leaky boots they carried through the march determined to arouse the guardians to a better sense of responsibility in connection with the needs of the unemployed.

Ulverston is a respectable residential centre, and the sight of hundreds of unemployed marching through the streets to establish their rights was something unprecedented and alarming to the residents.

Before the marchers reached Ulverston the police thought they had made every preparation to safeguard the well-established conditions of "law and order", and when the main body of demonstrators arrived at the institution where the board was meeting they were confronted with closed gates and a strong force of police drawn from the surrounding localities. The strategy of the unemployed had, however, outwitted the police. Anticipating that attention would be centred on the demonstrators, a picked body of men had previously succeeded in secreting themselves in the grounds of the workhouse, and, when the police were holding the demonstrators at bay, this group of workers proceeded quietly to the board room and took possession. At the same time groups of demonstrators were being quietly instructed by their leaders to make their way to the back of the workhouse building. They did so unnoticed by the police, and when there were about 200 demonstrators in the rear of the building they scaled the walls while the police were holding the main gates.

Pandemonium broke out when this crowd of demonstrators reached the board room. Ultimately the police realised how they had been outwitted, and the superintendent, along with a body of constables, came through the workhouse grounds and pleaded with the demonstrators to "be reasonable." The guardians, under pressure from the marchers, had agreed to hear a deputation of three, provided the remainder withdrew from the room, but the unemployed insisted upon six being received, and the police superintendent advised the chairman to receive the full deputation. They ultimately agreed to do so.

The raid took place at 1.30 p.m., and at 4.15 p.m. the guardians decided to fix a definite and increased scale of relief. The scale was increased to 26s. for man and wife; 5s. a child up to four children; and 3s. for every additional child. For single persons 18 years and over 15s. per week.

This still fell short of the national scale demanded by the unemployed movement but it was a big advance on the former position in this district where no fixed scale had been made but where the amount allowed to the applicant was subject to the discretion of the relieving officer, who always seemed actuated by the motive of giving as little as possible and saving the rates.

A similar action also took place on this day at Strood in Kent. The unemployed movement had asked the guardians to receive a deputation and they had refused, so 100 men from Gravesend and Northfleet gathered at the workhouse; as the gates were shut against them they scaled the walls but were prevented by the police from reaching the board room. Before leaving the grounds, however, they insisted on a statement being made by the chairman of the board, and when they were promised that their grievances would be inquired into they departed. An amusing incident occurred before the unemployed left the workhouse grounds. The leader of the deputation who was addressing them ended the meeting by calling upon the unemployed to sing the national anthem. The unemployed knew what was meant but the police did not. Instantly the police drew themselves to attention but when the demonstrators burst into song and the police heard the strains of the "Red Flag," their surprised expression can well be imagined!

Throughout the whole of February hundreds of demonstrations marched to boards of guardians throughout Great Britain, and many exciting scenes occurred. In the naval dockyard town of Devonport 1,000 unemployed besieged the guardians and compelled them to withdraw the order which they had made for reducing relief. In West Ham (London), as the unemployed were marching from the guardians' offices on 23rd February, a baton charge took place with mounted and foot police. The unemployed used their banner poles as weapons for defence. Several were injured and six demonstrators were arrested. At Aylesbury (Bucks) the guardians fled before a determined demonstration of unemployed, some of them even making their escape from windows under the protection of the police.

Throughout Scotland, under the leadership of Harry McShane, exciting agitations were taking place around labour exchanges and parish relief offices. In Greenock, where the unemployed raided the parish council, they were forcibly ejected by the police and subsequently four local leaders of the unemployed were summoned—Murphy, McDade, McGuire, and Ross—and they were all sentenced to three months' hard labour. On the night that they were sentenced the Greenock Trades and Labour Council passed a resolution "protesting strongly against the savage sentences passed upon their fellow trade unionists, which on the face of the evidence as reported in the local press was entirely unwarranted."

Although the struggles of the unemployed had forced the scales of relief up to a level exceeding any previous scale in the history of poor law relief, it must be remembered that the cost of living was at this time exceedingly high, so that the unemployed were actually enduring severe poverty even where the best scales were applied.

Many of the unemployed organisations were appealing to the churches to join with them in their struggle against starvation. They sometimes met with sympathetic response and sometimes only with pious verbiage. The two following letters received from ministers of the church in the Vale of Leven provide interesting evidence of this. The Vale of Leven branch of the unemployed movement wrote to these ministers and invited them to participate in the activities of the movement or at least to address a meeting of the unemployed. They replied as follows:

17th January, 1922.

Dear Mr. Watterson,
Your letter of the 11th reached me when I was very busy, hence my delay in answering. I fear the suggestion of your committee is one that I cannot, however sympathetic, entertain.

The question of unemployment is almost entirely economic, and only a man of ripe business experience could offer any valuable information regarding it.

Why not approach someone with that needful qualification?

With kind regards,

ROBERT S. MACMORRAN.

Wesley Manse,
Bowhill.
18th January, 1922.

Dear Mr. Watterson,
Your letter dated 14/1/22 arrived on the 16/1/22 and found me in bed with the flu. I am still very unwell, that is my reason for not answering you sooner. I am sorry that I cannot accede to your request to give a lecture on "Unemployment: Its Causes and Cure." Lecturing is not in my line.

I think most people will agree that the great war which has cursed the world is one cause of much of the unemployment in the world to-day. Another cause of much of the unemployment in our own land, I believe, is the great amount of money spent on strong drink, gambling, sport, theatres, pictures, dancing, etc.; in 1920 we spent as a nation nearly £470,000,000, over £9,000,000 a week on drink alone. *No nation can waste money like this and prosper.* If the money spent on these things were spent in Ships, Motor Cars, Houses, Furniture, Clothes, Boots, Food and other COMFORTS, and necessaries of life, we should soon have Better Trade, Happier Homes, Better People, a Better Land.

In an old book which many despise, but which I believe in more and more, we read: "He hath shown thee O man what is good and what doth the Lord expect of thee, but to do justly, to love mercy, and to walk humbly with thy God." When we all do these things we shall have a better world.

We cannot have a new world until we have a new people; men and women with a new heart and a right spirit; a heart to fear God and keep His commandments. Jesus Christ said to men in His day: "Seek first the Kingdom of God and His righteousness and all these things (that is, food and raiment and all the necessaries of life) shall be added to you."

When we do our part God always does His. He never fails.

The only cure for the wants and woes of this old war-worn sinful world is the religion of Jesus Christ believed in and lived up to by the people.

I trust the day will soon come when all who want work will get work to do and do it cheerfully and well.

Kindest regards,
Yours sincerely,
HENRY ANDREWS.

In our agitations against the local authorities on the question of relief scales we were also fighting against the pernicious system of slave labour known as task work. Under the poor law of this country an applicant for poor law relief could be ordered to perform task work as a condition of the receipt of out-door relief, the applicant receiving no wages for the work performed—the grant of relief being his only payment.

The militant attitude of the unemployed had scared most of the boards of guardians and local councils into dropping any attempt to impose task work, but the Ministry of Health, which was beginning to exercise more and more control over the local authorities, attempted to rectify the position by an order laying down that the local authorities should endeavour to provide work schemes for the unemployed at which they would be paid not at trade-union rates but at seventy-five per cent of the trade-union rates.

Our movement conducted a relentless fight against this and broke the scheme down in nearly every place where it was attempted. Some exciting activities took place around this question.

On 7th December, 1921, the Bexley Heath Urban District Council met for the transaction of its business, one of the items on the agenda being proposals for starting district work schemes on the seventy-five per cent trade-union wage basis. The unemployed branches in the surrounding areas sent delegations to protest against this scheme. These delegations, numbering about forty in all, entered the council chamber. They were allowed to remain and listen to the discussion of the other items on the agenda but when the chairman opened the discussion on the work schemes the unemployed representatives requested that they be heard before the matter was voted on. The chairman thereupon declared the meeting closed, saying he was not prepared to allow the unemployed to interfere with the business of the council. The unemployed appealed to him to hear their views but he would not do so.

The meeting had begun at 8 p.m. It was now 9.30 p.m. The chairman of the Council attempted to leave but before he could do so the unemployed delegates took possession of the chamber. They barricaded the doors and windows and again appealed to the chairman to re-open the business. He refused to do so, so the unemployed delegates appointed their own chairman and proceeded to call upon their speakers to state their case, the councillors being invited to participate in the discussion if they so desired. Some of the councillors were sympathetic and repeatedly appealed to the chairman to re-open the meeting and put the business in order. The unemployed made it clear that they intended to remain until they got satisfaction. They emphasised that they were not going to allow scab work schemes to be introduced.

They were still in possession, with the councillors as prisoners, when midnight struck. The speech-making having been finished, they proceeded to the singing of songs. The fire brigade and the police were brought, but as there was division amongst the council itself there was apparently nobody ready to give the order for the police to take action. Time went on and still the unemployed held firm. At 3.15 a.m. councillors who wanted to get home endeavoured to persuade the chairman to re-open the proceedings. It was moved by one Councillor and seconded by another that a chairman be elected and the council resume business. Others spoke in favour of re-opening the proceedings. The chairman, however, remained adamant, and said he would not open the proceedings until the unemployed left the chamber. This they refused to do. Just after 6 a.m., however, councillors wishing to avoid a conflict with the police and at the same time wishing to get home to their beds or get to their work, decided by eight votes to nil, many abstaining from voting, to re-open the business.

A vice-chairman was elected and hurriedly brought the proceedings to an end by taking a resolution which laid down that no work would be undertaken at wages below trade-union rate and that a deputation from the council along with two representatives of the unemployed committee should visit the Minister of Health in respect to this question of work schemes below trade-union rates.

This decision satisfied the unemployed representatives and when the chairman of the council declared the meeting closed the unemployed departed for their homes.

In West Bromwich the unemployed marched to a relief job where seventy-five per cent of trade-union rates were being paid, and succeeded in stopping the job. It resulted, however, in five of the West Bromwich leaders being arrested and imprisoned, by the names of Rigby, Baggart, Swaine, Connor and Carpenter.

In Basingstoke, too, the unemployed moved into action against a relief-work scheme. On 28th December, 1921, I went down to Basingstoke to address a mass meeting in one of the local cinemas. I found that the unemployed had organised strike action on a road job which was being run as relief work, but thirty-four other workers had been persuaded by the authorities to blackleg. From the mass meeting in the cinema we decided to march on to the job to persuade the blacklegs to stop work.

Three hundred unemployed took part in the march—a distance of nearly three miles. When we reached the job I appealed to the blacklegs to stop work. More than half of them did so; the others, however, refused, so the order was given to confiscate the tools from the job. This was very quickly done, not only taking the tools which the men had been working with, but also collecting from the hut all the spare ones, mostly picks and shovels. We then decided to march back into the town of Basingstoke and the men set off with about 200 picks and shovels on their shoulders.

We were not clear what we were going to do with the tools. Some suggested dumping them in the river, but I suggested that, as our grievance was against the conduct of the district surveyor and the town hall authorities, we should march to the town hall and deposit the muddy instruments of labour there. The shopkeepers and pedestrians were astonished when they saw us marching through the streets. The police were bewildered and did not know what to do. We went straight to the town hall and there the order was given for the picks and shovels to be thrown into the district surveyor's office. In disposing of his pick one of the demonstrators accidentally picked out a plate glass window in the door, but nobody bothered very much. The surveyor's office certainly looked a wreck with 200 muddy picks and shovels heaped up in it. After a short meeting outside the town hall, the unemployed dispersed to their homes, having successfully stopped the job.

A similar action followed at Rochdale (Lancs.) on 3rd January. The unemployed marched to a job where only seventy-five per cent of trade-union rates were being paid and stopped it by taking away the tools and barrows. The Rochdale *Observer* in commenting upon this, called the unemployed "work-shys." This roused their anger and a demonstration marched to the premises of the *Observer*. Whilst an interview was taking place between the unemployed representatives and one of the proprietors of the paper, a stone was thrown at the *Observer* offices, breaking a plate-glass window valued at £30.

For this the police served a summons upon Dawson, the organiser of the Rochdale unemployed branch, and when the case came before the court a big demonstration took place outside. Percy Kealey, who was the divisional organiser for the N.U.W.M., demanded to be allowed to defend Dawson in the court, but the bench refused this on the grounds that he was not a qualified solicitor. The case ended in Dawson being bound over to keep the peace for twelve months in surety of £10, or to go to prison for one month.

At Gravesend, on 30th January, the unemployed marched to a relief work scheme, held a mass meeting on the job and succeeded in putting a stop to it.

By these methods our movement broke down the seventy-five per cent relief-work schemes all over the country. There can be no doubt about where our movement stood in the fight for the maintenance of trade-union standards and conditions. We also showed this by the actions of the movement in strikes and lock-outs. Solidarity with the employed workers was in fact one of the rules of our movement. It was clearly stated in the programme laid down at our national conference in 1921, which said: *"All Unemployed Committees are pledged to assist in every possible way workers who may come out on strike or who are locked out.*

The unemployed to act as pickets in support of the workers in their dispute, and the unemployed committee to seek representation on all strike and lock-out committees."

A strike took place on 3rd February, 1922, amongst the workers of a transport firm in Reading. The Reading branch of the unemployed movement immediately offered their support to the workers in picketing and demonstrations. The employers were seeking to reduce wages to 6s. below the district rate. The effective picketing, sometimes taking on a mass character, prevented the firm from obtaining the services of blackleg labour. The strike resulted in a victory for the workers: not only were the wages maintained but an agreement was made that only union labour would be employed. The unemployed organisation received a letter of thanks from the Transport and General Workers' Union for the part that they had played in the struggle.

In Ipswich a strike of Transport and General Workers' Union members took place at the docks. The organised unemployed stood loyally to the programme of their movement and rendered full support to the strikers. After the dispute ended the following letter was received by our movement from the Provincial Docks Group Secretary of the Transport and General Workers' Union.

To the National Secretary,
    National Unemployed Workers' Movement.

Dear Comrade,

We have recently run a very successful strike of dock workers in Ipswich, the success being largely due to the loyalty of the Unemployed Committee and their members. The dispute in question lasted a fortnight, but on the eve of the dispute I was able to get in touch with the Unemployed Committee and addressed about one thousand of their members the following morning, and as a consequence of the relations established and the pledge of the unemployed to assist strikers to every possible extent we were able to limit the amount of blacklegs obtainable to 20, some of whom came from outside the town.

There are some 5,000 to 6,000 unemployed in Ipswich and despite the fact that the employers advertised regularly in the local Press for scabs, and had their touts at the Labour Exchange and Guardians Relief yard, and although the average wages of the town would not exceed £2 per week as compared with the high earning capacity at the docks, the victory of the strike was obtained as a result of the energetic picketing of the unemployed both at the docks and at the Labour Exchange.

Yours fraternally,

F. THOMPSON,

Provincial Docks Group Secretary.

On 11th March, 1922, the national lock-out of the engineers started. The unemployed movement went into action in support of the locked-out workers in all parts of the country, and big solidarity meetings and demonstrations were held. We took the lead in picketing and in raiding factories where blacklegs were working. Under pressure of mass demonstrations of unemployed and locked-out engineers the boards of guardians in many of the big engineering centres were compelled to pay outdoor relief to the engineers on the same scale as the unemployed, although this was illegal.

Coventry in particular was a storm centre during this dispute. I was invited to speak in Coventry in the Baths Assembly Hall on 12th March. I did so, and plain-clothes officers were present taking notes of my speech. From Coventry I continued my campaign in other industrial centres and on 26th March, whilst I was in Birkenhead, the police came to my lodgings and placed me under arrest on the charge of having made a seditious speech in Coventry.

I appeared in the police court at Coventry on 28th March. After hearing the charge and the police evidence I demanded an adjournment in order that I could prepare my defence and call witnesses. The court gave an adjournment until 4th April. When the proceedings re-opened on this date, 5,000 unemployed demonstrated outside the court. I cross-examined the police witnesses for over an hour and the decision of the bench was that I should be bound over to keep the peace for a period of six months. I challenged the bench on whether this meant preventing me from speaking on the public platform, but their ruling was that I would not be prevented from speaking but must not use words of a nature likely to incite people to break the peace. The alternative to the binding over was one month's imprisonment.

Before giving my decision I asked the bench if they would permit me to discuss the matter with my committee in an ante-room. To my surprise they agreed and I re-entered the court and announced that I would accept the binding over.

Now at the same court on the same day five committee-men of the Coventry unemployed branch were being charged with having taken an active part in a demonstration outside the house of a certain person who had used insulting remarks about the unemployed in a Labour Party conference in Coventry on 25th February. The Coventry Unemployed Organisation had demanded an apology which had been refused; hence the demonstration which took place on 20th March. After the demonstration this man took out summonses against Tom Dingley, who was an N.A.C. member of the unemployed movement, R. Heard, F. Preece, H. Whiteley and W. J. Arden. The charge against these men was "that complainant is afraid of some bodily harm being done to him or a breach of the peace being caused, and therefore craves not for malice or ill-will, but merely for the safety of his person."

The case came on immediately after my own, and each of the defendants was found guilty and ordered to find sureties in the sum of £10 to be of good behaviour for six months. They decided that they would not put up the sureties and that they would do the alternative of twenty-eight days' imprisonment. I felt that this decision of my colleagues altered the position in regard to myself and I thereupon stepped forward in the court and announced that I also would refuse to be bound over. We were taken below to the cells and later removed in police cars to Winson Green gaol, Birmingham.

Huge protest demonstrations were organised on the streets of Coventry. A torchlight demonstration of 7,000 marched through the streets during the evening. The police were seriously alarmed. A Free Speech Committee was set up and pressure was brought to bear upon the party concerned to apologise. He ultimately did so in the following statement:

To the Secretary of the Coventry Unemployed
    Committee and whom it may concern.

I have been accused of making a statement inimical to the unemployed. May I explain that at a meeting held on Saturday, February 25th, the unemployed were mentioned by a speaker in a manner which I considered entirely irrelevant to the purpose of the meeting. I then used an objectionable phrase concerning the unemployed which I sincerely regret, more so in that it was uttered with no intention of disrespect to anyone. The remark has been taken in a sense never intended by me and was only heard by less than half a dozen immediately around me, and I very deeply deplore the sequence of events leading to the imprisonment of the Unemployed Committee leaders. If my remark has been misunderstood by the unemployed in general, I apologise.

This apology considerably eased the situation, and the writer of the letter along with the unemployed and delegates to the Free Speech Committee, interviewed the chief constable of Coventry, and demanded the release of the prisoners.

The police were alarmed about the size of the demonstrations which were marching the streets in protest against the imprisonments. We had been in prison several days, and one evening, when we were quietly settled in our cells, we were surprised at being unlocked and taken to an ante-room to meet a representative from the Coventry police, along with members of the Free Speech Committee and the Unemployed Committee, who informed us that they had come over with an order for our immediate release. In half an hour we were outside the gaol again.

The engineers' lock-out lasted four months and during that period many members of the National Unemployed Workers' Movement were arrested and imprisoned, or fined for their activities, the charges against them mostly being: "seditious speeches"; "obstruction"; or "acting in a manner likely to cause a breach of the peace." Amongst the numerous arrests which were occurring throughout the country was that of Mrs. Thring on the charge of "inciting to disaffection amongst the metropolitan police." She was at the time editor of a national paper which the unemployed movement was publishing known as *Out of Work*, which had a large circulation, and after one of the big battles with the police in London an article appeared in this paper appealing to the police not to use their batons against the unemployed. She was ordered to pay £10 at Bow Street. This was refused and she was imprisoned for three weeks.

In addition to our activities of solidarity with the locked-out engineers, the wave of arrests and imprisonments was also occasioned by the fact that in April 1922 the government introduced a new feature into the unemployment insurance scheme in the form of a five weeks' gap in the benefit payments. By the Act of March 1921, the government had raised the period of statutory benefit from fifteen to twenty-six weeks and introduced a system known as "uncovenanted benefit" to meet the needs of those who had exhausted their statutory benefit. The five weeks' gap condition applied to the latter claimants only, but they constituted more than half of the total claimants at the labour exchange. The gap system meant that when they exhausted their statutory benefit they would be unable to draw any further benefit at the exchange for a period of five weeks. If they were still unemployed at the end of this period they could claim five weeks' uncovenanted benefit, followed by another gap of five weeks, and so on.

The operation of the gap system drove hundreds of thousands of unemployed claimants to the boards of guardians, so that not only were the unemployed conducting big struggles to smash the system, but the local authorities were also compelled to make strong protests at the new burdens thrown upon them. Within three months from the introduction of this system the agitation had become so strong that the government had to modify it, and from 20th July the gap was reduced to one week in five. Many of the boards of guardians in this period tried to ease their financial position by refusing relief to many claimants, particularly those who were in receipt of labour exchange benefit. This action, of course, led to intensified struggles on the part of the unemployed throughout the country and in many centres street fighting with the police took place.

At the beginning of May the Birmingham authorities made a definite ruling that no relief could be paid to those receiving labour exchange benefit. The unemployed claimed that the labour exchange scales were inadequate to meet their barest needs, and after a series of big demonstrations thousands of Birmingham unemployed were organised by our movement to demand admission to the workhouse. On 10th May, 1922, a crowd of 5,000 Birmingham unemployed assembled on the famous meeting-place known as the Bull Ring—the place which our forefathers had used nearly one hundred years previously in the Chartist agitations. From the Bull Ring the demonstration marched to Summerfield Park to meet other Birmingham contingents, and by the time that they reached the workhouse their numbers had increased to nearly 20,000. As the demonstration marched up to the locked gates of the workhouse, the police endeavoured to disperse them. After a short conflict the ranks of the demonstrators were reformed to march back through the main streets of Birmingham. Reinforcements of police were being rushed up almost every minute. When the demonstration reached Great Charles Street the police tried to prevent it from proceeding any further and as the unemployed pushed forward batons were drawn, and the police rushed into the ranks to club down unarmed men and women. But they could not disperse the crowd; over and over again they rallied and reformed their ranks, and ultimately they again reached the Bull Ring, where a huge protest meeting was held and where copies of the *Birmingham Daily Mail*, which had made scurrilous statements in regard to the unemployed, were burned in public. This meeting did not end until 10.30 p.m. The Birmingham unemployed had therefore been meeting, marching, and fighting from one o'clock in the day until 10.30 at night.

Seven days later another great demonstration of the Birmingham unemployed took place, on 17th May. The police had previously notified the leaders that they were placing a ban upon the demonstration unless it conformed to a particular route. This route, of course, was well away from any of the important streets of Birmingham. When the unemployed assembled in the Bull Ring, the police refused to allow the ranks to be formed. They drew batons immediately the order for fall-in was given, and in the famous Bull Ring the blood of the workers was again shed. It happened that part of the roadway in the Bull Ring was under repair and after the first baton charge the unemployed rallied their forces and seized paving-stones and other missiles with which they met the second charge. Both sides suffered severe casualties, but the strength of the unemployed resistance, now that they had some means of defence, had a steadying effect upon the police and the order was given for them to withdraw and to put away their batons. Although the demonstration had not marched out of the Bull Ring, the battle had not dispersed them, and a tremendous mass meeting was held whilst the police looked on.

On 29th May another big London demonstration was held to support a deputation to the Minister of Labour and Minister of Health to protest against the five weeks' gap system. Contingents from all over London marched to the central point of mobilisation, which was Victoria Embankment. The arrangement was that we should march to Hyde Park and that en route the deputation should fall out and proceed to Whitehall, returning to Hyde Park to report the result of the interview. To our surprise, however, the police refused to allow the demonstration to march to Hyde Park, even though we were prepared to conform to the one-mile condition. It was clear from the outset that the police had been mobilised in very big forces and appeared to be eager for a conflict, probably because the demonstration was not as large as had been anticipated. It was only with the utmost difficulty that we managed to avoid a conflict on the Embankment.

The head of the procession, refused the right to proceed to Hyde Park, turned towards the city, and when we reached Cannon Street it was decided that we should disperse and that the marchers should make their way to Hyde Park individually. The bugle for the fall-out was sounded, and immediately the police, mounted and foot, charged down upon the unarmed and helpless half-starved demonstrators. Men and women fell before the blows of the police clubs, some were trampled under hoofs of horses, men were caught up and beaten to the ground and left there bleeding. Four were frogmarched to the police station near by and charged next morning with "assaulting the police"! One of those arrested was a Battersea borough councillor by the name of Wheeler. The chief police evidence against him was that he had a water-bottle in his pocket and the police claimed that he carried this as a weapon to use against them. He was sentenced to two months' hard labour.

Immediately following this conflict the headquarters of the N.U.W.M. decided upon a national week of struggle against the gap system. From Monday, 19th June, to Sunday, 25th, every branch of the unemployed movement was called upon to organise mass demonstrations culminating in big rallies on the Sunday. The call was taken up with enthusiasm everywhere and there was hardly a town or industrial village which did not witness during that week mass meetings or demonstrations against the gap. This week of struggle was undoubtedly the crowning-point in our offensive against the gap system, and in July the government reduced the gap period to one week.

During the beginning of the year 1922 the eviction of unemployed families from their homes for failure to pay rent and rates became a burning issue. The national conference of the unemployed which had been held in November 1921, charged the movement with the task of resisting evictions. Within a few days of the conference an eviction struggle occurred in Smethwick. Three unemployed families were evicted from their homes for arrears of rent. The unemployed organisation immediately called the unemployed together. A demonstration marched to the house, broke open the doors, and reinstalled the furniture. Two of the local leaders by the name of Grant and Swain were later arrested, but the police evidence was not strong enough to secure a conviction.

During May and June, 1922, Glasgow and the whole of the

Clyde witnessed stormy scenes in the fight against evictions, which were becoming almost daily occurrences. The unemployed movement led the way in forming special tenants' organisations which took on a highly-organised form. A system of scouts was developed, and when an eviction was about to take place the scouts would run or cycle through the neighbouring streets blowing whistles or ringing bells, calling the workers out to the address where the eviction was to be attempted. Crowds of men and women and children would rush to the scene of eviction and prevent the bailiffs from removing the furniture. Of course, before the day of eviction, every effort would be made by the unemployed and the tenants' defence committee, by constitutional methods, to persuade the landlord and his agents to abandon this inhuman practice of throwing a family and its goods on the streets. But often negotiations proved fruitless, especially where the landlord or agent had already made arrangements for new tenants who were prepared to pay a higher rent than the old tenant. Not infrequently one came across a case of eviction where a family had lived in the house for very many years—in one case in Glasgow as long as thirty years—yet the landlord, seeing the prospects of a few extra shillings a week from new tenants, had secured an eviction order on the grounds of a few weeks' arrears of rent.

The biggest eviction fight in Glasgow took place on 17th May, 1922. It gave a lead to many other parts of the country and led to the Glasgow City Council having to set up a special rent fund to relieve tenants who were in danger of eviction. About 7.30 on the morning of 17th May, one of the Glasgow leaders of the unemployed called upon Harry McShane to inform him that an eviction had taken place in South York Street, in the Gorbals district. McShane, Duffy and another worker immediately proceeded to the scene. They found that the furniture had already been placed on the stairs and the door of the house had been nailed up. One was sent to rouse other supporters, and McShane and Duffy forced open the door and replaced the furniture in the house. Crowds quickly gathered at the call of the movement, and mass meetings were held in the street outside the house. McShane spoke at these meetings, and during the meeting in the evening three detectives took notes of his speech. After the meeting ended the committee of the unemployed movement was called together and met at midnight, in a house close by. After discussion it was decided that the whole of the committee would proceed immediately to the house where the eviction had taken place and occupy it along with the tenants and resist any attempt at entry by the police or the bailiffs. Twelve men and two women took up positions in the house.

In the early hours of the morning of 19th May police came to the house and knocked at the door. They were informed that the door was barricaded and that the inhabitants intended to resist their entry. They were advised to go away as the defenders were at that time busily engaged in a draughts tournament. The police departed and came back with large reinforcements. The scouts went out and aroused the workers in the neighbourhood; within a short space of time big crowds had gathered.

The rooms that were now in siege were in a tenement two stories high. Expecting a conflict, McShane knocked on the wall to call the tenant of the next house to the window. He asked her to go out and call a Labour magistrate by the name of James Buchan to the scene, so that he could be a reliable witness of any foul play by the police. Mr. Buchan was known to be very friendly towards the unemployed movement and he immediately answered the appeal and stood outside the house during the morning. In the besieged room the defenders chalked a notice on a piece of floor-cloth and hung it out of the window announcing that McShane would address the crowd from the window at 10 a.m. By the time the meeting was due to start a tremendous crowd had gathered and a huge force of police was present. Every two hours short speeches were made from the window by McShane and others. The crowd was so dense that their voices could not reach to everybody assembled and speakers of the movement held other meetings outside on the streets. When a red flag was hung out from a window of the besieged room great cheers arose from the crowd.

The police meanwhile were taking no action to eject the defenders. They were probably relying on the defenders having to surrender through lack of food. They were surprised therefore when they saw a bag being lowered from the window by a rope with a note requesting food. The police attempted to snatch the bag, but the crowd prevented this. Several workers went away and came back with the bag loaded. The rope was lowered again from the window and up went the food. The police attempted to bring up a Black Maria, but the crowd refused to make a gangway and the van had to go back.

Late in the afternoon, when a number of the demonstrators had gone to their homes for a brief period to get tea, the police took their chance. A van, accompanied by hundreds of policemen, came into the street. They rushed the house and smashed the door to splinters, entering the rooms with batons drawn. The news spread quickly and crowds of workers came running to the spot from all the side streets. As the police broke into the room McShane threw the red flag to the crowd. A scuffle took place for the possession of the flag and the police were defeated. The fight outside alarmed the police who were breaking in, and they entered the room white with fear. A warrant was read in the room charging the defenders with taking possession of the house without permission of the rightful owner and in addition charging McShane with giving two seditious speeches the previous day. The defenders were taken down the stairs to the waiting police van and as they emerged the crowd rushed forward to prevent them from being taken away. Bottles and stones were thrown at the police and it was only after a severe battle that the defenders of the house were got into the van and driven to the police station.

Next morning the accused appeared in court and large crowds gathered outside the police station. The accused were remanded to prison, bail being refused. After remaining in prison three weeks all the accused were released from Duke Street prison on bail, with the exception of Harry McShane, who was refused bail. The trial took place on 4th July. McShane, after persuasion, agreed to allow himself to be defended along with the other accused by a famous K.C. named Craigie Aitchison, who later became chief justice for Scotland. During the period of imprisonment awaiting trial, the lawyer had made a very important discovery, namely, that the real tenant of the house was Mrs. Shaw, and that the order for ejectment was given against her husband, James Shaw. This was kept quiet until the day of the trial and when the prosecution opened their case it collapsed within ten minutes on the grounds that the order of eviction had been wrongly made out against the husband who was not the actual tenant. The accused were therefore discharged, on the grounds that the order for eviction had never been properly issued.

Then came the second charge against McShane—that of sedition. Practically the whole of the statements attributed to him by the police were admitted, the only part denied being reference to rifles and bayonets. The only witnesses for the prosecution were police officers, and although they said that their notes had been taken in long-hand the remarkable thing was that every note was identical. They had to admit in cross-examination that there was no disorder at the meeting; they tried to colour their case by reference to the eviction scenes but every time they raised this it was objected to by the defence. The lawyer Aitchison made a great defence and McShane made a statement of working-class principles from the witness-box. The jury retired and brought in a verdict of "Not proven."

The following September McShane and three others were arrested and again a properly prepared defence was successful in securing an acquittal.

Eviction fights flared up in many towns during this period. In the south-east of London in particular the resistance to evictions became very strong. It took on the form, at times, of the unemployed seizing empty dwelling-houses, and putting the furniture in for families who had been evicted from other places. Whilst the police were watching the old house where the eviction had occurred, the furniture was often being unloaded from a van into some other house which the unemployed had decided would be a suitable residence. Then of course, there frequently followed prosecutions for unlawful seizure of premises, but sometimes the family was able to retain possession if a satisfactory arrangement with regard to the rent could be made with the landlord.

In Walkley, Sheffield, a particularly bitter fight took place. The scene of the eviction was a house at the end of a yard off Providence Road. The unemployed committee were informed of the eviction and a body of workers were mobilised for restoring the furniture to the house. Crowds gathered to watch the furniture being taken back in. The entrance to the yard was a narrow alley-way, like a bottle-neck. Workers crammed into the yard, and suddenly the police drew their batons and there was a panic as many of the unemployed fought to get out of the yard, whilst others were locked in combat with the police. Severe injuries were inflicted upon the workers.

Deep indignation at the conduct of the police was stirred up throughout the Sheffield district amongst the workers, and when the funeral took place thousands of unemployed marched in procession behind the cortège.

The struggles of the unemployed against evictions undoubtedly stayed the hands of many landlords who were eager to evict tenants for small arrears in their rent, in the hope that they would get higher rents from new tenants.

.   .   .   .

At the end of July 1922, the Birmingham branch of the unemployed movement decided to organise a march of thirty unemployed workers to London to meet the Minister of Labour and the Minister of Health. They set out from Birmingham on 9th August and arrived in London on the 17th, where they were welcomed by a big demonstration of London unemployed.

They were received by Dr. MacNamara, the Minister of Labour, and Sir Aubrey Simmons, representing the Ministry of Health. They spoke on the conditions of the unemployed in Birmingham and urged more consideration by both ministries to the needs of the unemployed. After Dr. MacNamara had spoken sympathetically about the conditions of the unemployed, he explained in some detail the financial difficulties of the unemployment insurance scheme. He said that in principle he quite agreed that if persons were willing to work and could not obtain it, they were entitled to adequate relief, but he claimed that he was doing as much as he could with the funds at his disposal and that already many millions of pounds had had to be borrowed to meet the demands on the scheme. The interview terminated with Dr. Macnamara inviting the marchers to take tea in the Ministry of Labour.

During the time these Birmingham marchers were in London —a period of ten days—they were officially accommodated and fed in Poplar by the local authorities. On the night that they arrived, they were given a civic reception at a mass meeting in the Poplar town hall. Charlie Sumner, the mayor of Poplar, speaking at the meeting, said he was indeed pleased to be able to welcome the marchers from Birmingham. He said "It is a sign of the times and a tribute to your organisation. I hope that this will be but the fore-runner of many other such marches. Let them all march to London and perhaps the government would then wake up to its responsibilities." It was not long before this wish was to be fulfilled.

Armistice Day, 11th November, 1922, was approaching, and the London District Council of Unemployed decided to organise a big procession of a fitting character to march past the cenotaph, The conditions of many ex-service men were now terrible. The specially "generous" treatment which they had received immediately after the war had long ago ended. On the streets of all the big cities ex-service men could be seen with their medals pinned to their breasts, standing in the gutters endeavouring to raise a few coppers for food by selling matches or bootlaces.

The following is a letter which was published in the *Daily Herald* about this time, from an ex-sergeant:

Sir,

Life has reached the stage when it is an overwhelming burden. Those for whom we fought in the War have taken from us our means of existence. We are informed that we are not wanted. Industry can carry on quite nicely without us.

This, then, is our reward; to exist on a pauper's pittance, helped out by what we can borrow from a lean and uncertain future.

I look at the wording on my Victory medal. I think of my hopeless present and doubly hopeless future, and I curse the system under which I must deny my children and myself even the bare necessities of existence, until, worn out, my mortgage perhaps still unpaid, I sink with a sigh of relief to the grave.

The day of anxiety is past. We reap our reward in terms of hunger and misery; yet the day may come when they will want to call on us again. May that call be as vain as the despairing cry of our hungry children to-day. May the experience we are so hardly buying be of sterling service to us when the reckoning comes.

Yours faithfully,

UNEMPLOYED EX-SERGEANT.

This ex-service man's cry of despair expressed the feeling that existed amongst many thousands of ex-service men who found themselves reduced to terrible conditions of penury through unemployment.

One ex-service man, however, who wanted to prevent his comrades from falling into despair and apathy, wrote a poem which was published in the *Out of Work*, as follows:

> When you are down, and for a while
> All things, and people, seem to rile,
> Just try and summon up a smile,
> —and organise.

> When you are down, and hope appears dim,
> No job for Bill, or Dick, or Jim,
> You've tramped, and ache in every limb,
> —then organise.

> When you are down, you've just been "fired,"
> You're feeling hungry, cold, and tired,
> The landlord's pinched the "sticks" you hired,
> —why, organise.

When you are down, and Guardians say,
"We've nothing here for you to-day,"
You'll make them skip if you'll but say,
    —"I'll organise."

When you are down, and the world seems hard,
Don't despair; be on your guard,
And just take out that small red card
    —Be organised.

(The red card referred to is the membership card of the National
Unemployed Workers' Movement.)

.   .   .   .   .

It was in this spirit that the London movement decided to march
to the cenotaph on 11th November, 1922. We informed the
police of our intention to march and to lay a wreath at the war
memorial in Whitehall. They decided that, whilst we could not
be allowed to march in the official procession, we would nevertheless be permitted to march past the cenotaph at the end of
the official ceremony.

Twenty-five thousand London unemployed marched to the
Thames Embankment. Many of the contingents came from outlying districts in London and had to start very early in the morning to be there before eleven o'clock. Towards the end of the
official ceremony the unemployed contingents formed up in one
huge procession and moved up Northumberland Avenue, waiting
for the signal to enter Whitehall.

Whitehall and the streets surrounding it were densely packed
with mourners and sightseers. This time they saw a sight that
they had never seen before. As the banners of the various contingents were raised ready for the march, it was seen that each
banner had hundreds of ex-service men's medals pinned on to
it. Thousands of ex-service men took pawn tickets from their
pockets and pinned them on to the lapels of their coats. The
bands of the unemployed movement were draped in red and
black, and at the head of our procession was carried a large
wreath with an inscription that read: "From the living victims
—the unemployed—to our dead comrades, who died in vain."

The police were seriously alarmed at the way in which we had
organised this procession, especially the display of pawn-tickets
and medals. But it was now too late for them to prevent the
march down Whitehall, and, as the last of the official procession
moved out, we marched in. It was an impressive sight; in the
hush of the occasion and with dense crowds packed on the pavements in Whitehall, the unemployed ex-service men marched

under the banners of the N.U.W.M. to pay their tribute to the dead. Clearly the authorities were excited; large bodies of police received their orders to take up their positions unostentatiously on the flanks of the procession.

Then out of the grey mist came the wail of the fifes from the unemployed bands and the measured tread of tramping men. Into Whitehall came the long trail of drab humanity, with their medals hanging from the red banners and the pawn-tickets pinned on their coats, as an indictment against the system which praises the dead and condemns the living to starvation. On they came, steady and inevitable. Be-medalled and bearing obvious signs of poverty they stirred the dense throng of sightseers to a sense of deep emotion and a realisation of the injustice which was being meted out by man to man.

"Who are these people?" asked one young woman to another on the sidewalk. "Why—they're the unemployed." "Then good luck to them," said the first girl bitterly, almost savagely. "Disgraceful," snorted a red-faced old man, with a fur-clad young creature on his arm. "Those men are Bolsheviks," he said. "But look at their medals," said the girl. A woman in a black shawl turned on the old man. "Shut up your bloody gap! If you'd been out of work as long as my old man, you'd be a Bolshevik." A murmur of approval went through the crowd.

The head of the procession was now nearing the cenotaph, the banners dipped, the big drum boomed, punctuating the strains of the "Dead March." On came the phalanx of unemployed, the living indictment against the system which they had fought for, but which had now cast them on to the streets to starve.

On they came, almost inch by inch, the police horses curvetting before them. Then as the first ranks reached the foot of the cenotaph, and the wreath bearers dropped out to lay the wreath of the unemployed amongst the many others that were already there, the leading band played "Auld Lang Syne." It was a tense and unforgettable moment. As each contingent passed the cenotaph, men dropped out to place their floral tributes in position, and as the last contingent filed past the "Red Flag" and the "International" were struck up on the bands of the unemployed, and with a quickened step the living ex-service men passed out of Whitehall on their way to cold and hungry homes.

Chapter IV

THE FIRST NATIONAL HUNGER MARCH

"WHY all this unrest? What ails the workers? It seems that, in the rebound from the anxieties of the war, we are all trying to get something for nothing. Too much selfishness exists; that is the result of all the evil. We must not ask for the impossible."

This astonishing statement was made by the lady mayoress of Southport in her speech of welcome to the 1922 Trades Union Congress.

It was effectively replied to by Mr. Bob Smillie, the miners' leader, who said: "The lady mayor would never have made that statement about unrest had she been aware of the real facts that caused it. She had asked—why this unrest? One answer was that over two million men and women were asking leave of their brethren of the earth to give them leave to toil. They found themselves refused this right. That was one reason for the unrest."

George Lansbury said in the course of his speech to the congress on behalf of the Labour Party: "There ought not to be a slum in the land, and there ought not to be a hungry person. Yet these things exist all around us." A delegation from the National Unemployed Workers' Movement was received and permitted to address the congress. The official resolution of the congress on unemployment expressed

"strong condemnation of the Government for its failure to take timely and effective action either to prevent or diminish industrial dislocation and trade depression. The Congress protests against large masses of unemployed being left absolutely idle when their labour power could be organised and used on productive service to the national benefit. The Congress further condemns the inhuman treatment of the unemployed shown in the reduction of benefits under the Unemployment Insurance Act, and in the persistent refusals to meet reasonable claims for the maintenance of the people wholly unable to secure employment."

79

Whilst the Trades Union Congress was meeting, the National Unemployed Workers' Movement was preparing for its biggest national activity—the 1922 Hunger March.

The conditions of many of the unemployed can be judged from the following reports of suicides which appeared in the press at the time. "John Wright of Rotherhithe cuts his throat at the second attempt. His widow says he was depressed through unemployment for months." "George Bidwell took poison after being unemployed for eighteen weeks. He left a message for his family which said 'I can't stand it any more. My money is stopped at the exchange and I cannot see hope of any work. So good-bye.'" "John Burford of Acton attempted to take his life. He was found with his throat cut and he murmured: 'Let me die—I am out of work.'"

It was to fight against the conditions which were driving men to such desperation that the National Unemployed Workers' Movement undertook the organising of the national Hunger March of unemployed from all parts of Great Britain to London. It is of interest to note that in the *Daily Herald* of 21st August, 1922, the following passage appeared in a leading article on unemployment, referring to the Birmingham march to London:

"Nor would it be amiss if half a dozen of the unemployed from every town set out to meet the Premier on a given day."

The *Daily Herald* was at that time under the control of Mr. George Lansbury, and the paper gave sympathetic and favourable publicity to the unemployed struggles. Our movement took the cue from this *Daily Herald* suggestion, and we circularised our branches to ascertain what response we could get to such a proposal. Mass meetings of the unemployed were held at which the question was raised and found a ready response. Within a week letters were pouring into national headquarters declaring support for the march on London. The work of recruitment began, and by the end of October a considerable body of unemployed were eager for the start.

Looking back on the march from the experience of subsequent marches, I see how much we were lacking in knowledge of what was required for such a big undertaking. There was no proper equipment prescribed as was the case in subsequent marches; many men took the road even without overcoats, much less blankets and other necessary kit. There were no food kitchens for the contingents. There were no assurances of food or guarantee

p: Engine-Shop Stewards' Committee, Slough, 1920 ; Hannington and Dingley in the centre. *Bottom:* Burial of the White Elephant, Slough, April 30th, 1920.

Top: Defendants in the famous Communist Trial, 1925. *Left to right:* From second left: J. T. Murphy, Harry Pollitt, William Rust, T. Wintringham (*behind*), J. R. Campb Wee Arthur Manus, Wal Hannington, Tom Bell (*behind*), Wm. Gallacher. *Bottom:* Welco to released Communists in Hyde Park, September, 1926.

Top: Welsh miners march on London, 1927. *Bottom:* Marchers' roadside cookhouse.

Unique Publicity methods!

op: The late A. J. Cook addressing the miners' march, Trafalgar Square, 1927. *Bottom:* The crowd!

Contrasts in reception! *Top:* Macdonald at Lord Mayor's Banquet. *Bottom:* Hanningto
and the Unemployed Deputation's reception at the Ministry of Labour.

Top: On a cold and frosty morning, Hunger March, 1930.   *Bottom:* A battle for the Banner in Oxford Street, October, 1931.

Top: An arrest. *Bottom:* Bricks versus batons.
Incidents in the fight against the Means Test, October, 1931.

p: Deputation to 10 Downing Street, 1931. *Third from Left:* David Kirkwood, M.P.,
mes Maxton, M.P., Hannington extreme right—previously injured in street battle.

Bottom: Scots on the road, 1932.

Top: Women's Contingent from Burnley to London, 1932. *Bottom:* . . . a well-deserve
meal!

Top: Durham and Northumberland marchers setting out, October, 1932. *Bottom:* Scots on the Lancashire cobbles, 1932.

Top: Head of the Yorkshire column, 1932. *Bottom:* First-aid on the road.

Man for Man

Battle at Bristol, February 23rd, 1932.

Top: Scots entering Hyde Park, after five weeks' marching, October 27th, 1932.
Bottom: ... batons drawn, a memorable fight, see page 248.

Top: Police block Whitehall against hunger-marchers' demonstration in Trafalgar Square, October 31st, 1932. *Bottom:* The County Hall.

of places to sleep. It was an adventure which only men with deep-seated grievances would be prepared to undertake. We realised, of course, that severe hardships, even with adequate preparations, would be involved in such an undertaking, and this was made clear to all who volunteered to march. Only a few drew back.

The spirit of the movement is expressed in the following oath which members of the movement were taking at that time:

"I, a member of the great army of unemployed, being without work and compelled to suffer through no fault of my own, do hereby solemnly swear with all the strength and resolution of my being, to loyally abide by, and carry out the instructions of the National Unemployed Workers' Committee Movement, with the deliberate intention of pressing forward the claims of the unemployed so that no man, woman or child suffers hunger or want this winter.

Further, realising that only by the abolition of this hideous capitalist system can the horror of unemployment be removed from our midst, I here and now take upon myself a binding oath, to never cease from active strife against this system until capitalism is abolished and our country and all its resources truly belong to the people."

The first contingents of hunger marchers set out from Glasgow for London on 17th October, 1922. Glasgow had been the mobilisation centre for over three hundred marchers from the unemployed branches in Scotland. The routes and time-table had been prepared by headquarters, and the various contingents from different parts of the country took the road on dates fixed according to the distance that they had to cover. The whole of the marchers, numbering 2,000, had to arrive in London on the same day—17th November—practically one month from the date when the first contingent took the road.

As the dates for starting arrived, the respective contingents set off, and soon every main road in Great Britain had its quota of marchers plodding on towards the capital. These men knew the hardships that they would have to face on the cold and wintry roads, often to be soaked to the skin after marching in rain, but their spirit remained undaunted. They marched knowing why they marched, bearing within their breasts a feeling of hatred towards the system which was slowly starving themselves, their wives and their children.

They moved from town to town, depending upon the local authorities for the provision of food and sleeping accommodation. Just after the Scottish contingent started, the Lloyd George government resigned, and during the month that the marchers were on the road, we were in the throes of a general election. There can be no doubt that the agitation of the marchers in the towns and villages through which they passed contributed largely to the considerable increase in the number of seats gained by the Labour Party in the election, bringing their total from 61 in the previous parliament up to 142.

Mr. Bonar Law became prime minister, and the headquarters of the unemployed movement wrote asking him to receive a deputation from the hunger marchers when they arrived in London. He sent a reply on 3rd November, in which he declared that he could not receive the deputation and said, "I consider no useful purpose can be served in proceeding with this march any further, in view of the fact that a special Unemployment Committee has just been formed to investigate the whole problem of unemployment afresh, under the chairmanship of the Ministry of Health."

To this letter we sent the following reply:

Dear Sir,

With further reference to my letter addressed to you on 1st November and in answer to yours of the 3rd November, wherein it is stated that you feel that no useful purpose can be served by proceeding with the proposed March to London.

I have first of all to inform you that the March has now been in progress for three weeks. Secondly, the announcements made in the Press written by you, were made in order to influence the Marchers to return. The mere fact that the Government had set up a Committee of the Cabinet to deal with the whole problem of unemployment conveys nothing to our minds.

There has been in existence for some considerable time a Cabinet Committee on Unemployment, their achievements still leaving between two and three million unemployed. The relief scales that have been forced from the various Boards of Guardians by the agitations of our Movement are, we contend, still too low, the late Ministry of Health being responsible for attempting to force them yet lower. The benefit paid by the Labour Exchanges is absolutely and totally inadequate, and with the most vivid imagination nobody can possibly visualise the millions at present unemployed being absorbed into industry during this winter.

In view of the above, and also the fact that the Marchers have more than half covered their journey, I am again instructed to inform you that the deputation from the Marchers will wait upon you on November 22nd and we request you to make the necessary arrangements to receive them.

Of this letter we received a curt acknowledgement, but no intimation that the prime minister would receive the deputation.

Although during the first three weeks of the march the capitalist press had boycotted it, we found that, as the marchers pressed closer to London, the silence of the press broke down. A sudden change took place, and London woke up one morning to find startling news-posters being displayed about the "Hunger March to London." The papers contained double-column front page articles about the 2,000 men who were slowly but surely closing in upon the capital, and through each article ran a note of dismay and uneasiness about the consequences.

Some of the reactionary papers printed unfounded stories of preparations for riots when the marchers arrived. The London branches of the unemployed movement had made preparations for a big welcome to their comrades who were due to arrive in Hyde Park on 17th November at 2 p.m. Great excitement prevailed, not only amongst the unemployed of London, but amongst the employed workers also, and huge crowds began to assemble in Hyde Park and around Marble Arch soon after noon.

The London branches led demonstrations to the Park, with bands playing and banners flying. From every part of London they came to welcome the stalwarts who had faced blizzards and storms to march hundreds of miles in an effort to secure an interview with the prime minister. By two o'clock all the streets round Marble Arch were lined with thousands of sympathisers who had congregated and were anxiously awaiting news of the marchers' approach.

Just after 2.30 came news that the South Wales miners and the Plymouth men, who had joined forces at Staines, were half a mile away. Shortly after, the strains of one of the London unemployed bands could be heard in the distance as they led the Welshmen to the park. Cheer after cheer rose from the throats of the vast crowd assembled and many a tear trickled down the cheeks of the more emotional as they eagerly stretched for a glimpse of the men who were marching against starvation. As everybody was clamouring to shake hands with these first arrivals and to express feelings of appreciation, the news came that the Scottish marchers along with the men from the North of England were approaching. When they entered the park gates extreme difficulty was experienced in making a way for them—so anxious were the workers to welcome them. Other contingents followed within the space of a few minutes. After a great demonstration in the park the various contingents of marchers formed up with the London workers to march to the various localities where they were to be accommodated.

Twentieth November was the day fixed for the pompous ceremony of opening the new parliament. Two days later was to be the great day of demonstration of the hunger marchers to press for an interview with the prime minister. During these few days the whole of the capitalist press became hysterical, and news columns were filled with scare articles about "Secret meetings of the marchers," "Bolshevik gold," "Firebrand leaders," and so on, and, as the great day for the demonstration arrived, the hysteria became worse. No lie was too contemptible, no suggestion too sinister, for these organs that moulded public opinion.

On the evening of 21st November the *Pall Mall Gazette* had a disgraceful article headed "The Red Plot." The marchers were accused of bearing firearms, and the leaders were made out to be rogues and scoundrels of the worst type, and, of course, in the pay of Bolshevik Russia. Even the prime minister stooped to the contemptible depth of endeavouring to blacken the marchers by a statement to the press claiming that two criminals who had long prison records were amongst the leaders of the movement. That statement was, of course, totally untrue.

On the morning of 22nd November one was confronted with newspaper placards everywhere warning the people not to go near the Thames Embankment or within the vicinity of Whitehall. "Keep away from Whitehall," said one. "Barricades at Westminster," said another. The great demonstration was due to assemble on the Thames Embankment at 1 p.m. Special midday editions of newspapers were printed and people were eagerly buying them in order to acquaint themselves of the latest news. One morning-paper in particular became specially vehement, and foretold awful bloodshed. It said in one paragraph: "*One hundred thousand armed men are going to march on Downing Street, which they intend to take by storm. Telegrams have already been prepared for sending to Moscow, stating that the unemployed rebels have captured the Government Offices and compelled the government to capitulate.*" The paper went on to explain that the police had made elaborate preparations to deal with the insurgents. It spoke in terms of thousands of mounted police and tens of thousands of foot police. The government had had barricades erected in Whitehall and particularly at the entrance to Downing Street. The press laid emphasis upon these preparations, and some papers claimed that machine-guns were mounted on certain buildings in readiness to sweep the streets.

At one o'clock, when the great procession of London unemployed, along with the marchers, began to arrive on the Embankment, the feeling was intense. Huge forces of police, mounted and foot, were being moved to strategical positions. Nobody knew what was going to happen and there was a nervous tension on the part of both the police and the marchers. Just before one o'clock I walked into Whitehall with other leaders of the march to see for ourselves the state of the government preparations. Sure enough, there were barricades, and huge forces of police were in position at important points in Whitehall. Whether there were any nests of machine-guns on the Whitehall buildings, I cannot say; probably this was just another capitalist press lie; but the elaborate preparations made by the government, by the erection of barricades, by the stopping of all traffic through Whitehall, by the boarding up of government office windows and the obvious evidence of preparation for a battle, suggested that there might have been some truth in this report.

This elaborate display of force was made because the unemployed were marching for bread. It was obvious that there could be no chance of the marchers and demonstrators getting into Whitehall without suffering severe casualties, and the leaders of the march, anxious to avoid such an uneven combat, decided that the demonstration should march through the West End of London to Hyde Park, whilst the deputation proceeded to Whitehall. At 2 p.m. the bugles sounded the fall-in. The deputation on their own, headed by Tom Dingley of Coventry, quietly moved off in the direction of Whitehall, with a police escort. They were to proceed to the Ministry of Health buildings, where arrangements had been made by the Minister of Labour and the Minister of Health, together with other officials, to receive them.

I, along with others, was in charge of the demonstration. At 2.15 p.m. the great demonstration, numbering approximately 70,000, and headed by the drum and fife band of the Barrow-in-Furness contingent of marchers, began to move in the direction of Whitehall. Nobody in the procession, except the marshals, knew the point for which the demonstration was making; consequently much excitement prevailed. There was a look of fear on the faces of many of the spectators who lined the sidewalks. Were the unemployed going to force an entry into Whitehall or not? The moments were tense. Was this great army of ragged, half-starved, unarmed men going to dare to make battle against the great force of uniformed, armed and disciplined police? Such was the question in the minds of many thousands.

The great procession moved on until it came under Waterloo Bridge, which was the proscribed area laid down by the police. The head of the procession was now over the boundary and it seemed almost certain that a clash would take place. The police were obviously amazed and were looking for instructions from their officers. But suddenly the leading contingent, on instructions from the marshals, turned up Savoy Street, across the Strand and into Kingsway, and most people then realised that the demonstration was moving for Hyde Park via Piccadilly Circus, which also was in the proscribed area. On reaching the park it took well over an hour before the end of the procession passed in.

From a dozen platforms, speakers addressed the crowd, whilst we awaited the return of the marchers' deputation to give their report. When the deputation arrived, they stated that they had met the Minister of Labour, Sir Montague Barlow, the Minister of Health, Sir A. Griffiths-Boscawen, and other prominent officials, but they had, in accordance with our previous decision, refused to state their case before these ministers unless the prime minister was sent for. This had been refused and under protest they had therefore withdrawn from the conference room, but not before expressing in strong terms their opinion of the prime minister's attitude. As the deputation withdrew from the building, about two hundred police who had been in hiding in the building came out. The mass meeting in the park pledged themselves to carry on the fight to demand that the prime minister should hear their case; the banners were raised again and the contingents formed up for the march back to their localities. The great demonstration was over and London heaved a sigh of relief.

The refusal of Bonar Law to interview the marchers aroused bitter feeling, and prolonged the activities in connection with the march over a period of five months, whereas an interview would probably have led to an early return of the marchers to their homes. Sunday, 26th November, had in fact been fixed as the date for a farewell demonstration in Trafalgar Square, but because of the attitude of Mr. Bonar Law, the Marchers' Control Council decided that the marchers should remain in London and that the demonstration in Trafalgar Square should take the form of a protest against the prime minister. It was a tremendous demonstration, after which the marchers settled down to a period of varying activities directed towards changing the attitude of the prime minister.

On Monday, 27th November, a big poster parade was organised by the marchers in the vicinity of the House of Commons. This resulted in the Rev. T. E. Pickering, who had marched with the Sheffield contingent, being arrested on a charge of causing obstruction. He was tried at Bow Street next morning and a large crowd of marchers and London unemployed assembled outside the court. The magistrate ordered Pickering to be bound over to keep the peace for a period of six months. Pickering declared in the court that he refused to accept this, but in spite of his declaration he was immediately released. The crowd outside the court carried him shoulder high through the streets of the West End to Hyde Park, where a short meeting was held.

The Marchers' Control Council was meeting daily and planning various activities for the marchers in different parts of London. One activity that caused no little uneasiness was that of a large number of marchers crowding into a restaurant just before the busy hour, taking up seats at the tables and sitting for an hour or two over a twopenny cup of coffee. There was no law under which they could be ejected and there was no regulation defining the length of time a customer could stay.

Immediately following the decision of the Marchers' Council for remaining in London, a call was issued to all our branches for reinforcements, and we did not have to wait long before fresh bodies of marchers began to take the road to join their comrades in London. The start of these reinforcements was given full publicity in the newspapers and it was realised that the threat to remain in London until Bonar Law received the marchers' deputation was no idle one.

The Ministry of Health took serious notice of this start of the reinforcements and dispatched an instruction to the local authorities to the effect that any marchers entering their towns must be treated as "casuals"—in other words, as tramps and vagabonds, to endure the disgraceful treatment associated with casual wards. The marchers in London were keeping up a constant activity in the localities and from time to time in the West End of London. Several of the London local authorities were perplexed to know how to deal with the situation, as some of the local workers' reception committees which had taken responsibility for providing food and accommodation had now come to the end of their resources and were compelled to throw the burden upon the boards of guardians. The guardians were not desirous of encouraging the men to remain in London so they endeavoured to provide for them as meagrely as possible. This, of course, met with resentment on the part of the marchers, and exciting scenes occurred in some of the workhouses where they were accommodated.

Mr. Bonar Law, however, remained adamant on the question of the marchers' deputation, and night after night heated debates took place in the House of Commons over the premier's attitude. Mr. George Lansbury was particularly indefatigable in his persistence on our behalf. The Marchers' Control Council decided that they would press for a deputation to be heard at the bar of the House of Commons. A petition was prepared and signed by the leaders of each contingent, and Mr. Lansbury presented it to the House on Tuesday, 5th December, 1922. It was accepted, but the request contained in it was not conceded. On 7th December Mr. Lansbury indignantly protested against the attitude of the government towards the marchers and a scene took place in the House. During the scene Mr. Bonar Law blurted out, "I am sick and tired of hearing about the unemployed marchers, and I don't want to have anything more to do with them." This remark was, in fact, a tribute to the effective agitation which the marchers were conducting, and which was seriously worrying the government.

By this time there were another thousand marchers on the road to London. The capitalist press indulged in a campaign of vilification and demanded drastic measures by the police. Then a very interesting move took place. Some of the London local authorities who were having to house and feed marchers offered to pay their fares home in order to get rid of them. This certainly created a difficulty for the Control Council, and we appealed to the marchers to stand firm against this offer. A considerable number of the men, however, accepted, causing a split in the ranks. But the thing which more than anything else had caused them to accept the offer was the receipt of pitiful letters about the condition of their wives and dependants, who were not being properly treated by the authorities at home.

This position presented a serious problem to the March Council and there was a danger of a complete rout. In addition to the offer of fares to return home, there were individuals at work amongst the marchers endeavouring to stir up dissatisfaction, and not infrequently they succeeded. The Council, in face of the new situation, decided to introduce a relay system of marchers, whereby any body of men who desired to return home owing to domestic difficulties should do so, their places being taken by bodies of reinforcements now beginning to arrive in London, so that the front line should remain unbroken.

This system worked very effectively. Local authorities were spending hundreds of pounds in fares for the marchers only to find new bodies of men continually arriving. In fact, some of the men who had returned home, after making more satisfactory arrangements with their families, again took the road and marched back to London. This even happened in the case of the Scottish marchers, and by this means we kept the march activities going for a period of almost five months.

At the beginning of December 1922, one of the marchers, by the name of Walter Tompkins, from Luton, died. His death had taken place at Willesden, where his contingent were being accommodated. The Marchers' Control Council decided that the body should be returned to his relatives in Luton by train, and a funeral procession should take place from Willesden to St. Pancras station. About twenty thousand London unemployed, including the marchers, assembled at Hyde Park for the funeral, with bands and banners draped in red and black ribbons. As the funeral procession from Willesden came slowly down Edgware Road towards the park, led by the drum and fife band of Willesden, the huge crowd of marchers in Hyde Park formed up four abreast, and with the bands playing the "Red Flag" in funeral time, they wheeled out of Marble Arch and marched in behind the hearse.

The procession moved slowly through the main thoroughfares of the West End to St. Pancras railway station. Thousands of people on the sidewalks stood silent and bareheaded as the procession passed along Oxford Street, Tottenham Court Road and Euston Road, and many were moved to tears at the sight of 20,000 men and women marching behind the cortège, paying their last tribute to a dead comrade. Arrangements had already been made with the railway officials at St. Pancras, and on reaching the station the procession moved slowly through the main entrance on to a platform that had been specially cleared to accommodate them. Four unemployed marchers then bore the coffin from the hearse to the train, and as they did so the banners and flags were dipped as a last salute, and the buglers sounded the "Last Post."

An escort from the marchers accompanied the body of their dead comrade to his last resting place, and as the train steamed out, the thousands of unemployed marchers stood bareheaded singing the "Red Flag" and the "International." The scene was most impressive; no greater tribute could have been paid to one who had breathed his last whilst engaged in a great working-class activity. A demonstration of Luton unemployed, along with Yorkshire marchers who were in the town that day and who were moving towards London as reinforcements, met the train at the station, and escorted the body of their comrade to the burial ground. Will Tompkins had been one of the first recruits to the national march. He had suffered a long period of unemployment and was eager to join in the struggle for the amelioration of the conditions of the unemployed. When he left Luton he was practically unknown and unheeded, but he returned as a martyr in the cause of the working-class struggle for bread.

After the House of Commons turned down the marchers' petition to be heard at the bar of the House, the leaders of the march planned a campaign of varying activities, particularly in the vicinity of Westminster. On 12th December a body of picked men, numbering 150, proceeded to the House of Commons in two's and three's at intervals of a few minutes, taking approximately 1½ hours before the last gained admission. This was necessary in order not to arouse the suspicions of the police on duty at the House. The unemployed gathered in the outer lobby and various Members of Parliament were asked to come out to meet the unemployed. When about forty Members of Parliament were in the lobby, conversing in groups with the marchers, I gave the agreed signal and the marchers formed a big circle in the lobby and produced large posters containing suitable slogans. A dead silence fell over the place. Visitors, M.P.'s, detectives and police, stood for a few minutes looking dumbfounded. Then the whole of the marchers commenced lustily singing the "Red Flag" and the entire building rang and re-echoed with the singing of the workers' song, penetrating into the debating chambers of the Commons and the House of Lords. Several Labour members who were in the lobby at the time joined in the singing.

Then the police suddenly began to assault the unemployed. Police reinforcements were rushed up from all parts of the House and an exciting scuffle took place with men and police struggling all over the lobby. The police ultimately got the upper hand and the unemployed were forcibly ejected.

Three days later Parliament decided to rise and remain pro-rogued until 13th February, 1923. A number of Labour members of Parliament made stormy protests in the House against this decision of the government for such a long holiday when the

problem of unemployment was so urgent, and strong indignation was expressed throughout the country amongst the workers
against the government. The Marchers' Control Council immediately took up the question of organising an intense agitation
directed towards compelling Parliament to re-assemble before
the stipulated date, and as part of this activity it was decided to
organise a demonstration in Trafalgar Square on Sunday, 17th
December, and to petition King George V, asking him to use his
royal prerogative to reassemble Parliament to deal with the
question of unemployment.

From all parts of London great processions of unemployed and
employed workers marched to the square. We had considered
the advisability of marching the demonstration from the square
to Buckingham Palace, but we realised, of course, that every
conceivable measure would be taken by the authorities to prevent
this. Long before the processions arrived in Trafalgar Square, the
area surrounding it was black with police. The gates at the
Admiralty Arch, at the entrance to the Mall—which leads to
the palace—were closed, and a tremendous force of mounted and
foot police stood on guard at the gates to prevent any demonstration going through to the palace.

Whilst I was on the plinth, waiting my turn to speak, one of
the police inspectors called me aside and informed me that
nobody would be allowed to go through Pall Mall to the palace,
and that if any trouble occurred I, as leader of the march, would
be held primarily responsible. I discussed the matter with the
members of the Marchers' Control Council and we realised that it
was impossible for any procession to get through the Admiralty
Arch. We accordingly decided, in order to avoid a conflict in
the square, to urge the demonstrators to carry on with the meeting whilst a deputation went through with the petition.

We informed the police accordingly, and at first they refused
to consider even the question of a deputation going to the palace.
To this our reply was, "If that is refused, we cannot be responsible
for what will happen here to-day." The police reconsidered the
position and ultimately conceded our demand that fifteen members of the Marchers' Control Council should be allowed to pass
through to the palace with the petition.

We urged the crowd to stand firm in Trafalgar Square and to
await the return of the visit to the palace, but as the delegation
moved away from the square towards Admiralty Arch crowds of
demonstrators followed. The police became extremely nervous,
some began to draw their truncheons and it only needed one

policeman to lose his head and strike at a demonstrator for the vast assembly to become involved in a battle with the police. For several minutes it was touch and go whether this would happen, but as the delegation were allowed to pass through a small side gate at the Admiralty Arch, the tense situation eased and the crowd returned to the square.

When the delegation reached the palace they again found the gates closed and a strong force of police inside, ready for any emergency. The chief inspector stepped forward and informed the delegation that he had been instructed to convey the information to us that the King could not receive us, or accept our petition, but that it must be sent to him through the home secretary. The delegation, unable to make further progress, returned to report the result of their endeavours to the crowd in Trafalgar Square, who had been kept interested by a relay of speakers, including Mr. George Lansbury. The King's message was received with strong disapproval, but after the passing of a resolution declaring the intention to carry on the fight by every possible means for the reassembling of Parliament the great demonstration closed and the contingents marched back to their respective localities. Next day the press contained extensive reports and photographs of the demonstration, and the whole country was made aware of the fact that the marchers were now fighting for an early re-assembling of the House of Commons.

Our next step in the campaign was to approach the Trades Union Congress General Council, to endeavour to get the trade union movement to join with us in pursuing our objective. On 20th December the general council received a deputation from the marchers at which we stated our case for joint action against the government. After discussion they decided that they would organise, in conjunction with the unemployed movement, a day of national demonstration on 7th January, 1923, this day to be known as "Unemployed Sunday." A central organising committee was immediately set up, consisting of an equal number of delegates from the National Unemployed Workers' Movement, the T.U.C. General Council, the London Labour Party and the London Trades Council. Calls were issued to the trades councils, trade unions and labour parties throughout the country to establish similar joint machinery in every centre for the organising of powerful demonstrations on the day which had been fixed.

On 21st December, the day following our meeting with the T.U.C. General Council, the Glasgow branches of the National Unemployed Workers' Movement, having heard that Mr. Bonar

Law was due to arrive that day in Glasgow, organised a big demonstration. They marched to the hotel where he was staying.

The demand was made for a deputation to be heard, and ultimately Mr. Bonar Law gave way, and three representatives, Harry McShane, J. Mulligan and Allan Campbell were received.

Mr. Bonar Law tried to argue that he was not meeting them in his official capacity as prime minister, but as a Scottish representative. He had to listen to a forcible denunciation of his government in respect to its treatment of the unemployed. Mr. Bonar Law, in reply to demands for improved scales of benefit and conditions, protested that the government was doing all it could to help the unemployed and that he was unable to make any definite promises for the future.

The interview ended with a member of the deputation declaring, "Mr. Bonar Law, to-day you have demonstrated the inability of your government to aid the unemployed. We warn you that this fight will go on in the streets. This is a fight of the classes, and the unemployed can only express their indignation against your indifference on the streets. We say beware! There will be trouble this winter."

Whilst preparations for the national day of demonstration were being organised, a series of exciting activities were carried out in London by the marchers. The Scottish and North of England marchers were steadily moving forward to London, and a considerable number of reinforcements from English towns had already arrived. The northern reinforcements numbered 340, and arrangements were made for a demonstration of welcome to be organised for them in Trafalgar Square when they entered London on 30th December. As these reinforcements began to get nearer London, strenuous efforts were being made by the Control Council to arrange accommodation for them, but since the call for reinforcements had gone out the struggle for accommodation between the marchers and the local authorities in London had become daily more bitter. The Ministry of Health was bringing pressure to bear upon the local authorities to compel them to refuse accommodation to the marchers, other than in the casual wards.

A deputation from the Marchers' Council met officials of the ministry, but the interview was fruitless. The night before the Scottish marchers arrived, the Metropolitan Asylums Board, which then controlled the casual wards in London, held a special meeting, and a deputation from the leadership of the march waited upon them. The board offered to accommodate the new arrivals and to remove the casual ward restrictions; in the words of the chairman "they would be treated as guests." This offer was joyfully accepted by the deputation and we had no reason to doubt the good faith of the board. Whilst a demonstration was welcoming the Scottish marchers in Trafalgar Square on 30th December, news came through that a body of marchers staying in the Battersea baths had that day come in conflict with the police, and a baton charge had taken place, resulting in five marchers and one London man being arrested. This conflict occurred because the Battersea guardians had refused to supply any more food to the marchers. The marchers thereupon decided to enter a restaurant with the intention of ordering meals and having the bill sent in to the guardians. But the police apparently had an informer in the ranks, and as the marchers were nearing the restaurant a body of police made a baton charge upon them. Two hours after the arrests took place, the accused appeared in the court. One of them, a marcher from Sheffield, was sentenced to twenty-one days' imprisonment, the others receiving lighter sentences.

When this announcement was made at the welcome demonstration in Trafalgar Square, the crowd pledged themselves to carry on an agitation for the release of the prisoners, and during the period of imprisonment several demonstrations were organised to Wandsworth gaol.

The day following the arrival of the Scottish army we received complaints to the effect that the men were being given casual diet. This was a breach of faith on the part of the Metropolitan Asylums Board, so the Marchers' Control Council arranged that all the Scottish marchers should leave the casual wards next morning and march to the Metropolitan Asylums Board building on Victoria Embankment, to demand an explanation. We made it known that unless the men were satisfactorily accommodated and fed we should be prepared to march them into the West End of London where they would remain all night, and if necessary sleep on the pavements. The men were ready to carry out this threat. In an interview that took place with the Asylums Board it was clear that after our first meeting with them the Ministry of Health had brought pressure to bear on the board and succeeded in causing them to rescind the arrangements which they had offered to us. They now cited rules and regulations and virtually admitted that their hands were tied by the ministry. The deputation therefore withdrew and we marched the men to the Ministry of Health. This move had taken the police unawares and the

Marchers' Control Council were able to get inside the Ministry of Health, but only to find that they were received by a minor official whose duty was obviously to act as a stop-gap and to commit himself in no way in respect to arrangements for accommodation.

It was 11.45 a.m. when we entered the building and proceeded to a room on the first floor. After an hour's discussion with the official who received us, we realised that we were up against a solid wall of officialdom and that no progress could be made unless we could reach somebody in higher authority. I was leading the deputation and demanded that the Minister of Health should be called to the room. At first we were met with excuses, but as we continued to press for the presence of the minister, we were ultimately met with a definite refusal. We were now confronted with a desperate situation for which we felt entitled to apply desperate remedies. Amongst the unemployed marchers who were outside in Whitehall, there were over 300 for whom we had no accommodation. We were determined that, as the ministry had been responsible for smashing the arrangement which we had made with the Asylums Board, they must now face the responsibility and find suitable accommodation for these marchers.

At noon we therefore announced to the Ministry of Health officials who were in the room that we did not intend to leave until we got some satisfaction. They thought we were jesting, but when they saw men take up their positions at the door and seize the telephone they realised that we were in earnest. The officials quietly accepted the inevitable. From then onward we played the game of patience, no attempt being made by either side to reopen negotiations. We just held tight. Other officials of the ministry who came to the room found that they were unable to enter. The police were brought to the building, but they were no doubt puzzled as to which was the best course to take; they did not wish to upset the dignity of the ministry by a baton charge inside with the unemployed, and so apparently they just waited.

Meanwhile inside the board-room we not only prevented the officials using the telephone, but we used it ourselves to telephone the news of what was happening to the *Daily Herald*. We also telephoned to a number of workhouses and endeavoured to get satisfactory arrangements made for the accommodation of the marchers, but all to no avail. At 3 p.m. crowds began to gather in Whitehall; the news of the marchers' action was attracting attention. By 4 p.m. the whole of London was informed by newspaper placards that the marchers had seized the Ministry of

Health building. We heard the newspaper sellers shouting the news in the streets below.

We wondered how long it would be before the police decided to smash their way in and eject us. At 4.30 we telephoned to the House of Commons and asked to speak to Mr. George Lansbury. We stated the position at the ministry and asked if he could help in any way. He said he would come over immediately. When he arrived the men on the door admitted him to the room. A heated argument then took place between Mr. Lansbury and the ministry officials concerning the powers of the local authorities, but Mr. Lansbury soon realised that all the reasoning in the world would not shift the officials who were present from their attitude. Mr. Lansbury then discussed the question with us and said that Poplar would take 100 of the marchers in addition to those whom they already had. He thought he could persuade Shoreditch and Southwark to take the remainder between them. Telephone calls were thereupon made to both these places; Shoreditch said they would take 150 and Southwark agreed to take 50. This still left 23 outstanding.

By this time all departments of the ministry were closed for the day and we realised that it would not be long before the police decided to take action. At 6.15 a number of police inspectors came up to the room and forced an entry. We told them that there were still 23 men for whom accommodation had got to be found. The inspectors replied that this was no concern of theirs, and when they failed to remove us by persuasion, threats were resorted to. Still we held firm. The police inspectors then left the room and in a few minutes returned with a strong body of police. There must have been 150 police in the room and the passage outside. We were overpowered by sheer force of numbers and ejected into the street. We should undoubtedly have been much more roughly handled had it not been for the presence of Mr. Lansbury who hotly protested against the drawing of batons. There were crowds in Whitehall when the police rushed us out, after we had been in the building for nearly seven hours. The marchers then proceeded to the localities where accommodation had been arranged.

During the next week the country was flooded with literature relative to the national demonstrations on 7th January, organised by the T.U.C. and the National Unemployed Workers' Movement. The demonstration that took place in Trafalgar Square stands out as one of the greatest ever witnessed in Great Britain. Unemployed and employed gripped hands in comradeship and marched in their tens of thousands from every district in London to demand that Parliament be reassembled in order to meet the demands of the unemployed.

The following is the resolution which was put to the assembly and carried with acclamation:—

This mass meeting of workers and citizens protests against the action of the government in declaring the prorogation of parliament until 13th February, 1923. We denounce this declaration of a prolonged holiday for legislators and regard it as a manifestation of indifference to the chronic suffering of thousands of men, women and children directly affected by the long-continued unemployment. We call upon the prime minister at once to take steps to summon parliament to deal with this problem as a national emergency of vital importance, and we also call upon the government to take such action as will secure employment for willing workers, or the alternative of utilising the full resources of the state in order to provide a standard of maintenance such as will prevent the deterioration of those who continue to suffer the consequences of our industrial stagnation.

This meeting also urges individual electors to communicate personally with each member of parliament representing their constituencies, calling upon them to support the terms of this resolution and to give effect to the decisions of this meeting.

After this demonstration, which was typical of those held throughout the country, we began to experience new difficulties in regard to the marchers. The Ministry of Health were apparently bringing pressure to bear upon the local authorities in respect to the dependants of the marchers, and relief was either being completely stopped or severely cut down. We therefore arranged that several hundred of the marchers who were faced with these difficulties should return home, but others who were in the position to carry on the fight should remain to continue the activities of the march.

In the third week in January we decided that two armies of marchers should undertake a march for securing new recruits. One was to march north as far as Birmingham and the other was to go south along the coast. The northern army was under my command and the southern under that of Tom Dingley. Both armies assembled on Tower Hill on the morning of 24th January and were given a send-off by the London unemployed. Before we started the press announced that the Ministry of Health had sent instructions to the local authorities on the routes of the marchers, insisting that the marchers must be treated as casuals. On Tower Hill we pledged ourselves to break down these regulations and to stop at nothing in order to do so. Both armies were to arrive back in London on the day that Parliament reassembled, 13th February, and although we knew that we had three weeks of strenuous struggle on the roads in front of us we set out full of confidence and determination.

The northern army experienced no difficulty in breaking down the regulations of the Ministry of Health until we reached Luton. Here the board of guardians declared that they were not prepared to break the instructions of the ministry on the question of food, although they were willing to accommodate us in the Plait Hall. After we entered this hall, bread, margarine and tea were sent from the workhouse for the marchers. We tried to persuade the chairman of the board of guardians and other members to augment this diet, but they refused. We thereupon asked them to leave the premises, and they did so. The men were called together and we discussed our line of action. It was decided that the marchers should go out in batches of tens into the town, enter the high-class restaurants, order meals, and, after having gratified their hunger, pass a note to the proprietor stating that the bill would be paid by the Luton board of guardians.

This plan worked out very effectively, and all the marchers had good feeds and succeeded in returning to the hall without any arrests; although several attempts had been made when proprietors had called the police. After the marchers had all returned we had to lock and barricade the doors because the police began to mobilise their forces outside, and we were not certain what they intended to do. But they took no action. Next morning, when we formed up to march from Luton to the next town, we read the local press placards which called the marchers "The Poached Eggs Brigade." Apparently many of the marchers had two eggs on toast! Later, when the Luton board of guardians met, they were faced with bills from cafés and restaurants all over the town, and they decided to meet these claims. That is how the Ministry of Health instructions were defeated in Luton!

Next day the southern army at Brighton pulled off a similar manœuvre, but in their case it resulted in ten marchers being arrested; they were subsequently released after a fine of £2 had been imposed upon one of them.

Two days after leaving Luton, on 31st January, we entered the town of Rugby, and here again we experienced difficulty about the diet offered by the guardians. A sub-committee of the guardians was called together to discuss whether they could give a more liberal diet than that laid down by the regulations governing casuals. The committee, however, decided against this. At this time the marchers were in the Drill Hall, Rugby, where they were to sleep, and the clerk to the guardians and several members of the board came to the hall at 6.30 in the evening to inform us of the decision.

We explained to them that it was a matter not merely of food, but of principle, with us; that we had pledged ourselves to break down the Ministry of Health instructions and we intended to do so. We said we did not want expensive meals, but we still pressed for some addition to the ordinary casual diet. On finding that we could gain no concessions by discussion, we announced to the guardians that we would have to resort to our own methods for obtaining our demands. The guardians thereupon left the hall, and informed the police that there was likely to be trouble. The police placed a guard on the private houses of the guardians and reinforcements from surrounding localities were sent for; but in spite of this the strategy of the marchers defeated them.

From a local worker who was sympathetic to the movement we secured a rough plan of the workhouse, which was about three-quarters of a mile from the centre of the town. We decided that we would raid the workhouse and take what food we needed to augment that which had already been sent to us by the guardians, but in order to do this it was necessary for us to engage in a little strategy. We decided that a demonstration of the marchers should be held through the centre of the town that evening, and groups were sent out to chalk the streets, informing the populace that a meeting would be held at the Clock Tower at 7.45 p.m. At 7.30 all of the marchers, with the exception of fourteen, marched through the main streets to the Clock Tower in the centre of the town.

George Cook of Manchester was in charge of the demonstration and I instructed him to be the speaker at the meeting, and not to leave off talking until he received instructions from me to do so. This function I knew he could perform admirably. The police, of course, concentrated upon the demonstration and the meeting, expecting action to come from there. The marchers themselves did not know what the plan was, so there was little likelihood of the information getting to the police. When the meeting was in full swing, the little group of fourteen "direct actionists," whom I had held behind, proceeded by a circuitous route to the workhouse. There were no police there; they were all at the meeting, or guarding the houses of the guardians. We therefore had no difficulty in gaining admission. Immediately we got inside, the front door was closed behind us, and men guarded the telephones to prevent the master from communicating with the police.

One of the matrons, alarmed at our bold methods, and no doubt expecting us to murder everybody in the institution, dropped to the floor in a faint. The workhouse master and his assistant were asked to hand over the keys of the stores; they refused to do so. Before resorting to taking the keys by force from the master, we decided to try the lock of the stores; a few hefty shoulders were put against it and it gave way. There in front of us on the shelves were large pots of jam. We were not particular about what we had; our intention was to get something over and above the casual diet in order that we could claim to have successfully broken down the Ministry of Health instructions.

Twenty-eight pots of jam were taken from the shelves. As we attempted to leave by the front entrance, somebody was at the door, knocking to get in. We therefore decided to retreat to the back and escape that way. In doing so we had to climb over walls and hedges, and in the process two pots of jam were lost. As soon as we had taken our departure, the police of course were sent for. Dozens of police rushed in by motor-cars and every other kind of available vehicle; but they were too late.

After leaving the workhouse I instructed the raiders to return quickly to the hall with the jam and to put guards on the doors. While the police were searching for us in the vicinity of the workhouse, I went to the meeting at the Clock Tower and spoke, informing the crowd that we were having jam for breakfast next morning, and I hurriedly brought the meeting to a close, so that we could get back into the hall before the police returned. That is how the marchers defeated the authorities at Rugby.

All night long the police were outside the Drill Hall where we were sleeping. We had the doors barred and guarded, but no attempt was made to force an entry. Our next stopping-place was to be Coventry, and in the morning, before we set off on the road, the Marchers' Control Council met and decided that we would carry our audacity a stage further in Rugby, by marching back to the workhouse with the empty jam-pots on the end of sticks. The men lined up and twenty-six of their number were called out to carry the jam-pots at the head of the column. The police looked on and made no interference. It was certainly an amusing sight as the marchers proceeded through the main streets of the town on their way to the workhouse. The news of our approach reached the workhouse authorities before we got there, and when we arrived the workhouse master and his staff, along with members of the board of guardians who had been summoned to an emergency meeting that morning, were gathered together on the top of the high steps leading to the entrance.

The marchers lined up in orderly fashion outside on the roadway. The pot-bearers were ordered to fall out, and with a red flag in front of them they marched up the long gravel path leading to the steps where the workhouse authorities were gathered. At the word of command the jam-pots were deposited on the steps in pyramid form, and with as much solemnity as the occasion would permit I handed a letter to the workhouse master, ironically thanking him for "the jam which we had so much enjoyed at breakfast." He was a quiet, good-natured sort of fellow, and he read the letter with a benign smile. I then took the red flag from the bearer, mounted the steps, and over the top of the jam-pots he was presented with the flag in military style. The marchers then gave the guardians and the police a vocal entertainment by singing the "Red Flag" and the "International" and at the word of command they marched off on the road to Coventry.

Before reaching Coventry, cyclists came to us from Rugby, to inform us that the board of guardians at its meeting decided to issue a warrant for my arrest; we smiled, and marched on. We expected that the Coventry police would have this warrant forwarded to them and that they would attempt to effect an arrest as we entered the town.

The marchers prepared for a struggle, but we met with no interference from the Coventry police. During the evening messengers came to us from Birmingham and notified us that reinforcements in that town had already been broken up by the police. We also learnt that the warrant for my arrest had been forwarded to Birmingham. Birmingham was our next stopping-place after Coventry, and from there we intended to turn back upon London via Warwick, after joining the reinforcements. The warrant for arrest had no doubt been sent to Birmingham because of the strength of the Birmingham police, and their reputation for brutality towards the workers.

We sent out scouts to Birmingham that evening and they reported that there was evidence of strong police preparations. The Marchers' Control Council decided that we would miss Birmingham, rest a day in Coventry, and then march across country to Warwick—this would put us in order with our time-table. We wondered what the police would do now about the warrant.

In Coventry we were staying in a big hall which formerly had been a church, but had been converted into a two-story building. On the morning that we were due to march out to Birmingham, we went to the municipal restaurant for our breakfast, supplied by the Coventry board of guardians, and to the surprise of the police, we returned to our hall. They waited about for an hour or so and then became agitated and began inquiring what time we intended to leave. At first we gave evasive answers, but then, as dinner-time approached, we announced to the chief of the police that we were unable to march to Birmingham that day as so many of the marchers were suffering from strain and sore feet. We said we would be going to Birmingham the next day. We sent a deputation to the Coventry poor law authorities informing them that we would be unable to leave Coventry and that we must ask them to provide us with further meals until next morning.

At first they refused to do so, but ultimately, on a definite promise from us that we would not delay our departure for more than a day, they consented to our request for meals. Then the police came to us again and were very anxious to be sure that we would be going to Birmingham next morning. We told them that we would, but they were evidently suspicious. Maybe information concerning the Control Council's decision had leaked out, or possibly they had guessed our intentions as a result of messengers which we had sent over to Warwick.

However, that evening we held a big demonstration in the Market Place. There were signs of special police activity and during the evening we saw van-loads of fresh police being brought in to Coventry—they were coming from Birmingham. After I had spoken at the meeting in the Market Place some old acquaintances in Coventry invited me to go to their home for supper. I quietly slipped away, thinking that I had done so unobserved, but at 11.30 at night whilst I was sitting in the house of my friends, a gentle knock came at the door. It was one of the marchers who had come to inform me that the police were surrounding the block of houses where I was. He asked what should be done, and I told him to hurry back to the hall and to rouse up the marchers, to bring them down to the house, and I would return to the hall with them. They came, many not even waiting to put on their jackets. This move had taken the police by surprise. I came out of the house, joined the marchers, and returned back to our hall. Police watched the hall all night, and next morning when we marched from the hall to the municipal restaurant for our breakfast, it was obvious by the police activities that something was going to happen before we left Coventry. As we left the restaurant a group of detectives stepped forward and closed in around me.

They informed me that they had a warrant for my arrest and that I must accompany them to the police station. I demanded to see the warrant, but they said they could not produce it in the street whilst the marchers were there. An Irishman, by the name of Jim Murphy, who had marched from Greenock, shouted "No warrant—no arrest!" This slogan was immediately taken up by all the marchers who gathered around and refused to allow the arrest to take place. A heated argument ensued and when the police endeavoured to drag me away a fight quickly developed.

The marchers, who were all carrying heavy walking sticks, met the police batons blow for blow. Several times, the police were driven back, but they rallied, and ultimately I gave the order for our men to retreat to our hall, as fresh reinforcements of police were being rushed up to the scene of battle. Immediately we got inside the hall all the doors were barred and barricaded. We took a roll call and found that one of the marchers, by the name of William Hunter, of Edinburgh, was missing. We later learnt that he had chased a policeman up a side-street and had got cut off from the marchers when we retreated.

Inside the hall we discussed what our next move should be. We took up our position on the top floor, and, looking out of the windows, we saw a cordon of police shoulder to shoulder, double rank, being formed up all round the building. The police hammered at the main door, but it was strong, like most church doors. The chief of police looked up at the windows and called on us to surrender. This was met by a volley of unfriendly remarks from the marchers. Then the fire engines were sent for and the chief of the police shouted to us that unless we surrendered the hoses would be put on and we would be driven out with water.

It was an anxious moment for the Control Council. We realised that if the police did succeed in forcing an entry their treatment of the marchers would be merciless because of the bitter battle that we had already had on the streets with them, and in which a number of police had been injured. After an hour, when the police were getting ready to use axes on the door, and to put on the hoses, we decided that discretion would be the better part of valour and that we would surrender. I shouted to the chief of police that we would remove the barricades and I would be prepared to come out, provided he promised that no attempt would be made to rush the door as it was opened. We made this demand because we wanted to avoid the men being beaten up inside the hall, and without this guarantee from the police we were not prepared to weaken our defences by opening the doors to them.

At first the chief of police refused to discuss the matter or to make any promises, but ultimately he said that if I surrendered his men would not enter the hall. We thereupon sang the "Red Flag," and along with a group of six comrades, I emerged into the street, to be surrounded immediately by a huge force of police who formed a procession with me in the centre, and marched to the police station. The solidarity and the spirit of the marchers in the hall had been splendid. They had been quite prepared to fight to the very last, but it would have been an unwise decision and the leadership advised against it.

I was taken to Rugby in a police car. William Hunter was tried in Coventry two hours later, and, although as a result of the man-handling which he had received he was still in a state of semi-consciousness in the dock and no witnesses were called on his behalf, he was sentenced to two months' hard labour on a charge of assaulting the police. On arrival at Rugby I was brought before a local magistrate and remanded for five days, bail being refused. I offered the names of good securities but the police were not letting me go free again. I was then handcuffed and taken by train to Leicester gaol by two uniformed police. It was a Saturday afternoon and there were thousands of football enthusiasts waiting for trains at Rugby and Leicester stations, and they eyed me with curiosity as I was led before them handcuffed.

On 7th February I was taken from Leicester gaol again in handcuffs, and escorted to Rugby. At the Rugby railway station two lines of police were formed up at the exit and I had to pass through them to a waiting car. When I appeared in court I learnt that the charge against me was that I had been guilty of "feloniously stealing twenty-eight pots of jam." In the court I strongly protested against the wording of the charge, pointing out that if I was found guilty on such a charge I would be recorded as a common thief. I then went on to explain that the action which we had taken was an action dictated by principles; that we had not regarded the matter as one of stealing, but one of carrying out our pledge to break down the instructions of the Ministry of Health, which we regarded as having been issued with the deliberate intention of starving the marchers into defeat. I dealt with the principles of the national hunger march; I spoke of the character of the marchers themselves, many of whom had been decorated for services during the war, and resented the attempt to treat them as tramps and vagabonds. The bench retired, and, on returning to the court, the chairman announced that they had to find me guilty and that they would impose a fine of five pounds. In announcing the verdict, he said, "I have no doubt that you have been actuated by high principles, yet all right-minded people would regard what you have done as stealing. You were the organiser of the raid where twenty-eight pots of jam were feloniously removed from the workhouse."

On hearing the verdict I announced that I would not pay the fine and the magistrate stated that the alternative would be twenty-eight days' imprisonment. As I was about to go down to the cells, somebody at the back of the court shouted "The fine will be paid." The police seemed extraordinarily anxious to get rid of me. They wanted no more arguments about the matter, and in the space of only a few minutes I found myself outside the court again.

A group of Rugby workers greeted me outside. On inquiring who had paid the fine, I was introduced to a benevolent-looking gentleman, who informed me that he was a Quaker and that he was a member of the board of guardians which had issued the warrant for my arrest. He explained that, whilst he did not agree with what I had done, he realised that it was a question of a working-class action for principle's sake and he believed that the hunger march was doing some good to stir up the conscience of the people on the question of unemployment, and he therefore did not want to see me go to prison.

After my release from the court at Rugby I joined the marchers again at Bicester, on their return journey to London. They had carried out the plans which I had left with them when I was taken away from Coventry, and they were conforming strictly to time-table. I learnt that since leaving Coventry they had been treated splendidly by the local authorities in the towns where they had subsequently stayed. The incidents at Rugby and Coventry had therefore apparently had their effect on the other local authorities. The Ministry of Health were furious at the open defiance which these guardians were adopting towards their instructions, and when our advance party had got to Bicester and were making arrangements about diet at the guardians' meeting, two representatives from the Ministry of Health, direct from London, came in. They insisted that the regulations laid down by the ministry should be observed. The board, however, refused to obey the ministry's instructions and the chairman said to the representatives, "We don't want any trouble in this town." From then on the marchers continued to have good conditions right down to London.

The southern army had also been well treated in the places where they had stayed, after the incident at Brighton. Both armies, accompanied by reinforcements, arrived back in London on 13th February, 1923, and were welcomed by a big demonstration of London unemployed assembled in Hyde Park.

Following this return to London the leadership of the march reviewed the whole position. Owing to large numbers of marchers having been forced home by domestic hardship and the decision of the Ministry of Labour denying labour exchange benefit to the marchers, we found that the reinforcements were not sufficient to make up for the loss of strength, and that we now had only about five hundred marchers in London. Rather than allow the march to peter out, the Council decided to make an organised termination to it on 20th February, and on the Sunday previous to this, 17th February, a farewell demonstration was held in Trafalgar Square.

The local authorities in London were approached and agreed to pay the fares for all the marchers back to their localities. So ended the biggest organised activity of the unemployed movement up to that time. The tenacious manner in which we had carried on the struggle for nearly five months won the admiration of millions of workers throughout the country, and even our enemies were unable to deny that we were a foe worthy of their steel.

Although we did not succeed in securing an interview with Mr. Bonar Law, the march had undoubtedly seriously disturbed the government and shaken the country into a much deeper consideration of the problem of unemployment. Tory members in the House of Commons, fearing the development of such marches, actually pressed for a bill to be introduced into Parliament "to prevent more than twelve men marching together on the highways." The marchers answered this challenge by declaring, "Let them pass such a Bill, and we shall organise a thousand parties of twelve to take the roads. It will constitute a greater danger to them than one compact body."

Both before and during the march, the government had carried on considerable propaganda about the state of finances of the unemployment insurance scheme, propaganda undoubtedly designed to prepare the way for reductions in the standards of the unemployed. Therefore, whilst the march had not secured any positive concessions from the government, it no doubt had the effect of preventing the launching of new attacks upon the unemployed standards.

The intensive propaganda of the marchers in the towns and villages throughout the country, moreover, unquestionably played an important part in preparing the minds of the masses for the election of a Labour government in January 1924.

Chapter V

THE TRIALS OF A STOWAWAY

IN April 1923, following the national hunger march, the third national conference of the unemployed movement was held in Coventry. No outstanding national activity occurred during the remainder of the year. There were, of course, hundreds of demonstrations, meetings and deputations of a local character, and the movement settled down to a period of persistent and effective work around the grievances of the unemployed at the labour exchange and relief offices.

Shortly after the conference I was elected to attend an international trade union conference which was to be held in the Soviet Union. Lord Curzon was the foreign secretary in the Bonar Law government. He conducted a pronounced anti-Soviet policy, and workers connected with the British revolutionary movement who had applied for passports to visit the Soviet Union were either refused or experienced long delays before receiving permission.

My prominence in the national hunger march led me to believe that I should also experience difficulties in regard to a passport. Not wishing to warn the government of my intentions I therefore decided not to apply for a passport, but to devise my own ways and means of reaching the Soviet Union.

For reasons which will be obvious to the reader, I do not propose to go into details on this point, except to say that I had many interesting and exciting experiences over the borders of Holland, Germany, Poland, Lithuania and Latvia before getting into the U.S.S.R. and reaching Moscow.

I left London on 1st May, when all the attention of the London police was centred upon the May Day demonstration. I was not able to get back into England until the following October. After the conference in Moscow I again had to make my way as best I could through Central Europe. I reached Berlin during July and then pushed on to Hamburg to take my chance of jumping a boat and stowing away to England.

Germany at this time was in the deepest throes of inflation, and the most appalling poverty and destitution were evident amongst the whole German working class. The bottom had completely fallen out of the currency, and 100,000 marks would only buy a loaf of bread. Most of the middle class were ruined, and the scanty savings which some workers had been able to accumulate were completely valueless. One could stand in the streets and see the prices in the shop windows being changed almost every hour, rising by hundreds of thousands of marks. Strikes and struggles swept throughout Germany as the workers fought to secure wages that would keep pace with the fantastic rise in prices. These struggles quickly developed into armed battles on the streets in all the big industrial centres of Germany. Government troops occupied all buildings of strategic importance. Military control was established on the great docks of Hamburg, and this, as the reader can well imagine, made my task of stowing away from Hamburg a thousand times more difficult.

I established contact with the revolutionary workers of Hamburg and enjoyed the hospitality of a comrade who was a leader of a section of the Workers' Defence Forces, at the time known as the Hundertschaft. In later years they became the organisation known as the "Red Front Fighters." Most members of the Workers' Defence Forces at that time possessed arms, and as the struggle developed throughout Germany these men came into fighting action almost nightly on the streets.

I shall never forget the awful paradox which was to be witnessed in the St. Pauli district of Hamburg. Whilst actual famine prevailed in the homes of the workers, the bourgeois restaurants, cafés and cabarets, patronised by the wealthy class, were in full swing, and one could catch a glimpse of the most riotous abandonment on the part of men and women who frequented these centres. It was as though those who still had money to spend lived only for the next twenty-four hours; they saw everything collapsing around them and threw themselves into a mad frenzy of obscene and revolting pleasure. Hamburg became a new Sodom and Gomorrah for the upper class.

It was not surprising, therefore, that the honest, hard-working German toilers expressed their bitterness and disgust at such conduct, whilst they themselves were starving, by looting shops, smashing up cabarets, and beating up the social wasters. Masses of workers from the districts surrounding Hamburg would swoop down upon the St. Pauli district. Police and military would endeavour to disperse them. Men, women and children would fall on the streets bleeding from the wounds inflicted by rifle-fire, and the most heart-rending scenes were to be witnessed almost every night as the workers heroically fought against their oppressors.

The workers' armed defence forces would come on to the streets and in disciplined movements take up their positions against the police and the military. Under cover of fire from the workers' defence forces, the masses of unarmed workers would be enabled to retreat back to their homes, some hugging to their breasts scanty portions of food or other necessities of life which they had looted from the shops.

I was in hiding in the Altona district, and each day I had to make my way across the St. Pauli area down to the dockside, in an effort to make contact with English seamen to get through on to the docks to jump a boat. On three occasions I became involved in the fighting as I tried to make my way at night back from the dock area to Altona. I witnessed some magnificent and heroic actions on the part of the workers' defence forces.

When barricades were thrown up one night on the Reperbahn-strasse, I found myself trapped in a zone held by two firing lines of the workers' defence forces. Fortunate for me that I was not the other side of the barricades! The armed forces of the German workers were lying flat on the ground, directing their fire down the main street at a force of military and police. Once in the fighting zone there was no means of escape, except by taking the extra-ordinary risk of becoming an open target for the bullets of the enemy. I therefore lay on the ground with the German fighters. They were too busy to pay very much attention to me; I was one of a number of others who unfortunately had to lie there without a weapon to aid in the fighting. After a time the word of com-mand was passed down the line of battle-scarred workers, and a steady retreat began under cover.

A small section kept up a constant fire in order to deceive the enemy, whilst the main body of men retreated with their weapons. Then at a signal, the heroes who had covered the retreat of their comrades, themselves suddenly vanished, and when the barri-cades were stormed the working-class fighters had departed.

The order for the general rising of the German people had not at that time been made, and these were only skirmishes leading up to the rising that ultimately took place in October, in which the town of Hamburg was completely captured by the working-class.

The consuls of the various nations in Hamburg issued proclama-tions advising their respective nationals to leave the port in view of the civil disturbances. Armed police would pull up pedestrians in the street if they thought they looked in any way suspicious. Foreigners were frequently stopped and asked to produce their papers of identification, but as luck would have it I managed to escape this predicament. Had I been so challenged, I had a story ready, of course, but whether it would have gone down is another question. In appearance I made myself to look as German as possible by growing a moustache modelled on that of the ex-Kaiser.

I drank in German beerhouses and wherever possible made contact with English seamen. Many times I picked up with seamen and got on friendly terms with them, learnt what boats they were on and what their destination was to be from Hamburg. Of course, I was not greatly interested in boats that were going to other ports except English ports. Many times, after spending an evening drinking with seamen and telling them the story that I was an English stoker who had fallen into bad company, got drunk, lost my papers and lost my boat, I succeeded in getting promises of help to stow away on a boat.

I discovered that when men of the sea are on the way to becoming well and truly "oiled," there is no limit to the promises which they will make to a fellow countryman. But when the effects of drink are vanishing, the splendid promises vanish with them. Repeatedly I suffered disappointment when I went to meet an English seaman and found that he had apparently forgotten all about the appointment.

At this time special permits were required to get past the sentries on the docks. Several times I succeeded in obtaining such permits and got past the vigilance of the military authorities, only to find it impossible to steal on to a boat. After a few weeks I was beginning to feel that my chance of getting out of Germany was hopeless. Then one day, sauntering into a little German beerhouse not far from the waterfront, I called for a lager, and whilst standing by the bar discovered that the proprietor, although a German, could speak almost perfect English. I got in conversation with him. He was used to English seamen in his beerhouse. Certain seamen who regularly sailed between Hull, Grimsby and the Tyneside ports to Hamburg made a practice of visiting his establishment and were well known to him.

Being a stranger, he asked me what boat I was from. I was ready with my story, and even had the name of a boat which I learnt had been in the port several weeks previously, and had sailed to Canada. He advised me to go to the British consul and said, "If you explain that you have lost all your papers and tell him your story, he is bound to do something for you." I nodded my assent, but of course knew that I could not go to the British consul.

I mixed with seamen in this little beerhouse, but of course had to make my inquiries very carefully, and it was not to every man that one could divulge one's intentions. I told the beerhouse-keeper that I hoped to be able to jump a boat or get a job to work my way back to England, but he showed little interest in the matter.

I regularly used his house for making contact and again suffered many disappointments. I got particularly friendly at this place with an old German seaman, who before the war had lived in Hull and had had a fleet of trawlers of his own. We knocked around together quite a lot, but I never divulged to him my identity. I bought food for him frequently and probably he was secretly anxious that my stay in Germany should not come to an end. One day, he took me to the room where he lived and opened an old sea-chest. At the bottom of the chest was a pile of pre-war German notes. He dived in his hands and pulled out a large bundle, and said, "This is my life's savings. In pre-war values this would be worth about £600. To-day it won't buy me a pound of potatoes." Tears ran down his cheeks as he said this, and he exclaimed "Ruined—ruined, absolutely ruined!"

One day I was sitting with this German seaman—whom for safety against the Hitler régime I will call "Schmidt,"— and overheard a conversation between another English seaman and the beerhouse-keeper.

"Have you heard anything from Jackson lately?" said the seaman.

"Oh, yes," replied the beerhouse-keeper, "I had a letter from him only a week or two ago—he seems to be doing quite well out there. Says he's now working in a printing works. He also says that he's been up in an aeroplane with some delegates."

On hearing these remarks, I became alert, and listened carefully for the rest, but the conversation died down too softly for me to distinguish it clearly. But I had a clue, and intended to follow it up! I knew a Jackson who came from Hull—he was a printer in a printing works in Moscow, and he had been up in an aeroplane with me at an air display just outside Moscow. I felt sure from the little bit of conversation I had heard that it must be the same Jackson—but suppose I was wrong? One had to be very careful in Hamburg at that time. To fall into the hands of the police as a foreign revolutionary might have meant disappearance.

There was much suspicion prevalent and people talked carefully.

I didn't know whether the beerhouse-keeper would be prepared to help me if he knew who I was, or whether he would betray me, but I was ready to take the chance, so a little later engaged him in conversation, and said, "Excuse me, but I couldn't help overhearing your conversation just now and heard you mention a man by the name of 'Jackson.' "

As soon as I said this, he became all alert and looked me straight in the eye. Immediately I thought I knew what was running through his mind. He was wondering whether I was trying to trick him. He replied, "Oh, no! You don't know who I was talking about." I pressed my point and said I felt sure that he had been talking about a Jackson whom I knew. He said, "Why do you think that?" I replied, "Did your Jackson originally come from Hull?" "Yes," he said, "but Jackson is a common name in England." As I began to follow up the conversation I discerned that he became more and more guarded, almost bitter and hostile, but this only encouraged me, because it led me to believe that he had a good reason for not wanting me to know of his associations.

It was clear that he began to mistrust me, probably thinking that I was trying to draw out information that might have been useful to the police. Of course, this only strengthened my belief that he might be a sympathiser with the revolutionary movement but naturally I could not be sure. I wondered how much I dared tell him now. I knew that if he was a supporter of the revolutionary movement, many of my problems would be solved if I could tell him who I was, but to have told him and then found out that I had been mistaken in regard to his attitude might have meant disaster for me.

But I was determined to make or break, and so I persisted in my questioning and laid emphasis upon the fact that I knew the Jackson whom he knew. For a minute or two we engaged in word fencing, then he suddenly said, in the most peremptory manner, "Who the hell are you? What are you getting at?"

In an instant I took the risk and said, "I heard sufficient from your conversation to cause me to believe that you are friendly with a Jackson whom I knew in Moscow! It might interest you to know that I only recently met Jackson in Moscow and in fact it was I who went up in the aeroplane with Jackson!"

His two hands gripped the bar counter, and he looked as though he was ready to spring at me. But he just said "Go on—what's the full story?"

I replied, "The full story is, I'm not an English stoker stranded; I'm a revolutionary worker from Britain, travelling illegally, returning from an international trade union conference in Moscow."

He set his jaw and said, "What proof can you give me of that?" I replied, "No proof, only my own word. I'm not fool enough to be carrying any documents which show my identity."

He then asked me my name, and I told him, but still he expressed doubt as to my bona fides. He then mentioned the names of people connected with the British revolutionary movement and asked me if I knew them—Arthur McManus, Albert Inkpin, Willie Paul, Bill Gallacher and finally came to the name of ——
——. I said, "Yes, of course I know —— ——. He is at the present time in this very port, secretary of an important international organisation. The beerhouse-keeper then said, "Bring —— here and I'll believe your story." I said, "I'll bring him to-night."

I departed and went straight to the office where I knew I could find ——. I had not been able to use ——'s office because it had been raided several times by the police, but this time I chanced it. I met —— and said, "Do you know an old fellow by the name of —— (mentioning the name of the beerhouse-keeper) who was in America before the war?"

—— replied, "Of course I know him; we were great friends at one time. I haven't seen him for years."

I then told —— my story about the beerhouse and he agreed to go round with me that night. When he walked into the beerhouse the proprietor moved from behind the counter and with his face wreathed in smiles he stepped forward to grasp the hand of —— like a long-lost brother.

From that moment the whole atmosphere of the beerhouse changed for me. We went into the back parlour and told the full story and I found that the beerhouse-keeper was an old revolutionary who was only too anxious to help me in my difficulties. I was treated like a son and we often laughed over the way in which we had deceived each other before arriving at the truth.

But even with the help of my new-found friend and staunch comrade, escape from Hamburg was not easy. He talked with seamen, never, of course, telling them who I was, but there were always great difficulties, particularly the difficulty of getting past the sentries at the docks and then the difficulty of getting on a boat itself.

One day, however, he spoke to a seaman named Bob Owens, who was leading stoker on a tramp steamer that was regularly trading between Tyneside and Hamburg, and Owens promised he would arrange to get papers for me, that he would get me past the docks and show me where his boat was lying, and if possible help me to stow away. But he let me down. I was to have met him at night-time, but he did not show up. I had said good-bye to my good friend the beerhouse-keeper, and next day when I walked in he was greatly surprised to see me and said, "What happened? Did things go wrong?"

I explained that Owens had not kept his word.

"Too bad, too bad," said the beerhouse-keeper.

Then in the afternoon I was sitting drinking with my old friend Schmidt when who should walk into the bar but Bob Owens, so drunk that he could hardly stand. With him there was a young, rough-looking German. Schmidt turned to me and said, "Look at that! I would swear that fellow with Bob Owens is a beach-comber"—meaning one who preys upon seamen and gets an existence by cheating them.

The young German ordered Owens to call for a drink, but Owens was too be-fuddled, and the German, thinking that nobody was noticing, dived his hand into the inside jacket pocket of Owens and pulled out a wallet; then instead of calling for a drink he turned to walk out. Instantly, Schmidt—a man of about sixty years of age—jumped up to intercept the young beach-comber. The beachcomber pushed him on one side and as Schmidt clung to his coat he received a smashing blow on the jaw, and collapsed to the ground.

I had no special reason for interfering in a quarrel in which Bob Owens was involved. After all, was it not Bob Owens who had promised to help me and then broken his word? But what determined my action was the fact that my friend, Schmidt, had been struck down. I was in good physical condition, and having been a fairly strenuous athlete and amateur boxer I felt quite competent to take care of myself in such a battle. As Schmidt went to the floor, I stepped forward, and then it was the beach-comber or I who had to win. He could certainly fight, but he lacked the science of a trained boxer. He rushed in wildly with arms whirling like a windmill. I either parried most of these blows or stepped in beneath them with a straight punch before his blow could connect. But he was fierce. My lips were bruised, my nose was bleeding and my eye was swollen, but the honours went to me in the end; with a straight left to the face, and a right cross to the jaw, I put the beachcomber down for the count and there was no more fight in him after that.

Whilst he lay on the floor we went through his pockets and took the wallet which he had stolen from Bob Owens. During the fighting, Owens considerably sobered up, as drunken men will do when faced with danger. After throwing the beachcomber outside on the street, Owens retired to lie down for a couple of hours on a couch in the back parlour, to sleep off the effects of German lager. Later in the evening he emerged, and the first question he asked was, "Where's that bloke who helped me today?"

The beerhouse-keeper pointed to me, sitting in a corner and Owens came over and said, "I made a promise to you. I didn't keep it, but I'm keeping it to-night!"

He got seaman's papers for me and a docks pass and that night I passed the sentries again, on to the Hamburg docks, and following Bob Owens at a distance I came to the ship on which he was a stoker. He refused to put his own job in jeopardy and had said, "When I show you the boat and come back and give you the all-clear, you must do the rest." I stealthily hurried on board in the darkness and quickly stowed away in a filthy hole at the back of this North Sea tramp steamer.

I lay quietly for several hours. My heart jumped with delight when I heard the engines begin to throb and knew we were about to sail down the River Elbe. After a time the boat began to pitch and toss and I knew that we had entered the North Sea. I had no luggage with me of any sort, not even a change of shirt. I had only a packet of sandwiches. I was hungry and these I devoured and then dropped to sleep, to be awakened by a fierce itching sensation which told me that I was being bitten by bugs, lice, or some other kind of pernicious vermin. But I could do nothing about it, I just had to grin and bear it.

During the day Bob Owens came to me with a plate of some food. Although I was terribly hungry I found difficulty in relishing the food because of the conditions in which I found myself. On the second night out Bob Owens again came to me and asked if I would like to stretch my legs a bit.

"Yes, it would be welcome," I replied. But then he said "You are a stoker, aren't you? Perhaps you'll come down and give me a hand with the fires. It's my turn on." I couldn't very well refuse. He said "Follow me along the deck, the old man (meaning the captain) is on the bridge, but he won't recognise you in the dark. Pull your cap well over your eyes." Down into the stokehold I went. I stripped to the waist and with my eye on Owens and another stoker I watched the methods of toil and imitated them. The noise, the dirt, and the heat were terrific, the ventilation was terrible. When we spoke to each other we had to shout at the top of our voices.

Owens shouted, "Clean that fire!" I picked up a heavy iron rod about ten feet long with about six inches bent at a right angle at the end. I opened the furnace and a terrific white-hot heat burst out into my face. I had seen Owens clean the fire next to me and I did the same as he did. I drove in the iron bar beneath the white-hot coal, I turned it, drew it towards me, drove it in again, repeating this process several times. Then came the shovelling of more coal into the furnace, whilst the heat blazed through the open door.

After about an hour bells rang from the bridge announcing that more steam was wanted. I was not keeping my fire up to the pressure that it should have been, and the pressure gauge had been steadily dropping. Owens shouted, "You've got to send her up!" I opened the furnace door again and heaved in coal as fast as I could. Sweat was pouring off me, my face and body were almost jet black. So I toiled for four long hours in that hell-hole with Bob Owens. Not having handled tools for a long time, my hands had got soft and the use of the fire-iron had brought up huge blisters that broke and pained me as the dirt got into the punctured skin.

My relief when the four-hour shift came to an end can well be imagined. I was half blinded as sweat with the coal grime ran down my forehead into my eyes. I was getting a taste of what a stoker's life is like. I emerged as the next shift came down, and after a wash and something to eat I crawled away into my hole again, exhausted, to sleep like a log. The other stokers, of course, learnt that I was aboard, but they never betrayed me. We got friendly, but I naturally never told them who I was.

We entered the mouth of the Tyne some time during the evening of the third night out from Hamburg. I was pleased that we were coming in at night-time; I thought that darkness would be a great aid to me in avoiding the customs men and dock police. I was, however, to suffer a disappointment. There was a large amount of traffic in the river. A little while previously there had been a dock strike and the result was that the docks were congested and we were not able to proceed straight into our berth. We tied up in mid-stream alongside two other boats and there we lay all night.

Next morning the stokers said they still thought that we should not be able to go in with the next tide. One of the stokers on board was a temporary hand, the regular fireman having lost his boat on the last trip. About nine o'clock in the morning, I was down in the stokers' bunkhouse when a stranger came in. He looked at me and began to talk about the job. Bob Owens cut in and explained to him that I was not the temporary hand, I was a stowaway. By his demeanour he showed that he was friendly, and I asked him, "How did you get on to the boat?"

"Oh!" he said, "I came over across the river in a small rowing-boat to see the old man about my job."

I immediately seized this opportunity, and said, "You've got your seaman's papers and you'll experience no difficulty from the customs men or the police. What about me getting away in the rowing-boat that you came over in?"

He considered the proposition for a few minutes, and Young said, "That's a good idea." He held out his hand, I gripped it, and he said, "That's on!" Then he explained that to reach the rowing-boat I would have to go along the deck to where the next boat lay closest to ours, jump across, get over this deck, and so on to the third boat; on the port side of the third ship I would find a rope ladder hanging. I must untie the rope that held the rowing-boat, and then pull across stream to the steps that led down to the river. I would find a big iron ring on the side of the steps, and I must fasten the rowing-boat to this.

I said, "Am I likely to get stopped on the other two boats?" He answered, "No, nearly all the crew are ashore." Bob Owens then ran up on deck to make sure that it was all clear for me to go out. He came back, and with a few hurried final directions I went up from the stokers' quarters on to the deck. I ran to where the port side of our boat came nearest to the starboard side of the second boat, and leapt across on to the next deck. Then across that deck over on to the third boat. I found the rope ladder hanging just as had been explained to me, and I remember the very strange sensation that I experienced when I went to climb down it, the feeling that the rungs of the ladder are trying to escape your feet. It doesn't feel like treading on a ladder at all. Not being used to it, I almost pitched into the water, but I clung on with my hands and awkwardly made my way down the ladder into the rowing-boat. I pulled across stream as directed, found the steps, tied the boat to the ring, and ran up the steps. I found myself in the back streets of Jarrow or Hebburn—I don't remember which.

I made my way to the Central Station, Newcastle; I had just about £3 left, so went into an outfitter's and bought a complete change of underclothes and a shirt. I went to the wash-house and lavatory on Central Station, and told the attendant that I had just come off a boat and would like to change my clothes before going home. I dropped him half-a-crown and he raised no objection. I walked out of the Central Station wash-house feeling much better after having left behind many small friends that I had picked up on the boat. I advised the attendant to have the dirty clothes burnt, as the boat I had worked on was a filthy one. He seemed to understand and sympathised!

The next thing to be done was to go to the barber's. By this time I had not only a moustache but a stubble that almost amounted to a beard. I sat in the barber's chair and said "Take the lot off!" He said, "Do you want that nice moustache removed as well?" and I replied, "Yes—all of it!" Twenty minutes later I emerged from the barber's shop my normal self, and, with a feeling of joy at having been to the Soviet Union and emerged triumphant over my difficulties in Central Europe, I caught a train to London and dropped into a nice sleep, waking up to find myself in King's Cross station.

Chapter VI

THE TRADE UNION CONGRESS AND UNITY

FOLLOWING the National Day of Demonstration on 7th January, 1923, organised jointly between the National Unemployed Workers' Movement, the Trades Union Congress General Council, the Labour Party and trades councils, the N.U.W.M. put forward proposals for continuing this joint work.

On 24th January, 1923, representatives from the N.U.W.M. met the T.U.C. Unemployment Sub-Committee, consisting of Messrs. J. B. Williams, A. A. Purcell, Arthur Heyday, Ben Tillett, A. Conley, George Hicks, John Hill and Bob Smillie. We submitted to the committee the following three definite proposals:

1. Closer relationship between employed and unemployed by the establishment of a joint committee with equal representation from the T.U.C. General Council and the N.U.W.M.

2. That the General Council should circularise the trade unions and trade councils, encouraging the formation of unemployed committees in every locality, attached to the N.U.W.M.

3. That at the next Trades Union Congress the affiliation of the N.U.W.M. to the T.U.C. should be placed on the agenda.

The T.U.C. sub-committee considered these proposals and issued to the General Council the following statement of proposed action on the scheme we had put forward:

Proposal No. 1.

That steps be taken to develop a closer relationship between the organised workers who are employed and the organised unemployed as represented by the National Unemployed Workers' Movement, through the agency of the Trades Union Congress General Council.

That the closer relationship should take the form of establishing a Joint Advisory Council consisting of three representatives of the General Council and three representatives of the Unemployed Workers' Movement, with secretaries to act jointly appointed by both bodies.

The Joint Advisory Council shall be authorised to prepare

plans for joint action as considered necessary to be recommended for adoption to the Trades Union Congress General Council and the Unemployed Workers' Movement.

The Advisory Council shall not be authorised to incur financial responsibilities other than incidental expenditure in connection with the committee work of the Advisory Council without the sanction of the Trades Union Congress General Council.

The Advisory Council shall not be authorised to issue any statement as representing the Trades Union Congress General Council without first submitting the same for the approval and adoption of the Council.

Regarding Proposals Nos. 2 and 3, we have to make the following observations:—

Proposal No. 2.

We recommend that the General Council issue a circular advising local trades and labour councils to co-operate with the Unemployed Workers' Movement, for the purpose of calling public attention to the unemployed problem and acting jointly regarding representations made to public bodies on all matters relating to local effort to deal with the position of the unemployed. These committees to represent equal powers and representative authority on both sides. The General Council to decide what action should be taken to secure the co-operation of trade union branches through the executive committees of unions affiliated to the Congress.

Proposal No. 3.

We cannot recommend to the General Council this proposal, as we consider that all unemployed workers are or should be represented at the Trades Union Congress by the properly consti-tuted trade union bodies affiliated, and we are opposed to the principle contained in proposal No. 3 as likely to lead to dual representation at the Congress.

With regard to the note appended to the National Unemployed Workers' Movement's proposals, we have to state that this proposal is already covered, so far as we are prepared to suggest its adoption, in the recommendations we have made, and, in our opinion the Advisory Committee cannot be authorised to accept the executive responsibilities which appear to be implied in the note.

When the Trades Union Congress met at Plymouth in Sep-tember 1923, the statement of the sub-committee received endorse-ment, but it was not until 10th January, 1924, that the first meeting of the Joint Advisory Committee took place. The representatives from the T.U.C. were Messrs. John Bromley, Ben Tillett, A. A. Findlay and Fred Bramley; for the N.U.W.M. Messrs. J. W. Holt, H. Straker, P. Haye and myself. Later, when Fred Bramley, the general secretary of the T.U.C., became ill, Mr. Walter Citrine, who was acting assistant-secretary, took his place on the J.A.C.

At our first meeting we discussed the question of a national campaign around specific demands for the unemployed, and it was decided that a six point charter should be issued and popularised as the basis for joint agitation of employed and unemployed. The meetings of the Joint Advisory Council were held monthly, sometimes more often when urgent questions arose. By the end of February we had reached agreement on the points of the charter and an intensive campaign was begun leading up to a National Day of Demonstration, to be called "Unemployed Sunday," on 1st June, 1924.

The charter read as follows:

THE UNEMPLOYED WORKERS' CHARTER

represents a programme for immediate attainment by united action. We call upon all workers by hand or brain to help in our great National effort to rescue unemployed workers from continued starvation and despair.

WE DEMAND

1. Work or effective maintenance for all unemployed workers and increased Government assistance to be provided through Trade Unions. All unemployment relief to be completely dissociated from Poor Law administration.

2. The immediate development of Government schemes of employment to absorb the unemployed in their own trades at Trade Union rates of wages and conditions.

3. The establishment of State Workshops for the purpose of supplying the necessary service of commodities to meet the requirements of Government Departments.

4. The reduction in the hours of labour necessary to absorb unemployed workers, the normal working day or week to be regulated by the requirements of the industry.

5. The establishment of occupational training centres for unemployed workers, providing proper training with effective maintenance, particularly for unemployed boys and girls and able-bodied ex-service men.

6. The provision of suitable housing accommodation at rents

within the means of wage-earners, and the proper use of existing houses.

TRADE UNIONISTS, UNEMPLOYED WORKERS, LABOUR PARTY MEMBERS, and all Wage Earners must support the demand for just treatment of the unemployed.

The points of the charter were printed in leaflet form and circularised to working-class organisations throughout Great Britain. This was followed up by six explanatory leaflets, each leaflet advancing arguments in favour of one of the points of the charter. The demand for copies of the charter and the leaflets rapidly developed and over a million and a half leaflets were issued by the Joint Advisory Council, in addition to many more which the trades councils and labour parties issued themselves.

It is of historical importance to record the contents of the supplementary leaflets which were issued supporting our points in the charter. They are reproduced below:

Leaflet No. 1.
WHAT IS MAINTENANCE?

We demand work or effective maintenance for all unemployed workers and increased Government assistance to be provided through Trade Unions. All unemployment relief to be completely dissociated from Poor Law administration.

Government Maintenance for Poor Law Institutions.

Mr. Neville Chamberlain informed the House of Commons on August 1st, 1923, that the cost per head in Poor Law Institutions was £88 5s. 3¼d. a year.

On Poor Law scale two adults would cost	.	£176 10	6½
Two children (equal to one adult) cost	. .	88 5	3¼
Total cost per annum	. . .	£264 15	9¾
Total cost per week	. . .	£5 1	10¼

Mr. Bridgeman, late Home Secretary, informed the House of Commons on August 2nd, 1923, that the cost of maintaining a convict in H.M. Prisons was £111 a year.

On the convict scale two adults would cost	.	£222 0	0
Two children (equal to one adult) cost	. .	111 0	0
Total cost per annum	. .	£333 0	0
Total cost per week	. . .	£6 8	0¾

The Unemployed Workers have suggested the following scale for unemployed maintenance:—

Man and wife	per week	£3	0	0
Two children	per week	0	18	0
	Total cost per week . . .	£3	18	0
	Or an annual cost of . . .	£202	16	0

The question arises: Are Unemployed Workers entitled to Maintenance equivalent to that provided for Poor Law inmates and convicts in H.M. Prisons? The answer of British citizenship should be clear and definite—

SUPPORT THE UNEMPLOYED WORKERS' CHARTER.

Leaflet No. 2.

GOVERNMENT SCHEMES TO PROVIDE WORK.

We demand the immediate development of Government schemes of employment to absorb the unemployed in their own trades at Trade Union rates of wages and conditions.

The Government should devise Schemes for:—

IMPROVING THE ROADS AND BRIDGES OF THE COUNTRY. IMPROVING THE RIVERS, CANALS, DOCKS AND HARBOURS. SETTING UP A NATIONAL SCHEME OF ELECTRIC POWER SUPPLY, PUBLICLY OWNED AND DEMOCRATICALLY MANAGED. AFFORESTATION, LAND DRAINAGE, AND LAND RECLAMATION. RE-CONDITIONING, EXTENSION AND ELECTRIFICATION OF RAILWAYS.

A National Spring-Cleaning.

The Clearance, Cleaning and Planting of Open Spaces, the Pulling Down of Old and Obsolete Buildings to beautify and modernise Towns and Cities.

These schemes are necessary, would be remunerative, add to the resources and prosperity of the nation, and, above all, keep unemployed workers in a state of physical and mental efficiency.

The health and efficiency of the workers is a great National asset.

Work at Trades Union wages, and conditions, providing a reasonable standard of comfort, is essential for all citizens.

WE STAND FOR USEFUL WORK WITH EFFECTIVE MAINTENANCE. SUPPORT THE UNEMPLOYED WORKERS' CHARTER.

Leaflet No 3.
STATE WORKSHOPS.

We demand the establishment of State workshops for the purpose of supplying the necessary service or commodities to meet the requirements of Government Departments.

Private enterprise has failed to regulate industry in making provision for continuous employment for willing and capable workers.

The Government departments require commodities of all kinds. These should be produced in factories and workshops owned by the Nation, utilised for the Nation, and employed during periods of national emergency, such as exceptional trade depression, for producing Government requirements in advance as an alternative to providing unemployment benefits without a return.

WORK IS MORE SATISFACTORY THAN MAINTENANCE. WHEN PRIVATE ENTERPRISE FAILS, THE COMMUNITY MUST ACT.

All Government Departments should be compelled to place orders for Government requirements with State-owned factories, especially in relation to non-perishable commodities. Where possible, these should be produced in advance to avoid the payment of overtime rates with extra cost during periods of normal demand.

During the Great War, national factories were established employing one and a quarter million people, to increase the efficiency of the Nation for the purpose of War.

State factories and workshops are necessary for the regular employment of the workers, and the maintenance of their physical and mental efficiency to meet the dangers of a capitalist peace.

FULL EMPLOYMENT OF CITIZENS IS THE NATION'S RESPONSIBILITY. SUPPORT THE UNEMPLOYED WORKERS' CHARTER.

Leaflet No. 4.

We demand the reduction in the hours of labour necessary to absorb unemployed workers, the normal working day or week to be regulated by the requirements of the industry.

The development of our productive capacity, due to the application of steam, electricity, and a number of labour-saving inventions, has increased the productive power of the community to an enormous extent during the last 150 years.

The hours of labour have not been reduced in proportion to the increased capacity of the nation to produce wealth.

The normal working week of industry is not regulated by the needs of the community or the output power of the workers.

Every improvement in machinery has been utilised not to save labour but to scrap labourers.

Unemployment has become the natural economic consequence of increased productive efficiency.

THE HOURS OF LABOUR SHOULD BE REGULATED ACCORDING TO THE TIME NEEDED TO PRODUCE THE COMMODITIES THE COMMUNITY REQUIRES.

As improved machinery, new methods of production, and re-organisation of industrial activities are devised, a reduction in the normal working week should be the natural consequence.

The normal working week or day should, therefore, be reduced as a means of absorbing unemployed workers displaced by improvements in machinery.

Lord Leverhulme supports the unemployed workers' demand for a six-hour day.

This is the common-sense AND ONLY scientific method of regulating productive activities in accordance with social needs.

SUPPORT THE UNEMPLOYED WORKERS' CHARTER.

Leaflet No. 5.

TRAINING FOR UNEMPLOYED WORKERS.

We demand the establishment of occupational training centres for unemployed workers, providing proper training with effective maintenance, particularly for unemployed boys and girls and able-bodied ex-service men.

The continued industrial depression has not only thrown thousands of able-bodied men and women out of work, but has prevented thousands of boys and girls from entering any kind of occupation.

The most disastrous consequence of our unemployed problem to-day is the serious physical, mental and moral degradation of boys and girls who have never been employed since leaving school.

The war-time period limited, and in many industries destroyed, the chance of apprenticeship. The long-continued period of industrial depression, reducing the normal requirements of industry, has also limited the opportunities of occupational training.

The State must accept the responsibility for maintaining the efficiency of our industrial population by utilising periods of unemployment for the purpose of giving occupational training with effective maintenance for unemployed boys and girls.

Government action has been taken to provide inadequate and under-paid training for disabled ex-service men. In many cases for men so wholly disabled that they are unfit for remunerative occupation.

The Government has not provided proper schemes to give training with maintenance for able-bodied ex-service men. Such schemes are vitally needed and MUST be obtained by consultation and agreement with Trade Unions.

Prevent the ruin of boys and girls and the punishment of able-bodied men for their war service to the community BY INSISTING ON PROPER TRAINING AND MAINTENANCE FOR ALL. SUPPORT THE UNEMPLOYED WORKERS' CHARTER.

Leaflet No. 6.

HOUSING.

We demand the provision of suitable housing accommodation at rents within the means of wage-earners, and the proper use of existing houses.

The nation needs at least ONE MILLION new houses.

BUILDING WORKERS ARE UNEMPLOYED.

Private enterprise has failed to provide houses at rents which wage-earners can afford to pay.

Building rings and other profiteer agencies stand in the way.

Government factories could be employed in providing building materials on a large scale.

Profiteering interests would suffer but the community would gain.

CHEAP HOUSES ARE AS ESSENTIAL AS PUBLIC PARKS.

Healthy rooms are as necessary as well-lighted, broadly-constructed and clean public thoroughfares.

The workers' health can best be maintained by proper home conditions. All houses fit for habitation should be fully occupied, overcrowding abolished, and eviction of tenants suitably housed made illegal.

HOUSES ARE A VITAL SOCIAL NECESSITY.

A National Housing Scheme on proper lines would reduce the death-rate and produce healthier men and women. The efficiency, happiness, and general welfare of the community depends more on healthy houses than a powerful Army or Navy.

Support the Demand for Strengthening the Nation's First Line of Defence, namely:—

HEALTHY HOUSES.
SUPPORT THE UNEMPLOYED WORKERS' CHARTER.

The arguments contained in these leaflets were taken up by thousands of speakers of the working-class movement all over

Great Britain, and an intensive campaign was conducted leading up to the big day of demonstration, 1st June.

When this day arrived we witnessed a mighty display of working-class strength. In almost every town tens of thousands of employed and unemployed workers marched together under the banners of the trade unions, labour parties, co-operative guilds and the N.U.W.M. branches. The venue of the demonstration in London was Trafalgar Square and huge contingents poured into the square for fully an hour and a half. It was one of the greatest demonstrations ever held at this favourite spot. A uniform resolution was passed at all the demonstrations on this day. It was short and to the point, as follows:

That this demonstration of workers, employed and unemployed, approves the Unemployed Workers' Charter, calls the attention of the Government to the points contained therein, and urges that immediate administrative and legislative action be promoted to give effect to its proposals.

This meeting also urges individual electors to communicate personally with each member of Parliament representing their constituencies, calling upon them to support the terms of this resolution and to give effect to the decision of this meeting.

The government at the time was the Labour administration which had been established in January 1924. There could be no doubt that the charter agitations made a considerable impression and acted as a stimulus to the Labour government to make improvements in the conditions of the unemployed.

This government introduced a new Bill that became operative in August 1924, increasing the benefit scales from 15s. to 18s. for an adult man, and from 12s. to 15s. for a woman. At the same time it increased allowances for dependent children from 1s. to 2s. per week. Speaking on this Bill in the House of Commons on 18th June, 1924, the Minister of Labour, Mr. Tom Shaw, said, "The principle of this Bill is that an honest man shall not starve though he be unemployed; nor shall he be driven to the guardians; that he shall be paid a sum of money that at any rate will keep him from starvation."

The Labour government also responded to our demand for work schemes and an extensive plan of schemes was formulated and many were actually put into operation before the government were driven out of office in October. Steps were also taken to meet point six in the charter in respect to the provision of suitable housing accommodation, and many new housing schemes were launched. The agitation for the charter continued throughout 1924 and 1925.

Other questions relating to the conditions of the unemployed were raised by the N.U.W.M. representatives on the Joint Advisory Council; and joint deputations representing the Labour Party, Parliamentary Labour Party, and the General Council, were appointed to meet the Ministers of Labour and of Health, to urge the importance of remedying the conditions complained of. The grievances which were raised were as follows:

1. The granting of outdoor relief to unemployed applicants on loan, which means that when they do secure employment, they have a heavy debt to meet to the guardians. This operates, not in all but in many localities.

2. The payment of all relief in kind. This means that no money is granted to meet necessary expenditures in the home.

3. Task work for bare relief.

4. Guardians refusing relief and offering the workhouse.

5. Disqualification of recipients of relief from standing as candidates for boards of guardians and urban and borough councils. This means a loss of civic rights through unemployment.

6. Belmont Colony and Hollesley Bay. These are institutions maintained by certain London guardians to which they send unemployed men who apply for relief. It is asserted that there is little difference between these institutions and an ordinary prison.

7. The loss of national health insurance benefits through unemployment. This applies to men or women who have been unable to secure employment for a considerable time.

It must be recorded that no effective steps were taken by the Labour government to remedy these grievances, in spite of the protest which came from their own ranks. Mr. Philip Snowden was the chancellor of the exchequer and Ramsay MacDonald prime minister of the Labour government; this probably helps to explain the failure of the government to take effective steps to remedy the grievances which we had raised through the Joint Advisory Council, and which had become the subject of a national deputation from the Trades Union Congress and Labour Party.

At the 1924 Trades Union Congress, held in Hull, I was appointed by the J.A.C. to attend and address the congress as a fraternal delegate from the organised unemployed. The question of affiliation of the unemployed movement to the T.U.C. unfortunately was voted upon before I had spoken, but in the course of my address I spoke on the importance of the organised unem-

ployed in relation to the struggle of the workers as a whole, and to
the protection of trade union standards. I gave examples of the
way in which the organised unemployed had assisted workers
engaged in industrial disputes. On this point I quoted the
following letter which we had received from Mr. Ernest Bevin,
general secretary of the Transport and General Workers' Union:

February 29, 1924.

Dear Sir,

I am directed to convey to you the best thanks of the Dockers'
National Delegate Conference for the splendid and valuable
assistance rendered by your Organisation during the recent
struggle.

The Conference feel that the action of your Movement helped
considerably in effecting a quick victory.

With best wishes,

Your sincerely,

Ernest Bevin.

I emphasised the need for continuing the work of the Joint
Advisory Council and, in fact, of going a step further by a system
of membership transference from the unemployed movement into
the trade unions, when a member of the unemployed movement
obtained work. I dealt with the struggles which the movement
had gone through since its inception and instanced the improvements that had been obtained by agitation in respect to the unemployment insurance scheme and poor law relief. In conclusion
I laid emphasis upon the need for following this up with still more
powerful agitations and strengthening the bonds of unity between
the employed and unemployed.

The transference scheme which had been put forward by the
N.U.W.M. representatives received the support of the T.U.C.
representatives who sat on the Joint Advisory Council, but when
it came before the full General Council for consideration it was
turned down. The Trades Union Congress upheld the rejection
of the General Council. The scheme which we had proposed
was as follows:

1. That the unions make provision either by amendment of
their rules where necessary or by other means, for retaining their
members during periods of unemployment, either without payment of trade contributions or the payment of a nominal contribution sufficient to cover administrative expenses.

2. That the unions be requested to make arrangements

through their branches by which their unemployed members can be linked up with the Unemployed Workers' Movement for the purpose of maintaining a unified policy in relation to the activities of unemployed workers.

3. That the unions be requested to recognise the Unemployed Workers' Movement card of membership for the purpose of transfer to the unions without entrance fee when such workers obtain employment.

4. Further, the committee agreed to recommend to the General Council that steps should be taken to set up a permanent Joint Committee of the General Council and the National Unemployed Workers' Movement charged with the responsibility of securing administrative effect for the above proposals and also the initiation and control of special campaigns or other activities promoted in the interests of unemployed workers.

The leaders of the trade unions which opposed the transfer scheme and the affiliation of the unemployed movement to the T.U.C. advanced as their main argument that the transfer scheme would be resented as an interference with the internal affairs of the unions, and that the affiliation was not possible because an unemployed movement was not a trade union and therefore that it was not necessary because the unemployed had representation in the Congress through their unions.

I answered this criticism in my speech to the congress in the following manner: "There are hundreds of thousands of men who went into the army in the early days of the war as youths, and came out of the army as men, and they never really entered industry proper at all; they never had the opportunity of settling down in a trade. Many of these men have been tossed about from one industry to another as common or casual labourers and consequently have never really felt the urge to become members of the trade union movement. The very fact that unemployed men see the necessity of getting into the ranks of the organised unemployed movement and playing their part in the general agitation on unemployment is clear evidence that they understand and appreciate the need for working-class organisation. It will be possible for many of those who are in the unemployed movement to be made real good trade unionists. Under the transfer scheme we now suggest that it should be made easy for men and women holding a membership card of the unemployed movement to gain access to the trade union movement, and, when they do secure employment, to obtain full status as trade unionists, without having to meet heavy initiation or entrance fees. I suggest that the heavy initiation and entrance fees in many unions to-day are an obstacle to bringing renewed strength to the trade union movement.

"In answer to the criticism that such a scheme would interfere with the autonomy of the respective unions, can we get over that difficulty by suggesting that the executives of the different unions endeavour to arrive at an understanding as unions with the unemployed movement, with a view to operating such a scheme?"

Following the congress, the Joint Advisory Committee continued its work, and on 1st June, 1925, another national day of demonstration, known as "Unemployed Sunday" took place, with tremendous support from all sections of the working-class movement. The success of this day led the T.U.C. General Council to organise a special Trades Union Congress on unemployment, which was held at the Central Hall, Westminster, on 24th July, 1925. The National Unemployed Workers' Movement put forward a proposal to the Conference Arrangements Committee, urging a twenty-four hour general strike against the government in regard to unemployment, and proposed that this should be embodied in the official resolution. The proposal, however, was rejected.

The Conference Arrangements Committee met in the Labour Party room at the House of Commons. Jack Holt and I met Mr. Citrine after the meeting, in the lobby of the House and in conversation with us he expressed disappointment at the fact that the twenty-four hour general strike proposal had been defeated.

Mr. Citrine has travelled a long way from the Left attitude of which at that time he expressed his support.

When the conference met I was permitted to address it in the name of the organised unemployed. Mr. Ben Turner was in the chair. In concluding my speech, I put forward the following proposals in the form of a resolution:

That this Special Conference of Trade Unions instructs the General Council to immediately form a special committee consisting of representatives of the General Council and representatives of the N.U.W.M. for the purpose of jointly organising a Great National March upon London.

A programme of demands upon which the March shall be organised shall be as follows:—

1. That the Premier and Members of the Cabinet shall meet a deputation from members of the General Council of the T.U.C. and representatives of the N.U.W.M. to discuss the following demands on behalf of the unemployed.

2.   That the scale of benefit at the Labour Exchanges shall be 30s. per week for adult workers (the same scale for unemployed women), 10s. for wife of unemployed workers, 5s. for each child up to 14 years of age, 15s. for unemployed juveniles between the ages of 14 and 18.

3.   The State shall bear full responsibility for maintenance of unemployed, and the local authorities shall be relieved of this burden.

4.   Benefits shall be continuous while the applicant is unable to find employment and there shall be no disqualification from benefit on the grounds of not genuinely seeking employment, unless the Labour Exchanges are able to indicate work for the applicant to go to.

5.   No work shall be offered by the Labour Exchange or Local Authority under trade union rates of wages and conditions, and there shall be no compulsory domestic service for unemployed women.

6.   That the six days waiting period shall be abolished.

7.   That as a means of providing work for the unemployed, the Government shall grant complete recognition to the Government of Soviet Russia with extension of credits and the full use of the Trades Facilities Acts.

8.   Also as a means of absorbing the unemployed into industry, the Government shall introduce legislation for the establishment of a 44 hour working week along the lines laid down by the previous Trade Union Congress.

The Conference should call upon the Labour members of Parliament to immediately commence a campaign for holding up all business in the House of Commons until the Government gives satisfaction on the question of unemployment.

There was, however, an official resolution and this was the only one upon which a vote was taken. It dealt with the conditions of the unemployed, but proposed no positive line of action. It did, however, contain a threat of action by ending with the following words:

" If redress is not speedily forthcoming, the trade union and labour movement will be compelled to take such action as conditions and opportunity dictate."

But this was subsequently overshadowed by the development which rapidly took place in the dispute in the mining industry.

Chapter VII

THE COMMUNIST TRIAL AND THE GENERAL STRIKE

IN the summer of 1925 the mine-owners threatened a lock-out of all mine-workers to enforce lower wages and longer hours. It was to begin on Friday, 31st July, unless the miners surrendered to the owners' terms. The whole trade union movement undertook to support the miners by general strike action.

The Baldwin government adopted a stubborn and unhelpful attitude throughout the negotiations, but on the day before the struggle began they retreated by an agreement to give a financial subsidy to the industry for a period of nine months in order to obviate reduced standards for the mine-workers. This was a notable victory for working-class solidarity, and 31st July, on which the government's decision was announced, became known as "Red Friday."

The government intervention in this dispute was purely a matter of expediency and intended to gain time in order to prepare effective machinery for a smashing resistance to the workers. The well-known statement of Mr. Baldwin during the negotiations clearly indicated this, when he said "All the workers in this country have got to face a reduction in wages." This statement was publicly endorsed by Mr. Joynson Hicks, home secretary, a few days later, when he said, "In order to compete with the world, either the conditions of labour-hours or wages would have to be altered in this country. Sooner or later this question has got to be fought out."

After the victory of "Red Friday" a number of prominent right wing trade union and Labour leaders clearly expressed their uneasiness, and showed by their statements where they stood even at that time in relation to the struggles of the workers. Mr. J. H. Thomas, speaking on the subsidy given by the government, was reported in the *Daily Herald* of 17th August, 1925, as saying "There has been a lot of talk about the magnificent victory of the miners, but I am far from happy over the whole business, because nothing is more dangerous to the future of this country than when employers of labour and the government are compelled to concede to force what they have refused to concede to reason." Mr. Ramsay MacDonald accused the government of having "handed over the appearances of victory at any rate, to the very forces that sane, well-considered, thoroughly-examined Socialism feels to be probably its greatest enemy."

On 6th August, when Mr. Baldwin announced the subsidy in the House of Commons, he declared, "I am convinced that if the time should come when the community has to protect itself, with the full strength of the government behind it, the community will do so, and the response of the community will astonish the forces of anarchy throughout the world. I say it merely as a warning."

Lord Londonderry was even more definite. He said, "Whatever it may cost in blood and treasure, we shall find that the trade unions will be smashed from top to bottom." Mr. Winston Churchill is reported on 10th December as saying, "We therefore decided to postpone the crisis in the hope of averting it, or, if not averting it, to cope effectually with it." These statements of the government representatives should have left no doubt in the mind of any person that the government granted the subsidy only in order to gain a nine months' breathing-space for the preparation of its machinery, to defeat any united struggle of the workers.

In the Labour ranks this purpose should have been countered by intensive preparation for the struggle which appeared to be inevitable in May 1926, when the nine months' truce came to an end. But the strange thing is that outside the ranks of the miners and a left-wing group of the Trades Union Congress General Council, there was an almost complete absence of preparation for a struggle on the part of the general trade union leadership. The "Red Friday" victory was followed by a period of inertia and fatalism.

The Communist Party of Great Britain, however, opened an intense campaign in support of the miners and in preparation for victory in the event of a general strike taking place in May 1926. Instead of this being welcomed by the Labour Party, we had the remarkable spectacle of the National Labour Party Conference on 29th September, 1925, at Liverpool, attacking the Communists and deciding to expel them from the Labour Party, and to bar them even as delegates to Labour conferences when elected by their trade unions. The decisions of this conference were not lost upon the Baldwin Tory government. Within a fortnight they followed it by a vicious attack upon the Communist Party, raiding its premises, seizing its documents and arresting twelve executive members, of whom I was one.

The government no doubt thought that the decisions of the Labour Party conference provided them with an excellent opportunity of smashing the revolutionary vanguard of the workers, and they seized their opportunity. After warrants for arrest had been issued by the home secretary, my house and the houses of other members of the executive of the party were raided by the police and searched from top to bottom. The day before the police came to effect my arrest, I had gone to Plymouth to speak at a working-class conference. After the police had searched the house, they asked my wife where I was to be found. She said I had gone away the day before, but she did not know to what district; she said she thought it was Scotland. This led the police on an anxious chase for the next twenty-four hours, but while I was speaking the following evening in the Dockers' Hall at Plymouth the police quietly entered the hall. I saw them come in and guessed their mission, because I had already read of the arrests of other comrades the day before. I went on with my address and the police waited until I had finished. At the end of the meeting I was placed under arrest, and, followed by a big demonstration from the meeting, I was marched to Plymouth police station.

The crowd refused to disperse while I was held in the station. The police inspector had a bright idea. He announced to the crowd that I should be taken to London on the 8.35 train next morning. The crowd were deceived by this and decided to disperse and to re-assemble next morning in a demonstration of protest at the station. Then, just after midnight, when all was quiet outside, I was hustled into a police car and driven to the station to catch the night train to London, accompanied by two detectives.

Arriving at Paddington just after seven o'clock in the morning, I was met by a police van with a squad of police and driven to Bow Street police station. While I was in the station they brought in Arthur McManus, who had evaded arrest up to that time. The other ten arrested were Harry Pollitt, Albert Inkpin, William Gallacher, William Rust, Tom Bell, Ernest Cant, J. R. Campbell, R. Page Arnot, J. T. Murphy and T. Wintringham. We were all committed for trial at the Old Bailey. There were three charges preferred against us by the attorney-general, Sir Douglas Hogg. They were "preaching sedition," "uttering seditious libels," "incitement to mutiny amongst H.M. Forces."

The trial lasted three weeks. Our speeches at meetings, literature of the party, and the *Workers' Weekly* were all extensively quoted by the attorney-general to secure a conviction and to prove that we were preparing for struggle against the ruling-class in defence of the miners. The charge of incitement to mutiny amongst his majesty's forces was made on the grounds that in our speeches and in our press we had urged that in the event of a general strike and the soldiers being called upon to use their arms against the workers, they should remember their working-class origin, and not be ready to shoot their own brothers. The summing-up of the judge, Rigby Swift, was nothing short of a clear direction to the jury to find us guilty. After an hour's retirement they returned with a verdict of guilty on every charge.

Pollitt, Gallacher, Inkpin, Rust and I were each sentenced to one year's imprisonment on each charge, making a total of three years; fortunately the sentences were to run concurrently. After we had been taken below to the cells, the remaining seven accused had the astonishing proposition put to them by Judge Rigby Swift that, if they would give a declaration in court to the effect that they would have no further association with the Communist Party, and that they would not engage in any further political activities similar to those upon which they had been charged, they could walk out of the court free men. They were each asked in turn if they would give such an undertaking. One after another they emphatically declared "No!" They were then sentenced to six months' imprisonment.

We were taken to Wandsworth prison where we served our sentences. Our treatment was the same as that of the ordinary criminal. When we protested that we were political prisoners, we were told that there is no political division in the English prison system. We therefore did the same work, wore the same clothes and had the same food as the ordinary criminals, and had no privileges beyond those provided under the ordinary prison regulations. I make this point because there is a general impression that political prisoners are allowed to wear their own clothes, have their own food and enjoy certain privileges. This is an entirely wrong impression and a knowledge of the truth should stimulate agitation to secure prison reform.

Life in the gaol was, of course, the usual round of dreariness and monotony, and there is not much to be written on this question. We did, however, experience moments of joy when demonstrations of London workers marched with bands and banners to the prison gates on Sundays. The week-end in a prison means solitary confinement from twelve o'clock on Saturday until seven o'clock on Monday morning, with the exception of two hours' exercise and attendance at the chapel service. On Sunday afternoons, long before the demonstrations arrived, we would be eagerly waiting in our cells for the first faint sounds of the approaching workers. On these occasions there would always be, inside the grounds of the prison, large forces of mounted and foot police, and, of course, outside the prison gates the guardians of law and order would also be well in evidence.

Although we had been placed on the opposite side of the prison, the singing and cheering which went on at these demonstrations could be distinctly heard. It gave us a warm feeling of confidence and faith in our class as we heard the singing of the "Red Flag" and the "International" by thousands of workers demonstrating their solidarity with us outside the prison.

Sometimes the prison would be in a state of uproar, as prisoners answered the cheers of the demonstrators. Warders would run along the corridors and peer into the cells, and where they found prisoners had climbed on their tables to get nearer to the window to catch the sounds of the demonstration more clearly, they would unlock the door, rush into the cells and remove the tables into the corridors. We learnt that many prisoners were punished for climbing up to their windows on the occasions of these demonstrations, but, although the communist prisoners regularly did it, the governor evidently thought it wise not to punish them for this offence.

The release of the six months' men took place in April, just before the General Strike, which began on 3rd May, 1926. During the General Strike the five of us who remained in prison were, of course, eager to get news of the struggle, but it was extremely difficult. Then information trickled in about the betrayal of the strike on 12th May. We could not believe it; the warders taunted us about the workers having been beaten. Still we refused to lose hope. Later, when we were able to obtain reliable information in respect to the termination of the strike, I well remember our burning indignation and sense of bitter disappointment. We also sensed the effects of the betrayal upon the workers outside the prison, because from the time of the General Strike the demonstrations to the prison became less frequent.

On 11th September, 1926, we were due for release. The Home Office, however, wishing to avoid a demonstration outside the prison, released us during the afternoon of the 10th. The

London Trades Council, of which I was an executive member, organised a splendid "Welcome Home" social the following evening in the Holborn Town Hall. Special souvenir programmes were printed with broad arrows that read, "Welcome home to Wal Hannington and his fellow jail-birds." In the programme a history of the London Trades Council was given since its inception in 1860 and this concluded with the words, "The welcome home to Wal Hannington and his election to the Executive of the Council whilst he was in prison proves that the Council still loves a bonny fighter. In spite of the operation of the Emergency Powers Act, in spite of the animosity of the workers' enemies, the Council invites the Communists to be the honoured guests of the evening."

I was presented with a beautifully bound volume of copies of the *British Worker* which had been issued by the General Council during the General Strike. Attached to the volume was an official message of welcome, signed by the executive members of the Trades Council, which read as follows:

To Wal Hannington, who, whilst in Wandsworth prison, was elected to the Executive Committee of the London Trades Council.
Presented to him on his return to the Movement at the Re-union, Holborn Town Hall, September 11th, 1926, as a token of esteem from the London Trade Unionists through their affiliated organisations to the London Trades Council.

Later, when I had time to read the *British Worker*, I was struck by the mildness of the propaganda and the evident hesitancy and weakness of the General Strike leadership from the outset. It was very noticeable that, with each edition of the paper, the strike leadership proclaimed louder and louder, "The General Council *does not* challenge the constitution"; "It is *not* seeking to substitute unconstitutional government"; "It is *not* desirous of undermining our parliamentary institutions"; "The Council is engaged solely in an industrial dispute. There is no constitutional crisis."

Yet, whilst such declarations were being made, and were being printed in bolder type as the days went by, the government was standing four-square with the mine-owners and placing the forces of the state at their disposal to smash the strike.

The policy of the T.U.C. General Council after the General Strike is well-known history. The miners fought on alone for many months, whilst members of the General Council declared "never again." The big industrialists, led by Sir Alfred Mond, seized upon this statement of the trade union leadership, and propaganda was advanced in favour of "no more strike action," "co-operation with the employers," "peace in industry," and assistance in the carrying through of capitalist rationalisation. From that moment, the Trades Union Congress leadership swung more and more to the right, embracing the policy of co-operation with the employers, by what was known as the "Mond-Turner negotiations."

This swing to the extreme right carried with it the severance of all negotiations or sympathies with organisations that expressed a militant policy, and in place of the fight against the employers the T.U.C. opened the fight against the militants. This involved the severance of connections with the National Unemployed Workers' Movement, and the breaking-up of the Joint Advisory Council, which had done such good work.

In the early part of 1927, when the N.U.W.M. pressed for a meeting of the Joint Advisory Council to discuss the reform in poor law administration, which the Tory government was pressing, and to prepare to resist the attacks which we understood were to be made upon the unemployed in the Blanesburgh commission report, we received the following reply, over the signature of Mr. W. M. Citrine:

"In view of the fact that the questions of unemployment are now dealt with by the Special Joint Committee of the Labour Party and the T.U.C., no useful purpose can be served by continuing in existence the Joint Advisory Committee on Unemployment."

So ended the Joint Advisory Council. At the same time there began a new reactionary role on the part of the T.U.C. General Council in relation to the struggles of the unemployed.

Chapter VIII

POLICE SPIES AND *AGENTS PROVOCATEURS*

THERE is a pernicious toad-like species which occasionally reveals itself in the working-class movement. It is the person who sells his birth-right to manhood for a mess of pottage. It is the type that, although belonging to the working class, is ready to stoop to the practice of betraying the workers who are striving to improve working-class conditions. I am referring to persons commonly called "police informers," "spies" and *agents provocateurs*.

Throughout history there have been such types carrying out their vile work in the working-class movement. We can find records of them in the early trade union movement, when trade unionism was illegal under the combination Acts of 1799 to 1824. When our forefathers, who were the pioneers of trade unionism, met in secret conclave, they were sometimes betrayed by police spies and suffered long terms of imprisonment and transportation to the fever-ridden convict settlements of Van Diemen's Land and Botany Bay.

In the stormy days of the Chartist Movement in the first half of the nineteenth century, we can find evidence of the spy and the *agent provocateur* ready to send their fellow-men to the gallows for fighting for the franchise for the common people. All militant movements in conflict with the powers that be are subject to the treachery of the unprincipled wretch who worms his way into the movement and secures its confidence only in order to betray those who have trusted him.

During the war, the socialist movement became a special target for this creature. One of the most outrageous cases was that of the Wheeldon family. A government *agent provocateur* known as Alex Gordon joined the socialist movement, gained the confidence of the Wheeldon family and became their lodger, suggested to them acts of violence which they rejected as foreign to their policy, but nevertheless he managed to involve them in a charge of having plotted to poison Lloyd George.

141

The war fever was fanned up against all those who were opposed to the war, and in such an atmosphere the prosecution provided effective propaganda against the socialist movement. Sentences of up to five years' imprisonment were imposed upon the Wheeldon family.

Since the Communist Party of Great Britain was formed in 1920, a number of police spies and *agents provocateurs* have been discovered. On one occasion, in 1924, whilst a central committee meeting of the party was being held in a rehearsal theatre just off the Strand, noises were heard under the platform. A trap-door was opened, and there, quietly sitting on the steps, taking notes, were two police agents.

The National Unemployed Workers' Movement, like other active working-class organisations, has not been free from these pernicious people. During the 1922 Hunger March a spy succeeded in winning his way through to the Control Council of the march. Our suspicions were aroused when he repeatedly proclaimed that he was more revolutionary than anybody else, and that we were not doing enough desperate things to satisfy him. One thing which he proposed was that all the leaders of of the march should arrange a plan whereby they would individually be responsible on a certain night for dropping inflammable material into certain letter-boxes in a particular district. The area proposed was a working-class district and the night a Sunday night, which meant that working-class correspondence, not business letters, would be consumed by the burning.

We saw through this proposal, and, whilst we had no positive proof of his treachery, we took steps to remove him from the Control Council. He had a glib tongue and gained a good deal of support in the London area. Further proof that he was an *agent provocateur* came when, in 1923, a demonstration was held by the movement in Trafalgar Square. The usual Scotland Yard shorthand-writers were present taking notes of the speeches delivered from the plinth. After the demonstration had dispersed, some reliable comrades, looking for a place to get tea, went into the back streets of Westminster and entered a small out-of-the-way café. To their surprise they found this person sitting at a table whilst one of the Scotland Yard officers was audibly transcribing the notes of the speeches he had taken in the square.

The *agent provocateur* was immediately challenged and was at a loss to find an explanation, except to say that the detective had

sat down at his table uninvited. When this incident was reported
to the movement, action was taken and the *agent provocateur*
was expelled, but we had difficulty in getting members of the
movement to believe that he was an *agent provocateur*. It is
always very difficult to produce any documentary proof about
such persons. It is usually circumstantial evidence upon which
they have to be judged. For a long while the man in question
succeeded in holding many of his supporters, and he split the
London movement. But his supporters were very soon able to
judge for themselves, on a certain occasion when he led a raid
on a board of guardians; the police were brought in and every
member of the deputation had to run the gauntlet between a
double line of police, who batoned them down with their truncheons, but the *agent provocateur* walked quietly out, untouched,
with the police inspector.

His followers had their eyes opened by this, and soon he found
himself completely deserted. When his last foothold in the
movement had gone, he revealed his hand by attending subsequent demonstrations in the open company of police detectives.

I well remember an occasion when the head office of the
unemployed movement was on the top floor of a high building
in Hatton Garden; a stranger came one morning with a remarkable proposition. He furtively entered my office and said that
he wanted to speak with me alone. I asked him to sit down and
he then said, "I have come to you with a proposition that will
make the ruling class sit up."

Such an opening, of course, immediately put me on my guard.
He said, "Have you read about the two country mansions which
have recently been burnt down?" I said I thought I remembered
noticing the headlines in the paper. "Well, of course, you undoubtedly know all about that, and why it was done, and I have
come to you with a list of very big mansions which I think you
would agree should also be burnt down."

I promptly informed him that he was barking up the wrong
tree and that we did not believe in such methods of terrorism.
He said, "Oh, I thought you would be ready to discuss the
matter." I then said, "Who sent you here?"

Immediately he began to show signs of extreme nervousness
and in a shaky voice replied, "It is only my own idea."

"Have you any connections with the working-class movement?"

"Oh yes," he answered with confidence.

But when I began to question him further and asked him to
produce some evidence of even trade union membership, he was

completely unable to give any satisfactory reply. I felt certain that he was an *agent provocateur* and I told him so. He suddenly jumped up and made for the door. I followed him, and, just as he reached the stair landing, I got just close enough to lift my boot behind him and helped him to travel down a long flight of stairs much quicker than one normally descends! He picked himself up at the bottom and rushed down to the main door without even stopping to answer.

Another nasty practice of Scotland Yard is to put plain-clothes officers outside your house on occasions when they think that you are going to some important meeting connected with the movement. Several times I have had extreme difficulty in getting away from these persons, and avoiding leading them to the place where the meeting was being held.

On one occasion I found that to jump buses as they were passing, dodge down tubes and round corners, were efforts all in vain; the detective on my trail was something of an athlete. The meeting was to be held on a Sunday morning in the East End of London and after several unsuccessful attempts to get away from him, I suddenly had the bright idea of going into Petticoat Lane, where I knew there would be dense crowds of people. As I moved amongst the crowds he followed behind, elbowing his way through. Several times he narrowly escaped being assaulted by workers, who resented his impolite pushing.

Even in the mass of people down Petticoat Lane I could not get away from him. If I got a few yards ahead he would be straining his neck keeping my hat in view, and taking no notice of anything else around him. As long as he could keep my head in sight he relied upon catching up again, even when I got a lead. Then I realised that something must be done to cause me to disappear from sight, so I suddenly bent my knees to shorten my height by about eighteen inches, and pushed my way through the crowd. Many people, thinking that I was a cripple, made way for me. The detective lost sight of me, and I turned into a side street and found that I had successfully evaded him.

Imagine my disappointment, however, when on arriving at the meeting-place, I found detectives already outside, apparently having been successful in following some other members of the committee!

A much more amusing incident occurred during the summer of 1930. I happened to have a free Sunday, and decided to take a stroll over Hampstead Heath, accompanied by my little daughter, aged eight, and her friend. We wandered on to the Spaniards

Road, and the children said that they wanted to play hide and seek, so we decided to go down into a part of the Heath where there was dense shrubbery and bramble.

As we were making our way along narrow paths and through the bushes, I became aware of somebody following at a short distance. I doubted whether Scotland Yard would be so foolish as to spend public money in putting a man to trail me over Hampstead Heath, when I was obviously only taking a pleasant Sunday morning stroll. But I decided to make sure, and so turned round and walked back to where we had come from, passing the stranger in my path. The sleuth turned, and followed us back, and my doubts were immediately dispelled.

We then played handball whilst the detective looked on. I sat on a seat; he sat on the grass twenty yards away. The children played hide and seek behind the bushes. They asked me to join them in the game and I decided to do so, wondering what the Yard man would do now. Sure enough, when I went to hide, he followed; the children did not know who he was and thought he was joining in the game with us. We made the detective chase us all over the Heath.

Then, when I sat down for a rest, he approached me and asked, "How long are you going to keep this up?"

"What right have you to put such a question to me?"

"I am a Scotland Yard man," he said.

I freely expressed my indignation about his contemptible spying methods and he came back with the usual answer, "I am only doing my duty. I have been put on to watch you and I have to follow you wherever you go."

"What can you gain by following me over Hampstead Heath?"

"I don't know myself, except that I have to report your movements," he answered plaintively.

But then he came back to his first question and said, "Are you likely to remain over here long?"

"I'll remain as long as I wish, but why are you so curious about this?"

Then, greatly to my amusement, he informed me that he had been standing outside my house since eight o'clock in the morning, and that he was breaking his neck to "do a piss!" I roared with delight, and said, "Well, you don't expect me to have any pity for you, do you—if you must go to the lavatory, go behind the bushes."

"But if I do you'd run away?"

I promptly informed him that that was exactly what I would do.

"Well, I can't stand it much longer, I'm simply bursting."

I felt politically and morally justified in increasing his uneasiness, and I knew that in his condition running would not help matters. So I played at long running races with the children, whilst the poor detective, in agony, tried to keep up with us. Then I got the children together and asked them if they knew where the "Bull and Bush" was—an old Hampstead Inn. They said they knew the way, although it would be nearly a quarter of a mile distant. I told them I would give them a long start and see who could get there first.

They set off, and five minutes later I followed, with the detective straining himself to his last ounce of energy to keep up. I had a good lead on him, and I remembered that there was a gentlemen's lavatory just on the corner, next to the "Bull and Bush." I slowed down a little to allow him to come closer, and I figured that if I allowed him to see me going into the bar of the public-house for a drink, he would not be able to resist the temptation of entering the lavatory. My plan worked out just as I expected. As he saw me step into the bar he thought he had time to relieve himself. He dashed into the lavatory, but I only stepped into the entrance of the bar, allowed a few moments to elapse, and came out, telling the kiddies to follow me. We redoubled our steps back across Hampstead Heath, having successfully lost the Scotland Yard man in the lavatory. I wonder whether he reported this to his superior officers?

The most interesting spy case occurred in the summer of 1927. On 3rd June, a woman by the name of Mrs. Taylor, who was connected with the Bromley branch of our movement, came to headquarters and stated that she had discovered that a member of the branch by the name of Harry Johnstone was an informer for Scotland Yard, and that his main activities were concentrated on the N.U.W.M. The full story is as follows:

She had known Johnstone for nearly two years and had associated with him a good deal in the work of the unemployed movement, and they had been on friendly terms. On certain occasions, in her presence, he quarrelled with his wife, and on such occasions his wife had often made statements, within her hearing, to the effect that the "movement ought to know where you get your money from; that would finish you." Mrs. Taylor became suspicious about these remarks, and wondered whether Johnstone was playing a straight game.

So, one evening while she was in his company she decided to sound him out on this question. She led him to believe that she knew he was not playing a straight game. He bit the bait and immediately jumped to the conclusion that his wife had conveyed certain information to Mrs. Taylor about him. He said, "So she's ratted on me! What did she tell you?" Mrs. Taylor shrewdly answered, "A still tongue makes a wise head, but it's quite enough for you to know that I know all about what you're doing." Of course, at this time, she did not know any particulars, but the ruse proved to be so successful that he made a complete confession to the effect that he was in the pay of Scotland Yard, and had been submitting reports to them on what had happened in various sections of the working-class movement, particularly the unemployed movement, over the last three years.

He told her that when he first became an informer for the police he was only receiving £2 a week, but later this was raised to £3 regularly, with special payments in addition for special reports. On a certain occasion when he had embezzled £14 belonging to the Lewisham branch of the unemployed movement, he told the police that he was to be expelled from the movement for this, and they gave him the money to pay it back and prevent his expulsion. But although he repaid this £14 he was nevertheless expelled from the branch. At the time he was also a member of the Communist Party and the information in respect to his defalcations in the unemployed movement also led to his expulsion from the party. Later, however, he regained his connection with the movement by establishing a branch of the unemployed at Bromley in Kent, and became the branch secretary. It was from this branch that he continued to attend as a delegate to the meeting of the London District council of the unemployed movement.

On the occasion of the national conference of the unemployed movement held in Stoke-on-Trent during 1926, he had received a special grant of £8 from the police for his report. He had also received a special payment for attending the reception given to the released communists by the London Trades Council at the Holborn Town Hall. He informed Mrs. Taylor that on occasions when he did not have sufficient spicy material for his reports, he wrote it up out of his own imagination, very often giving statements and extracts from speeches that had never been made.

On one such occasion the police had called him to account and challenged the authenticity of his report. He therefore had to be more careful following this, because he believed that, in addition to himself, there was another police informer in the London

District Council, each of them acting as a check upon the other, without knowing each other.

After fully revealing himself to Mrs. Taylor, and no doubt relying upon his close friendship with her to stop the information going any further, he suggested that she should go into partnership with him; as she was still a member of the Communist Party, she could convey news to him from inside the party, and add a little more to it, and by so doing she could earn "no end of money." She encouraged him to go on with his story, leading him to believe that she was ready to agree to his proposal. He said her money could be sent in the same registered envelope as his. When asked why it could not be sent direct to her, he said, "Oh, let it come to me and what's over £3 will be yours." He then told her that he dealt with an officer of the Yard by the name of McBrien, who went under the alias of Francis, and that when he had occasion to meet him it was either in Wimbledon or in Putney. He said his understanding with McBrien was that in the event of the movement discovering his connections with the police, he would receive from McBrien a lump sum of roughly £100 down to enable him to clear out of the district or abroad, if necessary.

When Mrs. Taylor divulged this information to us she wanted to sever all connection with Johnstone immediately. But although she gave us a sworn statement containing this information we wanted to follow it up and obtain more. Under our persuasion Mrs. Taylor agreed that she would continue to keep on friendly terms with Johnstone and at the same time keep us informed of his movements.

Headquarters decided to send a letter to Johnstone on 9th June asking him to come along to discuss a number of important questions. On the morning of the 9th Johnstone telephoned headquarters and stated that he would not be able to arrive until late in the afternoon; he failed, however, to put in an appearance. On the morning of the 10th, whilst Mrs. Taylor was at headquarters, Johnstone telephoned to say that he had been too busy to come along the previous day, and if convenient he would come along on Monday, the 13th. This he was asked to do. He appeared very agitated and repeatedly asked what exactly we wanted to see him about, but he was given evasive answers.

On Sunday, 12th June, there was a demonstration in Trafalgar Square, and an envelope was given to me by somebody in the crowd. It contained a letter from Mrs. Taylor, which read as follows:

Please find enclosed a note which was sent to me yesterday. On Friday evening Mrs. Johnstone sent a stranger up to my house, asking me to go round to her house. I was unable to go at the time. The same night, Johnstone along with his wife and a stranger walked past my house on the other side of the road. I saw them from my window; Johnstone and his wife walked on, but the stranger came over and knocked at the door. I was suspicious and did not answer the knock. The stranger then went back across the road and walked a little way down the street and then hurriedly came back, met Johnstone and his wife and cleared off. This was somewhere about 11.30 p.m. No doubt I am being watched, because early this morning I went into the front room and looked out from behind the curtain and the same man was watching the house again. The bearer of this note is my husband, and I thought it better for him to hand this to you than for me to be seen with you in the Square by Johnstone.

(*Signed*) Mrs. Taylor.

The note enclosed was in the handwriting of Johnstone. It was addressed to Mrs. Taylor and read as follows:

I am going away for good. As far as I can see a complete exposure is awaiting me at headquarters. Sooner than face it I am off. Can I see you at once?

(*Signed*) H. R. Johnstone.

The invitations for Johnstone to attend at National Headquarters had apparently aroused his suspicions, but there was nothing to indicate that he suspected Mrs. Taylor of having divulged information about him. On the contrary, he continued his association with Mrs. Taylor right to the last and apparently placed implicit trust in her.

When we found that we were unable to get Johnstone to come to headquarters, I decided to go after him along with a group of five other comrades. On Monday afternoon, 13th June, we sent a telegram to Mrs. Taylor informing her that we would call at her house that afternoon and that she should wait in for us. We discovered later that the telegram had arrived at her house whilst Johnstone was there, he had read it, had become very alarmed, and immediately left the house.

When we arrived, we asked Mrs. Taylor if she could find Johnstone for us and endeavour to persuade him to come back to the house. She went out and on her return stated that Johnstone had rushed to his home; that she had met him but that he had refused to come back with her as he thought we should be there. He had made arrangements for her to meet him at New Cross station. We suggested that we should all go to New Cross station, but, in order not to provide him with proof that Mrs. Taylor was in league with us, when we got off the bus about 500 yards from the station we allowed Mrs. Taylor to go on ahead.

As soon as Johnstone met Mrs. Taylor, he rushed her down on to the platform, and we just arrived in time to see him pushing her into a carriage as the train moved out. We caught the next train to Charing Cross but we had completely lost trace of them. What happened after this was later revealed to us by Mrs. Taylor. After leaving New Cross station they had gone to London Bridge. From there Johnstone had telephoned to McBrien at Wimbledon and made arrangements to meet him there at 8 p.m. The appointment was kept. I will let Mrs. Taylor continue the story in the words of her signed evidence:

I stood at a distance away, but sufficiently close enough to hear their conversation. Johnstone told McBrien that he was certain that an exposure was awaiting him at the headquarters of the unemployed movement and that he wanted a sum of money to clear out. McBrien said "How do you know that you're discovered? Go back and face it!" Johnstone replied that he could not do that. McBrien then informed him that he would get no more money out of him; that he was finished and added that £3 had already been sent to his address that day and that would be the last he would get. Johnstone, on leaving McBrien, was very much distressed and began to talk about suicide.

He then suggested to Mrs. Taylor that they should go to Southend-on-Sea. When they got to Southend, Mrs. Taylor made an excuse for leaving him and returned to London.

The next morning I went along with the group of comrades who were hunting Johnstone to Bromley. Outside Mrs. Taylor's house we met Mrs. Johnstone and she showed us a letter that she had received from her husband that morning, which read as follows:

Dear Florrie,

This is good-bye. You have forced me in my present position, whereby I have no alternative but to disappear. You have no one but your own tongue to blame. You have received £3 to-night from Mac, which will keep you going for the time being. The telegram received by Mrs. Taylor from Holt will explain my position.

It's good-bye; you will never have me back. It's the river for us.

(*Signed*) Harry.

Mrs. Johnstone before showing us the letter had tried to cross out the sentence about the "£3 from Mac" but she had not done it successfully and it was still decipherable. While we were talking to Mrs. Johnstone in the street, Mrs. Taylor came along. As she approached, Mrs. Johnstone said, "Where's Harry?"

"At Southend-on-Sea!" was the reply.

"Where did he get the money from?" asked Mrs. Johnstone excitedly.

Mrs. Taylor replied, "You had better ask McBrien!" This instantly had a calming effect upon Johnstone's wife and she said no more.

It was decided that we should all go to Mrs. Johnstone's house and talk the matter over. When we got into the house we informed Mrs. Johnstone that we had definite information that her husband was in the pay of Scotland Yard. She pretended to know nothing; we then pretended to Mrs. Johnstone that we wanted to interview her husband for the purpose of hearing what he had to say, and, if possible, give him an opportunity of a fresh start. Of course, we had no such intentions, but we said this in order to encourage her to persuade him to come to headquarters. We told Mrs. Johnstone that if he did not come along this time to headquarters we would publish our information concerning him as a police spy. Mrs. Johnstone agreed to impress the need upon her husband of coming to us as soon as he returned. We then departed.

Two days later we read in the newspapers that Johnstone had committed suicide at Southend-on-Sea on the evening of Tuesday, 14th June, by drinking a bottle of lysol. We telephoned to the police at Southend for the purpose of ascertaining when the inquest was to be held. The police informed us that the inquest had already taken place at 5.15 p.m. on the previous day, Wednesday, the 15th. I then decided to go with Holt to the house of Mrs. Johnstone.

After we had left our office a letter was delivered from a relative of Johnstone; the letter was as follows:

Dear Sirs,

As far as I understand you have some information to impart to the papers concerning Mr. Johnstone. As gentlemen, I beg of you to withold anything that will blacken his character more

than it is blackened at present. Not for his sake but for the sake
of his destitute wife and children. I may inform you that Mr.
Johnstone committed suicide at Southend on Tuesday, the 14th.
Will you give this your kind attention?

We arrived at the house of Mrs. Johnstone at about 2.30 in the
afternoon, and were informed by one of her children that she had
gone to the relieving officer. We waited until she returned and
then went into her house with her to discuss the suicide of her
husband. She now admitted that she knew that her husband
was in the pay of Scotland Yard as a spy on the unemployed
movement.

"I had enough to do," she said, "to look after the home and
my four children without bothering about my husband's affairs."

We asked if she would let us again see the letter which had been
sent to her by her husband on 13th June. We, of course, wanted
this to complete our proof concerning Johnstone.

She produced this, but just as I was about to read it she snatched
it away, apparently still having some fear about providing us with
evidence of her husband's police associations, and tore it into
three pieces, throwing it into the fireplace. I picked it up and
later pieced it together again.

This poor woman was, of course, in a terrible mental state.
Her husband was now dead, she had four children and no
resources, and the police had apparently washed their hands of
all responsibility once Johnstone had served their purpose and
was no longer of any use to them. She said she was destitute
and asked what we could do for her. We suggested that as her
husband had been a police spy she should attempt to get some
compensation from the police, and that if we could in any way
help her in making the police pay we would do so.

The following day she wrote us a letter in which she said:

You are aware that my husband has committed suicide at
Southend-on-Sea. At the inquest a verdict of "temporarily
insane" was returned. This was probably brought on by his
knowledge that he was about to be exposed by the Movement.
I know he was greatly worried about this matter, especially when
he knew that members of the Movement were already in Bromley
waiting for him. I knew he was in the pay of Scotland Yard, he
dealt through Superintendent McBrien. It appears that Johnstone
tried to get some money from McBrien, who refused it. You
will of course, condemn the action of Johnstone in accepting the
money from the police, but I think that you will recognise that

the responsibility for my husband's action in committing suicide
rests mainly on Scotland Yard, and as I have four little children
and expecting another, who along with myself are left destitute,
I think that Scotland Yard should make compensation to me.
Can you help me in this matter.

Yours faithfully,

Florence E. Johnstone.

This poor woman innocently believed that Scotland Yard
might do something for her. She apparently did not understand
that Scotland Yard uses such persons as Johnstone like hand-
rags and then throws them off without any compunction or
feeling when they have no further use for them. However, we
wrote to Scotland Yard, calling attention to the fact that one of
their police agents had committed suicide and his wife was destitute and demanding that they face up to their responsibilities in
respect to the family. Our correspondence was, of course, never
even acknowledged.

On the following Sunday, 19th June, a report of the inquest
on Johnstone, held at Southend, appeared in the *News of the
World*. It reported that Johnstone had been found dying on a
seat along the Southend front, after drinking a bottle of lysol.

Although it was known to the coroner—from a letter left by
Johnstone—that Mrs. Taylor was the last person to see him
alive, she was never called into the inquest– a most unusual
proceeding. The coroner stated that in the pocket of Johnstone
a notebook had been found, on which Johnstone had written:
"Please don't open but hand straight to the police." The full
contents of this notebook were never divulged in the court.

The coroner, in returning a verdict of "suicide whilst of unsound
mind" remarked that it was "not necessary to go further into the
other matters connected with the case." This remark can only be
taken to mean that someone was not desirous of the information
being publicly divulged in respect to Johnstone's position as a
police spy.

So ended the career of Mr. Johnstone, with no regrets from the
working-class movement which he had betrayed.

Chapter IX

REVEALING THE TRAGEDY OF THE MINEFIELDS

BEFORE the war, the mining industry seldom experienced any serious long-term unemployment. But following the 1921 stoppage unemployment began to affect seriously the social and economic life of the colliery workers. At first, only particular coalfields, dependent upon the export trade, were seriously affected. This was due in a large degree to the reparation coal deliveries from Germany to France, Italy and Belgium—countries which were previously customers of South Wales, Durham and Scotland.

During the first three years of unemployment in the coalfields this symptom of decline in Britain's basic industry was generally regarded as being temporary and passing. The occupation of the Ruhr by the French military forces in 1923 and the recovery of the British coal trade which was the consequence of the inability of Germany to pay reparations in coal deliveries owing to the strikes on the Ruhr, appeared on the surface to substantiate this view. With the resumption of systematic deliveries under the terms of the Dawes plan, however, it became increasingly clear that this depression, due to there being more coal than there were customers to purchase it, was a serious and permanent phase of the mine-workers' conditions.

From the end of the Ruhr occupation until 1925 conditions became steadily worse. In 1925 the subsidy given by the Baldwin government to the mine-owners provided a temporary revival, but with the termination of the subsidy period even the most indifferent were forced to realise that unemployment—assuming the retention of private enterprise in the mining industry—was permanent.

The attempt of the coal-owners in 1926 to enforce lower wages and longer hours was resisted as much because of the increased unemployment which would have ensued as because of the worsening of conditions for those in work. It was realised that the extension of the working day by one hour (from seven to eight hours) would automatically involve the throwing out of

154

employment of some 100,000 mine-workers. Even before the
1926 stoppage there were some 200,000 miners out of work; the
8 hour day not only sounded the death knell to their hopes of
re-employment, but added another 100,000 to their numbers.

In March 1926, there were employed in and about the mines
1,111,900 men. Over the six months' period from April to
September, 1927, the following numbers were employed:

April,	1927	.. ..	1,280,687
May,	,,	.. ..	1,250,670
June,	,,	.. ..	1,011,906
July,	,,	.. ..	995,127
August,	,,	.. ..	984,552
September,	,,	.. ..	982,555

There was a rise in employment up to May 1927, as compared
with that in March 1926; this is undoubtedly to be explained by
the fact that the coal reserves which had been used up in the
period of the miners' lock-out of 1926 were being replenished;
from June onwards we see the effect of the longer working day
and a rapid drop in the number of workers employed in the
mines.

By July 1927 there were 258,203 mine-workers registered as
unemployed. This did not include something approaching
100,000 who by this time had ceased to be recorded at the labour
exchanges, having exhausted their right to benefit. In addition,
many who were recorded as working were only working short
time. In 1926 the average working time was 5.41 shifts a week,
but from January to September 1927 it was only 4.8 shifts a week.

When unemployment strikes a coalfield on a large scale the
social effects are especially harmful, because there are no other
industries or trades to which the mine-workers can turn. They are
wholly dependent upon coal production for their domestic resources. The municipal bodies and the boards of guardians were
dependent for the bulk of their income upon the rates drawn from
the collieries and from the workers. With the closing down of the
collieries, the local authorities quickly became dependent upon
loans which had to be authorised by government departments;
at the time when their income was rapidly falling, the demand for
increased expenditure was rapidly rising, as more and more
colliery families were driven by poverty to apply for relief. The
result was that many families who were in dire poverty were
being refused additional assistance from the guardians, and the

heads of families who had been disqualified as recipients of labour exchange benefit were in many cases only in receipt of 10s. for adult dependents, and 2s. or 3s. per week for each child. To single men all assistance was refused.

Thus there were in such coalfields as South Wales thousands of men completely destitute, having absolutely no kind of support. Rent had to be paid as the only alternative to eviction and thousands of families were experiencing actual starvation. The Conservative government, though fully cognisant of the situation, declared that it had no means at its command to remedy the position. The regulations issued by the Ministry of Labour, under the Unemployment Insurance Act, led to mass disqualification of men from benefit for all kinds of reasons. Men were struck off benefit because "there was no reasonable prospects of securing work," while others were disqualified because it was alleged that they were "not making genuine efforts to seek work"; men were refused benefit because they were too old, and others because they were too young, and they were told their relations would have to maintain them, if there was coming into the house an income exceeding 13s. a week a head.

Every complaint, every endeavour to bring about an improvement in the conditions of the unemployed miners, was met by the local authorities declaring that they were helpless to remedy the position and that the responsibility lay at the doors of the Ministry of Health and Ministry of Labour in London. This condition of affairs—the existing horror of poverty and the threat of the future, the utter impotence to defend themselves owing to the inadequacy of local resources and the restrictions laid down when loans were granted—forced the miners in the Rhondda Valley, an area rendered derelict by the coal-owners' maladministration of the industry, to move towards action against the government, and to call upon the miners in other parts of South Wales to join them in an endeavour to arouse the working class of the country. At a great demonstration of miners and their families held on the Penrhys Mountain on 13th September, 1927, a call for a march on London was raised.

The late Mr. A. J. Cook, the militant general secretary of the Miners' Federation of Great Britain, was a speaker along with myself at the demonstration. In the course of his speech Mr. Cook described the conditions of the unemployed in South Wales and referred to the strangle-hold exercised by the ministries of Health and Labour upon the boards of guardians and labour exchanges; he said that the miners should go to the fountain-head of the trouble and proposed that the unemployed should march to London. Following Mr. Cook I supported the proposal which he had made. The idea of a march of unemployed miners to London struck the imagination of that great mass meeting held on the Rhondda Mountain, surrounded by the slag heaps and the derelict pits of coal capitalism. The chairman called for a show of hands in support of the proposal, and thousands of hands shot into the air as evidence of the readiness to march.

The following day, the Rhondda district committee of the Miners' Federation was meeting, and I was invited to attend and speak on this question. The district committee declared their support for the project, and called upon the South Wales Miners' executive to join with the unemployed movement in organising the march. Weeks passed, however, before the executive took heed of the question. Then they merely referred it to the Miners' Federation of Great Britain. The executive of the Miners' Federation in turn said that it was not their business.

The march was due to start on 8th November, the date on which Parliament re-assembled, so there was no time to be lost, and preparations were started while we were waiting for the decision of the South Wales Miners' executive and the Miners' Federation of Great Britain. A Marchers' Organising Council was formed, composed of representatives from the N.U.W.M. and from the Rhondda Miners' district council of the federation, and I was elected leader of the march.

The objects of the march were drawn up in the form of a programme as follows:

1.   To draw attention to the chronic destitution affecting unemployed and employed miners, arising out of the failure of private enterprise in the mining industry.

2.   To draw the attention of the government to the persistent closing of mines, thus causing further widespread unemployment.

3.   To demand the repeal of the Eight-hour Day Act in the mining industry.

4.   To urge the government to make satisfactory provision for the employment of those unemployed.

5.   To demand state aid to permit guardians to more effectively relieve distress.

6.   To protest against the continuous disqualification of men and women from benefit at the labour exchange and to urge more adequate scales of benefit.

7. To press for a system of adequate pensioning of miners over 60 years of age as a means of reducing the number of unemployed.

8. To protest against the continuance of the system of royalties and wayleaves.

9. To protest against the government attack upon the unemployed in the new legislation, based upon the Blanesburgh report.

In planning the march we knew that there would be no difficulty in raising a strong army of men, but we had to remember that the men would need feeding and accommodation on the road, and as the main road from South Wales to London has practically no large industrial towns, except Swindon and Reading, it was necessary to limit the number of volunteers for the march, in order that we should be able to feed and accommodate them properly.

We limited the recruitment to men who had been denied both labour exchange benefit and poor law relief; there were many thousands of these in South Wales. We barred recruits who were drawing labour exchange benefit because we did not want their families to be penalised, as there was no guarantee that they would be permitted to reclaim benefit on their return to South Wales. Many thousands of young men who were drawing benefits volunteered for the march, but were rejected on these grounds.

The men who were being recruited for the march were the least likely to be sufficiently clad and shod to take the road. Therefore, one of our first tasks was to establish in each village an equipment committee which made itself responsible for collecting clothes and raising money for the equipment of the men.

Considering the impoverishment in every village in South Wales, the response to the appeal for equipment was magnificent; the women in particular did excellent work in house-to-house collection, and at every miner's cottage they received warm words of praise and encouragement. That the miners and their families were behind the march there was not the slightest doubt, and thousands were expressing the wish to participate.

We knew the extremely reactionary character of the Tory government. Their readiness to resort to violence and the use of repressive measures was well known. We were therefore anxious that the working-class movement throughout the country should express their support for the march either actively or morally. Hundreds of trade union branches, trades councils and local labour parties wrote to the marchers' committee, expressing support. In view of the right-wing policy which the Trades Union Congress General Council had pursued since the General Strike, we were not very optimistic about receiving any support from them. We did, however, expect that they would at least refrain from open opposition, which could only incite the forces of the Baldwin government against us. We were, however, to be disillusioned on this point. On 13th October the London Trades Council, at its full delegate meeting, pledged its unanimous support for the march, as did the Bristol Trades Council. After these decisions, the general secretary of the Trades Union Congress, Mr. Walter Citrine, could apparently keep quiet no longer, and statements were published to the effect that the march was quite unofficial and had not the support of the official trade union movement.

Manœuvres began to be made to reverse the decision of the London Trades Council. Mr. A. M. Wall, the secretary of the trades council, in spite of the decision of his own trades council began to denounce the march as a communist stunt "fostered by the communists for the express purpose of augmenting their membership." This statement was of course completely untrue; it could not be substantiated in any way. Although the whole of the facts relating to the origin of the march were laid before Mr. Wall and the General Council, and Mr. A. J. Cook himself made a public statement in the press in support of the march, the Trades Union Congress leadership persisted in their opposition and misrepresentation.

The statement of Mr. Wall was a signal for an outburst of violent abuse and incitement by the coal-owners' press against the march and its leaders. They called for the government to ban the march and for the police to "show no mercy for the political incendiaries, who were organising it against the wishes of the respectable elements of the labour movement."

The *Western Mail* and *South Wales Daily News* tried to frighten the men who were recruiting for the march by warnings of how they would be left to starve on the road, and declared that "the organisers of the march were only concerned with frustrating the campaign of the labour leaders to promote goodwill between capital and labour."

Within twenty-four hours of Mr. Wall's statement appearing in the press, four miners' wives who were carrying out house-to-house collections for the equipment committee were arrested and fined, and the police began to harass the march organisers everywhere. The coal-owners' press and the right-wing Labour leaders united in denunciation of the march, and were supported by intimidation on the part of the police.

The Marchers' Organising Committee had, however, succeeded in establishing contact with trades councils and labour parties on the route of the march, and had received promises of support in the reception, the accommodation and the feeding of the marchers. Then, when these arrangements were practically complete, Mr. Walter Citrine sent a letter to the trades councils on the route of the march, instructing them not to render any assistance. As a result of this communication, trades councils and labour parties began cancelling arrangements which they had made. A few days before the day for starting the march the organising committee found itself confronted with a complete breakdown of the road arrangements. There were only two courses to adopt, either to call the march off and thereby encourage the government to intensify its starvation policy against the workless, or to go forward in face of the official labour opposition and appeal to the rank and file workers en route to give their support and make it possible for us to reach London. After serious consideration the decision was made to go on with the march. The members of the organising council realised that they had a tremendous responsibility, but each man took up the burden with a grim determination to see the job through.

8th November arrives, and the whole of South Wales is astir. People are asking, "Will they really go on with the march?" The press made a few mocking references to the impossibility of the men ever reaching London, some estimating that the march would not last three days, that it would collapse and end in disaster; but when the first body of marchers, led by Arthur Horner, from Mardy and the top end of the Rhondda Valley, came swinging into Porth, with overcoats rolled and full haversacks on their backs, people who had doubted and questioned whether the march would start realised that here were men with a purpose, ready to face the worst that might come without flinching. They knew that the march had started.

Contingents from other parts of the valley joined the Mardy men at Porth, and, accompanied by thousands of supporters, men and women, marched on to Pontypridd, where we were joined by other contingents. From Pontypridd we proceeded to Newport, which was to be the end of the first day's march.

Our reception in Newport surpassed all expectations. Men and women of the Newport labour movement overwhelmed us with their eagerness to serve food and provide every possible comfort. Here was the real heart of the labour movement beating to welcome us! Here were the typical men and women, examples of the great mass of hard-working folk who really constitute the life and vitality of the movement. During the evening contingents from other parts of the South Wales coalfield joined us in Newport, and before we got down to sleep on the hard boards of the labour hall the marchers were reorganised into companies of twenty, with company leaders, red cross corps, advance guards and other necessary sections.

The following morning, 9th November, we rose early for a twenty-mile march to Bristol. As we marched out of Newport crowds of workers looked with amazement at the even ranks and marching order of the men who were marching as the standard-bearers of the thousands of downtrodden men and women in the Welsh coalfield.

We arrived at the outskirts of Bristol in the dusk of the evening. There was a rest of ten minutes before the last three miles, and the men were instructed to light their lamps for the entry into the town. Every marcher was carrying a miner's lamp, and it was a remarkable sight as this army moved forward through the darkness of the country roads, with their lamps swinging in rhythm to their marching step. Before reaching the centre of the town we were met by officers of the Bristol trades council and thousands of people lined the side-walks to greet us.

Mass meetings were held in Bristol during the evening. Workers were continually coming from factories bringing the proceeds of collections that had been taken, and others were bringing boots and clothing.

After the strenuous march to Bristol, many of the men needed the attention of red cross corps, but their spirits were excellent. The control council offered to arrange for the return home of any men who wished to drop out, but there were no faint-hearts.

Again, as we marched out from Bristol, thousands escorted us to the outskirts of the town. Then, while we were on the road to Bath, we received news that an official reception from the trades council was awaiting us. We were now feeling confident that the sabotage of the march was being defeated by the response of the rank and file workers in the towns through which we passed.

Several halls were placed at our disposal in Bath for the night of 10th November. Next day was Armistice Day, and a big town procession had been arranged, to march to the war memorial to lay wreaths in memory of the dead. Whilst thousands of people lined the streets, the marchers—many of them wearing rows of medals on their breasts for services rendered in the capitalist war—marched through the centre of the town, demanding bread for the living.

Many of the sightseers must have pondered long over the sight which they saw. The residents of the respectable town of Bath were given a second shock after the armistice ceremonies, when the marchers decided to line up at the public fountain so that each man could take a cup of the famous mineral waters. Crowds gathered round the Roman baths to witness this strange spectacle of rough, hard sons of toil, with packs on their backs and their safety-lamps swinging from their belts, silently and solemnly partaking of the waters, for which wealthy people visit Bath from all parts of the world. The process of taking the waters lasted approximately an hour, and the *elite* of Bath looked on with serious faces.

Here were people seeing, probably for the first time, an army of miners. They were being brought face to face with the grim realities of men in revolt for bread. The lamp swinging from the belt of each man—a reminder of their hazardous and strenuous calling—must have brought to the mind of every onlooker the terrible disasters which from time to time have blown to pieces and entombed in the bowels of the earth relatives and comrades of these men who now stood before them.

After this ceremony the miners re-formed their ranks and set out on the road again for Chippenham. Here again the trades council prepared a meal and accommodation. From Chippenham to Swindon (our next resting-place) is a distance of approximately twenty-three miles. It was dark long before we came in sight of the town on the evening of the 12th. All lamps were lit, and the men pushed forward with wonderful endurance for the last four miles. At the third mile-stone from Swindon, we were met by A. J. Cook and John Strachey, together with representatives of the labour movement of Swindon. Cook received a great ovation from the men, and his presence at the head of the army had a stimulating effect.

As the men marched into Swindon after their long trek, their ranks were a model of order and discipline. Thousands of Swindon workers gathered in the streets. Railwaymen in their working clothes, carrying red flags, marched at the head of the army; crowds lined the streets with tear-dimmed eyes as the marchers passed. The public baths of Swindon were placed at our disposal for feeding and accommodation.

The remarkable progress of the march apparently alarmed the

capitalist press. The *Daily Mail* in particular, having failed to prevent the march by threats, now turned to a more sinister method of trying to create dissatisfaction amongst the marchers by spreading lying stories concerning myself and the other leaders. The marchers replied to this clumsy misrepresentation by marching on Sunday morning to the public square and there in full ceremony making a bonfire with copies of the *Daily Mail*.

We were resting a day in Swindon, and on the Sunday night a great demonstration was held in the public baths. 3,000 persons crowded into the hall, and many thousands unable to get in formed overflow meetings outside, to hear the marchers' speakers describe the plight of the mining community. The message of the miners was received with outbursts of indignation against the Baldwin government and the system of capitalism. With cries of "Shame!" the great audience listened to the details of medical officers' reports, testifying to the enormous increase in starvation amongst the school children. In hushed silence they heard of the terrible famine area of Blaina and Brynmawr, where all the pits had lain idle for six years, and where dictators from the Ministry of Health were slowly squeezing the life-blood out of the people.

The great demonstration terminated with cheer after cheer for the marchers, and the vast audience sang the "Red Flag," meaning every word of it. A cheque for over £40 was handed up to A. J. Cook by the trades council, as a grant to the marchers' funds. On 14th November when we marched out of Swindon we no longer had any doubts of the readiness of the workers to assist us and to forward our objective of exposing the tragedies of the coalfields.

In Hungerford, a place not much more than a village, there was no hall large enough to hold the marchers, so we were accommodated in the workhouse. From there we pressed on to Newbury. As we were marching from Newbury to Reading on the 16th, we received the glad news that Tom Mann, the world-known veteran working-class fighter, along with A. J. Cook, was coming to meet us. A tremendous cheer rose from the ranks of the marchers as Tom came towards us on the outskirts of the town. A huge rally was held in Reading during the evening. After the meeting Tom Mann, in spite of his age, refused our persuasion that he should go to a hotel for the night, and insisted upon sharing the hard boards with the marchers in the various halls where we were being accommodated.

Next day, we again had to enter the workhouse at Maidenhead, as no hall was large enough to meet the needs of the marchers. All restrictions were waived by the local authorities, and after a hot meal of sausage and mash we marched out of the workhouse for a big demonstration in the town, returning again some time before midnight. After Maidenhead, we stayed in Slough, and the next day set out on our last march to Chiswick before going into London.

From Slough to Chiswick we marched in a constant downpour of rain and every man was soaked through to the skin. We entered Chiswick and were greeted by crowds of sympathetic workers. Huge fires were lit in the big schools where we slept that night and the marchers dried their clothes in readiness for the march to Trafalgar Square next day.

On Sunday, 20th November, the workers were astir all over London, gathering at the various mobilisation points for a march to Trafalgar Square to welcome the marching miners. Great crowds assembled on the streets in Chiswick to cheer the marchers and to fall in behind the banners, as we set out for the last march into the heart of the capital, headed by an Irish pipers' band.

When we reached Oxford Street, the heavy clouds which had been hanging over the city all the morning broke, and rain began to fall. But there was no damping the spirits of the marchers. Just before we turned into Charing Cross Road, cyclists came and informed us that huge crowds were already gathered in the square, and ten minutes later, as we approached Trafalgar Square, thousands of people who had stood long in the pouring rain rushed forward to greet us. The whole of the square was black with thousands of workers who had come from all parts of London to express their solidarity with the miners. Only after great difficulty did the column of marchers succeed in making an avenue through the throng in order to reach Nelson's column.

The great crowd of London workers were truly overcome with emotion as the marching miners with their lamps lit moved forward to the base of the plinth. In spite of the pouring rain the vast demonstration stood for two hours expressing with great enthusiasm their support for the miners in their fight against the famine conditions of the coalfields, as speaker after speaker gave descriptions of the conditions prevailing in the Welsh valleys.

One hundred and ten pounds was thrown on to the plinth in the collection to help the marchers' feeding fund and to make it possible to carry on the fight. The demonstration ended with thousands of people swarming along the Strand, escorting the marchers towards the East End of London, where they were to be accommodated in Bethnal Green town hall.

Next day a deputation from the marchers held a conference with the Welsh Members of Parliament in the House of Commons and arrangements were made for an approach to the prime minister and other ministers.   The prime minister, Mr. Baldwin, stated that he was not able to meet the marchers for the following reasons:

First, that as prime minister, he had no time to meet deputations and that the ministers of the departments concerned should first be approached.

Second, that he could not meet the marchers' deputation as the march, in his opinion, did not have the backing of the national trade union or labour movement.

Here we saw the interesting situation of a Tory prime minister using the reactionary behaviour of the official labour leadership as a justification for refusing to hear the story of the ruin and starvation which his policy had produced in the coalfields.

A similar attitude was taken up by Sir Arthur Steel-Maitland, the Minister of Labour, who said that he objected to seeing the marchers' deputation, lest it be interpreted as an encouragement to the continuation of such activities, and because he felt that by meeting the marchers he would be helping them to reduce the prestige and dignity of the official representatives of labour, who might complain that he was going over their heads in meeting such a deputation.

After pressure, however, he agreed to meet a deputation on 25th November, providing the Welsh Labour M.P.'s were present and that the members of the deputation resided in their constituencies.   A deputation of seven was accordingly elected by the marchers and three of their number were elected to state the case—Jack Thomas (Porth), Jack Jones (Blaenclydach), and D. Lloyd Davies (Mardy).   The minister, on receiving the deputation, informed them that he could only spare them half an hour, but they caused him to change his mind about this, and he listened to them for over two hours.

They portrayed to him the poverty of the minefields, and charged him as Minister of Labour with the responsibility for the starvation of thousands of claimants who had been denied labour exchange benefit.   They gave examples of the persistent closing down of pits, and demanded that, unless work could be provided for the unemployed, the government should take full responsibility for their maintenance.   They dealt with the effects of the eight-hour day which had been imposed in the mining industry by the Baldwin government, and they explained how the new unemployment Bill, which was at that time before Parliament, would drive thousands of men and women into revolt for bread.

The Minister of Labour admitted the seriousness of the mining situation and naively informed the deputation that the people of South Wales "are not alone in their suffering." He said the government hoped to be able to provide work for the miners in other occupations and urged that they should continue to sign on at the labour exchange, even though they were not receiving benefit. He said the ministry also intended to direct its energies towards establishing juvenile training centres in South Wales with a view to assisting the younger section who were unemployed. He said he thought "training centres would be a good thing for the unemployed miners as it would make them nimble with their fingers." The reply of Sir Arthur Steel-Maitland by no means satisfied the deputation and they spoke strongly about the evident lack of effective policy on the part of the government.

One of the deputation inquired whether the Minister thought that a man, wife and four children could live on 16s. a week, such as many of the miners' families were expected to do? In challenging tones he said to the Minister, "Could you exist on such a pittance?" But Sir Arthur only fidgeted in his chair and evaded the question. When the deputation demanded that all persons who had been struck off the exchange registers should be placed back on benefit, the minister said, "You are asking me to break the law."

"We don't care one jot about the law!" said the marchers. "We are concerned about saving human lives, and if the law has to be broken in order to do that, then the law should be broken!"

After several other heated exchanges the interview terminated in excitement, with the Minister, the members of Parliament and the marchers all standing on their feet getting in their last points, and the deputation challenging Sir Arthur Steel-Maitland to come into the coalfields and meet the mining communities in their starvation. The press, in reporting the interview, described it as "a heated exchange between the miners and the Minister," and had to admit that the deputation had obviously shaken the Minister.

Following this the marchers carried out an intensive agitation through the London area, with mass meetings and demonstrations by which they brought home to the people of London an understanding of the plight of the coalfields. The Marchers' Control

Council requested a meeting with the members of the General Council of the T.U.C. for the purpose of protesting against the way in which the Council had behaved towards the march.

Mr. Citrine and Mr. Ben Turner agreed to receive them at the offices of the T.U.C. in Eccleston Square, but when we arrived they declared that they could not proceed with any discussion if I was present. Arthur Horner and A. J. Cook were on the Marchers' Control Council deputation, and they immediately made a strong protest against this bureaucratic attitude and declared that unless I, as leader of the march, was present at the discussion, the other members of the Control Council would not remain. Ultimately Mr. Citrine and Mr. Turner withdrew their objection.

After a long discussion we demanded that a public statement be issued by Mr. Citrine withdrawing the unfounded allegations which he had made against the march. He replied that he had no power to issue such a statement without sanction from the General Council, but that he would communicate the opinions of the deputation to the Council. No statement however, was issued.

During the time the marchers were in London they had the sad misfortune to lose two of their comrades, one dying from pneumonia and the other being killed in a street accident. Their bodies were returned to their native soil. In the funeral procession which marched through London the coffins were covered with the red flag of the workers and on each stood an unlighted miner's lamp. The silent march to Paddington Station was most impressive; thousands on that great station stood hushed in silence as the marchers bore the bodies of their dead comrades to the van of the train.

On Sunday, 27th November, a demonstration of farewell took place in Trafalgar Square, and on the following morning all the marchers took their departure from Bethnal Green town hall, marching to Paddington station for the journey home. Sufficient money had been raised to make it possible to pay the fares home of every marcher. Great demonstrations gathered at the railway stations in South Wales to welcome back the men who had marched to London to reveal the tragedy of the minefields.

The march had had a tremendous agitational effect. It was the first serious endeavour that had been made to awaken the people of Britain to an understanding of the conditions which prevailed in the mining villages, and although no definite concession was offered to the marchers' deputation by the government, we soon began to see the results of the march in a number of ways. The Lord Mayor of London opened a special relief fund for the mining communities, which raised over £1,000,000; a committee of public men was appointed to inquire into the South Wales conditions; the Labour Party executive appointed three special commissioners to visit South Wales and to make a public report, and thousands of men were shortly afterwards placed back upon benefit, while there was a general improvement and more humane administration of the poor law.

The government had certainly been seriously shaken by the march, and the publicity which it had gained had focussed public attention on the terrible conditions prevailing in the coalfields, particularly South Wales. The nation had at last been compelled to take notice of the decay and ruin which had been created by capitalism in the areas which had once been flourishing and in the industry which had been one of the sources of British power throughout the world. Under the searchlight of publicity which we had shed upon the conditions of the coalfields, even the Tory Minister of Health, Mr. Neville Chamberlain, had to make the following admission: "Such conditions of destitution are without parallel in the memory of living persons. The devastation in the coalfields can only be compared with the war devastation of France."

This declaration of Mr. Chamberlain's amounted to nothing less than an admission of his own crimes, for the responsibility of these unparalleled conditions of destitution rested chiefly with the Baldwin government and in no small measure was the personal responsibility of the Minister of Health himself, who had consistently pursued a policy of forcing the local authorities to cut down or completely deny poor law relief to able-bodied unemployed. Whilst admitting the ravages of his policy, he nevertheless continued to refuse to treat the problem as one of the government's responsibility for relief. On the contrary, the government treated the plight of the coalfields as a subject for charity, and made the remarkable proposal that for every £1 subscribed by voluntary public subscription, the government should also give £1.

Chapter X

NEW MEASURES OF REACTION

IN the autumn of 1926, and during the whole of 1927, the Baldwin government indulged in a series of reactionary attacks upon the working-class. Chief amongst these were the report of the Blanesburgh Unemployment Insurance Committee, the poor law reform proposals emanating from the Ministry of Health, the Boards of Guardians Default Act, the Poor Law Consolidation Act, and the Trades Disputes Act, passed in July 1927, designed to cripple the trade union movement and make general and sympathetic strike action illegal.

The Blanesburgh Unemployment Insurance Committee was a body established by the Baldwin government in November 1925, owing to the insolvency of the unemployment insurance fund. The terms of reference for this committee were "to consider in the light of experience gained in the working of the unemployment insurance scheme, what changes in the scheme, if any, ought to be made." Lord Blanesburgh was appointed chairman; it consisted chiefly of titled persons and directors of big companies. It included Sir James Curtis, K.B.E., Sir Hugo Hirst, Bart., Sir James Lithgow, Bart., Sir William MacLintock, K.B.E., C.V.O., Sir Glyn Hamilton Wise, Viscountess Milner, Professor H. W. Carliss-Davis, C.B.E., Mr. J. Hamilton, and Mr. Laurence Holt, with Mr. J. A. Dale, C.B.E., as secretary.

In addition, the government appointed three representatives from the trade union and labour movement in the persons of Mr. Frank Hodges (ex-general secretary of the Miners' Federation), Mr. A. E. Holmes, and Miss Margaret Bondfield. The report of this committee was not issued until 31st January, 1927, and it contained many astounding proposals for further worsening the conditions of the unemployed. The report was all the more remarkable in view of the fact that the three Labour representatives signed it. A wave of indignation swept throughout the working-class movement when its terms were made known, and severe criticism was levelled at the Labour representatives.

The following are some of the outstanding points in the report.

169

In respect to labour exchange benefits, the committee recommended for:

Men over 21 years of age	1/-	per week reduction.
Young men 18 to 21 years of age ..	8/-	,, ,, ,,
Young women 18 to 21 years of age	7/-	,, ,, ,,
Boys 16 to 18 years of age	1/6	,, ,, ,,
Girls 16 to 18 years of age	1/-	,, ,, ,,

In only one case was an increase recommended, namely, for an adult dependent, wife or housekeeper, a 2s. per week increase was proposed, but 1s. of this was lost by the benefit reduction to the claimant himself. Further, where a family included an unemployed son or daughter, the adult dependent's increase would be more than lost by the heavy reductions proposed in the benefits of the son or daughter. If there were several unemployed in the family, heavy losses in income to the family would result. For instance, if there were two sons unemployed, the reduction in the income to the family would amount to 16s. per week; if there were two daughters unemployed, the reduction would be 14s. per week, and so on.

The committee also proposed certain reductions in the contributions to the scheme, but it was noticeable that, in each category of employees, the reduction in the contribution rate was larger for the employer than for the worker.

A debt of £20,000,000 had accumulated in the unemployment insurance fund since 1920; it had had to be met by loans from the government to the scheme at a fixed rate of interest. The committee proposed that for the purpose of extinguishing the debt on the existing scheme, the following additions should be made to the proposed new contributions referred to above:

1d. per week for man and young man.
½d. per week for woman, young woman, girls and boys.

Although the workers were not responsible for the existence of unemployment, they nevertheless were to be saddled with the responsibility of wiping out over seven million pounds of this debt to the national exchequer!

The report proposed the abolition of the system of extended benefit in the unemployment insurance scheme, and laid down the following conditions:

(a) That at least 30 contributions should have been paid in the previous two years in respect to claimant.

(b) That claimant is genuinely seeking work but unable to obtain suitable work, and is capable of and available for work.

(c) That claimant has not left his employment voluntarily without just cause, or been dismissed for misconduct.

(d) That claimant is not connected with a trade dispute.

The current condition for the receipt of benefit beyond the statutory period of twenty-six weeks in one year was that the claimant had to show thirty contributions at any time, or eight contributions within the recent period of two or three years prescribed by the Act. The report stated that "the cost of extended benefit is not separately shown in the accounts of the insurance fund, but it is officially estimated that about one-half of the persons now receiving benefit are receiving that form of it." The recommendation of the committee therefore meant that some hundreds of thousands of persons who were drawing extended benefit would be ruled out.

The committee, no doubt realising that suddenly to strike off such a large mass of claimants from benefit would create serious discontent and possibly disorder, proposed that the insured contributors should have good notice of the change, and that after statutory benefit had been exhausted the insurance authorities should have the power to grant what the committee termed "transitional payments" for an indefinite period. Exactly what this was "transitional" to, was not made clear; possibly the committee had in mind the transition to complete starvation but were not crude enough to state it. If it should be thought that they meant a transition to poor law relief, it is worth noting that the committee went out of its way to urge that workers who were struck off benefit should be prevented from obtaining poor law relief. On this point the report actually declared, "We understand that the poor law Acts and regulations made thereunder prohibit, except in special cases, the unconditional outdoor relief of able-bodied persons, and although the Minister of Health has found it necessary, during the extreme post-war depression, to assent to a widespread use of the regulation permitting unconditional relief in special cases, we think, both from the point of view of the parties to the unemployment insurance scheme and on general grounds, that in so far as it deals with the able-bodied unemployed, poor law relief should retain the deterrent effect which now attaches to it, or may be applied thereto." And adds:

"It would be unfortunate if a state of things were created under which anyone whom the authorities of the insurance scheme declined to pay, were paid at once by the board of guardians, since if anyone to whom the authorities of the insurance scheme properly refused benefit could be at once relieved by the guardians the refusal would be a matter of indifference to the claimant."

The committee urged more extensive application of the infamous principle embodied in the "not genuinely seeking work" clause by which hundreds of thousands of claimants were subsequently deprived of benefit. The committee recommended the continuation of the six days' waiting period under which the applicant receives no benefit when first unemployed.

Although the terms of reference of the Blanesburgh Committee were limited to a consideration of unemployment insurance, they actually went further, making a number of proposals which were extremely dangerous to the established trade union standards and conditions. For instance, there was a regulation in existence which permitted a claimant to draw benefit during an industrial dispute, if the dispute was due to the employer contravening an agreement, either locally or nationally. The committee recommended that this provision should be deleted and that any person engaged in an industrial dispute, irrespective of whether the employer had deliberately caused the dispute by the breaking of an agreement, should be disallowed benefit.

This was nothing short of an encouragement to the employer to break agreements if he thought fit, knowing that his workers would be under the intimidation of loss of labour exchange benefit. The report even advanced the impudent argument that the granting of benefit to an applicant who became involved in an industrial dispute caused by the employer breaking an agreement meant "discriminating against the employer with no corresponding discrimination against the worker. Although when an employer breaks an agreement his workers can obtain benefit, on the other hand, when the workers break an agreement, though they themselves be disqualified, the employer may be unable to fill their places, since the vacancies are due to a trade dispute and may, under the law, be refused by other workers with impunity."

There can be no doubt that this proposition amounted to nothing less than a defence of the employers who caused disputes by breaking agreements, and regarded the refusal of workers to blackleg in a dispute as "discrimination against the employer." It was a most astounding proposition for three trade union leaders to have appended their signatures to, particularly as one of them,

Miss Margaret Bondfield, was actually a member of the T.U.C. General Council at the time the report was issued.

On the question of labour transference schemes for the unemployed they went even further and proposed that "if after a reasonable period of unemployment there is no prospect within a reasonable time of the applicant obtaining re-employment in his own trade with sufficient regularity, he will be expected to seek suitable employment in some other trade, and where they are not possessed of the requisite experience to make their work at once of an adequate value to the employers, it is desired that such men should be willing and should be prompted to work for a few months at a wage somewhat less than the standard rate in the assurance that at the end of that period they will become sufficiently experienced to be worth the full wage." Not much imagination is required to realise how the employers would seize upon such a provision of cheap labour and for an indefinite period argue that the worker had not "become sufficiently experienced to be worth the full wage." A more dangerous proposition in its threat to established trade-union standards and wages would be difficult to find.

The publication of the report created a storm of protest all over the country. Many trade unionists found it difficult to believe that Mr. Frank Hodges, Mr. A. E. Holmes and Miss Margaret Bondfield had actually appended their signatures to such a document. It was not surprising that at public meetings these Labour representatives found themselves confronted by bitterly hostile audiences, and the proposal contained in the report that women should have their benefit reduced to 8s. per week led to Miss Margaret Bondfield getting the name of "Eight-bob-a-week Maggie!"

Numerous resolutions of protest were passed at workers' meetings, in trade-union branches, local labour parties, trades councils, co-operative guilds and other working-class bodies, and so strong was the feeling that the Trades Union Congress and the National Labour Party Executive convened a special conference to discuss the report in the Memorial Hall, London, on 28th April, 1927. At the conference a resolution was put forward in the name of the Miners' Federation of Great Britain severely censuring Mr. Frank Hodges, Mr. Holmes and Miss Bondfield for having signed the report, but the leaders of the conference would not allow this resolution to be discussed or voted upon, ruling that the official resolution, which made no reference to the Labour signatories, was the only motion before the conference. Although the delegates expressed themselves in bitter terms against the Blanesburgh report and pressed for lines of action to be organised to defeat it, they were compelled to accept the resolution, which did not go beyond the following proposal: "If the recommendations of the report are embodied in a government Bill, we urge the Parliamentary Labour Party to move a reasoned amendment on the second reading, expressing dissatisfaction with the provisions, which fall short of the proposals submitted to the Blanesburgh Committee by the Trades Union Congress General Council and the Labour Party Executive, and to use every effort to secure amendments in harmony with Labour policy."

The opposition to the Blanesburgh report continued throughout the whole of 1927 and the strength of the agitation was such that the government did not dare to embody the worst features of the report in the new Act which came into operation in April 1928. They did, however, impose a 1s. per week reduction upon the adult male unemployed workers, but they increased the allowances for an adult dependent from 5s. to 7s. a week. At the same time they seriously tightened up many of the regulations that led to disqualification of claimants from benefit, particularly the "not genuinely seeking work" clause which itself later became the target of big struggles and agitation led by the N.U.W.M.

The early months of 1927 also saw sharp controversy being raised over the question of poor law reform proposals which were being advanced by the Ministry of Health. The first poor law had been passed in the sixteenth century, at the time when the workers were being driven off the land by the enclosure Acts, and when many of them were rendered completely destitute as a result of this wholesale land robbery by the land-owners and cattle rearers. The poor law system had undergone many changes since that time and the Baldwin government now argued that there was a need for co-ordinating the whole system and tightening up its administration.

The great agitations led by the National Unemployed Workers' Movement that compelled the boards of guardians to grant outdoor relief to able-bodied persons had been a very disturbing factor to the government and the ruling-class, and in 1927 the government considered proposals for changing the whole structure of the administrative machinery of poor law relief and removing it from the control of the *ad hoc* elected bodies, the boards of guardians. The essence of the proposals were as follows:

1. That the boards of guardians should be abolished and their functions transferred to the respective county and borough councils, which were to establish public assistance committees to carry out the duties hitherto performed by the guardians.

2. That the relief to able-bodied persons should be limited and co-related with unemployment insurance.

3. That the county and borough councils have full control over the public assistance committee with complete responsibility for the consideration of applications for relief, the method of administration and the amounts to be paid.

4. The public assistance committees to consist partly of elected members of the county or borough councils and the others to be persons co-opted on the grounds of their experience in poor law relief work.

5. The county council to submit the scheme of arrangements proposed for the county to the Minister of Health for confirmation or modification.

The working class had little difficulty in seeing through the intentions of the government in respect to this poor law reform. In fact, the Minister of Health himself in a circular (No. 658) to the local authorities stated, "The present experience offers the greatest reason for apprehension as to the effect on sound local government of a continuation of elections turning on the one issue—whether out-relief is to be administered on a higher or lower level."

The unemployed movement organised a series of conferences against the poor law reform proposals, the London conference being particularly successful, held in the Bethnal Green town hall on 27th February, 1927, with delegates from trade union bodies, trades councils and other working-class bodies, representing over a quarter of a million organised workers.

In spite of strong working-class opposition, in March 1929 a Bill abolishing the boards of guardians and reforming the poor law system on the lines of the proposals, was passed by Parliament, becoming operative as from April 1930.

An earlier Act, known as the Guardians Default Act, was a measure which the government introduced in order that they should have legal power to remove any board of guardians that attempted to treat the recipients of poor relief too liberally. This brought a number of the boards of guardians and town councils into conflict with the central government authority. Particularly was this the case in respect to Poplar, Bermondsey, West Ham, Chester-le-Street (Co. Durham), and Bedwelty (South Wales).

In these places there were very strong Labour majorities on the boards of guardians and they had refused to observe the limited scale laid down by the Ministry of Health, but through the very acute unemployment in their areas they had been compelled to make application to the government for loans of money in order that they could continue to relieve the distress amongst the local residents. A central unemployment fund had been established for the purpose of extending loans at a certain rate of interest, and when the recalcitrant boards of guardians applied for loans the Ministry of Health attempted to dictate special terms on which they should be granted.

Even before the passing of the Guardians Default Act, the Ministry of Health, by special powers granted to it by Parliament, had taken action and removed the elected representatives of the people in the places mentioned above, and established in their place government commissioners, who went into the respective areas and pursued a policy of ruthless economy at the expense of the unemployed. This led to many big demonstrations of protest, and battles with the police took place in the streets of West Ham.

During the twelve months between March 1927 and March 1928, the drive against the unemployed by the government became intense. Hundreds of thousands of applicants for unemployment benefit were being wiped off the registers, disqualified under various regulations. The official figures of the Ministry of Labour show that in that period the total decisions of disqualification of applicants from benefit amounted to 441,387. The figures of poor law relief were soaring higher in spite of wholesale disallowances by the boards of guardians until they reached approximately one and a half millions.

Following the operation of the new Unemployment Insurance Act commencing in April 1928, the average monthly disqualifications of claimants went even higher than it had been in the previous twelve months. For the four months from 19th April to 14th August, 1928, it reached the figure of 204,511. Most of these disqualifications were made under the "not genuinely seeking work" clause. No indication was ever given by the Ministry of Labour of what was required of an applicant to prove that he was genuinely seeking work, and tens of thousands of honest workers found themselves robbed of the benefit which they had been compelled to pay for when they were in work.

The Scottish coalfields, like South Wales, were experiencing acute unemployment and extreme poverty. The great industrial

Top: Baton charge on November 1st, 1932, on the night-marchers attempting to present Means Test Petition to Parliament. *Bottom:* Hannington just after release from, gaol in 1933.

Top: "Lunch" in Cathedral Square, Edinburgh, Scottish march, 1933. *Bottom:* ... their beds were the flagstones, Princes Street, 1933.

p: The fountain is our bathroom, Princes Street, Edinburgh. *Bottom:* Setting out to London from Glasgow, a five weeks' trek, National March, 1934.

Top: Women marchers by the roadside, 1934. *Bottom:* No shortage of work here! Marche boot-repairing squad.

Top: Marchers entering Hyde Park, 1934. *Bottom:* . . . over a hundred thousand people welcomed them!

Top: Lancashire marches through the Strand, 1934. *Bottom:* 400 Scots have their fir
meal in London—is it haggis?

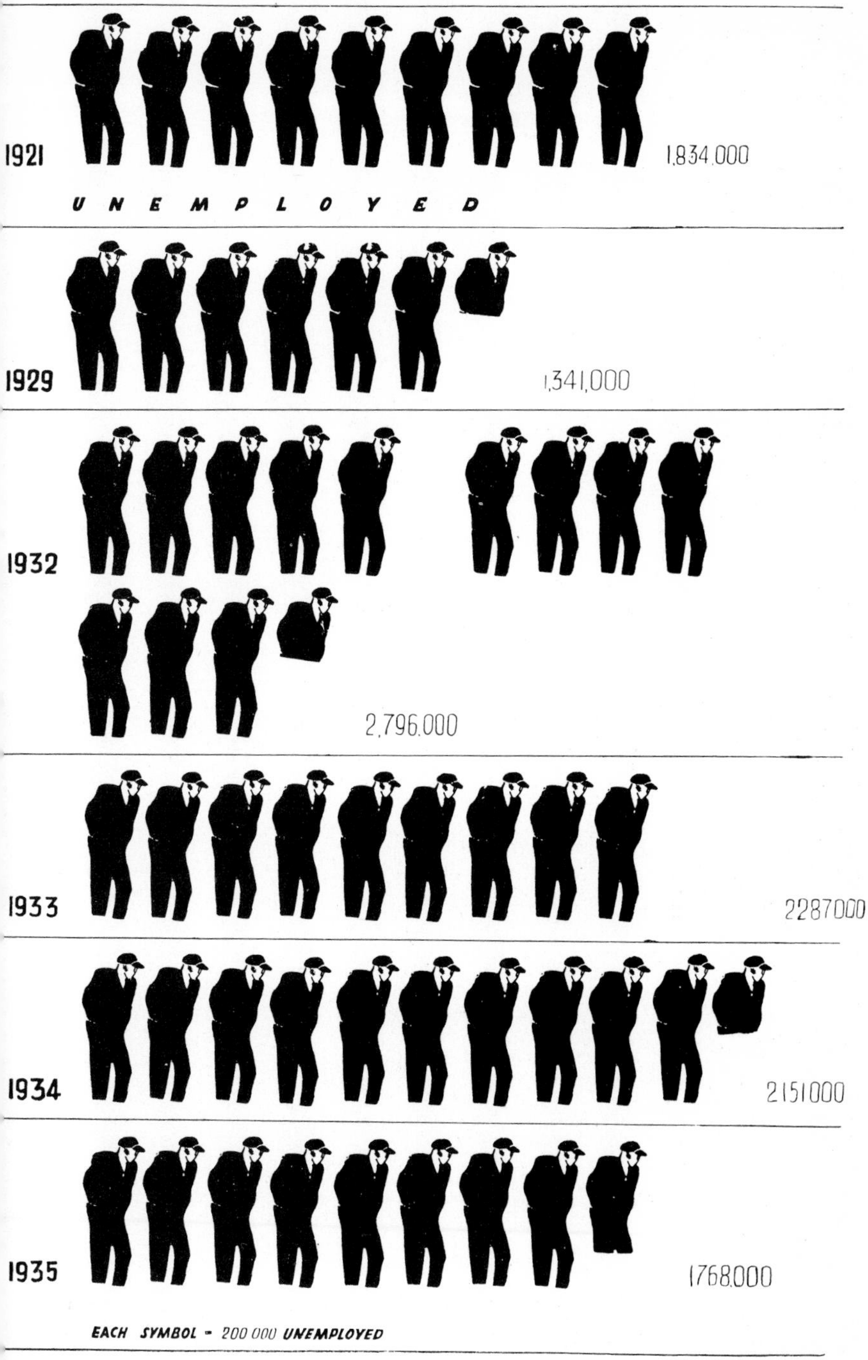

1921   1,834,000

U N E M P L O Y E D

1929   1,341,000

1932   2,796,000

1933   2287000

1934   2151000

1935   1768000

EACH SYMBOL - 200 000 UNEMPLOYED

Clyde was becoming more and more stagnant. Shipyard after shipyard was becoming derelict and the cranes and derricks were standing like gaunt monuments in this industrial graveyard, which had at one time been the greatest shipbuilding centre in the world.

The policy of rationalisation and "peace in industry" to which the T.U.C. General Council were giving allegiance was in fact leading to displacement of more workers from industry. When the policy of Mondism came up for further endorsement at the Swansea Trades Union Congress in 1928, the unemployed marched to the congress to protest against the effects of rationalisation. Over one thousand unemployed men and women marched from the West Wales coalfield to Swansea, only to be informed by the arrangements committee that their deputation could not be received by the congress.

Huge police reinforcements were mobilised in the town to bar forcibly the approach of the marchers to the congress hall. The *Daily Express* next day described it as being like "an armed camp." The *South Wales Daily Post* commented upon the police preparations against the marchers and reported as follows: "The Chief Constable of Swansea who had a conference with Mr. Citrine, Secretary of the T.U.C. and Mr. Arthur Henderson, Secretary of the Labour Party, had made all necessary arrangements for control of the situation. Further, to guard against any attempt on the part of the marchers to force an entry, some of the biggest and heaviest members of the trade union movement had been chosen to act as stewards at the main entrances to the hall."

But whilst the police and heavy stewards guarded the congress hall against the unemployed, the president of the congress, Mr. Ben Turner, was opening the proceedings with the following statement: "My first business is to welcome to the congress the mayor and corporation, the high sheriff and the lord lieutenant of the county"! The high sheriff of Glamorgan, chief officer for the crown, was invited to speak to the congress. He did so, and in the course of his remarks said, "I thank the congress for the invitation to be present, a privilege I shall not readily forget, although in a parliamentary contest I shall not be voting on the same side"! Nevertheless, the high sheriff was presented with a gold medallion as a souvenir of the congress.

The policy of Mondism received its endorsement in the decisions of the congress.

In consequence of the policy of rationalisation a big increase in the number of unemployed had taken place during the latter part of 1928. Pit after pit was being closed down under a scheme of the coal-owners known as the "pooling system." In short, this was a policy of restriction of output in order to force up prices, and it entailed the closing down of so-called uneconomical pits and the compensation of the owners out of a financial pool, the pool being raised by a general levy of sixpence a ton on all coal put on the market, with the exception of export coal. Whilst the coal-owners levied the consumer and drew tribute for laying the pits idle, thousands of miners and their families whose livelihood depended upon coal getting were thrown on the streets to starve.

In 1924 there had been over 140,000 miners employed in the Scottish coalfields, but on 25th August, 1928, the government reports showed only 90,016 so employed. Between August 1927 and August 1928 there was a decrease of 13.9 per cent in the number employed in the Scottish mines. This far-reaching extent of unemployment in the Scottish areas and the disgraceful conditions imposed upon the unemployed through the Ministry of Labour and the Scottish Board of Health gave rise to a proposal for a march of unemployed miners, shipyard workers and jute workers to Edinburgh in September 1928 to demand an interview with the Scottish officials of the Board of Health and the Ministry of Labour.

The National Unemployed Workers' Movement went ahead with the organising of such a march, and I travelled to Scotland from London to take over the organisation and leadership. On Sunday, 16th September, 1928, the first contingent of jute workers from Dundee took the road. Before reaching Edinburgh they were joined by miners' sections from Fife, Lanarkshire, Ayrshire and Stirlingshire, and shipyard workers from the Clyde. Dense crowds gathered on the streets of Edinburgh when the marchers entered the city on Saturday afternoon, 22nd September.

They were met on the outskirts of the town and led in by the Edinburgh silver trades band, receiving an official reception from the Edinburgh Trades Council. The *Evening Dispatch* reported that "the men who were bronzed and dusty marched in ranks of four in military fashion." The marchers remained in Edinburgh several days and the Scottish Board of Health and the Minister of Labour officials agreed to receive a deputation, numbering twenty, on the morning and afternoon of 24th September respectively.

The interview with the Scottish Board of Health in the morning lasted just over three hours and several times became a stormy encounter between the officials and the deputation. The outcome of the interview was that the secretary of the Scottish Board of Health agreed to the following three points:

1. To investigate immediately 200 cases which the deputation had with them of particularly harsh treatment by parish councils of unemployed families.

2. To receive any further cases of grievances in the future through the machinery of the N.U.W.M. for investigation.

3. To submit a complete report on all the points raised by the deputation for consideration of the secretary of State for Scotland.

In the afternoon, the deputation met the chief divisional officers of the Ministry of Labour. They hastened to inform the deputation that they were government servants and had powers to operate only within the Unemployment Insurance Act, and could not be expected to consider any proposals going beyond that.

At the end of the interview, however, the chief divisional officer agreed:

1. That there would be no victimisation of the miner harvesters who had migrated to Canada, and were now being forced by conditions to return to this country, and that if they were in receipt of benefit before leaving for Canada, they would come back upon benefit on their return.

2. That the cases of bad treatment by local officials and courts of referees, which the deputation had cited, would be immediately investigated.

3. That the divisional officers would investigate any further cases forwarded to them through the machinery of the N.U.W.M.

4. That a full report of the deputation's complaints concerning the administration of unemployment insurance benefit would be placed before a Scottish conference of labour exchange officials that was shortly to be held.

The results of the interviews were announced to great mass meetings held in Edinburgh, and the actions of the deputation received the endorsement of the workers. The following morning the marchers departed for their homes.

Chapter XI

THE NATIONAL HUNGER MARCH AGAINST THE "NOT GENUINELY SEEKING WORK" CLAUSE

IMMEDIATELY after the Scottish march to Edinburgh in September 1928, the National Unemployed Workers' Movement decided to begin organising the second great national hunger march on London.

The government was carrying out a ruthless elimination of unemployed workers from labour exchange benefit under the "not genuinely seeking work" clause. Tens of thousands every week were being deprived of their benefit by the arbitrary rulings of courts of referees under this clause. Not only were they suffering loss of benefit, but their character was being impugned, a decision against them under this clause being tantamount to declaring that they were wasters and ne'er-do-wells who did not want work. It was not surprising therefore that this clause was bitterly resented throughout the country.

The onus of proof under examination by a court of referees rested upon the claimant, who had to prove that he was genuinely seeking work; the court did not have to prove that suitable work had been offered and had been refused. The result was that unemployed applicants before the court would find themselves subjected to a rapid fire of questions about the places to which they had applied for employment (even several weeks previously) the dates and times of the applications, and proof that they were telling the truth. Many unemployed workers entered the courts in fear and trembling, knowing that the meagre labour exchange benefit for themselves and their family was in the balance. Trick questions were often put to the applicants in an effort to secure a contradiction of some previous statement, and under a gruelling cross-examination the applicant often lost his nerve and was unable to remember important points in his search for work which would have helped him to avoid disqualification. This procedure was even contrary to the elementary rights of a prisoner in a court of law, where, at any rate, he would be presumed innocent until the contrary was proved.

Often when an applicant was truthfully able to report that he persistently and daily searched for work, it was seldom possible to produce documentary evidence. Firms were not prepared to spend time in giving a note to all the workers who applied to them for employment and more often than not the applicant was either refused admission to the works, or was hustled from the premises by an officious commissionaire. Unemployed workers were reduced to the desperate necessity of tramping many miles from their homes each day, in a fruitless search for work which they knew did not exist, only in order to be able to supply evidence of their efforts.

It was common, however, even where claimants after long and painful searches for work were able to produce documentary evidence containing signatures of managers and foremen, for them still to be disqualified if the evidence was considered by the court not to be sufficiently abundant. It became quite customary to find men walking miles from their own district, such as from Halifax to Huddersfield, in search of work, whilst men from Huddersfield would walk to Halifax in search for work—often passing each other on the road, conscious of their fruitless mission, but doing it in order to satisfy the inquiries which they had to face at the court of referees.

Such senseless tramping was going on all over the country. Even in the derelict mining areas, where there was no other industry to turn to, and where there was no sense in going to a pithead which had been closed down, the unemployed had to give proof that they were genuinely seeking work. The result was that on the main roads leading from the coalfields to the big towns—particularly the Bath road, leading from South Wales to London—hundreds of men could be seen almost any day, footsore and weary, trudging towards London, having left their families behind at the mercy of the boards of guardians.

Whilst they were going up to London, others, who had gone before, would be returning, disheartened and broken. In the big cities they would wander for days, starving and destitute, before returning to their homes, where they would have the satisfaction of knowing that they could face the courts of referees and report that they had been to London on such and such a date, in search for work!

Such were the conditions which were arousing widespread resentment amongst the unemployed. Coupled with these was the threat of the Baldwin government to end the transitional conditions for the receipt of unemployment benefit in April 1929, which would have automatically struck hundreds of thousands of claimants off benefit.

It was in this situation that the National Unemployed Workers' Movement embarked upon the organising of the second great national hunger march to London. The march started when the Scottish contingent set out on the road in the dead of winter, 23rd January, 1929, to march in blizzards and snowstorms for five weeks before reaching London. Other contingents from all parts of the country took the road in accordance with the time-table, conforming to their separate routes, all leading to London.

Because of the hostile policy which the T.U.C. was pursuing and our experience of their treatment in the 1927 Welsh miners' march, we refrained from inviting their support on this occasion, because we estimated that such an invitation would provide them with the desired opportunity of attacking the march. We found, nevertheless, before the march started, that statements were issued to the press by the general secretary of the T.U.C., disclaiming any association with the march and denouncing it on the grounds that it would mean hardship for the men.

That there would be hardship was well understood by those vounteering to march, but it was something more compelling than personal hardship—the pain and anguish of witnessing their families slowly starving and sinking to despair—that prompted men to volunteer for the march, to make at least an effort to compel the government to mitigate that suffering.

Yet when the march started, the right-wing trade union and labour leaders who professed to be opposed to the march because of its hardships, themselves proceeded to create hardships by advising the trades councils and local labour parties on the routes not to render any assistance. At the same time, the Ministry of Health of the Tory government issued instructions to all the poor law authorities to the effect that marchers who sought shelter and accommodation in their workhouses were to be subjected to the ordinary treatment accorded to casuals and tramps. This meant that the following regulations were to apply:

1. That every man must be searched on entering, and that his name and address must be given.

2. That the regulation diet of food must not be exceeded (two slices of bread and margarine and a cup of tea for supper and breakfast).

3. That no man could leave the institution on the day of entering.

4. That a task must be performed next morning before leaving.
5. That no smoking, singing or meetings could be held in the institution.

We had, of course, no intention of accepting such conditions, and the marchers set out with the deliberate intention of smashing them down wherever they had to turn to to the workhouse for shelter. But in the face of the joint opposition of the right-wing trade union and labour leadership and the Ministry of Health, the march was certainly a daring and hazardous undertaking. But we placed our faith in the response and support of the workers on the roads and in the towns. We felt that the rank and file workers would instinctively come to our aid. The events certainly justified that faith. Every marcher before he set out knew of the serious difficulties that lay before him, but it only served to make him more determined to face the task and to battle through.

It is not possible here to give more than a glimpse into the conditions and experiences of the various contingents. One or two points, however, will serve to give the reader a picture of what the hunger march meant.

Before the march started, the capitalist press had as usual done its utmost to sow dissension by deliberately lying about the leaders, suggesting that while they called for men to march to London, they would not march themselves. As chief organiser of the march, I therefore decided to march with the Scottish contingent, which would be five weeks on the road, and to keep in touch with the other contingents by telegrams and letters through the post offices in the towns where the contingents were resting according to time-table.

On the morning of Wednesday, 23rd January, 1929, tens of thousands of Glasgow workers mobilised on Blytheswood Square, Glasgow, to give a rousing send-off to 200 men, representing the Scottish coalfields, shipyards, textile towns, fishing industries and others affected by the blight of unemployment in Scotland. The marchers were something more than individual volunteers; they were representatives, because they had all been endorsed at great mass meetings held in their respective towns throughout Scotland. Led by a pipers' band, we set out to blaze the trail for over five hundred miles on the roads of Britain, calling upon the workers of the land to stir their slumbering souls and to rise against the callous governing class responsible for the terrible plight of the unemployed.

In this second national hunger march, careful thought had been given to the question of equipment, and every marcher was fully equipped, with valise and haversack containing his requirements for the road, and with a blanket for sleeping at night.

Kilmarnock was the first resting-place from Glasgow, and here we were given a reception by the trades council and accommodated in the town hall. After leaving Kilmarnock we had to face a long dreary march for five days over the Scottish moors down to Dumfries with only small villages en route. But the contingent had its own field kitchen and cooking staff that went ahead on the road each morning, pitched up on the roadside and cooked hot stew for the marchers about mid-day. In the villages of Catrine, New Comnock, Kirkconnell, Thornhill, down to Dumfries, we found splendid men and women of the working class ready to give their help to the marchers by preparing food and attending to those in need of medical care.

At Kirkconnell, the local doctor gratuitously gave his services in attending to a number of cases of serious foot trouble and physical exhaustion. He examined over thirty men and highly commended the work that had been done by our own red cross corps. There were four cases that he refused to pass for proceeding with the march; he said that they must be returned home. Crippled and exhausted, these men begged to be allowed to continue with their comrades on the great journey, but the Control Council took the advice of the doctor as final and decided to pay the train fares of these comrades back to their homes. Two of the men pleaded with tears in their eyes to be allowed to go through with the march, but it was too dangerous in face of their condition.

Next morning, after sleeping on the hard boards in the biggest hall available in the village, we waked from our slumbers to find that we had to march in a heavy snowstorm. We had a fourteen-mile tramp before us. Thornhill was our destination, and we started off with our feet sinking two inches deep into the snow-covered ground. Napoleon said, "An army marches on its stomach," and our cooking staff took care to act on this epigram by providing a magnificent hot dinner of minced meat, onions, turnip and potatoes, served on the road after nine miles of the march from Kirkconnell had been covered.

We arrived at the small village of Thornhill at six o'clock in the evening. The day's march had been a severe test for the men. All day we had marched through open country in a blinding snowstorm; every man was dead beat, the heavy snow on the roads having made the march very difficult. But although there could be no great liveliness amongst the men that night, they were dour and determined. They knew that the following day the Durham, Northumberland and Tyneside contingent was due to assemble in Newcastle in readiness to take the road. The severe wintry weather was causing us to wonder whether it would affect the start of the north-east coast contingent. We decided to send a telegram of greetings to them, and the next day we were re-assured of their faith and solidarity, when we received a telegram back saying, "Greetings to the courageous Scottish contingent! Tyneside assembling ready for the road!"

As we were marching towards Dumfries on 28th January we halted in a small village for our mid-day meal of hot stew. There we met a band of strolling players who were travelling from village to village, booking halls and running their small theatrical shows. The party was a family group consisting of father, mother, one son and two daughters. Although they were smartly dressed, they had been doing very badly and were stranded with no money even to purchase food. As soon as we learned of their plight we welcomed them into our rough and ready company to partake of a hot meal from our field kitchen, the boys supplying them with plates and mugs. How long they had been without food we did not know, but they eagerly devoured three further helpings! They had heavy portmanteaux with their props and were wishing to go on to Dumfries—a distance of ten miles. Unable to pay their fares they had been anticipating spending a cold and cheerless night in a small hut that one of the local villagers had offered them.

They were full of gratitude when our hardy contingent of marchers decided to send them into Dumfries on our field kitchen lorry. We served them out with a ration of our cigarettes and bade them farewell and good luck. But we were to meet again.

Maxwelltown Braes, immortalised in the song "Annie Laurie," lies on the outskirts of Dumfries. As we approached Maxwelltown, crowds of people came out on to the streets to greet us and gave ample testimony of the wide sympathy and support which we were arousing in the hearts of our class. In Dumfries the town hall was placed at our disposal for the accommodation of the marchers, and here we had the pleasure of meeting the strolling players again. They came to give us a little show in return for our assistance. The boys joined in the singing of the choruses, and an enjoyable evening was spent, whilst heavy snow fell outside on the streets.

On the morning of 30th January the Scottish contingent set out from Annan for the border. There were many among the marchers who had never been over the border before; some middle-aged men who had toiled and wrought in the mines and factories, giving their lives in piling up wealth for the bosses, men who yearned to see something of the world, and who now for the first time were going to see England, even though they had to walk it!

Press photographers had waited at the famous Gretna Green blacksmith's shop, to take pictures of the Scottish army as it marched out of Scotland into England. On the small concrete bridge that marks the border, we halted and lustily sang the old Scottish rebel-song, "McGregor's Gathering" and the "International." After a short rest, we pressed on to Carlisle. Several miles out from the town we saw our cyclist-postman approaching. He had been into Carlisle to collect the marchers' letters. The practice was that the relatives of the marchers, knowing the towns where they would be on certain days, sent letters "care of the G.P.O." and marked "for the Hunger Marchers"; one reliable man was appointed as postman, who would collect the letters each day, return to the contingent, and distribute them.

Amongst the post that he brought this day, was a telegram from the Tyneside contingent with greetings of solidarity, announcing that they had reached Durham the night before. Just that short message had a wonderful effect upon the marchers; it made them realise that they were part of a great national movement, that was moving into action against unemployment.

In Carlisle, after a big demonstration on the streets, the marchers received a warm reception from the trades and labour council. They explained, however, that in view of the instructions from T.U.C. headquarters the reception had to be understood as unofficial.

Throughout the march the contingents experienced a mixture of treatment in the hundreds of towns through which they passed. Where the local labour party were under the domination of the reactionary officials there would be a blank refusal of any support whatever to the march. In other places, where they were more progressive, the ban against the march from their national right-wing leaders was openly defied, whilst in other places they overcame the difficulty by giving a reception, but calling it unofficial.

On 1st February, the Scottish contingent covered twenty-six miles from Penrith to Kendal, having to pass over the bleak heights of Shap Fell; every man arrived in Kendal soaked to the skin, as they had marched in a constant downpour of rain. After a day's rest, we took the road again for a twenty-one miles' tramp to Preston. We were now striking the great textile belt of England, and we arrived in Preston to be welcomed by thousands of textile workers lining the streets, and to receive a Lancashire hot-pot supper from the trades and labour council. From Preston the Scotties marched through the principal textile towns of Lancashire, and everywhere roused masses of the workers to tremendous enthusiasm.

The Durham and Northumberland marchers, however, experienced difficulties after being a few days on the road. They entered Thirsk on 2nd February, and went into the workhouse for accommodation. The master had promised the advance guard that no restrictions would be imposed, but once the men were inside the building there was an entire change of front. A heavy police guard was placed at the foot of the stairs and the marchers were told that no more than nine men would be permitted to leave the institution before morning.

This was strongly resented by the marchers, and the leaders of the contingent decided to make an endeavour to secure halls outside the institution for sleeping. Their mission, however, was fruitless, and when this was reported to the marchers, the workhouse master and Sir Henry Bowers, the chief constable of North Riding, listened with obvious amusement. They were taken by surprise, however, when the marchers decided to march out of the workhouse and to push on to Ripon, 11½ miles away. Special forces of police were brought up, but in spite of this, at ten o'clock at night the marchers, armed with stout ash sticks, demanded that the doors be thrown open.

As they marched out into the village square every form of intimidation appeared to be practised by the police to provoke trouble. The night was black and moonless and the rain began to fall heavily, but the marchers having once made up their minds to break down the casual treatment which the workhouse authorities attempted to impose, were determined to go through with it. At midnight the column of marching men were steadily tramping on towards Ripon, with police on cycles riding in the front and at the rear, and police motor cycles every now and again roaring past, and a packed police car following behind, its headlights stabbing the darkness. At intervals, the surging challenge of the "International" rose from the marching column as it pressed forward.

Thus it was that the Durham and Northumberland men crossed the Yorkshire moors on the night of 2nd February. They were still marching at two o'clock in the morning, and still the "International" rose in deep-throated singing; though their legs by now were moving mechanically, still they kept their regular marching step. It was not until two-thirty in the morning that they entered the small town of Ripon. As they reached the outskirts of the town, the police guard disappeared. Then a solitary constable detached himself from a doorway and came forward.

"Come on, boys—I'll show you where you are to go!" and to the great surprise of the marchers, they were led to the Constitutional Club, where hot tea awaited them, and where they dried their clothes before huge fires that had been specially lit! The grim determination of these north-east coast men had apparently startled the authorities after the march out from Thirsk, and the town of Ripon was informed that they were coming, and decided that it was best to treat them decently.

News of what had happened in Thirsk travelled right down the road of this contingent and their treatment from then onward was in the main satisfactory. When they struck the mining area of South Yorkshire, on 7th February, they received great receptions from the mining communities, many of whom were old Durham comrades who had migrated to Yorkshire for work.

On 8th February the Yorkshire, Plymouth and Liverpool contingents set out. Their experiences were much the same as those of the other contingents. Dense crowds met them in all the towns which they entered; sometimes, like the Scottish and north-east coast men, they had to march long distances in sleet, rain and biting wind; sometimes they encountered difficulties; but their persistence enabled them to overcome them. In some towns the workhouse authorities attempted to carry out the instructions of the Ministry of Health, but they found that that only meant trouble, and ultimately they gave in to the demand for humane treatment. Everywhere the marchers were smashing through the attempt of the Baldwin government to treat them as tramps and vagabonds. The message of the marchers was being carried into hundreds of thousands of working-class homes. Even in the numerous tiny villages and hamlets through which the marchers would pass in the course of their day's march, kindly aid was always forthcoming from the agricultural folk who knew of the hardships of life. Often small farmers would give free milk to the marchers whilst they were on the road; frequently, when the marchers halted for a rest in small villages, the cottagers would come out with jugs of hot tea; old and young would give small contributions to the marchers' fund, to enable them to secure food and to reach their objective. There were many touching scenes on the roads and in the towns, which revealed the admiration of the working-class people, who realised the importance of the stirring mission in which the marchers were engaged.

Sometimes the distances of the contingents would unavoidably be thirty or more miles a day in order to reach a town which could accommodate them. Always there were hard boards to sleep on; but there were no complaints; the men appreciated the difficulties of the march and understood why they were marching. Sometimes they would be almost dead beat before they reached the town, but it was a remarkable thing that, when they came on to the outskirts of the town, they would brace themselves smartly for an impressive march in. The contingents always marched in step in companies of twenty, taking the lead from their company leaders. Regular marching time was found to be the best and enabled the men to cover ground much more quickly than they would do otherwise.

Heavy responsibility, of course, rested upon the leadership of the contingents. They not only had to march and set an example to the men, even the example of taking their food after all the men had been served, and not before, but they had the job of attending to all the organising arrangements of the contingent in the towns and on the road. After the big demonstrations in the evenings, the Contingent Control Councils, consisting of the company leaders, would meet to discuss the arrangements for the next day. Sometimes it would not be possible to start the Council meeting until after midnight. There were the reports to be taken from the company leaders on the condition of their men; the reports of the advance guards about accommodation and reception in the towns ahead; consideration of the state of the marchers' funds and whether they had sufficient to purchase food and cigarettes for the marchers; the sending of regular daily reports to national headquarters; and a host of other problems which had to receive proper attention.

Many times the marchers would be down to sleep long before the leaders of the contingents were able to rest. The leadership also had to be up first in the morning in order to attend to the breakfast arrangements and other matters. Irrespective of weather conditions, the contingents had to march, in order to keep in line with their time-table; otherwise the reception arrangements would be thrown out of gear in the towns ahead. After breakfast, before setting out on the road, the marchers would all be called together and the press reports bearing on the march would be read to them. These reports often caused great amusement to the marchers, especially when such papers as the *Daily Mail* and *Daily Express* contained stories about the leaders riding in motor-cars whilst the marchers tramped; and about men who were deserting the ranks and so on, all of which were totally untrue.

The reading of these reports not only created much laughter, but it made the men proof against the effects of this anti-working-class propaganda in respect to the other contingents. Then, after the report on the state of the marchers' funds, and certain announcements about the march arrangements, the men would get ready for the road again. Before leaving, however, fatigue squads were always put on to clean up the halls where the marchers had stayed.

There was, of course, discipline in the march; orders of the contingent leaders and company leaders were readily accepted by the men. It was not a forced discipline, but a voluntary discipline, because our men understood the need for efficiency.

On fine bright sunny mornings we would take the road as early as possible and break the back of the day's march before mid-day. Marching in company formation of twenties, there would be a friendly spirit of competition between the various companies, as to which was the smartest. The whole column would swing along the country roads in perfect marching order, and this always became a subject of favourable comment on the smartness and efficiency of the men by all those who witnessed it.

The favourite marching song of the Scottish contingent was a song composed on the road to the tune of the "Youthful Guardsman." It ran as follows:

> From Scotland we are marching,
> From shipyard, mill and mine,
> Our scarlet banners raise on high,
> We toilers are in line.
> For victory we'll fight: we'll show the enemy our might.
> *Chorus:* We are the Hunger Marchers of the Proletariat,
> We are the Hunger Marchers of the Proletariat.
>
> We've met official sabotage,
> In village and in town,
> But with the workers' willing help,
> We've smashed the barriers down,
> This baby-starving government shall shake before our
> onward tramp.
> (*Repeat chorus*).

Now comes the day of reckoning,
No longer we'll endure
Starvation—we will conquer now,
Our victory is sure.
We are a strong determined band, each with a weapon
    in his hand.
(*Chorus*).

As the lines of the last verse were sung, the marchers would all raise their heavy walking sticks in the air, as a mark of defiance against the government. It was a striking sight when hundreds of ash sticks shot above the heads of the marchers as they sang their battle song.

Another popular song amongst all the contingents of marchers was the following, sung to the refrain of a military march:

> Now the unemployed are on the march,
> Marching forward on to London Town,
> Marching forward on to victory,
> Give us your help boys,
> We're fighting the battle for you.
>
> Men and women are starving in their homes,
> We're their standard bearers on the road,
> Marching forward on to victory,
> Give us your help, etc., etc.
>
> Millions of workers are starving in revolt,
> With our flag of red, we blaze the trail
> Marching forward, etc., etc.
>
> With the N.U.W.M. we fight,
> As the storm troops of the unemployed,
> Marching forward, etc., etc.
>
> Victory is certain for our cause,
> We call to arms the workers of the land,
> Marching forward on to victory,
> Give us your help boys,
> We're fighting the battle for you.

These songs were not only sung on the roads, but in the big halls, at the demonstrations and at impromptu concerts. They always received an enthusiastic response from the workers, and many times the local workers learned the words and sang the songs with the marchers. Then, of course, there was always Jim

Connolly's "Rebel Song," the "Red Flag," and the "International."

The Lancashire contingent took the road on 10th February. The second day out from Manchester they had to enter the workhouse at Northwich. They had their first baptism of the Ministry of Health's instructions. They stood up to it and succeeded in breaking down the regulations which the workhouse master attempted to impose. They got so far even as getting the workhouse authorities to provide them with hot stew for supper, porridge, fresh butter, jam and marmalade for breakfast. On their march from Northwich to Crewe next day they stirred up the new Melchett industrial centre, known as Middlewich, which was at that time the centre of the Imperial Chemical Industries. They marched round the town and received many gifts from housewives and small shopkeepers. They were informed that no meetings had ever been held in this place, so they halted in their march in order to start a free speech precedent in Middlewich.

On 11th February the Welsh marchers started out and by the 16th all the main contingents were on the road. It was on this day that the Lancashire contingent left Wolverhampton for Birmingham. On arrival at West Bromwich, about four miles from Birmingham, the police attempted to divert the contingent from the route previously decided upon by the Marchers' Council. Crowds of West Bromwich workers rallied to the support of the marchers, and ultimately the police had to give way. Two miles from Birmingham the contingent was met by the reception committee and a big procession of Birmingham workers with bands and banners. They marched on to the Digbeth institute where they were served with a splendid meal; during the evening, whilst the marchers' speakers were addressing mass meetings, the rest of the marchers enjoyed a concert in the institute.

At ten-thirty they formed up to march to the workhouse where they were to sleep that night. On moving off they were accompanied by an unusually large number of police who deliberately escorted them in a most roundabout way to the workhouse. Once inside the workhouse they found that they were to be locked in casual cells, and that there were a large force of police, stronger in numbers even than the marchers, who were deliberately making trouble. They refused even to allow the red cross corps men to carry out their work of attending to the feet of the marchers. The marchers therefore decided to leave the building, preferring to remain on the streets all night, rather than accept such treatment.

As the men were putting on their packs, the police rushed upon them with their batons drawn, and a serious conflict ensued. Several men were seriously injured and after a fierce struggle the marchers were finally overpowered and locked in the workhouse for the night. Next morning when they marched out they proceeded to the Bull Ring in the centre of the town, where a huge protest demonstration was held against the conduct of the police. They then set out, joined by Birmingham marchers, for their journey to Stratford-on-Avon, the sleepy town of Shakespeare.

Two days later the Plymouth contingent, which had been steadily pressing forward through the quiet countryside of Devon, Somerset, Hampshire, and Surrey, reached Aldershot, the headquarters of the southern command of the British Army. News of the approach of the marchers had spread through the camp amongst the soldiers, and when they entered the town they were greeted by crowds of soldiers who freely gave to the marchers' funds for food and cigarettes. The officials of the Aldershot Labour Party gave an official reception and the labour hall was placed at the marchers' disposal. In the evening a big demonstration was held in the town and soldiers and civilians listened attentively to the marchers' case.

So from town to town the various contingents closed in upon London. On Saturday, 28th February, the Welsh, Lancashire, Midlands and Staffordshire contingents moved forward to Chiswick, their last stopping place before entering London. The Scottish contingent after a magnificent welcome from the Watford Trades and Labour Council moved into position at Hendon, where they were accommodated in the schools. The north-east coast contingent took up their position in Tottenham, receiving a great welcome. Yorkshire, Notts and Derby were in Holloway, and Plymouth at Deptford. In the ranks of all the contingents enthusiasm bubbled over, and the men expressed their joy with singing and dancing that lasted into the early hours of the morning.

Sunday, 24th February, came; this was the great day to which they had all looked forward. For weeks the London reception committee had been preparing for this day of reception to the marchers. The marchers were early astir, smartening themselves up for their last march to Trafalgar Square, which was again to be the venue of a mighty demonstration.

The early morning had been dull and misty, but the sun broke through about eleven o'clock. In twelve centres round London the workers were assembling in thousands, with bands and banners; there was great activity and expectancy everywhere and the early reports of the London reception committee's scouts showed that the day was going to be a great success. Dozens of bands—drum and fife, bagpipes, silver and brass—took up their positions with the demonstrations. By 11.30 all the contingents of the marchers were on the road, heading for the centre of London, accompanied by thousands of London workers. By 1 p.m. all the London demonstrations had started and the tens of thousands of London workers were moving forward towards Whitehall.

The marchers were due to arrive in Trafalgar Square at 3 p.m., but those London demonstrations that were not accompanying contingents of marchers were due in at 2.30. An hour before this a big crowd began to gather in the square. Red rosettes and red flags were everywhere, and with every minute that passed the crowd grew larger. At 2.30 most of the crowd had formed up on to the main approaches in order to get a good view as the processions arrived. Then, at 2.45 p.m. bands were heard coming in the direction of the Strand. Masses of the workers swarmed down the Strand to meet them—it was the East London demonstration arriving. They poured into the square to await the arrival of the marchers. Before the tail end of the East London demonstration got into the square, other demonstrations began to arrive from all directions. On they came, swelling the crowd to immense proportions.

Then there was a lull, and everybody was excitedly striving to find a vantage point on all the main roads leading into the square from which they could witness the arrival of the marchers. At ten minutes past three the news spread that the Yorkshire and Notts marchers were approaching from the Strand. The great crowd surged forward in that direction; the bands could be heard in the distance and the excitement of the crowd was soaring higher as the banners came in sight. The marshals of the demonstration had extreme difficulty in holding the crowd back and keeping a gangway, and as the head of the marchers' column reached the outskirts of the square, the London workers, in their enthusiasm, rushed upon them with cheers and greetings. Crowds at the back pushed forward to get a glimpse of the hardy Yorkshire and Notts men.

In a few minutes another contingent is approaching; it is the men from Durham and Northumberland, accompanied by thousands of workers from North London. Down Charing Cross

Road they come, the crowd now swelling forward in that direction. The bands are drowned in the roar of welcome that rises
from the crowd as the marchers, in perfect military order, swing
forward, packs on their backs, to the plinth. Then come the
Plymouth men, approaching from the south side, accompanied by
a tremendous demonstration of South-east London workers.
Higher and higher rises the enthusiasm of the enormous crowd.
On the north side again the bands are heard approaching, and
again crowds of London workers stream up Charing Cross Road.
This time it is the South Wales, Lancashire, Midlands, Staffordshire and Liverpool marchers, arriving in one body, accompanied
by a big demonstration of West London workers. The South
Wales banner is leading, and as it appears within sight of the great
mass of people in the square, roars of cheers sweep up to greet
them. Thousands of cigarettes are pitched into the ranks of the
marchers as they pass. Cinematograph machines and cameras
are working furiously to get pictures of the march; tears of joy
and excitement swell up in the eyes of the marchers as the London
workers vociferously welcome them.

Across the plinth is stretched a great white streamer, amongst
dozens of working-class banners. The streamer throws out the
words in bold letters, "WELCOME TO THE HUNGER
MARCHERS!" The great square is chock-block full, and
thousands are compelled to remain on the streets around. Then
the dense crowd sees that someone is calling for order; it is the
veteran working-class leader, Tom Mann, chairman of the
Marchers' Council, declaring the meeting open. Immediately
there is a hush and from all sides of the plinth the marchers'
speakers begin to express their message to this vast London
audience.

But there is another contingent of marchers to arrive—the men
from Scotland! They are late, but they are on the road somewhere, heading for the square. At 3.45 p.m. the people on the
roadway hear the skirl of the Highland bagpipes; the news
spreads and the great crowd turn their heads towards the west.
From the west side of the square, the Scots approach, coming
via Piccadilly. They burst in at the north-west corner by the
National Gallery, and the dense crowds on the steps of the
gallery wave and shout their welcome to the marchers as they
swing past, headed by a magnificent pipers' band, along the
balcony of the square, turning into Charing Cross Road, making
for the bottom of the square.

A dense crowd is packed upon the steps of St. Martin's church;

it cheers continuously as the column of Scottish marchers wheels round. As they proceed towards the foot of the square, the great crowd sways and roars its welcome to the courageous men from Scotland who have marched for five weeks. With the kilted pipers leading and to the cries of "Good old Scotties!" "Well done, boys!" and numerous other such greetings shouted by an exultant crowd, the Scottish marchers try to clear a gangway to the plinth.

After this welcome to the last contingent, the speeches from the plinth begin again, and time after time are interrupted by cheers and singing, and at last the host of enthusiastic workers take up unitedly the singing of the "Red Flag," and the vast assembly roar out the words:

> Then raise the scarlet banner high,
> Beneath its shade we'll live and die,
> Though cowards flinch, and traitors sneer,
> We'll keep the red flag flying here.

From amongst the crowd on the centre plinth steps forward that wonderful and lovable Irish fighter Mrs. Despard, at that time eighty-five years of age. She is helped forward and begins to address the crowd. Her appearance is the signal for a new outburst of cheering that rolls like thunder round the vast assembly as they recognise the frail, white-haired Irish veteran. She addresses the crowd with a fervour almost unbelievable in one of such a grand age, and concludes by unfurling a small green flag which she had brought over from Ireland, inscribed "Ireland greets the Hunger Marchers." The crowd cheer to the echo, and again burst into song, this time the "International."

Then from all sides of the plinth speaker after speaker from the ranks of the marchers comes forward and is greeted with rounds of cheers. From the plinth one looked down upon a sea of faces, extending far beyond the balconies of the square, overflowing in a dense mass into the roadway on all sides. It was the mightiest working-class demonstration that had ever been seen in that historic meeting-place. It was a crowning triumph for the marchers. It was the thunderous challenge that the marchers had brought to the Baldwin government on the question of unemployment.

It was turned six o'clock and dark before the way could be cleared for the marchers to proceed out of the square, and then, as they moved forward in the direction of the East End of London, the vast mass of human bodies moved forward with them into Charing Cross Road, anxious to express the warmth of comradeship to the men who had set such a splendid example to their class. The sight of the square that day will surely live in the memories of all who witnessed it. Even the anti-working class capitalist press next day had to admit that it was "a remarkable scene and a striking success for the 'reds.'" They also announced that Lord Byng, high chief commissioner of the police, and Sir Thomas Inskip, attorney-general, were there to take an account of the demonstration.

Several large halls had been placed at our disposal by the Shoreditch Labour borough council and it was in the Shoreditch district that the marchers carried out their operations from now onward against the government. On Monday morning, 25th February, the Central Marchers' Control Council visited No. 10 Downing Street to present the marchers' petition to the prime minister and request an interview the following day. Next morning a letter was delivered to the marchers' headquarters, from Mr. Baldwin, refusing the interview.

Then began our agitation around the refusal of the deputation. That same day one hundred selected men from the marchers' ranks proceeded to the House of Commons to interview Members of Parliament to demand that the question should be raised on the floor of the House. Conferences took place with a number of Welsh, Scottish and English Labour M.P.'s, and they were asked to bring the matter officially before the Parliamentary Labour Party, so that the question of the deputation could be raised in Parliament. In the evening a group of Scottish M.P.'s made a scene in the House over the refusal of the prime minister to receive the marchers.

Next day the marchers followed up with another activity. We knew that special surveillance was being kept by the police on the movements of the marchers where we were billeted, and that precautions were being taken to prevent any scenes being created by the marchers in the vicinity of Westminster and Whitehall. By a little strategy, however, we succeeded in penetrating the defences of the police on four successive occasions. On Wednesday, 27th February, a squad of selected men succeeded in getting into the public gallery of the House of Commons. At a convenient moment during the debate they created a sensation by addressing the House from the gallery. Plain-clothes and uniformed police attempted to evict them and a scuffle took place. While this was going on in the House of Commons, we had drawn the attention of the police away from that neighbourhood by holding a big route march through the dock area of London.

The day following we held a big demonstration against the government on Tower Hill, that famous venue of old-time demonstrations. From Tower Hill we decided to march to the West End, to startle the well-to-do class by our presence. An enormous force of police were marshalled against us; we proceeded, however, to the West End, through the heart of the city, at 2.30 p.m. Several times during the march through the city arguments took place with the chief of the police concerning the route, and twice it nearly came to a clash over this question.

We finally succeeded, however, against the wishes of the police, in getting into the main thoroughfares of the West End. Before the demonstration had started, an arrangement had been made for a body of picked men to drop out when the demonstration reached Charing Cross Road, and escort the deputation to Whitehall. The deputation stepped quietly out from the ranks whilst the rest of the men proceeded to march into Oxford Street. This move completely threw the police off their guard, and whilst they escorted the marchers through Oxford Street, the deputation formed up in Charing Cross Road and marched into Whitehall.

In Whitehall one policeman asked us where we were going, and we told him we were going to meet Baldwin, so he accompanied us to Downing Street. When we arrived at Downing Street, the police who are usually on guard in Downing Street were bewildered, but they recovered themselves before we reached the door of No. 10. However, on inquiry at No. 10, two of the deputation were informed that Mr. Baldwin was "not at home." From there we proceeded to the Ministry of Labour. Unable to meet anybody there, we went on to the House of Commons, where, after a few more selected marchers had gathered with us in the lobby of the House, a scene was created by the singing of the "International." After a conflict, the deputation was overpowered and ejected on to the street, but in spite of the increased police vigilance, other marchers got into the gallery of the House again and created another disturbance the same night.

The following morning, the full contingent of Lancashire and Midlands marchers moved quietly out of the marchers' headquarters and assembled at a given point near Whitehall and marched to the Home Office, to protest against the police treatment that they had received in Birmingham. The contingent leaders actually succeeded in getting into the main entrance of the Home office and demonstrated their protest, whilst the marchers demonstrated outside in Whitehall, but ultimately the police arrived in sufficient strength to clear them from the streets.

On Sunday, 3rd March, another big demonstration was held by the marchers in Trafalgar Square, and three days later the Minister of Labour announced in the House of Commons that the Government had decided to suspend for twelve months the operation of the thirty stamps clause, by which thousands were about to be struck off benefit.

The response of the workers to the march, both morally and financially, made it possible for us to arrange for the conveyance of all marchers back to their home localities by rail. Special trains were put on from all the main London railway stations and the march terminated with big farewell scenes as crowds of London unemployed gathered at the stations to bid good-bye to the men who had roused the country on unemployment in the second great national hunger march on London.

The marchers were received back in their home towns with demonstrations, socials and suppers. They had arrived in London as an organised army, and had departed in the same organised manner. There were many enemies of the march who would have liked to have seen it fail and the men stranded, but the outstanding feature that runs through the experiences of all the contingents was the real rank and file working-class support which they met. It was the instinctive class unity of these workers which made the march victorious.

The power and value of the march lay not so much in an interview with the government as in the generation of mass feeling on the question of unemployment which in turn compelled the government to suspend the operation of the thirty stamps qualification and thereby saved a quarter of a million persons from being disqualified from unemployment benefit. This was the first retreat that the government had made in its unemployment policy since the 1927 Act became operative.

One cannot judge such activities as hunger marches simply by the standard of whether an interview with the government took place, or whether definite concessions were made at the time. One has to consider the cumulative effect of the propaganda conducted by the marchers. Through town and village, on all the main roads, the marchers had driven home into the minds of millions of the population the tragedy of unemployment and the failure of the government to grapple with it or to relieve its victims.

The government had sneered when the first contingent had set out to march over five hundred miles in severe wintry weather.

The capitalist press endeavoured to ridicule it and spoke of it as an impossible task, but as the army of marchers pressed forward from town to town, as contingent after contingent arose, according to plan, to take the road, as they swept in towards London from all parts of Great Britain, a ragged, grim, determined army of men, breaking down all barriers and battling their way forward against tremendous odds, the government had cause for alarm at the way in which the people were being stirred by the marchers.

The repercussions of that courageous tramp were heard when six weeks later the Tory government resigned, and, following the general election of 1929, the Labour government came into office.

Chapter XII

THE LABOUR GOVERNMENT AND THE UNEMPLOYED

THE establishment of the second Labour government in May, 1929, raised big hopes amongst the unemployed for improvement in their conditions. It was not a majority government and consequently the workers' criticism of its omissions and weaknesses was met by its apologists with the plea that it was a government only in office and not in power.

This argument appeared on the surface to be quite plausible, but in fact it was a mere excuse for the failure to attempt a serious policy of combating the evils which capitalism had created. When a party holds all the ministerial posts it is in power, and through its ministers it can change the whole policy of administration, even if it cannot carry through any parliamentary legislation involving basic changes in society. It may be said that any change in policy on the part of the departments designed to benefit the working class would be challenged in the House of Commons. Quite true, but a government ready to meet that challenge would rally the whole working class behind it, and would come out of the conflict strengthened, not weakened.

Mr. Ramsay Macdonald, who was prime minister, met the queries and criticism of some of the Labour back benchers on one occasion be declaring "The government intends to pursue a policy of continuity"—meaning that it was not breaking in any essential principle with the policy which had been pursued by its Tory predecessors. One might say that the characteristic of the 1929 Labour government was that of proving that capitalism was quite safe in the hands of the Labour administration. It was upon this rock that the Labour government was wrecked in September 1931. Had they given leadership and inspiration to the workers in the fight against the bankers and against capitalism generally, the results of the 1931 general election would have been altogether different. Labour would have gone back in power with a mighty working-class backing.

This history of the unemployed struggles would be incomplete and misleading if we did not record the experiences of the unem-

201

ployed under the Labour government from 1929 to 1931. I must confess that I should have been much happier if I had not had cause to write this chapter in the critical strain which the facts compel.

One of the burning questions, as previous chapters have shown, amongst the unemployed when the 1929 Labour government came in was that of the mass disqualification of claimants at labour exchanges by the "not genuinely seeking work" clause. Here we must record that this clause was introduced into the unemployment insurance scheme for those on statutory benefit by the Act passed by the first Labour government in 1924. Prior to the passing of that Act the condition applied only to claimants for extended benefit, and no question of disallowance of standard benefit arose, unless the claimant refused a definite offer of employment by the labour exchange.

I think it might in fairness be claimed that the Labour government of 1924 was not aware of the drastic manner in which this clause would be later used against the unemployed; it failed to appreciate its implications. The experiences, however, under the Baldwin government up to 1929 should have convinced the Labour Party of the iniquity of the clause. The official figures, issued in the *Ministry of Labour Gazette*, of the disallowances by local insurance officers under this clause for the twelve months immediately preceding the 1929 Labour government totalled 285,685.

There were a number of other injustices which the unemployed naturally expected the Labour government to tackle, and immediately following the formation of the government the N.U.W.M. prepared an unemployed charter. This charter contained twelve points, which were briefly as follows:

1. Raise the benefit scales of the unemployed.
2. Remove the "not genuinely seeking work" clause.
3. Restore to benefit all unemployed persons who were disqualified under the previous government's administration.
4. Make benefit continuous during unemployment; no disqualification unless suitable employment at trade union rates has been offered and refused.
5. Abolish the six days' waiting period; benefit to operate from first day of signing.
6. Introduce national plans of work schemes at trade union rates and conditions.
7. Abolish all test and task work under the boards of guardians.

8. Guarantee full trade union conditions for all unemployed transferred under the industrial transference scheme.

9. Give the lead for a general shorter working day without wage reductions, beginning with the mining industry, and government establishments and government contracting firms.

10. Introduce a system of adequate pensions for all workers over the age of sixty, in order that they can retire from industry.

11. Raise the school-leaving age to sixteen, with government maintenance grants.

12. Repeal the Guardians Default Act, and establish a national uniform scale of relief, not lower than the unemployment insurance benefit scale.

Here was a charter of elementary demands, which every worker would at least expect a Labour government to consider. The unemployed movement conducted a national campaign, and found tremendous support for the charter.

On Sunday, 21st July, demonstrations took place in all the chief centres of the country in support of this charter; and from fourteen areas representatives were elected to come to London the following day as a national deputation to seek an interview with the Minister of Labour, Margaret Bondfield, and the Minister of Health, Mr. Arthur Greenwood, to urge support for the charter. The headquarters of the National Unemployed Workers' Movement had previously written to the ministers, asking that arrangements should be made for this deputation to be received. Both ministers replied stating that our request was being considered; nearly three weeks elapsed without our receiving any definite reply. A further communication was sent, to which we received a reply informing us that they could not receive the deputation.

In spite of this refusal, we decided that the deputation should come to London and press the claim for an interview. Delegates came from all parts of the country. On the morning of 23rd July, the date on which we had asked that the interview should take place, we learnt that police were posted outside the Ministry of Labour in Whitehall. The deputation, therefore, realising that their entrance to the ministry would be barred, stayed away from Whitehall that day. They expressed their intention, however, not to return to their districts without making a determined effort to compel the ministers to hear their case.

We decided next morning that the members of the deputation should individually proceed to Whitehall just before noon; that they should stand watching the Horse Guards, or reading a newspaper, or casually sauntering along the street; and that, directly Big Ben struck the first chime of noon, this should be the signal for all the members of the deputation to make for the main gates of the Ministry of Labour.

There were no police outside the ministry this day; they apparently thought that, when the deputation did not show up the day previous, they had accepted the refusal of the ministers. As Big Ben boomed out, I, along with the other representatives of the movement, who were standing separately in Whitehall, quickly made a bee-line for Montagu House, the Ministry of Labour.

We entered without ceremony, not waiting to answer any questions by commissionaires inside the gate. I knew the lay-out of the building—I had been there before, leading a deputation to previous ministers of Labour. Once inside the building, we went straight up the marble stairway, turned to the left and entered the board room, which was empty. We took up our positions at the board table. There was consternation and alarm amongst the porters and officials, who had been caught unawares by this direct action of the unemployed representatives.

One of the under-secretaries entered the board room and inquired our business. We informed him that we were there to meet Miss Margaret Bondfield; he retired to make inquires and some time later returned stating that the Minister had already informed us that she would not receive the deputation and that she had nothing further to add to her communication. Had we known exactly where the Minister of Labour was to be found, we should certainly have made our way there, but, once inside the board room, we did not want to lose our strategic position by emerging into the corridors again. In reply to the message of the under-secretary, we then asked for Mr. Lawson, the parliamentary secretary to the Ministry, stating that we would be quite prepared to place our case before him. Again the under-secretary departed and returned to inform us that our request to see Mr. Lawson was also refused.

The official then ordered the deputation to leave the building; to this we replied that we intended to remain until we were received either by the Minister or by the parliamentary secretary. Half a dozen porters and minor officials were now in the room and it was obvious that they were seriously disturbed and hesitant about what they should do. They adjourned to discuss the matter, came back, and informed us that they had received instructions from the Minister that unless we departed immediately, police would be called in and we should be forcibly ejected.

Finding that their threat had no effect upon the deputation, the officials again left. Shortly after a police inspector and a sergeant entered, and ordered the deputation to leave. They met with the same answer, so they left. Twenty minutes later were heard a general hubbub in the corridors and words of command being issued. A big force of police were mustered outside the board room, and thirty of them marched in, headed by two inspectors.

The strength of our deputation numbered only fifteen, so there were more than two police to each member of the deputation, and many more in reserve outside the room! One of the inspectors stepped forward to me and ordered us to leave; we again refused, and the inspector ordered the police to clear the room. Two policemen tackled every member of the deputation, and ultimately, with arm-twists and half-nelson holds, the deputation was ejected from the building. Following this ejection, three members of the deputation evaded the police outside the ministry and proceeded to 10 Downing Street, where they again came into conflict with the police and were arrested. They were remanded in custody for a week, bail being refused. Finally they were fined £2 each and were bound over to keep the peace for twelve months.

This treatment of a working-class deputation by a Labour government surprised many people in the Labour movement, and there were numerous protests from all parts of the country. Back-benchers in the House of Commons began openly to express their dissatisfaction with the policy of the Minister of Labour, and when members wanted to know whether the government was going to end the "not genuinely seeking work" clause, Margaret Bondfield replied to the effect that the clause was considered to be a necessary protective qualification for the unemployed insurance scheme. She proposed, however, that additional machinery for the examination of claimants should be set up in the form of boards of assessors.

The unemployed movement claimed that this simply meant an additional inquisition and would not remove the injustice. These boards were not established until November 1929; in the meantime heavy disallowances of claimants under the "not genuinely seeking work" clause continued. It is true that in the four months from June to the end of September there had been a drop in the number of disallowances, as compared with the previous four months under the Tory government, but compared with the corresponding four months of the previous year the disallowances actually showed an increase. 58,185 were disallowed in the four months of 1928, but in the corresponding four months of 1929 79,526 claimants were disallowed. When the boards of assessors began to operate in November, there was certainly an improvement, but the anger of the unemployed was rising against the administration and there was a strong resentment against what we called "the new inquisition."

The establishment of boards of assessors involved an additional investigation of claimants disallowed under the "not genuinely seeking work" clause by the local insurance officers, before they went before the chief insurance officer for endorsement. The unemployed claimed that it was not new committees of inquiry that were wanted but the complete abolition of the clause that was robbing thousands of unemployed of their benefits every week.

The National Unemployed Workers' Movement led a nationwide campaign for a boycott of the boards of assessors. Many big protest demonstrations took place. The struggle became particularly intense in Yorkshire and Lancashire where angry demonstrations were held outside the labour exchanges against the administration of the new boards; in several places these demonstrations resulted in clashes with the police. In Yorkshire there was also an organised mass refusal of the unemployed to appear before these boards. Other districts followed the lead and this gave rise to an interesting contest with the Ministry of Labour.

The managers of the labour exchanges ruled that all claimants who refused to appear before the boards of assessors would be automatically disqualified from benefit and would have no right of appeal to the courts of referees. The question of the legal powers of the boards of assessors thus came into dispute, and in face of the intense feeling expressed by the unemployed movement the chief insurance officer was compelled to give the rule that refusal to appear before the boards would not mean automatic disqualification of claimants. This was actually the death knell of the assessors. Our agitation had the effect of considerably modifying the administration of the boards, and, when the new Unemployment Insurance Act came into operation in April 1930, this machinery was scrapped.

The unemployed also had grave cause for complaint against the Ministry of Health. The policy pursued by Mr. Arthur Greenwood not only staggered the unemployed but seriously alarmed many of the local authorities with Labour majorities. He opposed an established scale of relief, and instructed the local authorities that each case must be treated on its merits. This meant that the extent and amount of relief was entirely in the hands of the guardians and their relieving officers, and the applicant had no right to claim a definite scale. The minister also insisted upon test and task work being performed by able-bodied applicants, and he threatened to remove boards of guardians for discontinuing to recover relief debts incurred by the miners.

The term "test and task work" relates to local schemes of work operated under the authority of the guardians, on which recipients of poor law relief are compelled to work on roads, parks, sewerage, wood-chopping, stone-breaking, etc., in return for which they receive no recognised wages, but a scale of relief. Test and task work had its origin in the very early poor law legislation and has been carried forward ever since as a deterrent to the receipt of relief. The methods of operating test and task work vary considerably according to locality. In some places it means doing a full week's work for merely relief tickets; in others payment is made partly in cash and partly in kind; and sometimes a real wage rate is fixed and the applicant for relief works the number of hours necessary to equal the scale of relief that would be granted.

Refusal to perform test and task work not only means that relief to the applicant can be stopped, but that the local authority has the power to prosecute the applicant who can be imprisoned on a charge of refusing to maintain his family. There have been many such cases; one example was the case of Harry Homer, a member of the Amalgamated Engineering Union, during the period of the first Labour government in 1924. Homer was an active member of the unemployed movement who was receiving relief from the Dartford board of guardians. He was ordered to do task work and refused, stating that he would readily do the work if he was paid trade union rates for it. His relief was therefore stopped by the guardians, and he was summoned on the grounds of refusing to maintain his family, and received a sentence of six weeks' imprisonment. The London district council of the N.U.W.M. protested against this imprisonment and asked the Labour home secretary, the late Mr. Arthur Henderson, to receive a deputation to discuss the case. Mr. Henderson refused. A fortnight later, following the 1st May demonstration in Hyde Park, a large number of unemployed marched to Whitehall to press for their deputation to be heard, but they were unsuccessful and the deputation was eventually removed from the Home Office by the police.

From 1924 up to the time of the second Labour government there had been similar cases in different parts of the country, and there had been strong mass agitations and strikes of relief workers organised by the N.U.W.M.. In many places we had succeeded in stopping task work completely, although the Tory Minister of Health had insisted that the regulations should be enforced.

The whole system of test and task work is demoralising to the unemployed worker; it is a cheap slave labour system and a method by which trade union principles and rates of wages are violated by the local authorities. In many cases it is sheer waste of labour and energy, because men are put on work for which they are totally unsuited and which is often quite unproductive. It destroys the chances of the applicant securing suitable employment even if it were available, because he cannot be seeking employment elsewhere when he is engaged on task work. Such work is outside the scope of the unemployment and health insurance schemes, and consequently the worker's cards are not stamped for the period that he is performing this work; he is therefore placed in a much more difficult position for securing unemployment and health benefit at a later stage. Moreover, such work is not covered by the Workmens' Compensation Acts, so that if a task worker meets with an accident he cannot claim compensation.

With the advent of the Labour government in 1929 we fully expected that the pernicious system of task work would be strongly discouraged, if not completely abolished. But what was our experience? In August 1929 the Greenwich board of guardians, with a Labour majority, passed a resolution to discontinue their system of task work. A copy of the resolution was sent to the Minister of Health, and he refused to accept the decision, informing the board that their task work must continue and that a "labour test was imperative as a condition for the granting of outdoor relief to all able-bodied persons."

In September the Romford board of guardians received a letter from the Ministry of Health complaining of the large number of able-bodied men who were being granted relief in the Romford Union and asking for a full report with the particulars of the arrangements that the guardians had for imposing a work test as a condition for the receipt of relief. Then the Dewsbury guardians received instructions from the Ministry of Health insisting that task work must be imposed and that no departure from that regulation would be permitted. The letter further laid down that the Minister could not approve the practice of the hours of work being proportionate to the amount of relief granted as was proposed by the Dewsbury guardians; the recipients of relief must be kept in full employment irrespective of the amount of relief paid. In the discussion that took place at the guardians' meeting on this letter it was admitted that in some cases there were men in Dewsbury working on test work thirty-two hours per week in exchange for relief amounting to 10s.

On 5th November, 1929, the Gateshead guardians discussed a letter from the Minister of Health in which he insisted that task work must be started and declaring that he considered it desirable that an adequate labour test should be required as a condition for the granting of outdoor relief to all able-bodied men and that he would withhold approval of any payments of relief unless it was made clear to him that at least discrimination had been used and that there were special circumstances to justify exceptional treatment.*

An anti-working-class policy was also pursued over the question of relief debts. During the lock-outs of the miners in 1921 and 1926, many of them had been driven to apply for relief. It was granted in many cases for the dependents, but the miner himself had to accept the relief on loan and give an undertaking that it would be paid back. The total amount of debt in many mining areas ran into many thousands of pounds. The miners' wages were beaten down so low that following the lock-out of 1926 it was impossible for them to keep up their repayments.

There had been numerous prosecutions and orders made against the miners committing them to pay so much a week, but in spite of these the local authorities found it extremely difficult to recover the money. In some cases they actually resorted to the practice of stopping so much out of the miners' wages in the colliery pay office, and there were threats of strike action against this in a number of pits, particularly in Durham.

The boards were compelled to recognise how difficult it was for the miners to pay the debts out of the starvation wage which they were receiving. They realised that the repayment of the money meant taking the bread out of the mouths of the men and their families, who had already been reduced to starvation existence.

*The records of this and other such cases are to be found in the *Poor Law Officers' Journal* for that period.

The result was that many boards of guardians during 1928 and 1929 discussed the question of liquidating the remaining debts and making no further effort to enforce payment. This line had met with resistance from the Tory Ministers of Health, but the local authorities expected a change of attitude under the Labour administration; but what did they find?

The Swansea board of guardians applied to the ministry for permission to cancel their relief debt of £210,000. The ministry refused to permit any cancellation whatever. In Whitehaven (Cumberland) the guardians passed a resolution to liquidate their debt of £51,000. The Minister of Health threatened to surcharge the guardians if they did so, and compelled them to rescind their resolution and to continue to collect the debt.

The Mansfield guardians asked permission to cancel the debt of £110,000. They also were threatened with surcharge if they dared to do so. The Pontefract guardians owed the Ministry of Health £16,000 which they had borrowed for relief during the 1926 lock-out. The total amount borrowed was £180,000, and out of this the sum of £164,000 had already been paid back. In respect of the remaining £16,000 they sent a deputation to the Minister in October 1929, to ask for an extension of the time for the repayment which was due to be completed by March 1930. Mr. Arthur Greenwood, the Labour Minister of Health, refused point-blank their request for any extension of time, and the chairman of the deputation in reporting to the guardians declared "The Minister of Health, Mr. Arthur Greenwood, was as inaccessible as, and no more sympathetic than, his predecessor, Mr. Neville Chamberlain."

Coupled with this failure on the part of both the Ministry of Labour and the Ministry of Health to make a turn in their policy for more favourable treatment of the unemployed, was the fact that the number of unemployed month by month continued to rise under the Labour government. In May 1929, when the Labour government came in, the army of registered unemployed stood at 1,127,000. A year later it had risen to 1,770,000. In addition there were hundreds of thousands unregistered.

Whilst this rise was basically due to the deepening of the crisis in the system of capitalism, at home and abroad, which was unfortunate for the Labour government, nevertheless the government's own policy was in no small measure responsible for the increase. Mr. J. H. Thomas, who was at that time holding the new post of Minister for Employment, himself made this clear when speaking at the Oxford Union Society on 5th June, 1930, when he said, "I have deliberately, and will continue deliberately, to proceed on the basis of a process of rationalisation in industry, which must for weeks increase unemployment figures. I have got to do this in the interests of the country."

The whole policy of the Labour government in regard to unemployment can, I think, be summarised as follows. First, it was based on the belief that any substantial reduction in the number of unemployed depended solely upon the ability of British imperialism to defeat its rivals in the struggle for world markets; therefore the government devoted itself openly to help the recovery of British capitalist industry.

Secondly, it believed that, in order to effect this recovery, there must be an intensive drive for improving the organisation and equipment of British industry and for lowering the cost of production. Accordingly, wherever the employers were prepared to adopt measures of rationalisation, the government would help them to get credit on favourable terms by pledging government support for loans.

That, in brief, was the basis of the Labour government's policy. The encouragement and open assistance to the employers in their schemes of rationalisation fitted in with the line which the T.U.C. had embarked upon following the General Strike. In the drive for rationalisation the employers broke long-standing protective practices which had been established in the past by trade union struggles; this involved the intensive application of schemes for the sub-division of labour and simplification of productive methods, eliminating more and more the need for craft and skill which at one time had given to the workers who had acquired that skill a relative security in industry. It led to a greater displacement of workers who had formerly been almost indispensable because of their technical knowledge. The whole policy led to a rapid increase in the number of unemployed.

By December 1930 the number of registered unemployed had reached 2,643,127, under the pro-capitalist policy which the Labour government was pursuing. Mr. MacDonald attempted to excuse the increase in the number of unemployed by referring to the crisis which was sweeping the world.

The failure of the government to abolish the "not genuinely seeking work" clause and remove numerous other grievances which were driving more and more unemployed into desperate poverty led to the National Unemployed Workers' Movement deciding at the beginning of February 1930 to organise a national march to London.

We knew that this meant marching in the face of bitter opposition from the official leadership in the Labour movement, both nationally and locally, but we also knew that there was a very strong feeling of support for the march amongst most of the rank and file workers, who were openly expressing their discontent at the policy of the government. The march started on 30th March, 1930, and twelve main contingents took part, coming chiefly from the following areas: Scotland, Durham, Northumberland, Plymouth, Yorkshire, Lancashire, Notts, Derby, South Wales, Staffordshire, Midlands and Kent. In this march there was a special women's contingent from the derelict textile areas of Lancashire and Yorkshire. This was the first time that women had undertaken a hunger march in Britain, and it was significant that it should happen under a Labour government, with Margaret Bondfield as the Minister of Labour.

Chiefly because of the difficulties of accommodation and feeding, the number of marchers was limited to 1,100. Mr. Arthur Greenwood, the Minister of Health, followed the example of his Tory predecessor in issuing instructions to the workhouse authorities that they must treat the marchers as casuals. Every contingent came up against this instruction many times on the march, but nowhere did any contingent accept the casual regulations. The fight for sleeping accommodation had to be conducted by the contingents on the roads to a greater extent than in any previous march. Where halls were obtained they were in the main only given under the pressure of the marchers themselves. This was clearly borne out by the fact that frequently the advance guards were only able to report success on the day when the marchers were actually reaching the particular town, very often only a couple of hours before their arrival, and sometimes not until they had actually entered the town and demonstrated for the hall.

In spite of the difficulties, the whole body of marchers reached the borders of London on the evening of 30th April. It was while the unemployed were on the road marching that the Labour government abolished the "not genuinely seeking work" clause and raised the scale of adult dependent's benefit from 7s. to 9s. per week. The march into the centre of London took place on 1st May, the day of international demonstration, and it drew forth a great response from the London workers. About thirty thousand London workers took part in the demonstrations to Hyde Park, and at the entrance to the park another 20,000 waited to welcome the marchers as they arrived. When the meetings opened in Hyde Park a dense mass of people were gathered round the platforms cheering the speeches of the marchers. Many of the capitalist newspapers even estimated the crowd at 50,000.

Finding accommodation for the marchers in London was a most worrying problem for the London reception committee. Much time was spent in looking for suitable halls, and over two hundred applications were made to private proprietors and public authorities; but everywhere the committee met with refusals. The police had become alarmed about this question of accommodation and began paying frequent visits to the offices of the unemployed movement to ascertain whether we had been successful. Two days prior to the arrival of the marchers, when it was clear that there was a boycott against us, the London reception committee decided to throw the responsibility for finding accommodation on to the Ministry of Health.

A deputation met the responsible officials connected with the poor law administration in London and informed them that they must now make themselves responsible for the accommodation of the marchers when they arrived. Consultations took place between these officials and the higher authorities and we were informed that the marchers could not possibly be admitted to the workhouses without the casual conditions being imposed. After further discussion, however, they agreed to relax some of the regulations, though not all. On the morning of 1st May another interview took place with the Ministry of Health officials, but they refused to give an assurance that casual conditions would be waived. The contingents were informed of this position while they were on the road and they expressed determination to stand out against accepting any sort of casual regulations in London.

Plans were prepared the night before the marchers entered London for the carrying out of certain militant activities to compel the authorities to grant accommodation on our terms. The first move in this campaign was made when the marchers, after the demonstration in Hyde Park, marched with the support of the London workers to the Fulham Road workhouse to demand admission. This was announced from the platforms in Hyde Park and the London workers were asked to join in the march to the workhouse. The high chiefs from Scotland Yard were in the park during the demonstration, and, when they saw that the masses were enthusiastically behind the marchers, they sent a police officer to my platform to ask for an interview with me and other leaders. We met them and made it clear that the marchers were determined to find a place for sleeping and that they were going to the Fulham workhouse first, but that they would not enter unless all regulations were waived.

It was a most impressive sight as the whole of the marchers, backed by the London workers, marched out of Hyde Park to test out the question of accommodation with the authorities. Outside the Fulham workhouse the great procession halted, whilst I went inside along with other leaders to interview the authorities. Everything depended upon the reply which we received as to whether the marchers entered or remained on the streets to fight out the issue for accommodation.

Keen tension prevailed as the marchers and the great London crowd waited outside, confronted with huge forces of mounted and foot police. Inside the workhouse we met representatives from the London poor law authorities, whilst police stood in attendance. We briefly stated that we wanted to go into the workhouse for accommodation, but that we would not enter unless all regulations in respect to casual treatment were dropped. Immediately we were informed that our conditions would be granted and that the marchers would have complete freedom of egress and ingress during their stay in the workhouse!

We returned to the waiting crowd, thousands of eager faces watching the workhouse-door as it opened, and we came out to report. Briefly we stated the results of our interview and cheer after cheer rang out from the great crowd at the victory which the marchers and the London workers had achieved by their solidarity.

The main gates of the workhouse swung open and the whole army of marchers marched in, taking possession of a huge block of buildings. The London workers then marched to their respective localities. Once inside the workhouse the marchers began to sort themselves out for their sleeping quarters, and it was not long before the workhouse master came running to me with the complaint that the marchers had hoisted a big red flag over the marchers' quarters. The flag remained flying during the whole time that the marchers were in London, in spite of the repeated appeals of the workhouse master for it to be brought down. The accommodation which we had there was excellent; every man was provided with a bed and meals were served regularly in the big dining-hall. We even had our own cooking staff, with the assistance of the workhouse cooks, preparing our own food in the cookhouse. The workhouse staff served the meals to the marchers under the supervision of the Marchers' Control Council. Such a situation had never before existed in any London workhouse.

A campaign of route marches, demonstrations and mass meetings was carried out by the marchers during the next four days. Then, on Tuesday, 6th May, an attempt was made to secure an interview with Ramsay MacDonald, the Labour prime minister. Hundreds of police were specially mobilised in the vicinity of Whitehall when the deputation proceeded to Downing Street. Mr. MacDonald refused to receive the deputation. In the afternoon the main body of marchers marched through the West End to Hyde Park; special police precautions had been taken in Hyde Park to prevent any attempt to proceed to Whitehall. Our plans, however, had been carefully laid beforehand.

Whilst the police concentrated their attention upon what they thought was the whole army of marchers in Hyde Park, three big sections of picked men simultaneously raided the Ministry of Labour, the Ministry of Health, and the House of Commons. The raiding party at the Ministry of Labour were not successful; the police had anticipated our action and stood on guard behind locked gates, but the section that was tackling the Ministry of Health, only one hundred yards away, succeeded in forcing an entry and taking possession of the board room, where they locked themselves in for over an hour.

From the windows of the room they addressed a big crowd that had assembled in Whitehall; after a struggle with the police they were finally beaten out on to the streets. The raiding party at the House of Commons, at a signal given by the group leader, charged the police barrier in the inner lobby and attempted to force their way through to the floor of the House. This meant that they had to break through the first police barrier into the outer lobby, penetrate through a narrow corridor, pass the second police barrier, and across the inner lobby to the chamber. It was a most difficult attack to carry out; they broke through the first police barrier, but, as they rushed down the corridor, the police at the inner lobby tried to slam the swing doors, police rushed up from all parts of the House and a tough fight took place in the inner lobby, with a number of M.P.'s looking on. One marcher had his face very badly cut. After fighting their way right up to the door of the chamber they were finally overpowered by the police, and nine of them were placed under arrest.

At the same time as the attack was being made inside the House, another section of the marchers demonstrated outside the main gates. The large forces of police in Hyde Park were apparently informed of what was happening around Parliament, for they were suddenly withdrawn, but before they reached Parliament an order had been given for the marchers to disperse and join their comrades in Hyde Park. The police had certainly been out-manœuvred and the marchers were able to march back to the Fulham workhouse without the usual police "protection."

The following day the marchers' campaign terminated with a great demonstration on Tower Hill. Next morning they all returned to their respective localities by special trains, for which the Marchers' Control Council had been able to arrange.

The continuous rise in the number of unemployed and the increasing insolvency of the unemployment insurance scheme led to the Labour government appointing a Royal Commission on Unemployment Insurance, which received royal warrant on 9th December, 1930. A criminal court judge, by the name of Holman Gregory, was appointed chairman of this commission, much to the astonishment of the unemployed, and, out of the remaining eight members of the commission, only two of them were known to have any sympathies at all with the Labour movement.

Yet it was to such a commission that the Labour government entrusted the task of making recommendations for the future of unemployment insurance. Towards the middle of 1931 the Minister of Labour began to press the commission for its report and it responded with an interim report in June 1931. This recommended wholesale disallowances of claims in respect to four sections of the unemployed—married women, part-time workers, casual workers, and seasonal workers, estimated to secure a saving of £5,000,000 in the unemployment insurance scheme.

In the House of Commons on 22nd June, during the debate on unemployment, Miss Margaret Bondfield said, "The government agree in principle with the recommendations of the royal com-mission and we propose to place before the House proposals to give legislative effect substantially to these recommendations." This statement was followed up by the introduction of the measure known as the Anomalies Act, under which hundreds of thousands of unemployed were subsequently to lose their benefits.

Two months later, following the royal commission's interim report, the Special Economy Committee that had been appointed by the Labour government, with Sir George May as chairman, also issued its report. This report, coupled with that of the royal commission, played an important part in the events which brought down the Labour government in August 1931. The economy commission recommended 10 per cent cuts in all benefits of the unemployed, and similar cuts in the wages of civil servants, teachers, police and the armed forces. They also recommended heavy reductions in health services, maternity and child welfare expenditure, making a total saving of £96,000,000. The chief items in the economies were:

On Unemployment Insurance	..	..	£66,500,000
„ Education	.. ..	..	13,850,000
„ Roads ..	.. ..	..	7,865,000
„ Pay and Pensions	..	..	3,875,000
„ Health Insurance	.. ..	..	1,053,000

At the end of July 1931, when this special economy report was issued, the number of registered unemployed stood at 2,713,350. The report of the economy committee was a signal for an outburst in the capitalist press, which demanded quick and drastic measures against the workers. The cabinet met and began to draw up its plan of attack. The Tory and Liberal Party leaders were called in by the Labour government for consultation from the very beginning of the special cabinet discussions.

On 12th August, 1931, the *Daily Herald*, the official organ of the Labour movement, said in a leading article: "Mr. Snowden, the chancellor of the exchequer, has warned the nation with ever increasing urgency of the need for real national economy and it can be taken for granted that the Labour government will not shirk its responsibility." The fact that the Labour government was about to launch an economy campaign at the expense of the working class immediately drew forth nation-wide protests from the workers' organisations, and particularly the unemployed, who were to bear the greatest brunt. Demonstrations of the unemployed were quickly organised in many parts of the country. On 11th August, the Clydebank workers stormed the council chambers, and six were arrested on a charge of rioting.

In the cabinet a division of opinion developed; eight out of the twenty-one ministers stood out against the economy cuts, particularly that in the benefits of the unemployed. Messrs. Macdonald, Snowden and Thomas began to negotiate with the bankers, and it was soon very apparent that the bankers were running the show. The press developed a violent campaign designed to show that the Labour government had landed the country into a state of bankruptcy. The growing opposition of the workers throughout the country drove more of the cabinet ministers into the ranks of the opposition, and finally on 24th

August, 1931, the cabinet completely split and the government resigned.

The capitalist press campaign had had its effect, and four leaders of the Labour Party, Mr. Ramsay MacDonald, Mr. Philip Snowden, Lord Sankey and Mr. J. H. Thomas completely broke with the Labour movement and joined forces with the Tories and Liberals in forming the first National Government cabinet, along with Baldwin, Neville Chamberlain, Sir Samuel Hoare, Sir Philip Cunliffe-Lister, Sir Herbert Samuel and Lord Reading.

It was truly an ignominous end for the Labour government. The vested interests which they had so faithfully served now kicked them out of office, whilst in the mouths of the workers a nasty flavour remained over the pro-capitalist policy which they had pursued. Had they been true to working-class principles, repudiated the economy proposals, stood together and fought their enemies in the House of Commons in defence of the workers' standards, demanding that the deficiencies in the capitalist system should be made good by the capitalists themselves and not at the expense of the workers, we should have seen an entirely different situation and one in which the whole working-class would have rallied to their support.

Chapter XIII

BATTLES AGAINST THE ECONOMY MEASURES

THE new drastic threat to the standards of the unemployed in the form of the economy measures led the N.U.W.M. to organise a hunger march of Welsh miners to the Bristol Trades Union Congress at the beginning of September 1931, to call upon the congress to resist the attack. All over the country trade union branches were protesting against the new onslaught, but the T.U.C., still fettered by the Mond-Turner policy of peace in industry, was giving no lead for action.

The Welsh hunger marchers arrived in Bristol on the evening of Monday, 7th September. Mr. Walter Citrine, general secretary of the T.U.C., had announced that the marchers would not be permitted to state their case to the congress—an attitude which no doubt encouraged police hostility against the marchers. Following a demonstration in the Horsefair that evening, as the marchers were about to proceed peacefully to their sleeping quarters, the police tried to ban the march and launched a fierce baton charge; six workers were arrested.

The following day, 8th September, when Parliament re-opened under the provisional National government, a big demonstration of London unemployed mobilised in British Museum Square and marched to Parliament. Severe fighting took place in the vicinity of Whitehall and eighteen workers were arrested.

Two days later the Welsh unemployed marchers marched to the Trades Union Congress hall to press for the deputation to be heard. A powerful police cordon was drawn up to prevent them from reaching their objective, but a small deputation of six under my leadership were permitted to go through the cordon. When we reached the entrance to the congress hall we found our way barred by another force of police and hefty stewards. An altercation arose, and although there were only six of us we attempted to force an entry; a fierce fight took place at the top of the high steps, whilst the main body of marchers, 300 yards away, were being held back and threatened by the main police cordon. Our small deputation were finally overpowered by police and stewards and in the melée I received a blow which cut open my head and necessitated its being stitched at the hospital.

That night in Bristol the police attempted to ban a demonstration of the marchers and threatened to make another baton charge if the demonstration was not called off. We rallied 20,000 Bristol workers in the Horsefair; this greatly surprised the police, who evidently considered discretion the better part of valour, and the marchers, along with local workers, took possession of the streets in a mighty demonstration.

In London on 9th September the eighteen prisoners who had been arrested in connection with the demonstration to Parliament on the previous day came up at Bow Street police court. Several of them received short sentences of imprisonment for assault against the police, others were fined. Ernest Oliver, when sentenced to a month's imprisonment said, "Thank you, that will solve my unemployment problem for a month!" Outside the police court thousands of unemployed thronged the streets, expressing their support for the prisoners.

In Bristol police court the six who had been arrested in connection with the march to the T.U.C. were all bound over, in spite of the fact that the police prosecution did their best to secure a conviction by producing in the court sticks studded with nails, bars of iron, rusty choppers, legs of iron bedsteads and a host of other fearsome weapons, which the police declared had been used by the prisoners.

The look of amazement on the faces of the prisoners, when these instruments of battery were carefully laid out on the table of the court, was amusing. Where the weapons had been dug up from was difficult to judge, but the prisoners indignantly protested that they had never seen them before and the magistrate obviously doubted the police evidence.

By 11th September mass demonstrations were being organised throughout the country. Not only were the unemployed marching, but the black-coated proletariat—civil servants and teachers— were also on the move against the cuts in their pay. Protest meetings of the teachers were held on the evening of the 11th in the Kingsway Hall and the Central Hall, Westminster, and thousands of teachers embarked upon a new experience, marching through the streets from the embankment carrying banners in a protest against the economy measures.

Whilst at Bristol I received a telegram from the headquarters of the N.U.W.M. informing me that Ramsay Macdonald had agreed to meet an N.U.W.M. deputation on Monday, 14th

September. I returned to London immediately. Mr. Macdonald stated that he would meet representatives of the unemployed if they were accompanied by Members of Parliament so, accompanied by James Maxton and David Kirkwood, our deputation, consisting of six national representatives proceeded to Downing. Street on the morning of 14th September. We were admitted to the entrance lobby, and our names were sent in to Mr. Macdonald. Then there appeared to be a hitch; after waiting ten minutes a messenger came to the deputation and stated that Mr. Macdonald wished to speak first to Mr. Maxton and Mr. Kirkwood. When they returned to the deputation we were informed that Macdonald was objecting to the deputation being composed entirely of N.U.W.M. leaders, and that he had said, "I will not meet Wal Hannington."

We discussed the matter in the lobby, and the general opinion of the members of the deputation was that they should not meet Macdonald without me. I was anxious, however, not to allow the opportunity to slip by for representatives of our movement to meet Macdonald, and I therefore persuaded them to carry through the deputation without me. They ultimately agreed to do so, on the understanding that they made the strongest possible protest against my exclusion.

The interview with Macdonald lasted approximately 1½ hours; the deputation expressed themselves forcibly against the economy cuts, and Mr. Macdonald either sulked whilst he had to listen to them, or pleaded that the government could adopt no other course if the finances of the country were to be restored. The same night a great demonstration of London unemployed was held in Hyde Park, at which the deputation reported the results of the interview with the prime minister. Since Mr. Ramsay Macdonald was now a renegade from the working-class movement, as prime minister of the provisional National government, the workers rightly regarded his refusal to meet me as a tribute rather than a slight.

In the House of Commons on 12th September Sir Austen Chamberlain announced that a shilling a day reduction would be made in the pay of all naval ratings below the rank of a warrant officer. For the general ratings this meant a cut of as much as twenty-five per cent. There followed on 15th September the world-startling news that trouble had arisen amongst the sailors of the British Navy, Atlantic Fleet, at Invergordon. Twelve thousand men refused to obey the orders of their officers; they held mass meetings in the naval barracks and on the ships, and decided to strike against the pay cuts. Orders were given for the fleet to sail, but the men stood firm and refused to carry out the orders. Ships' officers tried to bully the men into submission, but they were helpless. One of the ship's captains said that "the action of the men was a blow to British prestige. You (the men) have ruined 300 years of British naval tradition."

The sailors drafted a manifesto which was forwarded to the Admiralty. It read as follows:

We, the loyal subjects of His Majesty the King, do hereby present to My Lords Commissioners of the Admiralty, our earnest representations to them to revise the drastic cuts in pay that have been inflicted upon the lowest men on the lower deck. It is evident to all concerned that these cuts are a forerunner of tragedy, poverty and immorality, amongst the families of the men of the lower deck. The men are quite willing to accept a cut which they, the men, think within reason, and unless this is done we must remain as one unit, refusing to serve under the new rates of pay.

This action of the sailors at Invergordon quickly forced the government to retreat and compelled a revision in the pay cut.

The revolt of the sailors was met with warm praise in the working-class movement and it greatly stimulated the struggle of the civilian workers against the economy measures. On 19th September another big demonstration of teachers was held in Trafalgar Square; then followed demonstrations of the unemployed and battles on the streets with the police. On 22nd September 30,000 marched in Dundee, and during a conflict with the police five were arrested. On the 23rd 20,000 marched in Glasgow, and this was followed by a still mightier demonstration in the same city on the 24th, when it was estimated that 50,000 participated. With the demonstration on the 24th 500 men marched as a defence force, carrying heavy sticks, which seriously alarmed the authorities; but the police did not attack on this occasion.

A rally took place on the same day in Birmingham; again, on the 25th, Dundee saw masses of workers on the streets and another baton charge took place. Sunday, 27th September, was made a National Day of Demonstration by the N.U.W.M., and tens of thousands marched in almost every town. Forty thousand marched to Hyde Park and from Hyde Park to Wormwood Scrubs prison, where several unemployed were serving sentences for their activities in demonstrations.

On 29th September the London unemployed, with the support of thousands of employed workers, rallied in Whitehall; 40,000 marched through the streets of Manchester to the public assistance committee.   On the 30th the London postmen marched from the Embankment to Hyde Park.   On 1st October 50,000 Glasgow unemployed mobilised at Glasgow Green; the police tried to ban the demonstrations, and as the ranks were being formed for a march through the city mounted and foot police charged into the multitude of unarmed workers.   The workers, however, fought back ferociously; iron railings around the Green were torn up and used as weapons.   The fighting spirit of the Glasgow workers had been stirred by the unprovoked attack and they fought their way out of the Green on to the main roads; the battle, which had started at the Green, rapidly extended throughout the centre of the city.   For hours it raged, shop windows were smashed and extensive damage was done, and not until after midnight did the struggle come to an end.   On the following day it flared up again in certain parts of the city.

Harry McShane, the Scottish leader of the N.U.W.M., and John McGovern, M.P. for Shettlestone, were arrested along with ten others, but when they appeared in court they were acquitted, whilst thousands demonstrated outside on the streets.

On Saturday, 3rd October, the National Administrative Council of the N.U.W.M. met at the headquarters of the movement; our offices were on the first floor of a building in Great Ormond Street, Bloomsbury, and during the afternoon session of the N.A.C. a knock came at the office door, and a police officer stated that he wanted to have a word with me.   Thinking that it was some inquiry in connection with particulars of a demonstration, I went outside the office on to the landing and found myself confronted by two uniformed police inspectors and four plain clothes detectives.   I quickly took in the situation, but before I could retreat into the office they grabbed me and stated that they had a warrant for my arrest.

My colleagues in the office were not aware of what was happening until I began to resist the arrest and the noise of the struggle on the stairs caused the N.A.C. members to rush out to protect me.   I insisted upon returning to the office to settle up important affairs before being taken to the police court, and incidentally to put on my jacket.   Ultimately the police gave way and agreed that this should be done.   Fifteen minutes later I was conveyed to Bow Street police court.

I went immediately into the dock, and to my surprise, without making any charge or calling any evidence, the magistrate demanded to know if I would be bound over in two sureties of £100 each, to keep the peace for six months. I immediately protested against this astonishing procedure and the magistrate asked, "Has the warrant not been read to you?" I replied, "Yes." "Then you know the charge?" "Yes, I know the charge, but it seems that you have found me guilty without any trial whatever." He then said, "Do you wish witnesses to be called?" and I replied, "I most certainly do." "Very well, the case shall proceed."

The charge was then read over to me, namely, that I had made a speech in Hyde Park at a demonstration, inciting to a breach of the peace. Police officers gave their evidence, which conflicted in a number of details; after I had made my cross-examination of the police officers and delivered my speech for the defence, we came back to the position we had started from—the magistrate declaring me guilty and re-stating his verdict as mentioned above. I had very reliable sureties who had rushed to the court immediately following my arrest, but I realised that this action of the police was intended to restrict my activities. I also felt sure that if I accepted the terms of the verdict the police would seek an opportunity of arresting me again and the sum of £200 would therefore be forfeited. After consideration, I announced my intention to the magistrate to serve the alternative of one month's imprisonment. I was taken away to Wormwood Scrubs prison; I remained there three days, but when the authorities learned that a big demonstration was being organised to march to the prison on the following Sunday, I was removed to Pentonville prison on the other side of London.

Whilst I was being conveyed across London in the police-van a strange coincidence happened. The van was not an ordinary Black Maria but was a covered-in motor-van with small barred windows at the sides. On the journey we got trapped in a traffic jam. I was looking through the grille, and on the kerb opposite stood one of my colleagues of the unemployed movement. He was looking at the van and when he suddenly recognised me he shouted his greetings. I replied, "They're taking me to Pentonville!" He understood what this meant, and no doubt was responsible for informing the movement and changing the arrangements of the demonstration for the following Sunday, but I only remained in Pentonville two days. When the authorities found that the demonstration was now to march to that prison on the 9th October, I was again taken from my cell to be removed to another prison.

I was compelled to have handcuffs fastened to my wrists in spite of my protests to the governor, and in the company of two warders I was conveyed in a taxi-cab across London to Waterloo station. I had no idea where they were now about to take me, but I strongly resented being escorted in handcuffs before the gaze of crowds of people whilst we walked the length of the train looking for an empty carriage. We were unsuccessful in finding a carriage without occupants and the warders wanted me to go back down the platform again so that they could find the stationmaster. This I refused to do; they attempted to persuade me and then to coerce me, but without avail. I then said, "If you want the station-master, one of you can go back up the platform whilst the other remains here with me." It was unlikely that I should be able to escape with my wrists in chains, and it seemed that this was the obvious thing for the officers to do, but the level of intelligence which this service calls for was not high enough for them to think of this, though when I made the proposal to them the superior officer said, "Oh, yes, we can do that"!

When the station-master was brought he entered a carriage in which sat a bearded gentleman and what appeared to be two elderly spinsters. What he said to them I don't know, but in great agitation they scrambled for their luggage and hustled out of the carriage. I then entered with the prison officers and "Reserved" notices were posted on the carriage windows. Even now I was not aware of my destination; this was the line that ran to Dartmoor, the penal settlement, and I began to wonder whether by some remarkable stretch of the legal code I was being deposited there. The passengers on the train must have formed many strange impressions of my identity and crime. Many possibly thought I was off to Dartmoor to serve a life-sentence for some foul deed against society! They all apparently took a great interest in seeking a glimpse of the criminal aboard the train, for soon after we steamed out of Waterloo it seemed that the whole of the passengers wanted to visit the lavatory and, strange to say, they all wanted to go to the particular toilet at my end of the train. There was a constant stream of morbid-minded humans passing along the corridor and gazing into our carriage, until I ultimately protested to the warders and caused the blinds to be drawn.

My destination, however, was not the penal settlement of Dartmoor, but Winchester gaol, seventy miles from London, where I was lodged and completed my sentence.

During this period the mass demonstrations and battles on the streets with the police gathered in increasing strength in all parts of Great Britain. Two days after my arrest 100,000 workers marched in a great united front demonstration of unemployed and employed in Glasgow. This was the biggest demonstration that had ever been seen in Glasgow since the days of the forty-hour strike struggles of 1919. Repeated demonstrations occurred in London, and fierce battles took place in the West End between the police and the unemployed. Sid Elias, chairman of the National Unemployed Workers' Movement, was arrested three days after my arrest for a speech which he had delivered at Woolwich, and he likewise was sentenced to one month's imprisonment.

In Manchester 80,000 unemployed did battle with the police on 7th October, when they attempted to march to the town hall. It was one of the fiercest fights that had ever been seen in Lancashire. Fire hoses poured tons of water into the crowd in an effort to disperse them. Mounted police repeatedly charged with their sword batons, clubbing down old and young. The resistance of the unemployed was such that the fighting lasted almost three hours. Several mounted police officers were dragged from their horses and received punishment from the demonstrators.

In Bolton 20,000 marched through the streets; then on 9th October, the day following the cuts in benefit to the unemployed, came the biggest demonstration of all, when 150,000 Glasgow workers marched at night-time through the centre of the city. London followed two days later, on Sunday, 11th October, with a demonstration of 100,000 in Hyde Park, when the civil servants, many of whom had never before "lowered their dignity" to march in street processions, demonstrated from the Victoria Embankment to Hyde Park. The unemployed in Derby marched in thousands to the town council. Port Glasgow on 15th October was the centre of bitter fighting between the unemployed and the police, and ten were arrested. On the same day at Blackburn unemployed marched, along with textile workers, against the economy measures and against the "more looms system" in Lancashire. This march also resulted in a baton charge. Next day the London unemployed in their thousands swarmed to County Hall to demand relief from the London P.A.C. Repeated baton charges failed to disperse them; the fighting spread from Westminster into Lambeth and Southwark districts and continued until past midnight, with many casualties on both sides. In Cardiff on the same day the unemployed were batoned and eight were arrested.

On the 19th 40,000 Manchester unemployed marched to Strangeways gaol where one of the Lancashire unemployed leaders was imprisoned. The lace manufacturing centre of Nottingham also came into line when 20,000 unemployed marched to the P.A.C. on 20th October.

Then on the 27th October came the polling in the general election, which resulted in a sweeping victory for the National government. To many it seemed strange that when there was such a strong tumult and agitation sweeping the country against the economy measures the National government should secure a victory at the polls, but the explanation is not very obscure. The ruling class had been clever; they had plunged the country into a general election when the masses were in a political quandary and were suffering from severe disillusionment over their experiences of the two and a half years under the Labour government.

By scares about post office savings being in danger, by lies, by a terrific capitalist press barrage, by slick manipulation of the electoral machine, giving a combination of the older reactionary parties under the label of "National," the masses were made to believe that the National government would represent all that was best in the three biggest political parties, namely Labour, Tory, and Liberal, and that this was a combination which had been formed to pull the country out of the critical position which had developed in the autumn of 1931—a situation in which the nation was represented as being on the verge of collapse.

The Labour Party went into the election in a most dispirited and unconvincing way. They were feeling the backwash from the reactionary policy pursued by the Labour government, and, although they had shed the chief traitors to the Labour government, they were hesitant to give a bold lead to the workers that would inspire them and rally them for victory. The *Daily Herald*, the organ of the official Labour movement, which could have done so much to stir the class feelings of the workers against the new alliance of the old leaders with Tory reaction, actually encouraged the workers to continue to have faith in these leaders, particularly Macdonald. The paper exhorted its readers not to indulge in "personal recriminations" and it declared that Ramsay Macdonald, in spite of what he had done, "was an honest man, actuated by the highest and purest motives of selflessness for the welfare of the nation." How could such propaganda have any effect but that of encouraging the belief that the National government was a new political combination which at least should be given a trial?

The new Parliament opened on 10th November. The means test, which was part of the economy measures, and which struck such a deadly blow at the family life of the working class, making aged parents maintain their unemployed sons and daughters, making sons and daughters maintain their parents, sisters maintain brothers, etc., came into operation on 12th November. At the same time the price of the quartern loaf, the staple food of the workers, was raised by one halfpenny.

A fresh wave of mass demonstrations broke out under the leadership of the N.U.W.M., against the means test and the economy cuts. In many parts of the country, particularly in Fife, North Staffs, West Riding, Wigan, Tyneside and Yorkshire, these demonstrations compelled the public assistance committees to hold up the operation of the means test, or to at least make modifications in its application. On 16th November a great demonstration of the unemployed marched in Wolverhampton to the mayor in order to protest against the means test. Next day, fighting took place between the unemployed and the police in Shoreditch, Coventry and Great Harwood. In an effort to stop the scenes around the London labour exchanges, Lord Trenchard, the high commissioner of the metropolitan police, ordered a ban against the holding of meetings of the unemployed near the exchanges. This led to some of the fiercest fighting that had been seen in London. Day after day the unemployed fought to maintain their right to free speech and assembly outside the labour exchanges. Severe battles took place and many arrests were made all over London.

At the Barnsbury exchange, Richard Thornhill, one of the unemployed men involved in the conflict with the police, had both arms broken by the police. A condition of actual police terror existed at all the exchanges. Even if a group of unemployed workers gathered in the roadway in conversation, the police would, without ceremony, draw batons and club them down, on the grounds that they were attempting to break the ban of Lord Trenchard. Yet, whilst the police were ready to obey the orders of their superior officers and unmercifully club down the unemployed, they were themselves disturbed over their own pay cuts; on 9th December 12,000 police attended a meeting in the Albert Hall and passed a resolution of protest against the cuts in their pay. The higher authorities of the police, however, were associated with the meeting and guided it in the channels of formal protest, but no action.

On 10th December 20,000 unemployed demonstrated to the

offices of the Northumberland P.A.C. in Newcastle. Next day, 5,000 Liverpool unemployed fought with the police, whilst in Wallsend a baton charge was made against a demonstration which attempted to interview the mayor. In London on 15th December 25,000 unemployed marched, in defiance of a ban by Lord Trenchard, to the County Hall, Westminster, to demand extra winter relief, but before they reached Westminster the police drew their batons and a severe conflict took place. The same day fights occurred in Leeds, Glasgow and Kirkcaldy.

The day after, Wigan unemployed were again in conflict and three arrests were made. Then, on 18th December, a great area demonstration of the unemployed in the Potteries district took place; contingents marched in to Stoke-on-Trent from Hanley, Burslem, Tunstall, Smallthorn and Longton, to demand a meeting with the lord mayor on the question of winter relief. Fierce fighting took place outside the town hall when the police attempted to disperse the demonstration; the city council, alarmed at the position, passed a resolution not to operate the means test, but two days later they reversed their decision. Then on 21st December the anthracite miners, the strongest organised district in the South Wales Miners' Federation, issued a call for a one-day strike against the means test. The same day the Bootle unemployed compelled the P.A.C. to grant extra winter relief for adults and children and a special coal allowance.

So ended the year 1931, with a new government, and with the masses in action against that government from the moment that it took office.

Chapter XIV

1932—BARRICADES IN BELFAST AND BIRKENHEAD

THE storm against the means test and the cuts in unemployment benefit continued to intensify in the year 1932. On
12th January police fighting against the unemployed took place
in Keighley and Glasgow. Three days later in Rochdale the police
charged an unemployed demonstration outside the town hall; the
conflict became so severe that territorials were called out to guard
the door of the town hall, and eleven unemployed workers were
arrested.

Again on the 18th, when Harry McShane and twelve others
appeared in the police court in Glasgow, thousands of unemployed
massed outside the court. While the case was proceeding, the
police drew their batons and charged into the crowd in an effort
to clear the streets, but before the fighting ended McShane and
the other prisoners had a verdict of "not guilty" returned.

The cause of the bitter resentment which was being expressed
by the unemployed was revealed in the figures given in the House
of Commons on 9th February by the Minister of Labour, when he
stated that in a period of approximately nine weeks, between
12th November, 1931, and 23rd January, 1932, there had been cut
off from benefit at the labour exchanges, by the operation of the
means test, 193,542 men and 77,995 women. Coupled to this was
the fact that those who continued to draw benefit had their scale
reduced from 17s. to 15s. 3d., and the amount of adult's dependent
allowance was reduced from 9s. to 8s., whilst the cost of living was
rising.

On 21st February 1,500 Scottish hunger marchers from all
parts of Scotland entered the city of Edinburgh, led by Harry
McShane, to demand the restoration of the cuts and the abolition
of the means test. 23rd February again saw the London unemployed in battle in Parliament Square, and 15,000 unemployed
against the police in Bristol.

The next day at Cardiff Assizes came the verdict of "guilty"
against the well-known miners' militant leader Arthur Horner, in
his trial. His crime had been that he, along with other miners in

230

Mardy, had endeavoured to prevent the eviction of a miner's family. A crowd had gathered outside the house and Horner went in to speak with the bailiff's men. The crowd were quite peaceful, when suddenly a large force of Glamorganshire police were rushed to the scene. Horner was negotiating with the authorities over the withdrawal of the eviction order, which was ultimately obtained. There had been a slight brush with the police, but nothing serious. Then later, to the astonishment of the Rhondda workers, Horner and twenty-eight well-known militant unemployed miners of Mardy were arrested on warrants. They were charged with riotous behaviour.

The police evidence, particularly against Horner, was of the most astounding nature—it even charged him with being responsible for the closing down of the pits in the Rhondda! It made him out to be an agent of a foreign power and asserted that he had terrorised the population of the Welsh valleys, breathing fire and revolution. Such utter nonsense was solemnly brought forward as evidence. Horner was sentenced to fifteen months' hard labour for the crime of having negotiated with the bailiffs to save a working-class family from being evicted on to the streets on account of arrears of rates caused by unemployment. The others in the trial were given sentences totalling seven years' hard labour.

From all over Great Britain protests poured into the Home Office. Under pressure of these protests the sentence on Horner was ultimately reduced to one of twelve months.

On 3rd March, 1932, a great demonstration took place in Dundee. The police opened the attack and seventeen arrests were made. The police made particular efforts to arrest McShane, the Scottish unemployed leader, but the crowds of workers protected him and succeeded in getting him away. The police knew that he had come from Glasgow for the demonstration and that night they watched all railway stations and main roads out from Dundee, but McShane kept under cover in Dundee that night and next day effected an escape.

Then in Birmingham 40,750 signatures were secured to a hurriedly-prepared petition and presented to the lord mayor of Birmingham calling for the abolition of the means test. On 14th March the greatest demonstration ever seen on Tyneside took place against the means test and the cuts on the Newcastle Town Moor; it is estimated that 100,000 participated. 3rd April was made a National Day of Demonstration against the means test by the unemployed movement. In spite of pouring rain, huge demonstrations took place in all the principal centres. In London, as the masses were converging on Trafalgar Square, the police made a baton charge on the East London contingent, but failed to break them up. Wholesale disallowances of claims under the means test were still continuing, and Sir Henry Betterton, the Minister of Labour, stated in the House of Commons that the claims disallowed up to 20th February numbered 377,512. About the same time the report of the Minister of Health was issued and showed that there were 1,143,025 persons (or 286 in every 10,000 of the population) in receipt of poor law relief in England and Wales on 1st January, 1932. This was an increase of 128,092 compared with the previous year. The Minister of Health stated that up to March 1932, there were 15,795 persons entering casual wards, this being 4,000 more than in the previous year, and the highest on record for twenty-five years.

In the early part of March the National Unemployed Workers' Movement began the organisation of a great national protest against the means test. A conference took place on 28th and 29th May, 1932, in the Shoreditch town hall. 657 delegates from all sections of the working-class movement attended, representing nearly half a million organised workers. Plans for the development of the campaign were laid down at this conference; these included the organising of a national hunger march to London, and the presentation to Parliament of a monster petition against the means test and the cuts.

Right through the summer of 1932 the agitation continued. At a demonstration in July at Castleford, an old worker by the name of Arthur Speight died, which caused intense indignation. Six Castleford leaders of the N.U.W.M. were sent to prison for periods ranging from six to fourteen months. Into all the branches of working-class life went the monster petition, and the workers eagerly signed. The petition read as follows:

We, the undersigned citizens, in view of the increasing poverty amongst the working class, arising from the operation of the present Economy Measures, do hereby speak our demands on the National Government for:

1. The abolition of the means test.
2. The abolition of the Anomalies Act.
3. The restoration of the ten per cent unemployment Benefit cuts.

4. The restoration of the cuts that have been made in the social services.

The pressure of the workers within the trade unions upon those leaders who were still clinging to the "peace in industry" policy of Mondism began to have its effect, and at the 1932 Trades Union Congress in Newcastle, which opened on 6th September, a district march was organised by the N.U.W.M. When a card vote was taken in the congress for or against receiving the N.U.W.M. only a few votes short of a million were cast in favour, and 1,570,000 against. The miners' card vote, representing nearly half a million trade unionists, was cast by the officials against the deputation being received; this led to strong protests being made by the rank and file miners' delegates from the districts, who knew that the vote of their Federation had not been cast in accordance with the wishes of the membership. Had it not been for the way in which this vote was cast, the voice of the organised unemployed would again have been heard on the floor of the Trades Union Congress, breaking the silence that had reigned since the right-wing policy had been introduced after the General Strike.

Shortly following the congress came the report of heavy battles on the Merseyside, particularly in Birkenhead. On 13th September 10,000 Birkenhead unemployed demonstrated to the Public Assistance Committee with the following simple demands:

Relief to all able-bodied unemployed and an increase of 3s. per week; immediate supply of boots and clothes and one hundredweight of coal during the winter; and the starting of work schemes at trade union rates.

The deputation was received and stated its case before the town council, whilst outside the town hall masses of unemployed awaited the results of the interview. Fuel was added to the fire of indignation amongst the people in Birkenhead over their poverty conditions when hundreds of police were drafted in from Liverpool and the surrounding areas. The great demonstration was, however, quite orderly, as the deputation, led by Joe Rawlings and Mrs. Barraskill, returned to report that the council had agreed to send a telegram to the government that day calling for the abolition of the means test. They had also agreed to institute work schemes at trade union rates to the total value of £180,000.

As the unemployed began to march away, the police interfered with the procession, a conflict took place, and a number of arrests were made. Two days later the unemployed again demonstrated outside the P.A.C. offices to secure improvements in their relief scales, and later outside the house of the chairman of the P.A.C. to express their dissatisfaction and to demand the release of the workers who had been arrested at the previous demonstration. The demonstration was quite peaceful and orderly, but suddenly large numbers of police were ordered to draw their batons and they began to club to the ground demonstrators and pedestrians, including men, women and children, the aged and the infirm.

This roused the feeling of the whole of Birkenhead, and that night a tremendous demonstration assembled at the park gates as a protest against the police action. After short speeches they formed up and marched round the town, returning to the park gates, and when the demonstrators were just about to disperse to their homes the police, without any apparent reason, made a baton charge. Unemployed and employed workers stood their ground, and one policeman was thrown through a plate-glass window. The crowd took up the offensive and the police were ultimately compelled to run; but they rallied again and a pitched battle ensued. Workers tore up railings to defend themselves, and the fighting went on until past eleven at night, thirty-seven policemen being carried to hospital.

Most of the wounded amongst the workers were taken into the homes of their class to have their wounds dressed, in order that they should not be marked for police arrest. Next day a further huge force of police were drafted into the town, coming from as far away as Birmingham, until the town looked like an armed camp. The police marched through the streets in military fashion in order to intimidate the workers. Another great demonstration took place, and again the police, now in great numbers, unmercifully beat up the demonstrators; but the courage of the workers was unbounded; handicapped and unarmed they fought back. The resistance of the workers appeared to drive the police frantic, and according to the reports, carefully verified afterwards, they began a campaign of terror.

At midnight they raided working-class streets, smashing the lower windows with their batons, in order to terrify the women and children. Joe Rawlings and the whole of the branch committee of the N.U.W.M. were arrested at midnight and taken away in a Black Maria. In the early hours of the morning groups of police forced their way into working-class houses and assaulted workers who were known to have been associated with the demonstrations.

The police terror continued the next night, and, as they entered working-class streets to beat up the inhabitants, the workers fought back by every possible means. Wire was stretched across the streets, over which the police stumbled, one falling into a man-hole, the cover of which had been conveniently removed. Ash-cans and other missiles were flung at the police in the streets from the windows of working-class houses. The night of Sunday, 18th September, was one that the workers of Birkenhead will ever remember. Lorry-loads of police descended upon blocks of thickly-populated tenements in the dead of night. Their pretexts were that they were "searching for loot," claiming that the workers had looted the shops in the demonstration. In the investigations afterwards, carried out by the International Class War Prisoners' Aid, women stated that their husbands and sons were dragged from their beds by the police, and beaten into unconsciousness, and then flung into the waiting Black Marias, with blood streaming from head, face and body wounds. They were carried off to the courts to be charged with riotous behaviour and assaults on the police, and then transferred to the hospitals to have their wounds dressed.

The severity of the police terror can be gauged from the fact that over one hundred workers were taken to hospital with severe injuries, including cases of broken pelvis, fractured ribs, broken arms and legs. One worker who had been badly beaten-up drank ammonia. He died later, and at the inquest it was stated that when the police were informed of what he had done, they replied, "Go back and tell him to take some more." This evidence was printed in the press without any coroner's comments. Further arrests on the Sunday night brought the total up to forty-four, one of whom appeared in court a week later on a stretcher.

Bob Lovell, who was at that time in charge of the I.C.W.P.A., went into the district to conduct investigations. He later reported the following evidence:

Mrs. Davin, the wife of D. Davin, an ex-service man invalided out of the Army, having been gassed, said:

"On Friday, Setember 16th, the police came at midnight to the houses of St. Anne's Street, smashing the windows back and front with their batons, entering the houses and batoning the occu-pants. This terror lasted until 4 o'clock in the morning.

"Next night, further attacks were made in St. Anne's Street, Payson Street and Victoria Street, and the screaming of the women and children was pitiful. Men fought back against this terror but were overwhelmed and arrested and bundled into the waiting Black Marias. The worst night of all was Sunday; we were fast asleep in bed at Morpeth Buildings, having had no sleep the previous nights, and my husband was very ill. My old mother, aged 68, is paralysed and could not sleep, she was so terrified. I have five children—a daughter 19, one 15, and sons 17, 12 and 6. Suddenly we were all awakened at the sound of heavy motor vehicles. Hordes of police came rushing up the stairs of Morpeth Buildings and commenced smashing in the doors. The screams of women and children were terrible, we could hear the thuds of the blows from the batons and the terrific struggles in the rooms below, on the landing and on the stairs. Presently our door was forced open with a heavy iron instrument by the police. Twelve police rushed into the room and immediately knocked down my husband, splitting open his head and kicking him as he lay on the floor. The language of the police was terrible. When I tried to prevent them hitting my husband they commenced to baton me all over the arms and body; as they hit my husband and me the children were screaming, and the police shouted: 'Shut up, you parish-fed bastards!' My eldest daughter, aged 19, also tried to protect me and her father. She too was batoned. In the next room my younger daughter, aged 15, and the other children were with my mother, too terrified to move. The police then smashed open their door and attacked the other children. They flung my husband down the stairs and put him in the Black Maria, where several other injured workers lay. I was in my night-clothes and rushed back into bed after they took my husband out, not knowing what to do. A picture of my husband in Army uniform, taken in India, was in a large frame, hanging on the wall, and before the police left they smashed this to smithereens with their batons. After taking my husband to the police station and charging him, he was then taken to the General Hospital, where it was found he had six open head wounds, one over the eye, and injuries to the body."

Interview with Mrs. Sullivan, who said:

"On Sunday, the night of the raid, I and my husband were in bed and my younger brother, 17 years of age, and older brother, were in another room. We were awakened by the screams and noise, but I was too terrified to move. One of my brothers opened the door, and the police pounced on him, batoning him right and left. They then set about the younger brother as he lay in bed; he had been working and could not have taken part in the recent demonstration. Ten officers came back and searched my house just as I was going back to bed. The door lock was smashed and they just walked in as I was undressing. I said, 'What have you come back for? Can't you see my condition—have you no

sense of shame?' They replied, 'You have some loot here,' and
they then commenced to search the room."

Such is the evidence that gives a glimpse into the character of
the terror which raged in Birkenhead, simply because the unemployed were demanding bread and work schemes. The resistance
of the workers was such, however, that at one time the mayor of
Birkenhead made an appeal for military assistance.

On the fourth day after the fighting had started, the P.A.C.
decided to raise the scales of relief from 12s. to 15s. 3d. for men
and from 10s. to 13s. 6d. for women. There were a total of forty-
five workers placed on trial in connection with the Birkenhead
struggles. The leader of the unemployed, Joe Rawlings, was
sentenced to two years' imprisonment, and Leo McGree, the
Liverpool unemployed leader, received a similar sentence for his
part in connection with the struggle.

During the battles in Birkenhead, Liverpool—just across the
Mersey—was quiet, but three days later, on 21st September,
20,000 Liverpool unemployed marched on the streets, and prolonged battles took place with the police; but the struggle in
Liverpool had come too late to help the Birkenhead workers.

Then came the start of the Scottish marchers, the first contingent in the great 1932 national hunger march, setting out from
Glasgow on 26th September with tens of thousands of Glasgow
workers mobilised on the streets to give them a send-off in their
great trek to London for the presentation of the monster petition
against the means test and the cuts.

Two days later fierce fighting broke out in West Ham between
the unemployed and the police, when 20,000 unemployed marched
on the streets against the means test. Hand-to-hand struggles
took place between the police and the unemployed, extending
late into the night, and several arrests were made. Then, on 3rd
October, came news of fighting in Croydon, a locality that had
always been regarded as quiet and respectable. Next day, West
Ham unemployed were again on the streets in a battle with the
police, and then North Shields came into the picture when the
police made a baton charge against a demonstration marching
to the P.A.C. on 5th October.

That same day information came to the National Unemployed
headquarters in London concerning the struggles that had
developed in Belfast, and within twenty-four hours the press were
full of reports of severe fighting amongst the Irish unemployed
against the police. It started over a strike of 2,000 Belfast unem-

ployed who were being compelled to do relief work in exchange for a poor relief pittance. The maximum outdoor relief even for a man, wife and family had been fixed at 24s., and single men and women had been completely refused relief. Negotiations took place between the Irish Unemployed movement and the mayor of Belfast, who offered some concessions with the object of dividing the strikers and the mass movement. These were defeated by the unanimous vote of the strikers; then commenced mass marches, and demonstrations and collisions took place with the police on several occasions. The movement spread to Derry, a small border town, between north and south, where there were over one thousand families in starvation. The strike of the task workers in Belfast met with a wide response from the workers in employment. In a few days a relief fund of over £300 was raised and large supplies of food and clothing began to pour into the strike centre. The struggle was gaining momentum hour after hour. On Monday, 10th October, the Relief Workers' Strike Committee called for a rent strike and a school strike, and demanded from the authorities an increase in the scales of relief.

Bonfires were lit in the workers' quarters and round them gathered thousands of workers who were addressed by the unemployed leaders. The city of Belfast became an armed camp, thousands of police being imported. They vainly tried to intimidate the workers, and, heavily armed, they dashed through the streets in armoured cars. At several points the bonfires were extinguished, but the workers relit them. A special mass demonstration of women was held in St. Mary's Hall; they pledged themselves to stand shoulder to shoulder with their menfolk in the fight. On the following day, Tuesday, 11th October, workers were gathering everywhere in groups to discuss the events of the previous night and everywhere expressing the determination to stand solid against their starvation conditions. The police began to charge the crowds as they gathered, but after the first shock the workers met them with a hail of stones, and when the police got within striking distance of any body of workers a series of fierce battles broke out. Armoured cars were called out and drove into the crowds wherever they assembled. Squads of workers rushed to the sites of the relief work jobs and seized the tools with which they had been compelled to slave for a starvation pittance; armed with these, they returned to the demonstrations and fought desperately against the police.

In the Falls and Shankhills districts very fierce hand-to-hand battles ensued; whilst the police used their batons, the workers used pickshafts and other weapons. Failing to intimidate and defeat the workers, the police then opened fire from rifles and revolvers. Five workers fell to the ground, so badly wounded that they had to be removed to the hospital, whilst others with lesser wounds were treated in the homes of comrades. The workers threw up barricades against the mounted police and the armoured cars; bravely fighting behind these barricades they repeatedly repulsed the attacks of the police. That night a police curfew was enforced in Belfast for the first time since the Irish struggles for independence in 1922.

On Wednesday, 11th October, the fighting continued. One of the workers shot down the day before had died in hospital; British troops now came into action against the unemployed and the workers. Seven lorry-loads of Royal Inniskilling Fusiliers, equipped with machine-guns, were drafted into the city. Two more workers who had been shot down on the Tuesday lay in a critical condition, but in spite of this display of armed force the surging mass movement of the hungry Belfast workers could not be quelled. Despite martial law, mighty demonstrations of unemployed and employed took place in the main streets. A police attack which was made in an effort to prevent a demonstration from reaching Balaclava Road was repulsed by the workers with volleys of stones, and again the police opened fire with rifles. In Albert Street workers were shot down and had to be removed to hospital. In Osmond Street the workers beat back the police and chased them; the police were stoned as they ran, and only when further reinforcements were brought, who opened fire, did the police hold their ground.

Barricades appeared in the working-class quarters, while lorries conveyed forces of police into the storm areas. In some streets, where the police got the upper hand, they compelled the workers at the point of the bayonet to remove the barricades. In the Falls area, workers actually tore up the flagstones and dug trenches across the streets. Before the day was over fifty workers were suffering severe injuries from gunshot wounds, while hundreds of other were injured by clubs and other weapons used by the police.

The lord mayor of Belfast and representatives of the Ulster government called a hurried meeting with trade union representatives to discuss whether anything could be done about the relief rates. The demands of the unemployed were for full trade union rates of wages for all those on relief work, workers to be employed a week-about; outdoor relief to be on the same scale as in England. The battle-cry of the Belfast workers was, "We want bread!"

Support for the unemployed in their struggle came from the employed workers in all parts of Ireland, irrespective of whether they were Catholic or Protestant. A mass meeting of 3,000 workers in the linen mills in Belfast declared for strike action in sympathy with the unemployed. On Wednesday night the Belfast Trades Council passed a resolution in favour of a General Strike, and called upon the unions to take up the issue immediately.

During the night of Wednesday another worker who had been shot down by the police died in hospital. The fighting continued through the night and into Thursday. Then the 2nd Battalion of the King's Royal Rifles arrived from Tidworth. During the day conferences were resumed between the Belfast authorities and the Northern Ireland government. The Falls Road district was an extraordinary storm centre, barricades were everywhere in the streets. In an effort to smash the resistance of the workers in this district the police stopped the delivery of food by any tradesmen. By Thursday night there were hundreds of workers under arrest. Then came Friday, 14th October; Tom Mann, the national treasurer of the National Unemployed Workers' Movement, went over to Belfast to represent the British workers in the great funeral procession of those who had been murdered in the streets. Tens of thousands marched in the funeral cortège on Friday to Milltown Cemetery. Large forces of police were in attendance and the military were being held in readiness. Armoured cars moved along with the funeral procession and the whole funeral took place under the guns of those who had shot down the unarmed workers for protesting against their starvation conditions.

Tom Mann marched at the head of the cortège. At the gates of Milltown Cemetery the police placed him under arrest. Let Tom tell the story in his own words, as it appeared in the workers' press at that time:

"I arrived in Belfast at 6.30 a.m. on Friday morning, October 14th, and my first surprise was to see 500 soldiers disembarking and lining up for marching. I had the attention of the 'tecs from the first jump off the boat; they didn't interfere with me in any way during the morning, beyond that of following me wherever I went. I joined in the great funeral procession of Comrade Baxter in the afternoon, the other comrade having been buried during the morning. I was by the coffin the whole 2½ hours—

the time it took to march through the city, whilst hundreds of thousands lined the sidewalks to the gates of the cemetery. Whilst the funeral ceremony was on, I turned away from the general body to proceed to an important meeting to discuss the arrangements for a big demonstration later in the evening. With the vast crowd unaware of what was happening, I reached the gates of the cemetery; a police detective touched me on the shoulder and said sharply, 'You'll come along with us, Mr. Mann.' I said 'What are you—the police?' 'Yes, the police station is only two minutes away. You'll accompany us there and will learn what is wanted.'

"On arrival at the police station I was informed that I must go at once to police headquarters in the city, and that a conveyance was waiting to take me. This conveyance turned out to be an armed police car, with a bird-cage arrangement. Suffice it to say this was packed with police, with their revolvers handy and only just room enough left for me. At police headquarters I was told by the chief superintendent that he was responsible for my arrest and that a deportation would follow. He asked 'Was it your intention to hold public meetings?' I said 'It certainly was,' and that I was intending to hold a meeting at the Customs House steps on Sunday night. He then said that would be impossible, as they could not allow such a gathering. A long talk ensued, but it finished by my being handed an expulsion order to be operated forthwith. This was at 5.30 in the evening, and at 8.30 I was taken in a car to the boat, which left at 9.15."

The same day that Tom Mann was deported from Ireland, the terrific struggles of the workers and the impressive funeral scenes compelled the Northern Ireland government to grant considerable concessions as follows:

The scale of relief for man and
wife was raised   ..   ..   from 8s. a week to 20s. a week
Man, wife and 1 child   ..   from 12s. a week to 24s. a week
Man, wife and 2 children ..   from 16s. a week to 24s. a week
Man, wife and 3 children ....   from 20s. a week to 28s. a week

Beyond that number of children up to a maximum of 32s., a week, as against a previous maximum of 24s. a week.

Concessions also had to be made in the character of the relief work. Following these concessions the struggle gradually subsided, but thousands of meetings and demonstrations were held thoughout Ireland and Great Britain to protest against the violence which had been used against the unemployed.

The heroic struggles of the Belfast unemployed will live long in the memory of Ireland. The blood of the workers killed and the hundreds wounded is on the hands of the Northern Ireland ruling class, who starved the unemployed into revolt and then mercilessly shot them down on the streets when they asked for bread.

Chapter XV

THE PETITION TO PARLIAMENT IN 1932

WHILST the struggles of the unemployed were raging in Birkenhead and Belfast, the army of hunger marchers from all parts of Britain was moving down the main roads to London, rousing millions of the workers in towns and villages against the means test and the benefit cuts. They were again having to smash through the casual regulations which the Ministry of Health sought to impose through the workhouse authorities, but the mass movement which was surging up and around the marchers everywhere was stronger than ever before. The events of Birkenhead and Belfast were rousing the fighting spirit of the British workers, and with their support the hunger marchers were breaking through to London, overcoming all obstacles.

The Lancashire contingent were due to arrive at Stratford-on-Avon on 20th October. This sleepy Shakespearean town has no big industrial population. The Stratford-on-Avon Labour Party refused to help the marchers, and so they had to enter the workhouse for food and accommodation. The authorities thought that there was a good opportunity to impose the Ministry of Health regulations in a town where the marchers would have to battle alone, without the support of any considerable number of workers. There can be no doubt that the move was deliberately planned by the authorities, for they brought into Stratford-on-Avon hundreds of police from the areas of Birmingham, Worcester and Gloucester.

Once the marchers had entered the workhouse they realised how they had been trapped; they demonstrated against the regulations and succeeded in breaking them down in respect to the meals that day. But at night large bodies of police were drafted into the building, and next morning, when the marchers demonstrated again against the casual diet conditions, the police suddenly opened an attack upon them in the grounds of the workhouse and battered them right and left with their truncheons.

The leaders of the contingent were seriously wounded about the head and face, as were many of the men. They were not even

243

permitted to have their wounds dressed in the institution, although many of them had their heads bleeding profusely after the stubborn battle which they had put up against the police. When they marched out from Stratford-on-Avon they were accompanied by huge forces of police on their flanks, while others trailed behind in lorries and vans. Their destination that day was Chipping Norton; the police left them before they reached the town, and the news of the struggle having travelled before them the authorities did everything to make them comfortable.

News of the Lancashire marchers' struggle in Stratford-on-Avon reached me on the morning of the 22nd, when I was with the Scottish contingent about to march from Banbury to Buckingham. Immediately the Scottish marchers heard what had happened to their Lancashire comrades, they wanted to divert their contingent in order to march to their aid, but it was then too late. Had we been informed of the tension which existed in Stratford-on-Avon we could have drawn into that town several of the north-country contingents which were all within a distance of twenty-five miles.

It would, of course, have been a great risk, but I think the men would have wanted to go to the aid of the Lancashire comrades. As it was, I decided to go across with a small group of Scottish marchers to meet the Lancashire men as they came into Oxford. We went to the outskirts of the town to meet them, and I shall never forget the sight of their approach. There were men with their heads swathed in bandages, others with arms in slings, and many, with leg injuries, limping along; but their spirit was undaunted. A magnificent reception committee had been set up in Oxford; many of the progressive-minded students, having heard of the condition of this contingent, had set up a special dressing-station in the Corn Exchange, where the marchers were to be accommodated. During the whole evening a fine group of militant university undergraduates attended to those who had been injured in the battle, and huge protest meetings were held in Oxford.

In this national march there was a women's contingent which had mobilised at Barnsley on 9th October. The women came from different parts of the north country and were on the road marching for a period of nearly three weeks. They also had to struggle against the casual regulations which some of the authorities attempted to impose. When they entered Burton-on-Trent they discovered that the letter from the National March Council which had been addressed to the trades council and labour party of this town, asking them to arrange a reception for the women marchers, had simply been handed to the police, who had been informed that the trade union and labour movement of that town would not be associated in any way with the march.

The authorities no doubt thought that the marchers were isolated from the rank and file workers and that casual conditions could be insisted upon. They discovered their mistake, however; the women marchers refused to enter the workhouse when they learned that casual conditions were to apply; they demonstrated through the town and held two of the biggest mass meetings ever seen in Burton-on-Trent, with wonderful rank and file support from masses of workers. The police endeavoured to persuade them to accept the regulations, but to no avail. During the evening the mayor called a special meeting of the Public Assistance Committee to discuss the matter. At eleven o'clock at night thousands of workers marched with the women to the workhouse to demand admission and the waiving of the regulations.

Negotiations took place between Maud Brown, who was in charge of the women's contingent, and the workhouse authorities, who were at first adamant. But the tremendous support of the Burton-on-Trent workers behind the marchers ultimately compelled the authorities to climb down, and the women entered the workhouse at 1 a.m. with all the regulations withdrawn.

Whilst these scenes were occurring on the roads, the London unemployed were not only preparing for a great welcome to the marchers, but were themselves carrying out a tremendous struggle against the means test, for higher scales of relief, and for work schemes at trade union rates. Tuesday, 18th October, was the day that Parliament reopened, and on this day the London unemployed marched to County Hall, opposite the House of Commons. The mobilisation centre for all the contingents was St. George's Circus, and all traffic was blocked as the demonstrators streamed into this circus from all parts of London. The time of assembly clashed with the rush hours of late afternoon, and soon the traffic of the circus was completely disorganised. By five o'clock about eight thousand workers had gathered in this circus, but still no full contingent of demonstrators had yet arrived. By six o'clock, the news came through that the police had attacked every contingent that was on its way to the centre, and there had been severe fighting in many districts. Despite this, the contingents that had been broken up in the localities began to pour into St. George's Circus by seven o'clock. Then the police opened an attack in the circus and tried to drive the demonstrators into the surrounding streets.

The unemployed rallied again and again and the foot police soon found that the task was beyond them, for as soon as they drove one section of the workers back, others surged forward, and the north side of the circus again became completely blocked to traffic. Mounted police then tried to ride their horses through the dense masses of workers, amid derisive shouts. They charged up and down the pavements, trying to drive the workers down the side streets. Many were injured in the fighting and had to receive medical attention. Then the order was given for the crowd to make for County Hall; the police did their utmost to prevent them from getting through, and a bitter struggle took place. In Oakley Street a pitched battle took place, the workers using bricks and stones against the police, who were compelled to run for shelter. Not until late in the night were the police finally able to disperse the demonstration.

The deputation from the unemployed had succeeded in getting through to the County Hall and had been met by Sir William Ray, the leader of the Council, Mr. Jacobs, Chairman of the General Purposes Committee, and Mr. Charles Latham, the deputy leader of the Labour Party opposition in the Council. Their case, however, was referred to the full meeting of the General Purposes Committee, which was not due to meet until the following Monday. The London District Council of the unemployed therefore decided to follow up with another great demonstration to County Hall on that day.

In the second demonstration to County Hall, the London unemployed raised a new demand, namely, that of providing proper accommodation for the hunger marchers when they arrived three days later. Up to that time the authorities had been adamant and would make no arrangement with the marchers' central organising committee. The police had obviously been alarmed by the severity of the fighting which had taken place on the 18th, and on this occasion police barricades were erected in the vicinity of the County Hall, in order that they could more effectively combat the demonstrators if they attempted to reach the building. Several thousand police, including mounted men, were on duty; some hundreds were inside the building; police were concealed even in St. Thomas's Hospital opposite.

When the first groups of demonstrators began to assemble mounted police rode into them, even though they were on the pavements, and broke them up. Some tens of thousands of unemployed tramped from all parts of London in a downpour of rain in order to back up the deputation. When the deputation entered County Hall the General Purposes Committee refused to receive more than five, but after heated argument they gave way and eight members were received. After the deputation had stated their case, the Committee agreed that accommodation would be provided for the hunger marchers and informed them that the other points in their demands would be further considered by the committee. There were a few skirmishes on this day, but the fighting was not so serious as it had been six days previously. Had the deputation been refused, then possibly the unemployed would have expressed their resentment, and clashes would have taken place with the police.

On the night of 26th October nearly two thousand five hundred hunger marchers from all parts of Great Britain reached the outskirts of London. The Scottish and North Staffs contingents were in Willesden; Northumberland, Durham and Teeside at Edmonton; the women's contingent at Holloway; Plymouth and Southampton at Acton; Lancs., Merseyside and the Midlands at Chiswick; Yorkshire, Notts and Derby at Tottenham; South Wales and Herefordshire at Hammersmith; Norfolk at West Ham; Kent at Deptford, and the south-coast men at Wimbledon.

Such were the positions of the men and women who had been marching for weeks in severe weather in order to present to Parliament the great petition, which now had a million signatures, against the means test and for the restoration of the economy cuts. They had steadily closed in upon London, like a besieging army, arousing tremendous enthusiasm amongst masses of the workers along all the roads through which they had passed. The battles in Merseyside, the shootings in Belfast, the bitterness of the struggles in London and other places, had created a tremendous feeling of agitation and class solidarity amongst the workers, and on the part of the government and the ruling class generally there was evidence of nervous tension and a feverish mobilisation of forces to combat the march of the workers.

Already large forces of provincial police had been brought into London, and thousands of special constables had been called up in readiness to take duty on the streets next day when the marchers were to move into the centre of London for a great demonstration in Hyde Park. The press, as on previous occasions, were calling again for drastic action by the government against the hunger marchers. Several of the most reactionary papers called upon the government to prevent the marchers from entering London. In the ranks of the marchers and the workers the final details in respect to the great Hyde Park demonstration were being attended to.

Next morning, 27th October, the general public of London, emerging into the streets, found that special constables had taken over all the normal duties of the policemen on patrol and on traffic duty. This was a clear indication of the elaborate preparations for struggle which the police had made. By mid-day approximately one hundred thousand London workers were moving towards Hyde Park from all parts of London, to give the greatest welcome to the hunger marchers that had ever been seen in Hyde Park. By two o'clock Hyde Park and the streets around Marble Arch were black with the multitude of workers who had arrived and were now awaiting the arrival of the hunger marchers. It is estimated that five thousand police and special constables were gathered round the park, with many thousands more mobilised in the neighbourhood in readiness for action.

The press had announced that morning that all leave had been stopped for the Coldstream Guards in Wellington barracks, and that they were being held in readiness in case of trouble. As the various contingents of marchers began to enter the park at 2.30 there were signs of tremendous enthusiasm. London's warmest welcome, shouted from 100,000 throats in Hyde Park, was the working-class reply to the impudent campaign of lies by the capitalist press against the marchers.

As the last contingent of marchers entered the park gates, trouble broke out with the police. It started with the special constables; not being used to their task, they lost their heads, and, as the crowds swept forward on to the space where the meetings were to be held, the specials drew their truncheons in an effort to control the sea of surging humanity. This incensed the workers; they felt particularly bitter towards the specials, whom they had dubbed "blackleg cops." The workers turned on the special constables and put them to flight, but the fighting which they had been responsible for starting continued throughout the whole afternoon, whilst speakers from the marchers were addressing huge gatherings on the green.

The workers kept the police back from the meetings; several times mounted police charged forward, only to be repulsed by thousands of workers who tore up railings and used them as weapons and barricades for the protection of their meetings. Many mounted men were dragged from their horses. From the streets the fighting extended into the park and back again into the streets, where repeated mounted police charges at full speed failed to dislodge the workers. The foot police were on several occasions surrounded by strong forces of workers, and terrific fights ensued. Many workers and police were injured. Inside the park one could hear the roar of the crowd as they fought tenaciously around the Marble Arch and along Oxford Street. At one juncture a plain-clothes detective stepped forward to speak to a chief inspector; as he did so a zealous special constable struck him down with a terrific blow on the head with a staff. He was about to kick him as he lay on the ground, but was prevented from doing so by the officer in uniform, who stepped forward to reprimand him for the foolish mistake which he had made.

As dusk came on fighting was still proceeding, more severe than ever. The police chiefs had established a post on the top of one of the high buildings in Oxford Street, and were directing the operation of their forces by a system of signals and telephones. Hundreds of police would move in formation against the workers down the main drive of the park, or up Edgware Road or along Oxford Street, but still the workers fought back and repeatedly broke through the police charges. As the great meetings came to an end many of the marchers had become involved in the fighting, along with the London workers, but as the bugles sounded the termination of the meetings, the marchers who were scattered around the area of Marble Arch began to make their way back to the centre to join their contingents.

The workers also pressed forward in order to reach the marchers and give them protection against the police as they marched out. The surge forward on the part of the workers broke through all police resistance, and tens of thousands who had been fighting all the afternoon poured into the park to line up again under their banners and march out with the hunger marchers. The Scottish contingent took the lead headed by their drum and fife band. All the marchers were to be accommodated in the Fulham Road and Wandsworth workhouses.

The moment was tense as the word for the march off was given, with thousands of cheering workers on the flanks. Harry McShane and I were leading the Scottish contingent; we felt that only a miracle could prevent a battle as we marched out of the park. We had to march out of the gates across the wide roadway by Marble Arch and turn into Bayswater Road. There was a tense silence as the head of the column reached the gates; everybody was expectant. A large force of mounted police was leading the way. The vast multitude of workers were holding their breaths expecting a clash. Suddenly, two bottles were thrown from somewhere and fell just behind the posse of mounted police and in front of the marchers. At that moment, it seemed that nothing could have prevented the reopening of the conflict; the one thing that saved the situation was the firm and steady determination of the marchers; nobody attempted to break rank —all marched forward, as the horses of the mounted police reared up. The slightest panic at that moment would have surely ended in a battle, and possibly the marchers being smashed up. It was the steadiness and discipline which the marchers had developed on the road that saved the situation.

That evening and the next day the press were full of reports concerning the bitter fighting which had taken place around Hyde Park. Three days later, another great demonstration, larger still, took place in Trafalgar Square. As it was a Sunday, the employed workers were able to participate in larger numbers. It was estimated that 150,000 people gathered in the vicinity of Trafalgar Square. Thousands could not get into the square at all, but were packed into all the surrounding streets. Again we witnessed a huge mobilisation of the police, the specials carrying out the normal police duties in all parts of London. From the plinth of Nelson's column one could see a large body of police in formation down Whitehall, waiting for an emergency call. Aeroplanes continually flew overhead, in wireless communication with the general staff commanding the police forces.

The gates of Pall Mall, leading to Buckingham Palace, were closed, and guarded by mounted and foot police. The crowd discovered a body of special constables hidden in the army recruiting depot, and they had to lock themselves in to escape from the fury of the workers. During the afternoon, whilst the speakers were addressing all those within hearing, fighting broke out on the outskirts of the crowd. A motor-cycle combination endeavoured to smash a way through the crowd; it was seized and overturned. Then a number of motor-cars that tried to break through the crowd were overturned. The police made repeated baton charges and the demonstrators fought back.

From the plinth of Nelson's column the speakers appealed to the crowd to hold their ground; every moment we expected that the fighting would extend into the square, but this did not happen, though it was taking place in the streets all around whilst the meeting was in progress. Every now and again could be heard the smashing of windows and the roar of the workers in Charing Cross Road, the Strand and towards Piccadilly, as the attacks of the police were resisted. The police had endeavoured to prevent banners from being carried in the demonstration, but there were

hundreds of banners of all sections of the working-class movement, nevertheless. Particularly fierce fighting took place at the
corner of Northumberland Avenue. About fifty police, with
their batons drawn, had been surrounded by the crowd and were
being severely handled; only after a fierce fight, in which the
mounted police charged from the rear, were they rescued.

Before the great demonstration was over and the workers
marched back to their localities, seventeen arrests had taken
place. The demonstration was certainly the biggest that had ever
been seen in Trafalgar Square. All the way back to the localities
the marchers and the London demonstrators jeered at the special
constables each time they came across them on point duty. It
even seemed that the ordinary constables enjoyed this bantering
of the specials. It was evident that there was a none too friendly
feeling between the paid policeman and the volunteer special.
In fact, the press commented upon this, and there was a general
impression that the fighting, both at Hyde Park and Trafalgar
Square, had been caused by the special constables.

The *Star* was particularly outspoken on the question and said
that "protests are being lodged in the right quarter. The constables want the specials' duties defined." The organ of the
Metropolitan Police, the *Police Review*, spoke strongly on the
question, and said:

This week witnessed a wholesale departure from the original
conception of what a special constable is for. He ceases to be an
emergency "ration." He is taking over the points, beats and
controls of regular constables, who are to be specially selected to
act as nursemaids. An excellent fellowship exists, but there is a
feeling that in this difficult time the appearance of the special is
calculated to cause trouble rather than avoid it. At the meetings
and hunger marches, the special is an irritant, rather than an anti-
septic. And why this sudden conversion to the employment of
special police? There have been equally difficult times for the
regular police, when they managed quite well without the special
constables. Fear and sound organisation are not good mixers
and if the real purpose for which the special constabulary came
into being is to be achieved, then the less they are seen and used
the better for everyone concerned.

Other papers made amusing comments about the specials.
Here is one:

Having got their traffic legs, the special constables came a
little further into the City to-day. They found that they needed

all their navigation for mastering the narrows, cross currents and the tides of the deeper waters. In the Borough, factory girls arrived, and screamed in unison to the special on point duty: "Kiss me, sergeant!" Then there were pedestrians who refused to stop with the traffic. The ordinary traffic cop seems to be able to take up half-a-dozen pedestrians under his cape whilst still directing four ways of traffic; the special finds this sort of extra gesture difficult, and in a natural anxiety to save women and children first, he allows a couple of lines of traffic to make a crossword puzzle.

Another problem presented itself in South London.

A passer-by collided with the special's arm and when the point duty man remonstrated, he elbowed him! The special then proceeded to arrest him, but the man refused to be arrested, and by the time they had walked down the street a bit, the traffic had tied itself into reef knots and looked as though it would never come unstuck.

Following the demonstration in Trafalgar Square we prepared for the next big move—the presentation of the million-signature petition to Parliament on Tuesday evening, 1st November. By this time the big national daily organs of the press lords were screaming for drastic action to be taken against the marchers and their leaders. Some claimed that the hunger marchers had deliberately come to London for trouble and rioting; others that they were "Moscow dupes," that they were being "exploited by heartless knaves whose one object it is to cause disturbance." There was foolish propaganda about the "emissaries of Moscow" and "riot leaders." The leading article of one big daily paper was particularly amusing. The following are extracts:

London may infer from the account given by the Home Secretary in the House of Commons of the serious rioting near the Marble Arch, what is intended to occur at some later date if a chance should offer. The abolition of the Means Test is a pretext; the presentation of a petition to Parliament is a blind. Hannington, professional organiser of this march, is conceited indeed, if he supposes that his Communist riff-raff could make a revolution; but that they could do incalculable damage by loot and pillage in an hour or two of mob excitement is undeniable, and that bloodshed would ensue is certain.

We urge the authorities not merely to take precautions to deal with the marchers. Let them deal not with the dupes, but with the organisers. A year ago this man Hannington was convicted at Bow Street for inciting the unemployed to riot. He is responsible not only for the behaviour of the marchers but for attracting the crowds which are certain to include the most dangerous elements in London, bent on the chance of mischief and rioting. It is foolish to take such unnecessary risks. These Communist organisers should be laid by the heels. What took place round the Marble Arch will certainly take place again; it is quite likely to be repeated on Tuesday. For Tuesday peremptory warning should be given that the rule against processions of any sort coming near the approaches of Parliament will be enforced to the letter. Sentimental weakness in handling this situation will only ensue in more disturbances and a longer list of casualties. These marchers are a public nuisance and a public danger.

Such quotations give us an indication of the fear which had been struck into the heart of the ruling class by the determination of the men who were simply marching against the means test and the benefit cuts, and by the great mass of the workers who were giving them their support.

A speech in the House of Commons by Mr. John McGovern, M.P., added fuel to the fire and strengthened the demand for the arrest of the leaders. A few days before the marchers arrived in London, Mr. McGovern had stated in the House that he would present the petition for the marchers; he made this statement without authorisation from the marchers' council and consequently we repudiated him in respect to this, stating that we intended to present the petition ourselves before the bar of the House. On the Monday, 31st October, he made a damaging statement in the House to the effect that the marchers were not willing to adopt the necessary constitutional formalities, but preferred "to rely on their massed strength to force Parliament to allow their deputation to appear." The *Evening News*, drawing the appropriate capitalist moral from this, said, "Mr. McGovern is to be congratulated on smoking out Messrs. Hannington and McShane," and thanked him for exposing the "Moscow methods" of the N.U.W.M. *The Times*, next morning, congratulated McGovern on his discovery that the marchers were out to "incite disorder."

After the marchers' arrival in London, a central marchers' control council was established, consisting of elected representatives from the various contingents. This council met regularly each day, and planned the activities of the marchers. On the evening of 31st October, whilst the council was in session, one of the members entered late, and handed to me a document in a sealed envelope, addressed to me and marked "by hand." At the moment, I was making a report to the council and was about to slip the document into my pocket, but fortunately did not do so, for I might have overlooked it afterwards and the consequences would have been serious, both for myself and the march. When I concluded my report I opened the envelope; having hurriedly scanned the document, I realised that it was a "plant."

It was a terrorist document, but it had been cleverly written in order to involve the march council and McShane and myself in particular. It opened with the words "Concerning the direct action activities which we have already discussed, the plans now are——" and then went on to set out a number of acts of terrorism, including the waylaying of cabinet ministers, the use of physical violence against them, and the burning down of certain government buildings. I immediately stopped the proceedings of the council and inquired from the comrade who had handed the letter to me where he had obtained it. He replied that he was stopped outside the hall by a stranger who asked if he was going to the meeting and whether Hannington would be present. When he replied in the affirmative he was given the letter and asked to deliver it to me personally. He said to the stranger, "Will you wait for a reply?" and the stranger answered, "No, there is no need to, Hannington knows all about it."

I read the contents of the letter to the council and pointed out that this was obviously a terrorist document being planted upon us for the purpose of involving the leadership of the march in a line of action which was entirely foreign to our methods and activities, and was intended to discredit the march. I warned all members against such acts of provocation; I said, "We do not know what is behind the planting of this document, and, whilst we would like to retain it as evidence against *agents provocateurs*, it is nevertheless too dangerous even to leave the building with it. Therefore, I propose that it be burned immediately." The members of the council agreed and the document was destroyed.

Next morning, 1st November, I had good cause to be pleased that we had not been careless with such a document. As I entered the head office of the N.U.W.M., I saw three or four plain-clothes detectives standing opposite; we had got accustomed to their being there, as they had been on duty outside the offices for the previous two weeks. Quite unsuspectingly I settled down to my work, when suddenly I heard a rush up the stairs, and into every room came detectives.

Detective-Inspector Kitchener approached me and stated, "You must come along with me, I have a warrant for your arrest." I demanded to see the warrant, and to have the charge read over to me; this was done. He then said, "I now intend to search the offices." I demanded to know whether he had a search warrant, but to this he gave evasive answers. I also insisted that if the place was to be searched, I, as the responsible head of the movement, should be there, to check up. This was refused, Inspector Kitchener insisting that I must go along immediately. It was useless to resist; there were about fourteen police officers already in the building, and even the staff were not allowed to move out of their rooms.

I was taken in the company of detectives, by taxi, to Bow Street police court, where I was charged with "attempting to cause disaffection among members of the Metropolitan Police, contrary to the Police Act, 1919." Mr. Charles R. V. Wallace was the prosecuting counsel on behalf of the Director of Public Prosecutions; the magistrate was Sir Chartres Biron. The charge against me related to a portion of my speech at the hunger marchers' demonstration in Trafalgar Square on the previous Sunday. The shorthand notes taken by Detective-Sergeant Ernest Oliver at the demonstration reported me as saying, "In this morning's *Reynolds* it is reported that there is going to be an inquiry into the incidents in Hyde Park, where seventy-five persons were badly injured. It is reported that there was a blunder on the part of the special police; let me address a few words to the police within my hearing. The government has made cuts in the pay of the police; the police should remember that they are drawn from the ranks of the working class. The government has already organised this blackleg police force (specials) ready to take the jobs of the men in uniform, if these men do as they did in 1919 (police strike). We ask the police to understand that what we are marching for is in their interests as well as the interests of the unemployed. We have marched to London for the abolition of the means test and the restoration of the economy cuts, and that means the cuts in the pay of the sailors, soldiers and policemen, as well as the unemployed. Let the working class in uniform and out of uniform stand together."

After the case had been opened and I had cross-examined police witnesses I was remanded in custody for a week, bail being refused. This was, of course, the critical period of the march; it was only a few hours before the great demonstration in the evening for the presentation of the petition, and the workers had no difficulty in realising that the arrest had been made with the deliberate intention of removing me from the leadership and disorganising the work of the march.

Afterwards, whilst I was on remand in Brixton prison, I learned that on the day of my arrest the police had not only searched the offices, but had removed in police vans five hundred-weight of material, including all documents, letters, even literature, and the account books. They had taken everything material to the work of headquarters, and no doubt thought that by doing so it would completely disorganise the work of the movement.

Whilst I was lying in Brixton gaol I reflected many times upon the terrorist document that had been planted on me on the eve of my arrest, and I could not help having more than a suspicion that the search which had been carried out of my person at Bow Street, and the search of the offices, were directed to the finding of this document. If the document had been found and put in as evidence against me, it would have been extremely difficult to convince people that it was a "frame-up"; the instigators had been very clever in the wording of it and I should probably have received a very heavy sentence of penal servitude and the movement would have been discredited. Whether the police were connected with the document we were never able to say, but it was certainly a strange coincidence that within a few hours of its delivery my arrest and the raid took place.

On the evening of my arrest all the newspaper placards contained captions such as "Hunger Marchers' Leader Arrested!" "Arrest of Wal Hannington!" etc. The marchers, the London unemployed and the working class in general were incensed, and everywhere the demand arose for my release. Huge groups of workers began to pour towards Westminster in the early part of the evening of 1st November, to support the deputation that was going to the House of Commons with the million-signature petition.

Every available policeman was mobilised for action against the marchers and the demonstrators. Police cordons were not confined to the Westminster area, they extended even as far as Holborn and Kings Cross. As a contingent of workers, more than eight thousand strong, came marching from the East End, police cordons were drawn across their path in Grays Inn Road. The mounted men charged and hundreds of workers clambered on to trams and buses in order to get through the police cordons and reach Westminster. The police stopped all traffic, and jumped on the vehicles after the demonstrators. Fights took place on the street cars and buses. In Farringdon Street, Holborn, where again the police tried to stop the workers, even though they were not in formation, from reaching the Westminster area, another serious battle occurred. A building job was in progress in Farring-don Street and the workers armed themselves with stones and bricks in the battle that ensued. Many plate-glass windows, including those of the big establishment of Gamage's, were smashed. In spite of the police cordons, it is estimated that about eighty thousand workers got through to Westminster.

By 8.30 in the evening mounted police were charging the crowds in Parliament Square in an effort to clear the streets. Police flying-squad cars drove at high speed through the streets, endeavouring to scatter the masses. The gates outside the House of Commons were all closed, with the exception of one, whilst inside this gate a strong force of police were posted. From the Battersea area, 6,000 workers marched to Westminster, led by the well-known working-class fighter, the late Shapurji Saklatvala. They reached Westminster whilst heavy fighting was in progress.

By 8.45, in spite of the repeated charges by the police, there were such dense crowds in the vicinity of Westminster that traffic was completely stopped. The workers were wondering why the deputation, numbering nearly fifty, along with the petition, had not arrived. Arrangements had been made for the petition to be taken to a convenient spot where the members of the deputation could then carry it through Whitehall to Parliament. The place selected was Charing Cross station. The petition was taken in taxis to the station. The members of the deputation, after difficulties with the police cordons, succeeded in reaching Charing Cross, and as they were about to emerge into the Strand with the petition, in order to lead the workers down to Parliament, the iron gates of the station were closed; the deputation was sur-rounded by a large force of police, and the petition was con-fiscated. When the deputation ultimately got away from the station, and the news spread amongst the workers that the police had seized the petition, there was bitter indignation. A baton charge occurred outside Charing Cross station as another at-tempt was made to march down Whitehall.

The fighting went on around the cenotaph in Whitehall, down Victoria Street, over Westminster Bridge, Cannon Row and Bridge Street. Then, just after nine o'clock, it extended into Trafalgar Square, where the most severe battle of all took place; men and women fought back tenaciously against the repeated charges of mounted and foot police. Many were clubbed down to the ground and trampled on by the horses. At 10.15 another terrific baton charge took place in front of the National Gallery and hundreds of workers were knocked down. The charge proceeded up Haymarket to Piccadilly; the streets were like a battlefield after the police had passed. On the Embankment, near Westminster, motor-cars were overturned and the destination boards on the side of tramcars were seized by workers for use as weapons.

The fighting continued throughout the whole area until midnight. At the end of it there were hundreds injured and more than fifty marchers and demonstrators had been arrested. Some of these received severe sentences on charges of violent assault against the police, although they themselves carried all the marks of having been assaulted when they entered the courts with their heads swathed in bandages. John Gellatly, one of the Scottish hunger marchers, received a sentence of six months, and a middle-aged one-armed man by the name of Edward James, who was also charged with assaulting the police, was sentenced to six months. Other marchers and demonstrators received lesser sentences. So ended the attempt of the workless to present their petition to the National government, of which Mr. Ramsay Macdonald, the renegade socialist, was prime minister.

On 3rd November the police arrested Sid Elias, the chairman of the unemployed movement, and on 5th November all the marchers left London, returning to their homes. In Glasgow the Scottish marchers were welcomed by a demonstration of 30,000 when they came off the special train on which they had travelled. Similar welcome-home demonstrations greeted the other contingents.

Whilst I was in Brixton prison, awaiting trial, a cable was received from the unemployed movement of America, which read:

On behalf of the American masses, who are deeply interested in the splendid British hunger march, we invite, you, Hannington, to come and address hunger march send-off demonstration at Bronx Coliseum, New York, November 29th. If still detained by Macdonald's police, other representative will be welcome. Warm fraternal greetings.

Benjamin, Secretary, Unemployed Councils.

I much regretted that my detention prevented my visiting the United States. Being a remand prisoner I was permitted to read the newspapers, and I read of the arrest of Elias. Before the hunger march Elias had been sent as a delegate by our movement to attend a workers' conference in the U.S.S.R. Before he came back to England he wrote a letter to our headquarters, expressing his views on the steps that he thought might be taken to strengthen the activities of the hunger march. When the letter arrived at the N.U.W.M. offices, I was out on the road with the Scottish marchers, and I did not in fact ever see or know of the existence of the letter until after the arrest of Elias. When the police raided headquarters they discovered this letter, which had a Moscow address on it, and they seized upon this in order to raise a red bogey against the march. They charged Elias with "attempting to cause discontent and disaffection and illwill between different classes of His Majesty's subjects and to create public disturbances against the police."

There was in fact, nothing in the letter of Elias which one could not read any day in the columns of the socialist press, and in agitational articles in working-class journals. The most serious portion of the letter was that which urged that we should follow up the agitation for strike action by the workers on the day that the marchers arrived in London. Other items of correspondence from Elias whilst he was in the Soviet Union were also put in as evidence to prove that there was continuous correspondence, although these letters contained no political statement, but referred only to domestic matters.

When I read the letter upon which Elias had been arrested, I knew that I had never seen that letter before, and on the morning that I was about to go to the court again for my trial I managed to get a few words with Elias expressing my surprise about the letter, and he informed me that he knew that I had not seen it, and that it was delivered in my absence. The facts were, as I learned later, that Elias had arrived back in London before the letter had been delivered, and that when it had arrived he had received it himself and nobody else had read it.

On Tuesday, 8th November, I was taken from Brixton to Bow Street police court for the continuation of my case. Immediately I entered the dock I asked that the magistrate, Sir Chartres Biron, should consider certain statements which had appeared on 6th November in the *Sunday Dispatch*. Right across the front page of the paper in heavy black type were the following words:

"HUNGER MARCH BACKED BY RED GOLD." "FIVE THOUSAND POUNDS IN HARD CASH SMUGGLED FROM MOSCOW INTO BRITAIN!" " 'FOMENT HATE!' COMMAND." "BOLSHEVIST AGENTS WHO PLOT TO COERCE UNEMPLOYED!" "SECRET PAYROLL!"

The article went on to make the most foolish statements in

respect to the hunger march. It said that the money for the rail fares for the return journey of the hunger marchers had been paid by money from Moscow. All these statements were absolutely untrue. The police knew that they were untrue because they had seized our account books, which showed the finances of our movement, which showed that the leading officials were paid a modest wage for our work in the movement out of its funds, and that the fares and other expenses in connection with the march had been met entirely from the money raised in the hunger march fund, every penny of which was traceable.

I claimed in the court that the statements of the *Sunday Dispatch* were made in order to prejudice the case against myself and others connected with the march, and that a grave contempt of court had been committed. I asked what action the court intended to take against this newspaper, but the magistrate said that I was not entitled to raise that question in the court. He said he had not read the paper in question and he could not therefore be accused of being prejudiced by it. For the rest of the story in connection with the trial I quote the reports which appeared in the press at the time:

Detective-Inspector Kitchener, the first witness, who gave evidence of the arrest, was cross-examined at length by Hannington on the methods and purpose of the police raid on N.U.W.M. headquarters on November 1.

Hannington: I want to suggest that the raid on the office was not to obtain documents in connection with the charge, but to disorganise the office at a vital moment. (To Kitchener): Are you one of the officers who for the past two months has been watching the headquarters of the National Unemployed Workers' Movement?

Kitchener: No.

Hannington: Would it surprise you to learn that for eight weeks before my arrest there was never a period in the day or late evening but what there has been observation on the N.U.W.M. offices by police officers, numbering sometimes nearly as many as ten?—That would surprise me.

Hannington: I would suggest that I have been under police surveillance for a considerable time amounting to almost police persecution. This charge levelled against me is the culmination of a series of attempts by the police to arrest me under some pretence.

At Hannington's request, Police-sergeant Oliver, who made a shorthand note of Hannington's speech in Trafalgar Square, was next put in the box.

He said at least six officers in uniform heard Hannington's speech.

Hannington (to Sir Chartres Biron): Would it be possible to call these six policemen as witnesses?

Sir Chartres Biron: Well, I don't think it would be relevant.

Hannington: I want to find out whether there are any policemen who feel disaffected as a result of my speech.

Hannington (to Oliver): What, in your opinion, constitutes disaffection?

Oliver: Disaffection?

Hannington: I am charged with attempting to cause disaffection. Can you define disaffection?

Oliver: I understand it to mean dislike, disruption.

Do you know whether there exists, or did exist before my speech any disaffection amongst the police concerning the wage cuts?—I have no knowledge of that.

Do you read *The Police Review*?—Occasionally.

You occasionally read *The Police Review*. Did you read it for November 4, in which, on page 314, occurs the following statement: "The Government turned a deaf ear to the definite statement that discontent and dissatisfaction was rampant throughout the service, caused by the unfair and unjust treatment meted out to members of the police service?"

Oliver: Yes.

Did you read this in *The Police Review* of October 28? In that there appeared, before my speech was made, a statement under the name of Jack Hayes, Parliamentary correspondent, in which it is stated: "The Police Council has been reduced to a farce." Did you read that?—If I remember rightly, I read it.

In the same article you will remember this statement: "The Desborough standards are your Magna Charta. It must be protected by all the power at your command, and the eventual restoration of those things that may have been filched from them in time of national stress." Do you remember that?—I think I read that.

Would I be correct in saying that that statement appearing in *The Police Review* is a much stronger statement concerning police action than the one I made in Trafalgar Square?—I cannot say.

Hannington (continuing his cross-examination): In *The Police Review* of October 21, among the letters to the editor, appears the following: "Has the Home Office forgotten that the reason for the appointment of the Desborough Committee was discontent as to pay and conditions of service, and does it not know that there is considerable dissatisfaction in the service to-day as a result of continual interference with pay and Federation matter." Did you read that?

Oliver: No, I did not.

Hannington: I am afraid you don't follow leading police matters closely. This happened before my speech was made in Trafalgar Square. Did you read *The Police Review* for October 14, under the heading of "Police Federation of England and Wales"? In that it was stated: "That in view of the very serious discontent that prevails throughout the service upon the introduction of the supplementary deductions, the lower rate of pay for new entrants . . ." Did you read that?

Oliver: No.

Well, that appears. In the same issue of *The Police Review* appears the statement: "The pay cuts have very naturally been the cause of much soreness, and I am aware that there has been a real effort to accept the cuts philosophically. Men have tried to believe that they are necessary; that everything possible had been done in other directions to effect economy before pay cuts had been considered. . . . There are men leaving the service to-day—men of high rank—sick to death of the treatment they have received." Do you remember that?—I think so.

Hannington: If you have yet a recollection of having read these things, why did you say you have no knowledge of disaffection amongst the police?

Oliver did not reply.

Hannington: An answer to the question, please.

Oliver (to Sir Chartres Biron): Must I answer that?

Sir Chartres Biron: Yes, you must answer the question. (To Hannington): May I point out that there is a very great distinction between dissatisfaction and disaffection?

Hannington: I will repeat the question. If you had read these statements in *The Police Review* to the effect that there is strong disaffection among the police over pay cuts, why, before I quoted these statements to you, did you reply to my question stating that you were not aware of any dissatisfaction or disaffection among the police in regard to the cuts?

Oliver: All I can say is as an individual I have no grievance.

Hannington was about to question Oliver further on this point when Sir Chartres asked him not to carry it further.

Hannington: I don't wish to take up the time of the court. I am only trying to prove that I could not cause disaffection among the police. It was already there.

Oliver denied he had received special instructions to take down Hannington's speech.

Hannington: At the time I was to speak some other officer was taking notes. It was only when I came on the scene that you came along, thinking my speech was important. I want to suggest that there were deliberate preparations on the part of the police to get me because of my activities in connection with the hunger march.

Wal Hannington then made his speech from the dock. He said: I want to make a submission to the court in regard to the case. My submission is that there is no case, and in support of that I wish to make the following statement:

"I do not believe that at any time in the history of political trials in this country has there been a case in which there has been less substance and proof pertaining to the charge than there is in this one. The case of the prosecution is so ridiculously weak that it obviously gives rise to an impression that this charge is simply a pretext for removing me from the scene of working-class activity —not for the speech I made in Trafalgar Square, but for the work I am doing amongst the unemployed.

"It has been admitted in this court this morning, from documents I have produced, that long before I made the speech in Trafalgar Square, there was a spirit of disaffection existing among the police in regard to wage cuts.

"I want to submit to this court that it is ridiculous to charge me with attempting to create disaffection when that disaffection already existed. I want to submit to this court that what I was doing in my speech in Trafalgar Square was making ordinary comment in regard to the conditions that exist among the working class, including the man in uniform. This 'ordinary comment' of mine has been presented by the prosecution in such a way as to almost represent sedition.

"There has been, in my opinion, an almost frantic effort on the part of the prosecution to secure a committal, to secure a conviction. I cannot possibly separate what the police have been doing concerning our movement for the past eight weeks from this prosecution. There has been constant spying at the headquarters of our movement; there has been a raid at headquarters, in which documents not relating to this case have been taken away. There has even been molestation and insult perpetrated against the ordinary typists on the staff of the movement. They have been molested and insulted in the street by police officers.

"There has been systematic spying on the correspondence of our movement. All the letters from our branches to headquarters are first of all delayed by the postal authorities for special inspection. Honest, straightforward working-class activity has been distorted to the public as being criminal, secret conspiracy.

"I further want to suggest that if this court upholds this charge against me, then the term 'free speech' in this country will become a mockery and a travesty.

"I suggest there is no working-class leader, if this charge is upheld, who would be able to speak in public about the condition of the working class. If this charge is upheld it must create a most dangerous precedent in regard to the conditions of a very large section of the working class. It would mean that their conditions could not be commented upon; it would mean the stifling of one expression of opinion concerning working-class conditions.

"I want the court to study the situation as I see it. What lies at the root of this prosecution? What, in effect, is the real offence I am guilty of?

"If we were to believe the big capitalist newspapers, notably the *Daily Telegraph*, the *Daily Mail* and the *Express*, I say definitely that I am not in this court this morning for a statement made in Trafalgar Square, but I am in the court this morning for my activities in connection with the great hunger march, because, before my arrest, these papers were clamouring for my arrest.

"According to this charge against me it seems that the demands of the marchers constitute a menace. The very demands of the marchers constituted an offence in so far as they called for the restoration of the economy cuts and the cuts in social service which affect the police.

"These demands were formulated by the National Unemployed Workers' Movement, of which I happen to have the honour of being national organiser, elected by national conference, and not delegated to that post and selected by the Communist Party, as the capitalist newspapers would suggest. I am a member of the Communist Party, and proud of my associations, but I hold my office as organiser elected by the branches of the movement. This movement that laid down the demands for the marchers has been represented in the Press as almost an illegal organisation.

"That speech was made in Trafalgar Square at the demonstration of the hunger marchers, and I suggest very definitely, and I am sure that this court will agree, that there can be no effects without cause; that the hunger march, which led me to make certain statements in Trafalgar Square, was the effect of certain conditions. I state that the cause of the march is to be found in the conditions of the working class in the country to-day.

"I am of the opinion that I have rendered services to my class in the work I have done in organising the march. I say that by the policy pursued by this Government the spectre of starvation has penetrated into millions of working class homes to-day. By this policy the conditions of the working class in the past ten years have been greatly lowered. There has been the inhuman means test applied to the unemployed, under which aged parents are compelled to maintain their unemployed sons, under which employed brothers and sisters are compelled to maintain their unemployed relatives, under which unemployed men have been robbed of war pensions, of trade union benefits, of workers' compensation, and even of gifts made to them by members of their family. I suggest that under the plea of economy this Government has stopped work schemes that would mean employment to hundreds of thousands of workers."

Sir Chartres Biron: Really, we are getting away from the point. It is a speech of some interest, but it is not relevant to the case.

Hannington: I am trying to explain my case. I don't believe that the economy measures that have been operated against the working class are necessary or fair. I can introduce into this court very strong, undeniable evidence to show that while there have been economies against the workers, there have been no economies at the other end of the scale.

"In defence of what I said in Trafalgar Square and what I say on many occasions, I would like to say that in my opinion these people who would urge the unemployed to starve in silence are rendering a terrible dis-service to this generation and are creating a terrible future for them. I don't believe there is any need for poverty and starvation such as exists to-day. I believe the working class has the power to produce in abundance. It is the system itself which is responsible for the state of affairs we see at the moment.

"The march organised by the N.U.W.M. was for the purpose of rousing this country to an understanding of the conditions that exist in working-class homes. I say that this Government does not mind there being millions of unemployed, provided these persons are willing to hide their rags and poverty; but when our movement brings into notice the rags and poverty of the unemployed, the leaders are not only vilified in the Press, but become subjects for police persecution, and are brought to court on charges which are only a pretext for bigger things.

"I am proud of the work I have done amongst the unemployed. I have led the unemployed in what might be described as an agitational war against starvation. I believe that is why I am in this dock this morning, and if my crime is that I have led the unemployed efficiently in the war against starvation, then I am quite proud to admit my guilt in that respect.

"I believe it is my duty to rouse the unemployed to constant agitation against conditions of poverty, starvation and degradation, which in my opinion are unnecessary. Whether I am sentenced in this court or not, I wish to make it clear—it is only right that I should—that so far as my work among the working class is concerned, it will continue.

"I don't feel that I have done anything wrong. In fact, on the contrary, I am quite proud of the work I have done. I ask this court to view the case as I see it—as a case that has no substance of proof as regards my speech in Trafalgar Square."

The magistrate, in summing up, commented upon my defence, in these words:

"Your case has not suffered through not being presented by counsel. Taking the speech in Trafalgar Square as a whole the question before the court is—was it likely to give rise to disaffection and to demoralise the existing police force? I cannot close my eyes to the circumstances in which that speech was delivered. I think its object and effect was likely to paralyse to a large extent the efforts of the police in saving the public from what was a considerable danger. I must find you guilty and I sentence you to three months' imprisonment."

This made my fifth term of imprisonment in ten years for my working-class activities.

In the trial of Sid Elias before Justice Charles at the Old Bailey every possible effort was made to represent Elias as an agent of a foreign power. The case was distorted by the prosecution and by the press. It now appeared that it was a crime for an official of a working-class organisation to visit another country and to write to his organisation concerning its activities, if the country visited happened to be the workers' Socialist Soviet Republic.

The judge, in passing sentence, said, "The maximum sentence I can pass upon you is in my judgment far, far too short. I sentence you to two years' imprisonment."

Five days later, 17th December, Tom Mann, the national treasurer of the N.U.W.M., and Emrhys Llewellyn, secretary, were arrested and sent to prison for two months. They were arrested under a six-hundred-year-old Act of Edward III and the Seditious Meetings Act of 1877, section 23. No charge was preferred against them, but 19th December was to be a national day of demonstration for the unemployed and so, two days before the demonstrations, Mann and Llewellyn were arrested on the grounds that if they were allowed to remain at liberty they might incite to a disturbance of the peace.

When they were brought before Sir Chartres Biron at Bow Street, he made the following remarkable statement: "There is no criminal charge and no question of imprisonment. The proceedings are merely to enforce a law which has been the law of the land from time immemorial for the protection of public order. It is merely a preventive measure." He then proceeded to order Mann and Llewellyn to be bound over in the sum of £200 in their own recognisances and in addition to each find two £100 sureties, the alternative being two months' imprisonment.

In reply, Tom Mann said, "If I am to be tied, if my mouth is to be closed, if I am not to participate in voicing the grievances of those who are suffering, while the incompetency of those responsible cannot find work for them, and is knocking down their miserable standards still lower, then whatever the consequences may be—if I am to be shot in the next five minutes—I would not consent to any undertaking. Regardless of my age or anything else I will not give an undertaking not to be identified with the further organisation of mass demonstrations and the ventilation of the troubles of the unemployed and of the workers generally. What am I here for? What offence have I committed to give anyone the right even to call me a 'disturber of the peace'? I believe that it is entirely unwarranted."

Llewellyn likewise declined to enter into any recognisances and made a statement to that effect from the dock. The magistrate, concluding the case, said, "There is nothing to prevent a petition to the House of Commons, but it is most undesirable that a petition should be presented by an organised mass of people marching on the House."

Both prisoners were then removed to Brixton prison. Throughout the country a storm of protest expressed itself in resolutions pouring into the Home Office from all kinds of working-class organisations, demanding the release of the four national officials of the N.U.W.M.

So ended the year 1932—a year of bitter struggles on the part of the unemployed.

Chapter XVI

LEGAL MURDER

LAST week, after vainly searching for work all day, William Castle, at his last call, pleaded desperately with tears in his eyes. He was turned away, and went sadly home. His wife met him with a brave smile. "Cheer up, Will!" she said, "here's a letter for you; perhaps it's a job for Christmas."

It was an intimation that his unemployment benefit had ceased. He hid it from his wife and lay awake all night. At 5 a.m. he got up and wrote a farewell letter. At 6 a.m. he took his wife a cup of tea and kissed her tenderly. Then he abruptly left the room. His wife heard a strange noise downstairs. She found him on the floor. He had cut his throat. The doctor came, but too late—William Castle was dead. He had passed through the horror of war and now he had the horror of a hungry wife, three hungry children, and an empty cupboard, and Christmas was near. It was too much for him to bear.

Such was the press report which appeared a few days before Christmas, 1932, concerning the suicide of an unemployed ex-service man.

The means test and the benefit cuts were producing appalling poverty and destitution in hundreds of thousands of working-class families. One frequently read of suicides caused by the means test. Here are two other cases that occurred during December 1932:

The body of a man named Taylor was recovered from the Birmingham canal near Smethwick Corporation Gas Works. The widow said that her husband had been very depressed and nervous on account of being out of work. There had been a decided change in his condition since 12th November when he had to go before the means test committee in connection with his benefit. A son said his father's benefit had been reduced under the means test, from 27s. 3d. per week to 10s. 9d. The coroner, Mr. A. Shakespeare, in recording a verdict of "suicide whilst temporarily insane," said "This man's worries following a 'means test' provided the last push sufficient to make him temporarily insane and in that state he threw himself into the canal."

"Please don't blame my poor wife—look after her!"

At the inquest at Cambridge on Christopher Saunders, aged 42, of Great Evesdon, whose body was recovered from the River Cam, Mrs. Saunders said she had found that note in his hand-writing. She said her husband had been very depressed since his unemployment benefit had been reduced under the means test from 25s. 3d. to 5s. 3d. a week. A verdict of "suicide whilst temporarily insane" was recorded.

Examples of the way in which the unemployed were being treated under the means test are to be found in the following cases which were collected during 1932 by the unemployed movement:

A Birmingham unemployed widower living with his only daughter had his benefit completely stopped under the means test because his daughter was working and earning 28s. a week.

In a family of five at Pontefract, Yorkshire, the father was unemployed and there was one son working, earning 14s. a week. The father's benefit was reduced to 8s. per week, leaving a total income to the family of £1 2s. 0d. for five persons to live on.

A Dalton (Cumberland) man and wife had their benefit reduced to 4s. because one son was working, receiving wages of £1 4s. 0d. a week, and another received 8s. a week unemployment benefit.

A disabled ex-service man in Sunderland had an income of 25s. 3d. from the labour exchange, plus 30s. army pension. He had a wife and one child, and another expected. Under the means test he was completely cut off benefit; the army pension had to maintain the family.

An Earby family of husband, wife and two sons, came under the means test. The husband and the two sons were unemployed, the wife working, earning £2 a week, and the husband received 10s. a week army pension. Under the means test the husband and the two sons were completely cut off benefit. The mother had to maintain the family.

In Sheffield, a single man receiving 7s. 6d. a week army pension was living with his married brother, who had a family of five children. The brother was a car conductor, receiving very poor wages, yet the unemployed man was completely stopped benefit under the means test, and his married brother forced to keep him.

At Hindley, near Wigan, there was a family of four, father mother and two sons. One son earned 11s. 6d. a week, the other son was blind and received 15s. 6d. a week blind pension and in addition earned £1 a week. Father was unemployed and under the means test his benefit was reduced to 2s. a week.

In Cumberland, an unemployed brother had his benefit reduced from 15s. 3d. to 10s. a week under the means test, because his blind sister was in receipt of a pension.

It is not surprising that during 1933 and 1934 alarming reports were issued by medical officers of local authorities, eminent medical men, schoolmasters and social workers, concerning the serious physical deterioration in the health standards of the people. Medical officers of health are usually very guarded in the language which they use in their reports, but so extreme had the poverty of the people become, that many of them, in the areas severely affected by unemployment, found themselves compelled to speak out in bold terms of condemnation.

In the report issued by Dr. Kenneth Fraser, the Cumberland school medical officer, in 1933, he said: "A large number of children are carrying on to-day in this county without adequate food." He then gave figures to show that there was an abnormally high infant mortality (number of children dying within a year of their birth) and he claimed that "under better economic conditions, many of these children would never have died."

The medical officer of health for Preston in 1933 stated that there was a general uniform decline in the health of the children in his county due to the unprecedented trade depression. He said that in the latter part of 1932 many more working-class mothers were driven to apply for free milk at the infant welfare centres, and he expressed the opinion that this was due to the operation of the means test. The Blackburn medical officer stated that the standard of nutrition amongst school children in his area continued to decline owing to the financial inability of the parents to provide the requisite sustenance for the children.

Dr. MacGregor, the Glasgow medical officer, reported an increase in rickets amongst the pre-school children, which he said was not an entirely local phenomenon. Dr. Howell, the Hammersmith medical officer, reported that there was under-nourishment of expectant mothers and referred to the malnutrition amongst school children in his area, which he said "is due to the small amount of money left over for food for the family after paying present-day rents." He quoted an examination of children in unemployed working-class families, which showed evidence of malnutrition in twenty-eight per cent of the cases examined, whilst seventy-six were below the average weight of children of the same age in elementary schools whose parents were working.

In November 1933 came a report by nine eminent medical

men appointed by the British Medical Association to inquire into the health conditions of the people. The report declared that after nine months' research they were unanimously of the opinion that the average unemployed family in Great Britain was not getting enough food to keep it reasonably healthy. Dr. O'Hara, medical officer of the Durham County Society for the Prevention and Cure of Consumption, speaking at a meeting of the society's governors in 1934, made the following statement:

"Most of our children are suffering not so much from tuberculosis as from starvation. Seventy-five per cent of the cases admitted to the society's sanatorium are definitely due to starvation."

A South Wales medical officer, writing on the question of tuberculosis, said:

"I should not be surprised to find an increase in the amount of tuberculosis beginning on the adult female side. There is not enough money available for adequate food and clothing to keep up the patient's resistance, whilst the worry entailed must have a deleterious effect."

A South Wales sanatorium superintendent said:

"Among the adults, there has been an increase in the number of young people admitted to the sanatorium, especially women, suffering from an acute type of tuberculosis. They appear to have no immunity and their resistance seems to be completely overcome."

In the 1933 report of the medical officer of health for the Gallygaer Urban District Council, issued in 1934, we read:

"The district has again had a continued epidemic of scarlet fever during the year, the majority of the cases being of a severe type and complications were common. The general want of resistance to the attack and the severity of the symptoms were in my opinion due to general malnutrition among the children, the result of the present unfortunate economic conditions prevalent in South Wales."

There followed the report of Sir George Newman, chief medical officer of health for England and Wales, issued in September 1934, in which the following sentences occurred:

"No fewer than two million homes in 1933 were stricken by death or disease during the year. There was distress and privation, physical and mental, in areas severely depressed by unemployment. Unemployment, under-nourishment and preventable malady and accident seem to be the unavoidable concomitant of current civilisation in Western Europe to-day.

In another report issued by Sir George Newman on 1st December, 1934, he said:

" I fear we are not doing all that is practical for the nutrition, physical education, nurture and health of the normal child. Yet if we are failing to ensure the physical health of the normal child under 14 years of age, we must not complain or be surprised if such neglect brings with it in later years hordes of preventable impairment or incapacity of body and mind. Medical science has proved that disease and incapacity in adolescence and adult life find their source all too often in the seed time of childhood. The state which allows its own people to degenerate physically and mentally, because of unemployment, is incurring a grave responsibility. Such young people are liable to become embittered and mentally depressed, and they lose the ground of hope. Have the authorities failed hitherto to recognise this?"

Further evidence of physical deterioration caused by unemployment and poverty in working-class homes is to be found in the British Army Council's report for 1933, which revealed the following:

During the year 95,270 men and lads offered themselves as recruits to the British army. 23,582 were rejected on sight, they were so obviously unfit. 71,688 were served with notice papers for a medical test. Out of that number 66,429 were rejected, leaving only 28,841 passing the test.

After the 1932 hunger march the National Council of Social Services came into prominence in an effort to organise social life amongst the unemployed.

The prime minister and the Prince of Wales spoke in favour of the social service centres, "to save the unemployed from demoralisation." Mayors of towns, councillors, magistrates and clergy were urged to associate themselves with the opening of social service centres, where the unemployed could play games, share out old clothes and possibly engage in schemes of voluntary work. The unemployed movement strongly opposed these social service centres. We pointed out that whilst many of the persons responsible for these schemes might be doing so in the honest belief that they were helping the unemployed, nevertheless the sum total of their effort amounted to keeping the unemployed quiet when they should be actively resisting their poverty conditions.

We were more than suspicious of the connection of the National government with the development of these centres. We found that nine government departments were represented on the National Council of Social Service, namely the Ministry of Health, the Ministry of Labour, the Ministry of Pensions, the Home Office, the Ministry of Agriculture and Fisheries, the Board of Education, the Charity Commissioners, the Development Commission and the National Savings Committee. We could not believe that the Ministry of Labour, which was operating the means test, had any true interest in the welfare of the unemployed; or that the Ministry of Health, which had superseded constitutionally elected local authorities for attempting to operate a comparatively decent scale of relief, would be any more sympathetic. Neither could we believe that the Home Office, which condones the clubbing down of unemployed workers on the streets when they march for bread, had suddenly become philanthropic towards the unemployed by its association with the National Council of Social Services. We were convinced that the big drive at that time for the development of social service centres arose from the fear which had been engendered in the ruling class by the struggles which had taken place in 1932 in Belfast and Birkenhead and in the hunger march.

We saw in the social service schemes not merely an effort to keep the unemployed quiet, but a clever move to prepare the way for a system of unpaid labour amongst the unemployed. Most of the social service centres were opened as purely games-playing centres; then gradually we saw the introduction of voluntary labour schemes, which the unemployed were induced to take up. These developments received the commendation of the Ministry of Labour which, in its report issued in 1934 covering the previous year, stated:

The activities of voluntary organisations on behalf of the unemployed developed considerably during the year, under the auspices of the National Council of Social Service, which undertook at the government's request the work of co-ordinating and stimulating this movement.

Here was a clear admission of the fact that the government not only encouraged this work, but requested that it should be undertaken. The report then went on to state that:

On the 31st December, 1933, the number of towns with welfare committees in operation was about 1,075, whilst some 1,243 occupational centres and 882 recreational centres were in existence at the same date. The latter figures disclose a significant feature of the year's development, viz., the increasing preponderance over purely recreational centres of occupational centres. The department (Ministry of Labour) continued to co-operate with the National Council of Social Service in fostering the movement for the voluntary welfare and occupational training of the unemployed, and also to experiment with a small number of demonstration physical training centres.

This report could leave no doubt that the National government was itself behind the development of the social service schemes and that these schemes were being used to initiate a plan whereby the unemployed would work without receiving wages.

Our suspicions were proved to be well grounded when in July 1934 the new Unemployment Act was passed, in which it was laid down that claimants who came under Part II of the Act must undergo compulsory attendance at a residential or non-residential labour centre, where they were to work in exchange for the benefit scale under the Unemployment Assistance Board, plus 4s. a week pocket money. I shall deal with the fight against this Act in my next chapter; I mention it here in order to show the connection between the government-inspired social service schemes of 1933 and the Unemployment Act of 1934.

The unemployed movement, whilst recognising the need for the development of social life amongst the unemployed, nevertheless rightly denounced the social service schemes instituted by the National Council of Social Service. We claimed that they were not only a danger from the standpoint of encouraging the unemployed to tolerate their poverty conditions, but that the voluntary work schemes in particular constituted a serious menace to the established trade union wages and conditions. We said that it was not games that the unemployed wanted, but food; it was not voluntary work schemes but employment at proper trade union rates of wages, in order that they could live a normal life like their fellows.

During 1933 many campaigns and agitations against the means test and the poverty conditions were carried out. A series of county hunger marches were organised. Two of the biggest of these took place in June and July 1933, when the Scottish unemployed marched to Edinburgh and the Lancashire unemployed marched to Preston. More than two thousand unemployed from the industrial areas of Scotland entered Edinburgh on 11th June, to demand the abolition of the means test, the granting of 1s. 6d. per week extra for the children and 3s. per week extra for adults, a twenty-five per cent reduction in rents and work at trade union rates of wages.

They were met in Edinburgh by 20,000 workers, and for several days intense agitation was carried on. To the amazement of the general public, they encamped and cooked food in their boilers in the main square outside the historic St. Giles' cathedral, and when the authorities refused to provide suitable halls for their accommodation they slept out on Princes Street, the main high-class shopping centre of Edinburgh. The authorities of Edinburgh were so shocked by 2,000 hunger marchers, wrapped in blankets, sleeping on the pavements of proud Princes Street, that next night they found suitable halls for the marchers. Fortunately it was a beautiful warm night in June and there was no immediate hardship involved for the marchers, but the spectacle of the streets littered with recumbent human bodies almost in the shadow of Edinburgh castle, and hunger marchers shaving and washing under the public fountain in the morning was too serious a blow to the dignity of the city for the authorities to remain unmoved.

Another shock to the traditions of Edinburgh was a surprise march into the grounds of the royal palace of Holyrood. They took not only the police, but the sentries by surprise; instead of turning to the right as they had been expected to do, they marched straight under the main archway leading to the palace and so into the grounds, with the Maryhill N.U.W.M. band leading the way, playing Connolly's "Rebel Song." It was a strange sight to see those 2,000 hunger marchers, with red banners flying, marching down the royal mile into the royal sanctuary. Inside the grounds the marchers sang the "International" and then marched out on to the meadows beyond the palace.

Before the hunger marchers left Edinburgh the authorities had to contribute towards the cost of transporting them back to their home town by a fleet of special buses. Later, in a financial statement issued by the Edinburgh town council, it was revealed that, in addition to these expenses, it had cost £550 for overtime pay for the police, and £82 for the hire of horses for mounted men standing by, all spent in trying to stifle the cry of the unemployed for bread!

In the Lancashire march on Preston nearly one thousand marchers took part. A deputation from the marchers met the

County Public Assistance Committee, and amongst the demands which they raised were: the unconditional feeding of necessitous school children; free boots and clothes for the unemployed; free maternity benefit for expectant mothers; the abolition of the means test and the provision of work schemes at trade union rates of pay. The P.A.C. agreed to set up a special committee to consider the demands and to make investigations into the conditions of the unemployed.

The struggles of the unemployed continued with varying success throughout the year 1933. The Royal Commission on Unemployment had issued its final report at the end of 1932; this was now under consideration by the government, and upon its recommendations the new Unemployment Act was being prepared. The report made recommendations for a further serious attack upon the conditions of the unemployed, involving reductions in benefits for men, women and youths, a reduction in the benefit period from twenty-six weeks to thirteen weeks, the reintroduction of the "not genuinely seeking work" clause and a new scheme to cater for the long-term unemployed, with allowances below labour exchange benefits.

The agitation against the royal commission's proposals continued throughout the year. The government framed new legislation, but in face of the agitation did not dare to embody in this all the new attacks which the commission had proposed. The new Bill, however, drew forth strong opposition from all sections of the working-class movement, and during the autumn of 1933 the N.U.W.M. resolved to organise another national hunger march on London to coincide with the holding in London of a National Congress of Action against the unemployment Bill. A National Congress and March Council was formed, consisting of many prominent persons in the trade union and labour movement, with Maud Brown and John Aplin as joint secretaries, and myself as organiser of the march, the object being to make the congress and march as representative as possible of all sections of the working class.

Whilst the work of preparation for the march was in progress, an important legal case was being fought by our movement in the law courts against Lord Trenchard. After my release from prison in the early part of 1933 the National Unemployed Workers' Movement decided to prosecute Lord Trenchard, chief commissioner of the Metropolitan Police, in respect of the raid upon national headquarters that had taken place at the time of my arrest during the 1932 march. We claimed damages for "trespass, conversion and detinue of documents seized by the police." The case came into the courts in December 1933. The attorney-general (Sir Thomas Inskip) and Mr. Wilfred Lewis defended the action on behalf of Lord Trenchard, whilst Sir Stafford Cripps, K.C., Mr. D. N. Pritt, K.C. and Mr. G. R. Mitchison appeared for the Unemployed Movement. The case was heard in the King's Bench Division before Mr. Justice Horridge. It was a keen legal battle that went on throughout December and January.

In his closing speech our counsel, D. N. Pritt, K.C., made the following remarks:

"What disturbs my clients and what they really desire to have stopped is that police officers can walk into the offices of a perfectly legal organisation and under the guise of arresting an individual, proceed to make a clean sweep of all documents, including books of accounts, collection cards, etc., and remove them to Scotland Yard. This is a shocking proceeding. The Commissioner of Police and his officers have committed ir-regularities in complete disregard of the law of the land."

Ultimately we won the day against Lord Trenchard, and on 23rd January, 1934, Justice Horridge awarded the plaintiffs (Llewellyn, Elias, Jane, and myself), damages amounting to £30 plus costs of counsel, and an order for the return of the documents which had been taken from the N.U.W.M. headquarters without search warrant and were still held by the police.

The recording of this verdict is of the utmost importance in respect to future possible action by the police against working-class organisations. It establishes an important point of law which will undoubtedly be a subject of further reference in future legal proceedings affecting the working-class movement.

Chapter XVII

THE GOVERNMENT COMPELLED TO RESTORE CUTS

OUR victory over Lord Trenchard took place at the law courts the day following the start of 500 Scottish marchers from Glasgow, under the leadership of Harry McShane.

In the organising of hunger marches we had now become experts, knowing every detail that was required in the preparation and the carrying through of the march. A manifesto was issued to the working-class movement by the congress and march council calling for support for the marchers on the road and for delegates to be elected to the congress of action which was to open in London on the week-end when the marchers arrived—24th and 25th February.

Tremendous support gathered throughout the country. We still encountered a measure of opposition from certain Labour leaders, but in the main this march rallied wider sections of the working-class movement in active support than we had experienced in any previous march. On this occasion Mr. John McGovern, M.P., was marching with the Scottish contingent.

As the contingents from all parts of the country pressed steadily on towards London, so the demand for the abolition of the means test, the restoration of the benefit cuts and the withdrawal of the new unemployment Bill rose louder. We again encountered intense opposition and misrepresentation in the daily capitalist press. The government also became alarmed, and in the House of Commons on 1st February, 1934, Sir John Gilmour, home secretary, in reply to a question, said:

"The right to hold peaceful meetings and processions is one of our most cherished rights, but if this right is to be abused in such a way as to lead inevitably to grave disorder or public disturbance, the government will have to ask Parliament to grant such powers as experience might show to be necessary to deal with such demonstrations."

This was intended as a threat against the marchers. The congress and march council issued a reply to the home secretary and challenged him to give a single instance in any hunger march where disorder was begun by the workers—at the same time offering to give him plenty of cases where his police chiefs had been responsible for conflict. We warned the marchers to guard against acts of provocation. Two days later, Sir Thomas Inskip, the attorney-general, speaking at a meeting in Hampshire, referred to the march and tried to frighten his audience by talk of bloodshed, saying that the government would be bound to take steps to stop it. The march went steadily on, gathering strength from day to day.

The route of the Scottish contingent lay through Birmingham. We had planned this deliberately because this was the strongest and most hardened contingent on the road, and would be better fitted to counter any police provocation such as had been experienced in the previous march by the Lancashire contingent in Birmingham. The Scots arrived in Birmingham on 13th February, and it was only by firm discipline that a conflict with the police was avoided. The police engaged in every conceivable act of provocation, attempting to interfere with the route of the marchers through the town, and interfering with them in the workhouse. They tried to prevent the marchers from leaving the workhouse after they had entered, and it was only after heated argument by the leaders of the contingent that this restriction was overcome.

Such acts of irritation by the police led to McShane, John McGovern, M.P., and other leaders of the contingent demanding an interview at midnight with the police superintendent and the P.A.C. officer. They demanded that the police and the attendants should be withdrawn from the sleeping quarters of the marchers. In reply, the argument was advanced that they were needed in case of fire! When the authorities saw the temper of the marchers over the question, they ultimately withdrew. A few minutes later the leaders were informed that a large number of police were still in a room upstairs. McGovern and McShane again approached the superintendent and demanded an explanation.

Not satisfied with the reply, they went to inspect the room and found it packed with policemen. The superintendent pretended that he was not aware of their presence and ordered the police downstairs. In a room downstairs a number of police were also found; Mr. McGovern reported that in this room there were glasses smelling of whisky and large glasses of beer. By persistence on the part of the marchers' leaders the institution was ultimately cleared of the police. If the Scottish men had had to fight that night they would have fought to the death; it was fortunate that this was avoided.

In the university towns of Cambridge and Oxford, progressive-minded students organised magnificent receptions for the Tyne-side contingent and the Lancashire contingent respectively. In Cambridge the police again tried to cause trouble with the marchers, arriving early on the scene at the Market Hall and ordering the marchers to leave before they had finished their breakfast. Some rough handling took place, but an open conflict was avoided.

While the marchers were on the road, the congress and march council organising committee met daily to review the movements of the contingents and to discuss preparations in London. Plain-clothes detectives were regularly watching the offices of the unemployed movement and occasionally following members of the council. At a meeting of the council held one evening in the club room over a public-house in Farringdon Street, when the members arrived they found four detectives outside the place of meeting. A little later two police cars drove up, a detective spoke to the occupants, and they went away again.

Then when Llewellyn, an official of the unemployed movement, arrived, one of the detectives spoke to him and asked if I would be at the meeting. Llewellyn refused to reply. I came along later and entered the meeting-place. After a few minutes we saw from a window a considerable number of plain-clothes officers assembling outside. One of the detectives came to the telephone, which was outside the door of the meeting-room, and started a conversation, talking in a code. We naturally became suspicious and thought that possibly the police were attempting to round up the whole march leadership.

So, instead of proceeding with our business, we decided to adjourn the meeting immediately and disperse in ones and twos, meeting at another place appointed, each man taking care to avoid being followed. The adjournment apparently took the police by surprise. Several of the delegates had difficulty in shaking off the detectives, who followed them, but ultimately they were successful, and late at night we reassembled and continued our work.

A few days later we arranged for the organising committee of the congress and march council to meet in a room, booked by Mr. Maxton, in the House of Commons. I knew that by order of the Speaker I was banned from entering the House of Commons. This ban had been in force for several years, arising from the disturbances with which I had been connected in the House. I thought, however, that my attendance at a meeting in a private room in the House, called by a Member of Parliament, would not be interfered with; I succeeded in passing the first group of policemen at the entrance without question, but, before I reached the outer lobby, several policemen ran towards me and informed me that I was banned from entering the House and must immediately leave.

I pointed out that I was to attend a meeting at which a number of M.P.'s were present, but still they declined to allow me to pass. Whilst I argued with the police, two sympathetic Members of Parliament came forward to ask what was the trouble. I explained, and in spite of their protests I was not allowed to proceed. The other members of the committee were already assembled; they were depending on my attendance at the meeting because I had most of the material concerning the march arrangements. It meant that either the whole of the committee would have to come out of the House and meet elsewhere, or I would have to find a way into the House surreptitiously.

I took the latter course, and walked away from the police along with the M.P.'s as though going out of the House; we discussed how I could get in; I gained certain information in respect to an entrance (then private) for Members of Parliament by a tunnel which runs into the House from Westminster underground station. Saying good night to the Members of Parliament, I led the police to believe that I had quietly accepted their orders and was departing.

I then proceeded to the entrance of the underground passage. Although there were police standing along the passage at intervals of a few yards, it is dimly lit and it is not easy to distinguish the features of a person passing through. I carried a satchel in my hand, similar to that carried by many M.P.'s, entered the passage and walked through with my head down as though in meditation. As I did so, the police saluted me with the words "Good night, sir!" at every few yards. I acted up to the occasion and replied "Good night, officer!"

Coming up the staircase into the House, behind the outer lobby, I made my way to the room where the committee were already sitting, and entered, much to their surprise. After the meeting I decided not to go out the way I had come in, but to walk out through the lobbies and the main entrance; the look of amazement on the faces of the police when I walked past them in the lobby was amusing. Two and a half hours earlier they had put me out and thought they had seen the last of me, and now they saw me coming from the inner lobby of the House. I did not give them a chance to put questions, and before they could recover from their astonishment I had passed out into the street.

As the marchers came nearer to London the clamour of certain capitalist elements for their suppression or for the restriction of their movements was increasing. The Duchess of Athol asked the home secretary if he would take suitable steps to prevent the hunger marchers from holding meetings in Trafalgar Square or other overcrowded areas. Three days before the marchers entered London, the police visited the Tyneside contingent and arrested five of the marchers on the grounds of "wife desertion." This action was instigated by the public assistance authorities because the wives of these men were claiming poor law relief whilst their husbands were on the march. Each marcher was able to prove that there was no desertion whatever, that the wives had been supporting the men going on the march, and that this was simply a high-handed action by the authorities in order to make difficulties for the marchers. Seven West Fife marchers were arrested on a similar charge after the march, when they returned to their homes. Their case was heard in the Dunfermline sheriff's court, and the men were acquitted amidst applause in the public gallery. I mention these things to show that whilst the home secretary spoke of what he would do to the marchers if they became disorderly, at the same time the authorities themselves were trying to provoke trouble.

The attempt of the government and the capitalist press to represent the marchers as disorderly persons led to the formation of a committee of eminent public men and women under the name of the Council for Civil Liberties. They combated the propaganda against the marchers and took steps to ascertain the facts of the situation in case trouble took place when the marchers arrived in London. The *Manchester Guardian* published a letter from this committee which read:

The present hunger march has been preceded by public statements by the Home Secretary and the Attorney General (who has already hinted at the possibility of bloodshed) which we feel justify apprehension. Furthermore, certain features of the police preparations for the present march—for example, instructions to shopkeepers to barricade their windows—cannot but create an atmosphere of misgiving, not only dangerous but unjustified by the facts.

All reports bear witness to the excellent discipline of the

marchers. From their own leaders they have received repeated instructions of the strictest character, warning them against any breach of the peace, even under extreme provocation.

In view of the general and alarming tendency to encroachment on the liberty of the citizen, there has recently been formed a Council for Civil Liberties. One of the special duties of this Council will be to maintain a vigilant observation of the proceedings of the next few days. Relevant and well-authenticated reports by responsible persons will be welcomed and investigated by the Council.

(*Signed*)

Lascelles Abercrombie	C. R. Attlee
Ambrose Appelbee	V. R. Brittain
C. H. Bing	A. P. Herbert
Dudley Collard	Kingsley Martin
Harold Laski	D. N. Pritt
Evelyn Sharp Nevinson	H. G. Wells
Henry W. Nevinson	Ronald Kidd
Edith Summerskill	(Secretary).

The foregoing letter clearly shows the state of apprehension which had come into being as the marchers came nearer to London. Tory Members of Parliament representing industrial constituencies became anxious about the attitude of the government to the new unemployment Bill, the restoration of the cuts and the allowances for children. On a proposition to increase the children's allowance from 2s. to 3s. a week, seventy Tory members voted for the increase against their own government.

When all the contingents of marchers were within three days' marching distance from London, arrangements were made for Harry McShane, from the Scottish contingent, and Lewis Jones, from the Welsh contingent, to meet one hundred Members of Parliament at a special meeting in the House of Commons, at which the marchers' representatives stated the case against the new Bill and urged support for the demand that representatives of the marchers should be permitted to state their case before the bar of the House of Commons. The M.P.'s listened attentively to the speeches of McShane and Jones; then they put questions which were promptly answered, proving that the marchers' representatives were fully conversant with the details of the new legislation. Warm support for hearing the marchers at the bar of the House was expressed by the members present and an assurance given that they would play their part in pressing the government to grant this request.

On 23rd February all contingents of marchers moved into position on the outskirts of London in readiness for the big welcome at Hyde Park which was to take place on Sunday, 25th February. Ten thousand special constables were called up for duty and strong forces of provincial police were drafted into London to supplement the metropolitan police. The Congress of Action was due to open at ten o'clock on the morning of Saturday, 24th February, in the Bermondsey Town Hall. During the Friday delegates were travelling from all parts of the country to represent their trade unions, labour parties, trades councils and other working-class bodies at the congress. On the evening of the 23rd, the eve of the congress opening, the government struck a blow at the march and congress by issuing warrants for the arrest of Tom Mann and Harry Pollitt, both of whom were members of the congress and march council. They were both charged with using seditious language in speeches they had made at meetings in the Rhondda Valley during the previous week-end. They were taken under police escort to Pontypridd, where they appeared in the court next day. Prominent publicity was given to these moves on the wireless and in all the newspapers. Tom Mann was to have taken the chair at the congress and Harry Pollitt was to have moved the main resolution. The action of the government in arresting Mann and Pollitt was a deliberate blow at the congress. Throughout the country the workers understood this, and within a few hours the government was made to realise that their action had called forth nation-wide indignation and a clamorous demand for the release of Mann and Pollitt. The arrests had the effect of stiffening the working-class movement behind the marchers and the congress. When Mann and Pollitt appeared in court at Pontypridd the police agreed to an adjournment and released them on bail.

One thousand four hundred and ninety-four delegates, directly representing three-quarters of a million organised workers, crowded into the Bermondsey town hall for the opening of the congress, with Alex Gossip, general secretary of the National Furnishing Trades Association taking the chair, and the Labour mayor of Bermondsey giving a civic reception to the delegates. The congress was one of the most enthusiastic gatherings of its kind that has ever taken place.

From Ireland came the veteran Mrs. Despard. In her speech to the congress she said, "I feel that this congress is the beginning of the fulfilment of the hopes I have cherished during my fifty years of struggle for the working class." The speech of Harry

Pollitt was read to the congress by William Gallacher. Mrs. Tom Mann attended the congress and was greeted with tremendous applause when she took the platform to speak. She told how the police had arrested Tom the day before and when she described how the police had stated they must search him in case "he might have drugs on him to commit suicide" the congress roared with laughter at the notion that this fearless and unbreakable fighter should think of committing suicide. Congress cheered her closing remarks to the echo, when she said, "Leaders may be taken away, but new leaders must grow up." Ivor Montagu brought a special message of solidarity to the congress from George Dimitrov, the great international working-class fighter who was lying in gaol on the false charge of firing the Reichstag.

The congress continued in session until late on Saturday evening. Before the congress closed that day, to the joy of all the delegates news was received of the release of Tom Mann and Harry Pollitt on bail. At the closing session of the congress on Sunday morning the resolution received the unanimous endorsement of the congress. It dealt with the fight against the new Unemployment Act and the way in which the struggle should be developed; made demands for the abolition of the means test, the restoration of the benefit cuts and increased children's allowances; advanced proposals for a forty-hour working week without wage reductions, and for work schemes at trade union rates of wages; and called upon the government to receive the marchers' deputation.

The following correspondence that had passed between Mr. Ramsay MacDonald and the congress and march council was read.

We, the representative members of the National Congress and March Council, respectfully request you to provide facilities for a deputation representing the marchers and the congress to be received by the Government on Tuesday morning, February 27th. The object of the deputation will be to state the case of the congress and the marchers against the new Unemployment Bill. We ask that all Ministers of the Government be present to meet the deputation.

(*Signed*) Alex Gossip, Tom Mann, Harry Pollitt, Wal Hannington, John Aplin, Maud Brown, James Lee, J. B. Figgins, James Maxton, M.P., Aneurin Bevan, M.P., Ellen Wilkinson, Dorothy Woodman, John McGovern, M.P., James Carmichael.

To this letter the prime minister replied as follows:

In reply to the letter sent from the National Congress and March Council, asking the Government to receive a deputation from the Unemployed Marchers, I have been instructed by the Prime Minister to say that it is impossible to accede to your request. The deputation can do no service to the unemployed. The communist purpose of these marches is common knowledge. The Government is responsible for a Bill which, when in operation, will facilitate the more satisfactory treatment of the whole question of unemployment, and that Bill is now receiving consideration by the House of Commons, composed of members whose knowledge and experience enable it to discuss the best way to achieve the objects of the Government. Individual members of the House are aware that Ministers are always desirous of helping them on any matter which they or their constituents wish to bring before the Government.

(*Signed*) J. A. Barlow,
Private Secretary.

This reply was received with ironical cheers in the congress.

During the session Tom Mann and Harry Pollitt, who had travelled up from South Wales, entered the congress hall and the whole congress rose to cheer. Both of them had to make short speeches before the delegates could be satisfied.

Despite the reply of the prime minister, a national deputation to the government was elected, including Members of Parliament and representatives from trades councils, co-operative societies and trade unions, together with representatives of the hunger marchers.

At one o'clock the congress terminated with the singing of the "International," and the whole of the delegates formed into ranks outside the hall, all the delegates affixing their red credential cards to the lapels of their coats, and, accompanied by thousands of Bermondsey workers, marching to Hyde Park to welcome the hunger marchers.

Hyde Park was again the scene of a mighty demonstration. Despite bad weather—drizzle, alternating with heavy downpours —over one hundred thousand workers from all parts of London mobilised in Hyde Park and gave an enthusiastic welcome to the hunger marchers as they began to enter the gates of the park at 3 p.m. The Scottish contingent was the first to arrive, with fifes, drums and bagpipes. They had been on the road for more than a month, and were leg-weary but full of enthusiasm. All through the afternoon the detachments of marchers trooped in—from

Tyneside, Cornwall, Lancashire, Yorkshire, Notts and Derby, Norfolk, South Wales, etc. Cheer after cheer rolled from the vast crowds as the contingents entered the park, headed by bands and banners announcing the areas from which they had come. A special cheer was given to the women's contingent, drawn from all parts of the country, which had mobilised at Derby and marched for two weeks.

There were thousands of police endeavouring to control the crowds; there were motor-cyclist police, flying squad cars, marchers' field-kitchens and ambulance cars all mixed up. On top of Marble Arch were police directing the marshalling of the crowds and the routes of the demonstrators into the park by means of specially-installed telephones. In addition to the huge forces of police on duty in the park, mounted and foot reserves were held in readiness in nearby streets, but it was noticeable that on this occasion all special constables were kept strictly away from the demonstration; they were being used solely for the purpose of relieving the ordinary policemen from point and patrol duty. The mistake made in the previous march was not repeated.

The demonstration made a tremendous impression; photographs appeared in most newspapers next morning, showing the vast crowds that participated, and all papers had to admit that it was one of the greatest demonstrations ever seen in this country. One capitalist newspaper, commenting upon the marchers, said:

Their will was strong and their spirits high. They marched in behind their bands with their packs on their backs, singing the "International" and shouting their defiance of the system against which they had gathered to protest. They brought with them an atmosphere of tragedy, for which the day, with its grey skies and drizzling rain, seemed made, but not a single policeman was called on for any duty other than that of escort. It was one of the most orderly demonstrations London has ever seen.

When the Welshmen came in to take their place behind their appointed platform, they were not smoking, because they had nothing to smoke. Suddenly, the crowd realised this and rained packets of cigarettes on them. That was typical of the attitude of the crowd all the afternoon.

In the park, speakers from the ranks of the marchers, along with M.P.s and other prominent persons in the British working-class movement, addressed the great crowds. "Down with the means test!" "Down with the National Government!" were the slogans that repeatedly rang out from all platforms. The crowd cheered to the echo when speakers demanded that the government should restore the cuts in the benefit of the unemployed and that the government should meet the marchers' deputation. The demonstration ended without any serious conflict, although with such a vast crowd it was not surprising that one or two incidents took place on the outskirts between demonstrators and police.

When the bugles sounded the closure of the meeting, the banners were raised, the ranks re-formed, and the marchers, accompanied by thousands of London workers, marched to their various sleeping quarters provided by the London County Council.

On Monday, February 26th, Mr. John McGovern, M.P., presented a petition in the House of Commons, signed by leaders of the marchers' contingents, which read as follows:

The petitioners as representatives of the unemployed men and women of the country and of the thousands of hunger marchers who have now arrived in London humbly desire to represent that great suffering has been caused to the unemployed and their dependants by the means test, Anomalies Act, and the cuts in unemployment benefit, and the declared intention of the Government to continue those hardships through the Unemployment Bill at present before Parliament, and even to worsen the present miseries of the working class thereby.

Wherefore your petitioners pray that they or some of their number should be heard at the Bar of this honourable House as representatives of the unemployed, to set forth their grievances and to urge on behalf of the unemployed men and women the withdrawal of the Unemployment Bill, and in its stead the introduction of a Bill to give decent maintenance or provide employment at trade union rates for the unemployed who are enduring such great hardships; and your petitioners as in duty bound will ever pray, etc.

> (*Signed*) HARRY McSHANE
> PETER NEVILLE HARKER
> JOHN SAMUEL WILLIAMS.

Following the presentation of the petition, Mr. McGovern announced that he wished to give notice of motion that the representatives of the hunger marchers be received at the bar of the House.

Next morning, 27th February, the national joint deputation from the congress and the marchers proceeded to Downing Street to press for an interview with Mr. Ramsay MacDonald, the prime minister. A large crowd had gathered in Whitehall to cheer the arrival of the deputation, and strong cordons of police stood across No. 10 Downing Street. The leaders of the deputation, including James Maxton, M.P., John McGovern, M.P., Harry McShane and myself, were admitted to No. 10, but were informed that the prime minister was not at home.

After spending fifteen minutes with Mr. Vincent, the prime minister's secretary, and strongly protesting against the refusal of Mr. MacDonald to receive the deputation, we left the prime minister's residence to report to the crowds outside. In spite of the police cordons, the demonstrators had steadily pressed forward into Downing Street, and were only a few yards from No. 10. We actually held a meeting in Downing Street and reported our interview with Mr. Vincent. During the afternoon Mr. McGovern again raised in the House of Commons the question of the deputation being heard at the bar of the House.

The prime minister replied to the effect that this was not necessary as the House represented all sections of the community and the unemployed could make representations through their members. He declared that in the opinion of the government no advantage would be gained by acceding to the request for marchers' representatives to appear at the bar of the House. A Conservative, Mr. Hannon, asked if there was any precedent for the appearance of commoners at the bar of the House. Mr. Maxton replied, "Yes—read the history of the House." Major Attlee, then deputy-leader of the Parliamentary Labour Party, asked if it was not a fact that the monied interests, represented by the City of London, had the right to come to the bar of the House. Mr. MacDonald replied that the City of London had been represented there, but not on account of any monied interests, but because of certain historical facts.

Mr. McGovern: "Has the prime minister definitely decided to close every constitutional approach for the unemployed to present their claims?"

Mr. MacDonald: "Quite the contrary; every constitutional approach is provided by the constitution and particularly by the fact that this is a representative assembly." (Tory cheers.)

Mr. McGovern: "I ask the prime minister, has he to sacrifice every principle and vestige of independence to retain his position as head of the government?" (Cries of "Order, order," and "Withdraw.")

The Speaker here intervened and claimed that the questioners were wandering from the point.

Mr. Maxton: "Surely it is legitimate to ask the prime minister,

as head of the National government, to give special consideration to the cry of men who, to a large extent, were responsible
for placing him at the head. I ask therefore that he concede to
these men a citizens' right, granted to nearly every other section
of the community. I ask him and the government to reconsider
this refusal."

Mr. George Buchanan then moved that the House should
adjourn in order that a discussion might take place on this point.

The Speaker asked if this motion had the support of the House
and he found that it had. He therefore announced that the
adjournment was carried and that the House would discuss the
question that same evening. When the debate was resumed at
11 p.m. bitter words of condemnation were hurled at the prime
minister for his refusal to listen to the case of the unemployed.
Stormy scenes occurred every few minutes, when Tory members
demanded that some statement made from the Opposition benches
be withdrawn. Not only did the I.L.P. and certain Labour
Members of Parliament make a fight for the marchers, but the
leader of the Liberal Opposition, Sir Herbert Samuel, also spoke
and urged the government to grant the request of the marchers.

Major Attlee said: "The marchers are fair representatives of
the great masses of unemployed. The injustice from which these
men and women are suffering is very widely known in all parts
of the House and the feeling in the country is now tremendous.
There is an ever-increasing volume of opinion that the unemployment problem should be grappled with. There is no reason
why these men should be refused a hearing by the cabinet."

Sir Herbert Samuel said: "No one can say that the grievances
of these men, who have walked to this city from many parts of
this island, are trivial or imaginary. The well-to-do are suffering
from a diminution of income and an increase of taxation, but
no one suffers anything in comparison with those hundreds of
thousands of men and women who have, month in and month
out, year in and year out, to exist on 15s. 3d. a week, 8s. for a
wife and 2s. for a child. What should these men do other than
what they have done, if they want to draw the attention of the
nation to their plight and shake Parliament out of its shameful
complacency in order to protest against the utterly inadequate
measures so far taken? Are we to say to them, 'If you are disorderly we cannot listen to you, but if you are orderly we need
not listen to you?' These men and women have walked from the
far ends of the country, hundreds of miles. It would have been
right for the prime minister to have received their spokesmen and

to have listened to their complaint. It would have been a fine and gracious act. Let them not go back thinking that every door is barred, every window shuttered, every heart closed against them. The government and Parliament would be wise to wish them well and show that we are anxious to help."

Mr. MacDonald endeavoured to justify the action of the government, and here he was able to fall back upon the reactionary conduct of Labour Party and T.U.C. leaders in connection with the organised unemployed. He referred to the fact that the Labour government had refused hunger marchers' deputations, and so also had the T.U.C. He went on to say that the march was "Placing a strain upon the over-burdened people responsible for the maintenance of public order," and went on to ask, "Has anybody who cares to come to London, either on foot or in first-class carriages, the constitutional right to demand to see me, to take up my time, whether I like it or not? I say he has nothing of the kind. If they think they have a constitutional right to compel me to see them, they are very much mistaken."

Following this rather undignified outburst the Tories were rallied and defeated the motion at twenty minutes to one in the morning. During the whole of the debate large forces of police guarded the House of Commons. There was fear of a demonstration by the marchers, and detectives filled the public corridors. Policemen were ready to slam the gates of Old Palace Yard at the first sign of trouble and were in close touch with Scotland Yard. One of the doors leading into the Chamber, which is normally closed only when it is slammed in the face of Black Rod, the House of Lords' messenger, as a sign of the independence of the other House, was kept bolted throughout the whole sitting.

The press reported that the "debate took place in an atmosphere of extreme bitterness, and tempers were raw." In the debate Mr. MacDonald had been taunted about the way in which he had deserted the Labour movement and turned Conservative. The *Star* next evening in a leading article said:

Mr. Macdonald may have made a good speech in defending his refusal to see a deputation from the hunger marchers. To what end? Conservative die-hards cheered him on! He may lay that flattering unction to his soul, but what practical purpose to humanity or efficiency did it serve? Far more of his own time was taken up in refusing to see the deputation of the marchers than would have been taken in seeing them. Hours of Parliamentary debate had to be devoted to the subject. The marchers came from areas where the black cloud of unemployment lies like a pall, where men are apt to feel that Parliament has forgotten them, where even empty words have some power to cheer. Mr. Macdonald's usual exordium to his speeches is "Ah, my friends!" Where could it have been employed more effectually than in receiving his fellow Scots who had come south. The marchers have shamed their detractors by their dignity and surprised those who know their grievances best, by their restraint."

If Mr. MacDonald thought that he had closed the subject of the marchers when he, along with the Tories, threw out the motion to give them a hearing at the bar of the House, he was very much mistaken. He had said that there was nothing to prevent the marchers from interviewing their Members of Parliament. We took him at his word, and next day, Wednesday, the 28th, the whole of the marchers, with some thousands of London workers, made their way in small groups to the House of Commons to ask for a meeting with their M.P.'s.

Had they marched with bands and banners, their way would have been barred long before they reached the House, but the tactic of proceeding in small groups resulted in a huge crowd gathering outside the entrance to the House before the police realised what was happening. The famous regulation that no group is allowed to assemble within a mile of Parliament when the House is sitting, was torn to shreds. Mounted police and foot police were sent for to try to control the crowds; all the time marchers were demanding admission to the House to meet their Members of Parliament. The police were flustered; they had apparently not received instructions on how to deal with this tactic, and the debate in the House of Commons the night before had made them wary about denying constitutional rights to the marchers.

Soon the marchers were singing the "International" and the "Rebel Song." A few were allowed to trickle into the House. Then Members of Parliament complained because they had to go on to the streets to interview their constituents. All the evening the crowd persisted. They formed into queues, broke up, and re-formed; the marchers steadily maintaining their rights to meet their Members of Parliament.

Inside the House of Commons heated protests were made by Members of Parliament against the marchers being kept out on the streets. The Speaker said he was sure that no differentiation was being made; the ordinary rules governing admission to the

House were being enforced; "There is a large number of people, there must be a limit." The demonstration was kept going until very late in the evening; then the order to disperse was given and the marchers returned to their sleeping quarters.

During the morning grave alarm had been caused amongst the authorities by the gathering of marchers outside Buckingham Palace. The gates of the palace were hurriedly closed, and large forces of mounted and foot police were rushed to the palace, but before they could arrive in full strength the marchers had dispersed, and reassembled again, much to the consternation of the police, in Piccadilly Circus, where they held a short demonstration.

Next day, the press announced that the Cabinet budget committee was giving serious consideration to the question of restoring either in whole or in part the ten per cent cuts in unemployment benefit.

The marchers again went to the House on Thursday, 1st March. Three hundred succeeded in getting into the outer lobby and twenty-four into the public gallery. Then suddenly a cry rang out from the gallery: "Meet the hunger marchers!" "We refuse to starve in silence!" "Down with the National government!" The House was startled; police rushed to the spot from which the disturbance had come, and when they attempted to evict the marchers struggles ensued. Members of Parliament, looking up, saw what probably few of them had seen before—uniformed police being used in the public gallery in addition to plain-clothes men. Suddenly, at the other end of the chamber in the Ladies' Gallery, above the Speaker's chair, a woman was heard shouting, "Don't knock those men about!" She was removed by the police.

When the news reached the central lobby that fighting had broken out in the gallery, the 300 marchers who had succeeded in gaining admission started vigorously singing the "International." Police reinforcements were rushed from all parts of the House and fighting took place in the lobby. The marchers were eventually ejected and the police thought that they had put an end to the disturbances, but there were still marchers in various parts of the House, and three times during the evening scenes broke out in the gallery and in the lobby.

On Sunday, 4th March, another great demonstration was held in Trafalgar Square. Early on Sunday morning the contingents of London workers began to form with bands and banners to march to this historic meeting-place, and long before the marchers had arrived enormous crowds had gathered in the square and the adjacent streets. A tumultuous reception was again given to the marchers when they arrived, accompanied by huge contingents of workers from the localities in which they were being accommodated. Large forces of police were held in readiness but there were no serious disturbances. A few slight clashes occurred in the surrounding streets as the dense masses tried to press forward to the square. All traffic had to be diverted as it was impossible to make a clearance for it in the vicinity of the square. The gates of the Admiralty Arch were closed and heavily guarded. When the police tried to clear the way for the traffic they were heartily booed by the crowds. A granite post on the east side of the square was knocked over under pressure as the police were endeavouring to clear the roadway. For a short time the traffic began to move again in Charing Cross Road and the Strand, but the police had a hopeless task and in the end had to give it up and wait until the demonstration ended.

Next morning the women marchers were informed by Miss Ellen Wilkinson that Miss Ishbel Macdonald had agreed to receive a deputation from them at No. 10 Downing Street. Miss Macdonald told the women that she did not agree with their marching and demonstration, as that would not help their cause. Maud Brown, who was leading the women's deputation, reminded her that in 1914 her father had been associated with demonstrations for peace. The women strongly stated their case against the benefit cuts, the means test and the unemployment Bill. Miss Macdonald asked many questions about the conditions of the workers in the various parts of the country from which the women had come. When she suggested that unemployed weavers, clerical workers, clothing workers and others should go into domestic service, the women marchers flared up and told her they wanted work at their own trades.

After a heated interview Miss Macdonald promised to speak to ministers of the government and said she thought something might be done to improve certain clauses of the Bill. The women left, very dissatisfied at Miss Macdonald's failure to offer any constructive policy.

During the afternoon the whole of the marchers joined forces at Hyde Park with full equipment, and inside the gates of the park they pitched their field-kitchens and cooked a hot meal; following this an impressive route march was carried out through the centre of London.

By Tuesday night sufficient money had been raised by donations from trade unions and other working-class bodies to make it possible for all the marchers to return to their home towns by train. Special arrangements were made for reduced fares by the railway companies, and on Wednesday morning, 7th March, all the marchers marched in full kit to the big London railway stations and departed to their homes. As the trains steamed out from Kings Cross, St. Pancras, Euston and Paddington, the London workers gave them a warm farewell cheer.

Telegrams were sent to the towns from which the marchers had come to inform them of the times of arrival, and big demonstrations gathered at the stations to welcome the return of the men who had carried the banners of revolt to the capital against the National government. The Glasgow demonstration was particularly large; over twenty thousand workers assembled outside St. Enoch station, and a mighty roar of welcome rose as the Scottish marchers entered the square. The sections from the outlying parts of Scotland remained in Glasgow overnight, and travelled to their homes next day.

In Lancashire, the North Regional station of the British Broadcasting Corporation approached the leaders of the Lancashire contingent for a short talk on the wireless to take place on 14th March. George Staunton, one of the contingent leaders, was chosen, but on the day that the talk was to take place it was cancelled by the B.B.C. authorities because Staunton would not speak of the march in the manner that they wanted. The speech which he proposed to deliver was, in the opinion of the B.B.C., "too political." They objected to Staunton referring to himself as "a victim of the means test," and said that that would suggest that the government was tyrannical.

The effect of the march continued long after the marchers had left London. Various organisations that had been aroused by the march continued to bring pressure upon the government to compel the restoration of the cuts and the withdrawal of the worst features of the unemployment Bill. Tory Members of Parliament had been severely shaken by the march, and as a result the demand for the cuts to be restored had grown day by day.

Mr. Neville Chamberlain, speaking at a Conservative banquet in Birmingham on 9th March, admitted that he was being overwhelmed with letters from all kinds of organisations and individuals urging restoration of the cuts to the unemployed. He particularly complained about a letter which the Archbishop of York had sent to *The Times* stating that all Christians should support the restoration of the cuts. Mr. Chamberlain said, "When I read this letter in *The Times* I thought it was a pity that the Archbishop should suggest, as it seems to me he did, by implication, that members of Parliament required to be reminded of humanitarian feelings which otherwise would not occur to them."

On 12th March a deputation representing an organisation known as the Children's Minimum Committee met the prime minister and demanded a daily ration of fresh clean milk for all children, compulsory free school meals for all those in need and increased children's allowance in the unemployment Bill.

On the same day a deputation from the British Chambers of Commerce met the chancellor of the exchequer and suggested that the government should put in hand public works schemes. Then three days later came the announcement in the press that 350 ministers of the church in the Lancashire area had petitioned the prime minister to increase the children's allowances.

The council of the Congregational Union of England and Wales at the same time passed a resolution urging more liberal allowances. The annual conference of the Co-operative Party, representing 4,000,000 co-operators, met in Glasgow on 1st April and passed a resolution demanding the immediate restoration of the cuts. The Rusholme (Manchester) division of the Liberal Association passed a resolution at its annual meeting declaring that "the association is deeply concerned about the welfare of the children of the unemployed and urges the government to increase the amount of children's allowance from 2s. to a sum consistent with their needs." Sir Donald Somervell, solicitor-general, was howled down at a public meeting in the Dulwich baths on the question of the government's treatment of the unemployed, and from all parts of the country ministers of the crown were being inundated with letters protesting against their treatment of the unemployed. The agitation culminated in a mighty day of national demonstration, organised by the N.U.W.M., on Sunday, 16th April, known as "Budget Sunday."

The hunger march had stimulated a nation-wide demand for humane treatment by the government. The government could not escape this; the march had been an extremely disturbing factor for them, and the agitation which it had aroused compelled them to retreat. Before the march Mr. Chamberlain, the chancellor of the exchequer, had stated in the House of Commons, in reply to questions, that there was no need to restore the cuts in benefit to the unemployed, as the unemployed, he claimed, were better off than they were in 1931, because of the fall in the cost of living. The march compelled him to eat these words, and when he introduced his 1934 budget on 17th April, he announced that the government had decided to restore the ten per cent cuts that had been made in the scales of the unemployed by the economy measures of 1931. This meant that the benefit was again to be raised from 15s. 3d. to 17s. per week for an adult male worker, from 13s. 6d. to 15s. for an adult female worker, and from 8s. to 9s. for an adult dependent.

Although the official leadership of the Labour Party had abstained from association with the hunger march, and in fact had discouraged local labour parties from associating, following the announcement of the chancellor in respect to the restoration of the cuts, the *Daily Herald* published a photograph of a queue outside the labour exchange with the caption: "These unemployed men will benefit by the concession which Labour, by its campaign, has won from the government"—a real case of hard-faced journalism!

The fight against the government did not end with the restoration of the cuts. The unemployment Bill was passing through its last stages in Parliament and new struggles were being prepared by the unemployed movement to resist its operation. In less than a year the government was again to suffer severe defeat at the hands of the unemployed in respect to this measure.

Chapter XVIII

GOVERNMENT BLUNDERS AND RETREATS

THE unemployment Bill passed its third reading in the House of Commons and became law on 14th May, 1934. It did not begin to operate until 26th July, when the cuts to the unemployed were restored. This delay in the restoration of the cuts met with strong criticism, and many demonstrations took place demanding immediate restoration.

Under the pressure of demonstrations many local authorities were compelled to increase their scales of relief. On 8th May, a London demonstration marched to County Hall and met the Public Assistance Committee, demanding increased relief allowances. The P.A.C. considered the demands, and later made a decision to increase the amount available for relief in the London area by £350,000.

On 4th July the trial of Tom Mann and Harry Pollitt at the Swansea Assizes ended with their acquittal. A great demonstration of workers in Swansea and the surrounding areas took place on the day the verdict was given.

The 1934 Unemployment Act made profound changes in the whole system of unemployment insurance. The Act was in three parts: (1) the Unemployment Insurance Act proper, dealing with all unemployed claimants on statutory benefit; (2) an entirely new scheme for creating an Unemployment Assistance Board, to deal with all claimants who exhausted their statutory benefit and all able-bodied persons in receipt of poor law relief; (3) the appointment of an Unemployment Insurance Statutory Commission to inquire into the working of the Act and to make recommendations every year as to changes in amounts of benefit or of contributions or in administration.

Only Part I of the Act came into operation on 26th July, the date fixed for the operation of Part II being 7th January, 1935. The Act lowered the age for entry into unemployment insurance from sixteen to fourteen years, although benefit was not payable to these contributors until they reached the age of sixteen. The scales of benefit laid down were as follows:

1. Workers of the age of 21 and under 65:
   s. d.
   Men 17 0
   Women 15 0
2. Workers of the age of 18 and under 21:
   Men 14 0
   Women 12 0
3. Workers of the age of 17 and under 18:
   Boys 9 0
   Girls 7 0
4. Workers under the age of 17 years:
   Boys 6 0
   Girls 5 0

The rates of benefit payable in respect of dependents:
For an adult dependent 9 0
For a child dependent 2 0

The first statutory condition for the receipt of benefit was that not less than thirty contributions should have been paid in respect to the two years immediately preceding the date of application for benefit. If satisfying this condition the claimant would be entitled to draw twenty-six weeks' benefit. At the end of this period, if still unemployed, he would have his case reviewed and be entitled to receive additional benefit on the following conditions:

An additional three days' benefit for every five contributions paid in the five years prior to the date of his first claim, less one day's benefit for every five days' benefit received during that five years.

In simple terms, this meant that if the claimant had been in regular insurable employment for the whole five years before the date of his claim, he would be entitled to a twenty-six-weeks' benefit. The period of additional benefit would graduate downwards according to the amount of unemployment in the five years. If he had had sixty weeks' unemployment in that five years, he would receive only eight weeks' additional benefit; if unemployed for eighty weeks in the five years, only two weeks' extra benefit; any longer period of unemployment in the five years would disqualify him for any additional benefit. The other regulations governing Part I of the Act did not differ much from those previously in force.

It was Part II of the Act which caused a storm against the

government in the winter of 1934. There were 1,250,000 persons on transitional benefit who, on 7th January, 1935, would pass under the control of the new Unemployment Assistance Board. The date for the transfer of the able-bodied unemployed in receipt of poor law relief under the scheme was fixed for 1st March, 1935. The board had separate machinery and separate finances for the administration of what were to be known as unemployment allowances. The board was to consist of six persons, with Sir Henry Betterton as chairman. Sir Henry Betterton had formerly been the Minister of Labour with a salary of £2,000; in his new post he received a salary of £5,000.

When the scheme came into full operation there would be over a million and a half persons under the control of this board. Detailed regulations governing the operation of Part II of the new Act were not made known until December 1934, but we knew enough about the main principles of the scheme to describe it justly as the most severe attack ever launched against the unemployed.

Following the defeat of the government over the restoration of the cuts in the early part of the year, the unemployed movement steadily conducted an increasing agitation against Part II of the new Act. By October a big movement was sweeping the country, demanding the withdrawal of this Act and the grant of increased winter relief for all unemployed.

A point in connection with Part II which aroused special resentment, even before the new scales of allowances were made known, was the provision for compulsory training for the unemployed applicants under the U.A.B. in either residential or non-residential training centres.

The drafting of the unemployed into labour camps meant that they would be removed many miles from their home towns and from their families; that they would live under semi-military discipline; that out-of-bounds areas would be laid down beyond which they must not go; they would have to perform a full week's work on road-making, land drainage, irrigation systems, new sewerage schemes, afforestation, improvement of canals and bridges, brickmaking, etc., for which they would be paid no wages, but would receive their meals in the camp, plus 4s. a week pocket money, whilst their dependents, if any, had to exist on the scales of allowances provided by the U.A.B.

We claimed that such a system of labour meant the creation of a new slave class in this country; a class of persons who would no longer be regarded as wage-earners, but who were expected to be content though their family life was broken up and they were compelled to work without wages.

We claimed that this would tend to create a slave mentality, and that the ruling class would use these workers to undermine established trade union standards and conditions; that the government would not hesitate, in fact, if it could create the right psychology amongst this mass of unemployed, to use them as an organised blackleg force, to smash any industrial struggle in which the workers were engaged. Such were our arguments against this proposed labour camp scheme which the government had adopted from the report of the Royal Commission on Unemployment. This report had referred to a similar labour camp scheme in operation in Germany, and we therefore claimed that this meant the application of Fascist methods in Britain by a constitutional government.

The attitude of the ruling class to the new scheme was revealed by their politicians. Mr. R. Hudson, parliamentary secretary to the Minister of Labour, addressing a meeting of the South Wales Conservative Association on 27th September, 1934, said, "The new unemployment Act is the best Act of our generation, because it would provide discipline and instruction to the unemployed youth." As early as 11th March, 1934, the *People* quoted Sir John Gilmour, then home secretary, as having described the proposed labour camps as "concentration camps." In our propaganda against the camp scheme we said, "If the government has work for the unemployed to do, we are pleased to welcome it, but we insist that such work must be paid for at full trade union rates of wages and conditions, so that the unemployed engaged on such work can live their lives as normal wage-earners."

Meanwhile the organised unemployed continued to demand improved conditions. On 1st October, 1934, 1,000 unemployed marchers from all parts of Monmouthshire marched to Newport. They demanded from the Monmouthshire County Council (1) that all relief scales should be increased to the minimum of standard unemployment benefit; (2) that there should be no task work or slave camps, and that full scales of relief should be provided for all those who refused to go to the camps; (3) a non-contributory medical scheme for all unemployed and families; (4) full relief scales for all miners when on strike.

Two days later a county march to Forfar took place, with contingents from Dundee, Blairgowrie, Montrose, Ferryden and Arbroath. The county council received a deputation and stated that the marchers' demands would be considered. At the end of the interview the deputation demanded that the fares of the marchers should be paid home, but the county council said that this was a matter for the P.A.C. The P.A.C. held out against the demand, and the marchers paraded the streets of Forfar throughout the day until in the evening the P.A.C. climbed down and paid the fares. On 8th October, a district march took place to Bridgend, South Wales, from Maesteg, Ogmore, and Garw Valley, to demand increased winter relief. Exactly twelve months previously a similar march had been broken up by heavy police cordons and the use of a police aeroplane that repeatedly swooped down to within twenty yards of the heads of the marchers in an effort to disperse them. On that occasion the marchers were prevented from reaching Bridgend. The use of the police aeroplane led to strong protests, particularly throughout South Wales; the miners discussed strike action as a protest, and demanded the dismissal of the chief of police responsible for these tactics.

In the 1934 march plans were made by the movement to overcome any similar attempt to disperse them. They succeeded in reaching Bridgend; their deputation met the Public Assistance Committee and demanded a ten per cent increase in relief scales; the refusal of the council to operate Part II of the Unemployment Act; no victimisation for refusing to enter the slave camps; and dismissal of the Caerau relieving officer for reducing the scales of relief. The vote was taken in the P.A.C. and the demands were rejected by twelve votes to nine.

On 10th October a march of Rhondda unemployed took place to demand extra winter relief from the urban district council. Next day, Glasgow was on the march to the city chambers. The city council, after hearing the deputation, agreed to appoint a special committee to deal with the demands. In the first week of November, under pressure of unemployed agitation, the Sheffield Public Assistance Committee granted 2s. a week extra winter relief to all applicants. Dumbartonshire County Council at the same time granted 2s. 9d. a week extra allowance for all unemployed.

So the agitation for improved scales continued in all the industrial centres, with varying successes. About this time the government began to conduct propaganda directed towards showing that the scales of unemployment benefit and relief were not low, but that the average working-class housewife lacked the knowledge of food values and therefore did not buy the right sort of food to keep the family healthy.

This brought forth a strong reply from Dr. J. R. Marrack,

professor of chemical pathology in the University of London, who, speaking at the Ruskin College, Oxford, on 9th October, said, "No amount of education in food values or instruction in cooking will make it possible to feed a child on 2s. or a family on 3s. a head per week. The best protection against disease is to be the child of well-to-do parents." Then came an article in the *Lancet* written by Dr. Helen M. M. McKay, physician to the Queen's Hospital for Children, London, in which she said, "It is scarcely necessary here to emphasise the fact that it is quite impossible for the wife of a man on unemployment benefit or relief to feed her family adequately unless she has some other source of assistance. An inadequate diet is, week in and week out, the daily lot of very many of our people."

On 8th, 9th and 10th December, 1934, the ninth national conference of the N.U.W.M. was held in the Keir Hardie Hall, Derby. Realising how grave was the situation facing the unemployed, particularly in respect to the operation of Part II of the Unemployment Act, the conference passed a resolution for united action addressed to the General Council of the Trades Union Congress. In this we said, "To secure the fullest co-operation of all working-class organisations for action against the Act in the various localities we strongly urge the General Council of the T.U.C. to give its support to the fight of the N.U.W.M. and to advise its constituent bodies to carry out, with the N.U.W.M., a proposal designed to ensure mass refusals of the unemployed to enter the slave camps with the guaranteed support of all employed workers."

The resolution also requested a meeting between representatives of the N.U.W.M. and the T.U.C. General Council. To this appeal for unity in face of the common danger which was threatening not only the unemployed but the employed workers, we received the following remarkable reply:

Dear Sir,
I am in receipt of your letter of the 13th December, forwarding the resolution passed by your organisation at its conference held in Derby from the 8th to 10th December.
Acting under instructions, I have to inform you that I cannot in future reply to communications from your organisation.
(*Signed*) Walter M. Citrine,
Secretary.

Immediately following this correspondence, the government made known the new scales and regulations in respect to Part II of the Unemployment Act. The whole country was shocked by the new conditions. The reductions per week in the scales of allowances were as follows:

	s.	d.
Man and wife	2	0
Single adult male, living with family	7	0
Second and subsequent members of family	9	0
Single female worker, living with family	7	0
Subsequent females living with family	8	0
Youths, 18 to 21 years of age	6	0
Girls, 18 to 21 years of age	5	0
Boys, 16 to 18 years of age	3	0
Girls, 16 to 18 years of age	1	6

To offset the severity of this attack the government cunningly endeavoured to make it appear that they were being liberal in respect to the children, to whom the following increases were made:

	s.	d.	
Between 11 and 14 years of age ..	2	6	a week increase
,, 8 and 11 ,, ,, ,, ..	2	0	,, ,, ,,
,, 5 and 8 ,, ,, ,, ..	1	6	,, ,, ,,
Under 5	1	0	,, ,, ,,

If there were more than five members of a family, then 1s. was to be deducted from the total payment for each member in excess of five. In addition to these heavy cuts in the scales, a harsher means test was to be imposed. Under the old means test local public assistance committees had certain discretionary powers. It is true that the National government persistently brought pressure to bear upon them to apply a uniform system, but they never succeeded in securing this.

Under the new scheme they sought to remedy this "weakness" in administration by laying down rigid regulations for the operation of the means test by the local officers of the Unemployment Assistance Board. Here are some examples of the way in which this means test was to operate. The whole family was to undergo an assessment, based upon the amount that would be received if all the members of the family were unemployed and without any other means of subsistence and in receipt of an Unemployment Assistance Board allowance. The Board would then inquire into the items of family income. Of the earnings of wife, husband, father or mother, all over the first 5s. earned must be counted, or one half, whichever was the less. This meant that only 5s.

of each member's wage was recognised as belonging to him or her; the rest must go towards maintaining the unemployed members of the family. In the case of the wages of son, daughter, brother or sister, two-thirds of the first 20s. was to be assessed and three-fourths of all over the first 20s. This meant that if a relative in this category earned £2 a week, only 6s. 8d. in the first £1 and 5s. in the second £1 would be recognised as belonging to him personally; all the rest would go to the family and become a determining factor in regard to the claim of the unemployed member of the family on unemployment allowance.

If the amount taken into consideration exceeded the amount of the scale allowance for the unemployed member of the family, then that member would receive no allowance whatever. Items of income other than wages—such as unemployment insurance, widows' pensions, old age pensions, superannuation pay, etc.— received by other members of the family were to be assessed at the full amount, less one-third of the difference between this amount and the allowance which would be received if the person in question was himself or herself receiving an unemployment allowance. This meant that if an adult male member of the family had an income of, say, 20s. a week in respect to the items mentioned, 16s. 8d. of this £1 would be assessed. In the case of any relative in receipt of poor law relief, the whole amount would be assessed.

Then there was a tricky regulation known as the "basic rent allowance." Many unemployed had been led to believe that they were going to have their rent paid as well as receiving a cash allowance, but they found that the basic rent allowance was in fact part of the scale payment and not something in addition to it.

The way in which this worked was as follows: where the assessment of the family was over 24s. and below 30s. an assumed basic rent allowance of 7s. 6d. was included in that scale. Where the actual rent paid was in excess of the assumed basic rent allowance the scale could be increased by up to one-third of the basic rent allowance, but no more. Where the assessment was over 30s. a week the assumed basic rent allowance was 7s. 6d. plus a quarter of the excess over 30s. The following is an example: If a family was assessed at 40s. a week, the assumed basic rent allowance would then be 10s. If the family were actually paying £1 in rent, as many families in the London area are, they could then be granted up to 3s. 4d. on top of their allowance. If the rent was below 10s., as it is in the provinces in some cases, then the difference between the assumed basic rent allowance and the actual rent paid was deducted from the scale payment, which meant that if the rent they paid was 6s., 4s. would be deducted. The same principle applied if the assessment was below 30s. An example of the way this would work out is as follows: The total scale received by a man, wife, son twenty-one years of age, and one seventeen years of age, would be 40s. per week. If that family was paying a rent of 6s. a week, their scale would be reduced by 4s.

In the case of claimants assessed below 24s. a week, the assumed basic rent allowance would be 7s. 6d., less a quarter of the amount of the difference between the assessment and 24s. For example: If the assessment were 14s. (such as a female householder would receive) the difference is 10s. In that case the basic rent allowance would be only 5s. If more than 5s. was actually being paid in rent, no matter how high it was, no more than one-third of the 5s. could be granted on top of the scale allowance.

The reader will easily realise that this system of complicated computation was extremely confusing to many of the unemployed; they simply did not know what they were entitled to, and very little effort was made by the government to explain the matter to them. They saw the U.A.B. officials working out tables of assessments which, with all the involved additions and subtractions, left them bewildered. There can be no doubt that the effect of this assumed basic rent allowance was to assist the landlords to obtain their rent. There was, in fact, a condition in the Act that, although the rent allowance was only an assumption, the U.A.B. could demand the production of the claimant's rent book for examination, and if it was found that the rent was not being paid the amount could be deducted from the allowance, and arrangements made with the landlord for its payment. Such was the Act which Mr. Hudson, the parliamentary secretary to the Ministry of Labour, had described as the "best Act of our generation."

On 17th December, immediately following the publication of the U.A.B. regulations, a big demonstration of unemployed marched to the Glasgow P.A.C. Following an interview the P.A.C. sent telegrams to the prime minister and members of parliament, declaring their opposition to the new scales. At the same time, in Monmouthshire, a conference of local authorities denounced the scales as "additional brutality." In Hull, the home of Councillor T. Ellis, who was a member of the Public Assistance Committee, and who had publicly advocated support for the means test, was attacked by an unemployed demonstration, walls and railings being smashed down before the police could disperse the crowd.

The Norwich City Council, at its meeting on 19th December, passed a resolution denouncing the new scales. Similar protests were coming from all parts of the country. On Saturday, 5th January, 1935, a special meeting of the executive of the South Wales Miners' Federation decided to call an All-South Wales conference against the new scales and to decide on lines of action. 7th January, 1935, the date for the operation of Part II, saw the unemployed responding everywhere to the call of the N.U.W.M. for a national day of demonstration. In sleet and rain the unemployed marched in protest against these new attacks. The agitation gathered momentum day by day: at the end of the week, when the unemployed received their allowances under the U.A.B., they were staggered at the severity of the cuts that had been imposed. In places where the whole family were unemployed, such as the distressed areas of South Wales, Tyneside, Cumberland and Scotland, the cuts imposed were drastic. For instance, a father, mother, two adult sons and two adult daughters would have their family income reduced by at least 33s. There were many cases reported where the family income was reduced by as much as 36s. a week.

In addition to the heavy cuts in scales, wholesale disallowances from benefit took place by the operation of the new rigid means test. By the middle of January thousands of unemployed were marching daily in every town throughout the country. Harry McShane was arrested on a charge of obstruction after a huge meeting on the 16th January outside the Springburn labour exchange. When he was taken to the police station a demonstration of 2,000 marched behind the police.

On Sunday, 20th January, 60,000 unemployed and employed workers marched in the Rhondda Valley to Pontypridd in a great united front demonstration. In all the pits and miners' lodges strike action was being discussed. At this time I was conducting a campaign in Cumberland. Thousands were rallying to the meetings to hear the message of the N.U.W.M. On the evening of 21st January, I was addressing my last meeting in this campaign in Maryport. A telegram arrived just before 10 p.m. and was delivered to the chairman of the meeting. It was a request that I should be in Merthyr, South Wales, next day, for a great demonstration. The telegram was read to the meeting and a resolution of solidarity from Cumberland was sent to Merthyr; but the chairman announced that it was now too late for me to catch a railway connection that would enable me to reach Merthyr in time. Then a well-dressed man in the audience rose and said that it could be done if I caught the Night Scot from Carlisle to London and then caught the 8.55 train in the morning from London to South Wales. He offered to drive me in his car from Maryport to Carlisle in an effort to catch this train. The audience warmly responded to this suggestion as evidence of their solidarity with their comrades who were marching in Wales. I was informed that the man who had offered help was an employer of labour who was warmly sympathetic to the working-class movement.

We terminated the meeting by the singing of the "International" and I made a dash for Carlisle, reaching the station just as the train steamed in. In the Merthyr demonstration next day 40,000 workers marched from the outlying mining villages into Merthyr. For many this meant a march of sixteen miles there and back, yet many women took part in that march along with their menfolk. All sections of the working-class movement participated, and the demonstration had to be accommodated on the Pendaren football ground, which was next to the U.A.B. offices. But the Labour Member of Parliament, Mr. S. O. Davies, had apparently under-estimated the feeling of revolt which existed, and when, a few days previously, he had been invited to join the demonstration he had refused to do so, declaring that it was a communist activity. His absence from the demonstration caused widespread hostile comments by the workers.

The deputation, headed by Jack Williams of Dowlais, met the U.A.B. officials and demanded the withdrawal of Part II and the restoration of the cuts. Williams said: "The Act is so rotten it cannot be amended; it must be ended."

The U.A.B. officials took shorthand notes of the speeches made by the deputation and promised that a full report would be forwarded to the government. Great mass meetings were held on the football ground whilst we awaited the return of the deputation; then a pledge was given by the crowd to keep up the fight until the Act was withdrawn.

Two days later 20,000 Glasgow workers marched to the city council, and 20,000 workers in Pontypridd marched the streets demanding the withdrawal of the Act. Tory members of parliament who had ventured into their constituencies to attempt to explain the Act were being howled down everywhere. The whole country was aflame against the government. Hundreds of thousands were now marching. In South Wales, particularly in the Rhondda Valley, the tramp of tens of thousands was heard day after day. Even the shopkeepers closed their shops and joined the demonstrations. They knew what this new attack would mean to them, that more little shopkeepers would be driven out of business by the poverty of the people and their inability to purchase goods. Doctors also marched; they knew that the new scales meant increased difficulties for them in their desperate efforts to protect the health standards of the people against the ravages of poverty. Teachers, who had the difficult problem of endeavouring to educate half-starved children, knew that their task would become still more onerous under the new scales, so they too joined in the demonstrations. Employed workers, who found that they were being compelled to maintain their unemployed relatives out of their meagre wages, joined with the unemployed. Reactionary trade union officials who had stead-fastly declared that they would not stand on a public platform with revolutionary workers found themselves caught up in the stream and carried forward to participation in great united front demonstrations.

On 26th January 1,600 delegates gathered at the All-South Wales conference in Cardiff, called by the South Wales Miners' Federation, against the new Act. The anthracite miners came to the conference calling for a twenty-four hours' strike in South Wales. They found great support amongst hundreds of the delegates, but the platform urged that strike action should not be supported at that juncture, but that a council of action should be set up to develop the agitation further and to send a deputation to the Ministry of Labour.

On the same day the Scottish national council of the N.U.W.M. decided to organise a Scottish hunger march of 3,000 unemployed to arrive in Glasgow on 17th March. On Monday, 28th January, the London unemployed invaded the House of Commons to protest to their M.P.'s against the new Act. In the gallery of the House fighting broke out when unemployed shouted, "You cowardly lot of rotters!" "Down with the Unemployment Act!" Then the Cambrian Combine miners, in the Rhondda, raised a call for strike action on 25th February if the government did not withdraw Part II. In the House of Commons on 30th January Members of Parliament quoted astounding cases of reductions in family income in their constituencies and called on the government to withdraw the Act.

When the U.A.B. regulations had been issued the government had declared that they were final and unalterable, but under the pressure of the mighty agitation which was sweeping the country the government now began to wilt. It announced that it was issuing instructions to the local U.A.B. officers to ease the situation in the following way:

1. Related families living together to be relieved of full rigour of family means test.
2. Slightly increased assessments for large families.
3. Where the U.A.B. assessment was lower than the old P.A.C. scale by a small amount, the old allowance to stand.

But this niggardly concession did not touch the fringe of the problem. The storm continued and became stronger.

On 31st January 10,000 unemployed marched on the streets of North Shields, breaking the police ban which had stood for a long time against any demonstrations in this town. The police were helpless to maintain the ban in face of the deep resentment amongst the workers. The unemployed marched to the docks and called for strike action of the dockers. In the evening they marched to the town council and the deputation declared at the interview that the workers would hound out of the town all councillors who refused to fight the new Act.

On 1st February an attempt was made by the U.A.B. authorities in the Rhondda to send fifty lads to a labour camp. Within half an hour of this being known a demonstration of protest marched on the streets. The lads were already in the bus about to depart, but they were persuaded to refuse to go, and were promised protection in their refusal.

Up to 1st February, in spite of this nation-wide agitation, which surpassed anything of its kind ever known before, the Trades Union Congress General Council and the Executive of the Labour Party had given no lead whatsoever to the workers. T.U.C. headquarters had, in fact, threatened the disaffiliation of the Abertillery Trades Council for participation in the great united front demonstrations in the Monmouthshire valley. To the credit of the trades council, they defied this threat, and Mr. J. T. Davies, at a trades council meeting, declared: "I would welcome being thrown out of an organisation which could not stand up for justice for the working class."

In a letter to the T.U.C., the trades council said:

"In our opinion the T.U.C. has been, to say the least of it, very timid indeed and has taken the line of least resistance. When the Bill had passed through the House of Commons it seems that the official movement had accepted the defeat and the only hope that they gave was 'Wait for a Labour Government with a majority.' That, in our opinion seems to be the policy of the T.U.C. They never gave a lead to the workers to fight and resist this attack. They let the matter slide out and hoped for the best, but the workers, employed and unemployed, wanted and demanded action. They wanted to fight and resist this damnable and iniquitous measure. . . . The workers were roused and embittered at this attack on them and they wanted a lead.

Take our local position; before the Council took an official part in this present movement, seven thousand employed and unemployed demonstrated to the Unemployment Assistance Board offices on this matter. The N.U.W.M. initiated this movement and it gained mass support. Then the Council associated itself with the united front, which embraced all organisations, including ministers of the church and shopkeepers. This movement has extended right throughout the country. . . .

We call upon the T.U.C. to get on with the fight and continually demand the entire repeal of this act, even to the extent of calling a one-day general strike. In the meantime our people are suffering hardship. All we ask for is action. . . ."

The letter was signed by L. Hill, secretary of the Abertillery Trades Council. To this letter, Mr. E. M. Harris, secretary of the organising department of the T.U.C., sent the following astonishing reply:

Dear Mr. Hill,

I have your letter informing me that your Council consider that the actions of the General Council over the regulations issued by the Unemployment Assistance Board have been slack and without vigour and that your Council have consequently allied themselves with the united front. It appears that your Council feel that the action taken by a few Communists in South Wales is of more importance than the deputation to the Minister of Labour and the debates in the House of Commons—a point of view with which I can only express surprise.

I also note with astonishment that you appear to blame the General Council in some mysterious way or other because the National Unemployed Workers' Movement took the local initiative in organising agitation against the regulations issued by the Unemployment Assistance Board. It is surely not unreasonable to ask that our Trades Council themselves should be capable of taking initiative in a local situation and should not always depend upon instructions from Headquarters. . . .

The fact that your Council are connected with the united front will be reported to the appropriate committee of the General Council at their next meeting.

Such was the remarkable correspondence passing between the T.U.C. and a trades council at the very time when millions of workers were stirring and marching throughout England, Scotland and Wales against the National government. It seemed that political bias was completely blinding such men as Mr. Harris to the ferment in the country. The *Manchester Guardian*, which was not likely to exaggerate the position, in its issue of 4th February, estimated that no less than 300,000 workers were marching in South Wales on Sunday, 3rd February. Yet Mr. Harris calls this "the action of a few Communists!"

The National Council of Labour, representing the T.U.C., the Labour Party and the Co-operative Society, broke the silence in regard to the fight against Part II on 1st February, when it issued what it was pleased to call an "Appeal to the Public Conscience." It was the most empty and harmless document that had ever been issued in the working-class movement. It called for no action whatsoever, the strongest passage in it being an appeal to the clergy to focus public attention on the hardship caused by the new unemployment regulations. It contributed absolutely nothing to the struggle which was raging against the government.

On 4th February a big demonstration of women to the U.A.B. took place in Merthyr. Mothers with babies in arms marched many miles to protest against the new starvation conditions which had been inflicted upon them. Whilst they were outside the offices of the U.A.B. somebody pointed to an official who was looking out of the window and who appeared to be sneering at them. This incensed the women, whose cup of bitterness was already overflowing, and instantly a rush took place leading to the smashing of the windows and doors of the U.A.B. offices. The police made several arrests, but the women fought with such determination that they compelled the police to release every one of those under arrest. Only with the greatest of difficulty were the police able to protect the U.A.B. officials from violent assault.

The same day unemployed stormed the town hall in Llanelly, West Wales; in Tyneside, 30,000 marched on the streets till late at night. Similar great demonstrations were marching throughout the towns of Scotland, Lancashire, Notts and Derby, Cumberland, Cheshire, Yorkshire and the Midlands. Day by day the demonstrations were increasing in size, the bitterness was becoming deeper and an almost reckless determination was growing amongst the workers.

On 5th February the National government had to bow before

this mighty storm. In the House of Commons, Mr. Oliver Stanley, Minister of Labour, announced that the scales and regulations under Part II of the Unemployment Act would be withdrawn, that the old scales would come back into force, and that the cuts that had been taken from the unemployed would be repaid. The mass action of the workers had conquered over the forces of reaction represented by the National government! A wave of rejoicing swept throughout the country, but the agitation was continued to demand the complete repeal of Part II of the 1934 Act.

Mr. Oliver Stanley, in announcing the withdrawal of the scales and regulations, had stated that it would not be possible to restore the cuts by the next pay-day, but that the change would be effected in approximately two weeks. Next day a demonstration was due to take place in Sheffield, with contingents from the outlying areas. Learning of the government's withdrawal of the scales, our Yorkshire district secretary, Len Youle, sent a telegram to national headquarters, asking for advice whether they should go on with the demonstration.

We wired back: "Carry through demonstration, make the demand immediate restoration of the cuts." This order was obeyed, and 40,000 unemployed iron and steel workers of Sheffield, along with Yorkshire miners, marched to the city hall to demand that the city council should immediately make up the cuts to the unemployed and recover this expenditure from the government. Huge forces of police had been drafted into the town, but the unemployed succeeded in pressing their way forward to the city hall. A deputation went forward in an effort to secure an interview with the Public Assistance Committee; this was refused, and the police were called in to eject the deputation.

As the deputation were being removed, large forces of police suddenly opened an attack. Mounted and foot police rode in freely, using their batons on the heads and shoulders of the crowd. The workers fought back desperately; so determined was their resistance that they held the streets against the police for over three hours, again and again rallying their forces and engaging in hand to hand fights with the police. Many on both sides were seriously injured. The word was put round that the demonstrators should mobilise at Barkers Pool, a favourite public meeting-place in Sheffield. The message spread from mouth to mouth, and within half an hour it is estimated that thirty thousand workers had gathered at the Pool.

Len Youle and George Fletcher rose to address the crowd and

to arrange for an orderly march out from Sheffield. The chief of the police, with other officers, pushed forward to the platform and gave the order that no public meeting was to be held and that the crowd must immediately disperse. An angry shout went up from the workers and they made ready to fight again; they insisted on their right to hold this great protest meeting and then to march to their respective localities. The police were compelled to give way, and the workers, who had fought for three hours on the streets of Sheffield, were not dispersed like a disorderly army, but marched out as they had come in, in an orderly fashion, with banners flying. Twenty-two workers had been arrested.

Sheffield is a great iron and steel town; it is the centre of the war industries of Britain, and the severity of the struggle which had raged that afternoon between the unemployed and the police caused grave alarm amongst the Sheffield authorities and at Westminster. The city council, which had refused to receive the deputation and thereby caused the battle on the streets, appointed a deputation of city councillors, headed by the lord mayor, to travel to London that night in order to meet the Minister of Labour and the U.A.B. and urge that they be granted powers immediately to make up the cuts in Sheffield. They went back to Sheffield with the authority of the government to do so, and in the House of Commons on 8th February the government announced that it had given this authority.

The unemployed movement followed up with telegrams to all its sections to raise the demand for the same treatment throughout the country as had been granted in Sheffield. Within twenty-four hours huge demonstrations were taking place in all the principal towns of the country. The Cumberland Public Assistance Committee, at its meeting on 8th February, defied the orders of the U.A.B. and decided to pay the full scales. On 10th February, Mr. Oliver Stanley, Minister of Labour, visited Newcastle-on-Tyne, to speak in the city hall. A great demonstration of unemployed marched through the streets to the hall and no meeting was held; the Minister of Labour was howled down.

The same day, which was a Sunday, the Stoke-on-Trent Public Assistance Committee offices were opened all day making up the cuts to the unemployed. It was another big day of demonstration. Next day in Maryport, Cumberland, the local Public Assistance Committee refused to carry out the decision of the Cumberland P.A.C. to restore the cuts immediately. A demonstration marched to the relief offices; they broke through police cordons, smashed the relief offices and chased the police through the town. At the end of the day the P.A.C. gave in and agreed to make up the cuts. Nobody had been arrested; the workers had prevented this; but the N.U.W.M. committee expected that some attempt might be taken by the police to effect the arrest of the leaders during the night. They therefore had made arrangements for street stewards to blow horns and whistles if the police took any action. Shortly after 11 p.m., when all was quiet in the streets, the police visited the homes of three leaders—Rafferty, McCowan and Telfer—and placed them under arrest.

The signals were immediately sounded throughout the town, and before midnight thousands of people had turned out and marched to the police station to demand the release of the prisoners. The demonstration continued through the night, increasing in size. At 1 a.m. the police superintendent attempted to address the crowd and to urge them to disperse; he was howled down. Before morning, the prisoners were all released on bail. Next day, a severe baton charge took place against a demonstration in Dundee, and six leaders of the N.U.W.M. were arrested, five men and one woman—Stewart, McCaffrey, Mathers, George Stalker and Mrs. Stalker.

The case of the Maryport workers was to be heard in the court on 15th February. Huge police reinforcements poured into the town the night before. The whole town was in a ferment. Headquarters of the movement arranged with the Council of Civil Liberties for the lawyer, Dudley Collard, to travel up by the night train in order to defend the men in the court. A big demonstration met him at the station, at eight o'clock in the morning; they later marched to the police court. All prisoners were found not guilty and were shouldered high through the town. On the same day the government had to agree that the cuts should be restored everywhere immediately and a standstill order had to be introduced into Parliament to legalise the suspension of the scales under Part II of the Unemployment Act.

On 19th February the twenty-three Sheffield workers appeared in court. Most of them had their heads swathed in bandages; they alleged that they had been subjected to severe police beatings in the police station after their arrest. They were all subsequently fined and released. The case of the workers arrested in Dundee came up in court on 22nd February. The cross-examinations and the speeches of the prisoners took nearly twelve hours; the court did not rise until 9.40 in the evening; the press claimed that it was a record Dundee trial. At the end of the case four of the accused were fined £1 each, one was fined 10s., and the other was admonished. There can be no doubt that these light sentences were due to the tremendous feeling which was being expressed by the workers everywhere against the policy of the government in relation to the unemployed.

The government was severely shaken and on the verge of collapse. The Minister of Labour had to admit that a blunder had been made, but he tried to hedge by stating that "the new regulations were sound in principle, but the grievances were due to the rigidity in administration and the mistakes inherent in a large and new measure." News leaked out that the Unemployment Assistance Board's original scales had been rejected by the government as too liberal. When the government had to answer this charge, it twisted and squirmed in an effort to avoid its responsibility. Scenes took place in the House of Commons when demands were made that the government should publish the facts and show who was responsible.

An attempt was made to pass the responsibility off on to the U.A.B. officials, and this drew forth strong protests and letters in the press from the civil servants' associations. The civil servants pointed out that the Unemployment Assistance Board had insisted that the regulations should be strictly enforced and that they had to obey orders from those in higher authority. The government were in a very dangerous position; they had had to retreat before the mass attack of the workers, and now they were endeavouring to shift the responsibility on to the shoulders of others. They ultimately found a scapegoat in the form of the Minister of Labour, and some time later he was relieved of his position and replaced by Mr. Ernest Brown.

I think it is unquestionable that, had the official leaders of the T.U.C. and the Labour Party clearly identified themselves with the great struggle which was raging and given leadership in the struggle, the government could have been overthrown at a moment when it was thoroughly discredited and could no doubt have been replaced by a strong Labour government, pledged to a policy of protecting and advancing the standards and conditions of the working-class.

The National Unemployed Workers' Movement continued the struggle against the government, long after the scales had been restored, with the demand that the whole of Part II of the 1934 Unemployemnt Act should be repealed. 24th February was again a national day of demonstration for the complete repeal of the Act; in towns throughout the country unemployed and employed workers marched side by side under the slogans of "Down with the Slave Act." The towns which were outstanding in big demonstrations that day were Liverpool, Manchester, Aberdeen, Glasgow, Sheffield, Bolton, Nottingham, Southampton, Hucknall, Port Talbot, Kilmarnock, Cowdenbeath, Arbroath, Saltcoats, Kirkcaldy and Newcastle-on-Tyne. In Hull a big demonstration came in conflict with the police. In Cumberland a district march took place to Workington. In London thousands marched to Hyde Park. Clashes occurred with the police in the park and eight arrests were made.

Next day, the national deputation, consisting of representatives sent to London by the big provincial demonstrations, made an effort to meet Sir Henry Betterton, now Lord Rushcliffe, at the central U.A.B. offices. The deputation got into the U.A.B. offices at Thames House, but only minor officials were available for the interview. In the evening, a demonstration broke the police ban and marched through Whitehall; there were scenes in the House of Commons and protest leaflets were showered on the chamber from the public gallery. Now that the government had restored the scales, the strike of the Cambrian Combine miners had been postponed for one month, awaiting the new announcement of the government.

On 26th February 8,000 unemployed marched in Wigan to the P.A.C. offices. In Glasgow the city chambers were rushed by a demonstration of unemployed, and the authorities compelled to relieve immediately many cases of destitution. In Nottinghamshire a county march was taking place and on this day entered the town of Nottingham, where they broke the police ban against organised marches to the shire hall. The county council met a deputation and heard the demand for full maintenance for all who refused the slave camps, and the complete repeal of Part II.

On 8th March thousands of Welsh women marched in the Rhondda Valley to the U.A.B. offices demanding complete abolition of the means test. Next day the first contingent in a great Scottish hunger march on Glasgow took the road from Aberdeen. As the days went by, other contingents from all parts of the Scottish industrial areas set out for Glasgow, 3,000 marchers in all. When the Aberdeen, Fraserburgh and Peterhead marchers reached Dundee, there were difficulties placed in their way in respect to accommodation. The mass support of the Dundee workers, mobilised on the streets behind the marchers, were so enthusiastic that at the end of the day the corporation authorities were forced to give accommodation to the marchers in Dunhope Castle, which had but recently been used as a military barracks. The marchers had created a tremendous stir in the jute town of Dundee, and, when they set out again to march to their next destination on the road to Glasgow, 25,000 Dundee workers marched with them on to the outskirts of the town. It was a fitting answer to the less militant workers in the Labour movement who were saying that the fight was over now that the scales had been withdrawn by the government.

On 18th March I visited the Monmouthshire valley for a campaign of meetings against the Act. Huge meetings were held in Blaina, Brynmawr, Nantyglo and Abertillery. I found that the unemployed in this valley were preparing for a big demonstration to the Public Assistance Committee to raise a number of local grievances in regard to the administration of relief. This demonstration was to take place on 21st March. Two days before this police-inspector Davis of Blaina visited the branch offices of the N.U.W.M. and read to the branch leaders a proclamation banning the demonstration. The news of the ban spread like wildfire throughout the valley. There was deep resentment at the attempt to deprive the workers of the right to march on the streets. I went from village to village throughout the valley addressing great meetings, at which the workers unmistakably displayed their determination to break the ban. Sometimes the meetings went on until late in the night. I was due to travel to Glasgow for the Scottish hunger march on the day that the demonstration was to take place, but, in view of the new situation which had arisen by reason of the police ban, it was my intention to remain in Monmouthshire. On the morning of the demonstration, however, the police informed the N.U.W.M. leaders that the ban had been lifted and that the demonstration would be allowed.

When I was informed of this I hurriedly arranged to depart for Scotland. Next morning, to my great surprise, I read in the newspapers of a terrific battle which had taken place in Blaina. The leaders of the march had been informed that the police ban was lifted and it would appear that this was a deliberate move on the part of the police to catch the demonstrators unprepared. The Nantyglo contingent, as they were marching into Blaina, were suddenly attacked and beaten up by the police. At this moment thousands were marching up the valley from Abertillery, and half-way to Blaina they found themselves confronted by huge forces of police who stood across the road and ordered them to disperse.

Before the workers could do this, the police opened an attack, mercilessly clubbing down men, women and youths. The Monmouthshire valley has great mountains rising up on either side of the road, and the workers took up their stand on the mountain-side and fought desperately with stones and boulders against the police. The press reported that over eighty policemen were seriously injured, but many workers were also badly hurt. After this battle, the Abertillery workers did not retreat, but scattered over the mountains to make their way in groups into Blaina, arriving to find that other contingents had been broken up in a similar way by the police.

No arrests had been made at that time, but twenty-one were later arrested. They were committed to the Monmouthshire Assizes, and when the trial ended several months later, on 19th July, four of the leaders, Abrahams, Madden, George Brown, and Langdon were sentenced to nine months, six months' sentences were passed on Jenkins, Legge, H. Lloyd, Thomas, C. W. Lloyd, and Jack Jones, the others receiving lesser terms of imprisonment. The defending counsel in the trial declared that there was evidence to show that the police had sought to inflict the most severe punishment upon the demonstrators in the baton charges.

On 24th March the whole of the Scottish hunger marchers arrived in Glasgow to demand a meeting with the Secretary of State for Scotland, Sir Godfrey Collins. It was a mighty demonstration, the biggest Glasgow has ever seen, which welcomed them into the city. The police estimate of the number of demonstrators was one hundred and sixty thousand. They marched from George's Square to Glasgow Green; the tail end of the demonstration was still coming into the Green when the big mass meetings were ending at 5.30 p.m.

Next day a demonstration of 80,000 marched to the city chambers and a deputation met the lord provost of Glasgow. The deputation consisted of Harry McShane, Stewart of Ayrshire, Chalmers of Edinburgh, Cooney of Aberdeen, Kerrigan of Glasgow, John McGovern, M.P., Councillor James Carmichael and myself. We protested against the failure of Sir Godfrey Collins to be present to meet us, and we stated our case for the complete withdrawal of Part II.

At the end of the interview the lord provost said, "I will communicate immediately with Sir Godfrey Collins and Lord Rushcliffe in London, and lay before them your demands, and immediately impress upon them your request for a deputation to be met by them." That same evening, tens of thousands of Glasgow workers marched, with bands and banners, along with the hunger marchers to the Kelvin Halls, where huge meetings were held before the marchers returned to their homes.

Such was the character of the agitation that continued against the government. For more than fourteen months the government was afraid to lift the stand-still order and make another attempt to reintroduce the scales and regulations for the full operation of Part II. On 4th July, 1935, the Unemployment Insurance Statutory Committee recommended an increase in the child dependent's allowance for all claimants drawing statutory benefit under the unemployment insurance scheme. It meant raising the allowance from 2s. to 3s. a week. The government was preparing for a General Election in November, and they deliberately held back the information concerning the extra shilling to the children until a few days before the election, then announcing that the increase should come into operation as from 31st October, 1935.

They could have granted the extra 1s. to the children immediately following the decision of the Unemployment Insurance Statutory Committee, but they were mean enough to withhold this from the families of the unemployed for three months and then to release the decision for vote-catching purposes. There can be no doubt that the persistent agitations conducted by the National Unemployed Workers' Movement in respect to the children's allowance was responsible for the decision which led to the increase, small as it was.

Chapter XIX

CONCLUSION—WHAT OF THE FUTURE?

IN the course of the past sixteen years many men and women have been driven to despair and suicide by poverty. How many more have suffered premature death as a result of starvation it is difficult to say, but there is sufficient evidence to indicate that the number must be staggering.

I have often heard it said that the unemployed are much better off to-day from the standpoint of benefit and relief scales than they were before the Great War. This is quite true; before the war only a small section of the workers were covered by unemployment insurance and the benefits were only 7s. a week with no dependents' allowance. But the point that has to be borne in mind in this respect is that since the war unemployment has been a constant problem in the lives of millions of our class, whereas previously the periods of unemployment were much shorter and the numbers affected were smaller.

The small improvement in unemployment relief may well be contrasted with the spectacular increase in the wealth of the capitalist class as a whole since 1913. Figures collected by the Labour Research Department from official government sources show the astonishing rise in the value of estates assessed at sums over £1,000 for estate duty. In 1913-4 there were 22,561 estates assessed at £263,000,000; the corresponding figures for 1933-4 showed 48,866 estates assessed at £486,000,000. From the stupendous increase in their wealth which these figures indicate the capitalist class has been forced by working-class pressure and their own fear of revolution to concede pitiful improvements in unemployment benefit to the masses who live on the borders of starvation.

The widespread and prolonged unemployment of the last fifteen years, which has meant that hundreds of thousands of workers have been out of work from one year to another, has undermined the whole family basis and slowly dragged these unfortunate workers into deeper and deeper poverty. The resources they may have had when their unemployment began

321

have now been completely exhausted, so that unemployment to-day, even though the scales are more generous than formerly, means much greater hardship and suffering.

In spite of this obvious fact the National Unemployed Workers' Movement has had persistently to force attention to the human needs of the unemployed when governments have sought to evade their obligations. Thousands of humans are alive to-day who would have been dead from starvation had there been no unemployed movement and no struggle.

Those who reveal their ignorance of past and contemporary working-class history by the question, "What good can these hunger marches and demonstrations do?" would do well to reflect upon the facts which I have endeavoured to record in the foregoing chapters. From these they will discern how the various governments in Britain since the world war have had to be compelled by organised mass pressure either to make concessions or to stay their hand when they were about to launch a new attack on the standards of the unemployed.

In fact, the whole of working-class history proves that the workers have never gained anything by way of improved standards, liberties or democratic rights, without persistent organisation and struggle. The ruling class have never given concessions to the subject class out of good-heartedness or human consideration. Right down the ages all improvements have had to be wrung from the ruling class by the organised strength and action of the workers. Every item of the boasted progressive or protective legislation of the past hundred years—the provision of public health, education, and the other social services—has been preceded by intense agitation, sometimes extending for years, on the part of the workers outside of Parliament. The enactment of such measures has always been simply a crowning triumph to the demands around which the workers have previously agitated. This has been the case in the past and will continue to be the case in the future, so long as control of the government rests in the hands of persons whose interests are inimical to those of the workers.

When unemployment reaches dimensions such as we have witnessed in this country since 1920 and persists from year to year the organisation of the unemployed within the general ambit of the working-class movement becomes an imperative necessity. But the task of organising the unemployed is not a simple one. One has first to contend with the fact that it is difficult for a person to think of his unemployment as a permanent feature in his life. It is a condition from which he is always striving to get away. The same person when working at his trade would readily recognise the need for organising in his trade union, because his trade is his means of livelihood and he knows that he needs to be permanently organised to protect his interests in industry. But in the field of unemployment it is only at critical moments when his standard is being attacked that he feels the need for the strength of organisation which he can gain by combination with his fellows who are in a like position.

Millions of workers have passed through membership of the National Workers' Unemployed Movement, but at no time has the standing membership approached even ten per cent of the vast masses of the unemployed. It is true that its influence extends far beyond its actual membership, as has been shown repeatedly in the struggles which the movement has conducted. There have been big achievements as a result of the work of the N.U.W.M., but how much more could have been done if the vast masses of the unemployed had been united in constant organisation and action!

The unemployed are constantly faced with the handicap of their domestic conditions. They are worried about their failure to secure work, and the effects of deepening poverty in their home. An organisation of the unemployed such as the N.U.W.M., which aims at keeping the unemployed in constant action against their conditions, is an important factor in preventing demoralisation.

One often hears well-intentioned persons remark that the unemployed are exhibiting a noble and courageous spirit by their passive endurance of poverty. I thoroughly disagree with such a sentiment. In fact, I contend that the peaceful toleration of poverty in an era of superabundance of all the common necessities of life is a certain sign of social degeneration on the part of society, and a form of demoralisation on the part of the unemployed who are the sufferers.

When a human being uncomplainingly endures pain and suffering that cannot be avoided he is certainly expressing a spirit which is courageous and praiseworthy. But to suffer grinding poverty through unemployment, for which he is not responsible; to feel the cold grip of destitution tightening about him day by day; to see his home wrecked and the health of his family broken, when he knows that the things which he so urgently needs exist in such quantities as the world has never known before—and yet to endure such a state of affairs without struggle amounts to demoralisation and might even be called cowardice.

Those who would persuade the unemployed to fit themselves passively into their conditions of poverty are simply perpetuating a system of injustice which is undermining the standard of life of the whole working class. In this age of plentiful production there is no justification for poverty. Therefore it is our duty to fight strenuously against poverty and not to treat its toleration as a virtue.

An even more serious danger is now revealing itself in Britain in the schemes of the government and of certain social service centres to encourage the unemployed to work without wages. This is particularly evident in the distressed areas. The government commissioners will make grants of thousands of pounds for such schemes of unpaid labour, but will not spend money on providing work for the unemployed on socially necessary schemes of employment at trade union rates of wages.

The government and the social service leaders advance the argument that it is better that the unemployed should be working, even though they are not receiving wages, than hanging about and doing nothing and becoming demoralised. But such an argument means that there are only two conditions from which to choose—complete idleness or work without wages. But one might well ask the question, "Have we arrived at the stage where vast masses of workers in this country are no longer entitled to work and earn their livelihood as they have normally done in the past?" If so, I can think of no stronger indictment of the system which presents such a situation for the working class.

Whatever the motives of those associated with the "work without wages" schemes may be, we cannot escape the fact that such schemes really mean demoralising the unemployed, de-classing them, turning them into a new slave class expected to toil in exchange for nothing more than their meals. Such a situation constitutes the gravest menace to the established wages and conditions which have been fought for and won by trade unionism in the past.

If we had in this country a government that was really determined to tackle the problem of unemployment from the standpoint of providing work for wages to the unemployed, there is much that could be done. Plans of socially necessary schemes of work have been drawn up from time to time by various bodies, but these plans still lie in the pigeon-holes of Whitehall. The National Unemployed Workers' Movement has itself put forward constructive proposals whereby at least a million unemployed workers could be provided with work at trade union rates of wages on public works schemes. It may be objected that the starting of such schemes would involve an enormous expense. We claim that a government concerned with solving the problem of unemployment should not boggle at raising the money for this purpose. It would, in the long run, prove to be very sound economy.

In addition to public works schemes there are other steps that could be taken at least to reduce unemployment, even though its ultimate removal may not be possible within the system of capitalism. There is the demand for the forty-hour working week without wage reduction. Such a demand is not only justified as a means of finding a place in industry for those who are now unemployed, but also on the grounds that the productive capacity per worker has been enormously increased in the last twenty-five years, and that this should carry with it shorter hours of labour and more leisure time, because of the greater intensity of toil.

Improvements in the old age pensions scheme could be used to mitigate unemployment. There are many thousands of aged workers who are still compelled to work in industry; otherwise they would starve. The amount of the old age pension should be increased and the age limit lowered to sixty years, so that these workers would be enabled to retire from toil in the autumn of their days and make way for young men in industry who are now unemployed. The extension of higher education for children and the raising of the school leaving age with government grants to the families would remove hundreds of thousands of juveniles from the labour market. Even legislation to grant holidays on full pay to all workers each year would not be without its effect in reducing unemployment.

All these measures are a rightful inheritance which the workers should enjoy. The Popular Front government in France has already tackled these questions and set an example to other nations. In the fight against unemployment in Britain we must not be content with developing the struggle to resist attacks upon our standards or to secure small improvements in scales of benefit, but we must energetically advance such constructive proposals as will rally the widest possible support for effectively combating unemployment. Organisation of the unemployed is essential if these questions are to be persistently pressed forward. But organising the unemployed has also taken on a new importance in the last three or four years. Germany has shown how, when capitalism has produced hopelessness and despair amongst the masses of the unemployed, the Fascists exploit their miseries, make specious promises to them which they never intend to keep, enrol them in the armies of Fascist storm troops—subsidised by the capitalist class—and use them to win power for the Fascist dictatorship over the working class. Having so used them, Fascism reduces them to deeper levels of poverty and starvation and drives them into forced labour camps.

Unless the unemployed are organised under the leadership of the working-class movement there is always the danger of their becoming the pawns of Fascist adventurers. The unemployed are naturally seeking a way out of their plight, and unless the working-class movement harnesses their discontent and directs it along correct working-class lines, providing them with leadership in their fight against starvation, they can easily become the victims of Fascist demagogy, with disastrous results such as we have seen in Germany.

I claim that where the unemployed exist every unorganised locality is a breeding-ground for Fascism. The question therefore arises—what sort of organisation should be created for the unemployed? It should be an organisation which can embrace the widest masses of the unemployed on a non-party programme directed towards removing the grievances of the unemployed and leading the struggle to compel the government effectively to combat unemployment

The seizure of power by Fascism in Germany was made possible by the disunity, hesitancy and doubts in the ranks of the workers, and in no small degree to the lack of real working-class organisation amongst the unemployed. In Britain equally there is division and disunity. There is, on the one hand, the National Unemployed Workers' Movement, which has been the only organised force that has consistently led the struggles of the unemployed for the last fifteen years. On the other hand there are the bodies known as "Unemployed Associations" under the control of the Trades Union Congress which were set up in 1930 with a constitution that makes them purely local bodies and which discriminate against Communists and other known militants. Then there are various unemployed clubs which serve no other purpose than that of providing on a small scale a social life for the unemployed. There are the social service centres, under the control of the National Council of Social Service, which are undoubtedly government-inspired and serve the purpose of helping to keep the unemployed quiet and even assist the government in its schemes of getting the unemployed to accept work without wages. A few trade unions have special unemployed sections, but they give only occasional attention to the question of leadership of the unemployed. All this means disunity. It causes perplexity in the minds of the unemployed themselves, so that by far the largest masses of the unemployed are not enrolled in any organisation, with the consequence that the struggle against unemployment is restricted and weakened.

There is an urgent need for ending this division and working towards the creation of one national movement of the unemployed with local, district and national machinery which can become an integral part of the trade union and Labour movement of this country.

The National Unemployed Workers' Movement has already pledged itself to the policy of unity, and it only requires the Trades Union Congress General Council to convene a conference of all unemployed organisations, out of which a united movement can emerge. Such a movement, with a national committee that is part of the Trades Union Congress machinery directing its activities, would become a powerful factor in the general working-class movement. Unity means something more than merely bringing together the existing organisations into one body. It would have an immediate psychological effect amongst the unemployed and the working class generally. It would stimulate and inspire the unemployed with a new confidence and new hope. It would ensure proper co-ordination in the struggles of the unemployed and the employed. It would draw the masses of unorganised unemployed into organised activity, and it would be the means of extensive recruitment of new members to the trade union movement.

Who in the ranks of the working class could dispute the importance of such an objective? The issues which are before the workers of Britain and every other capitalist country are so grave to-day—with the deepening effects of poverty through unemployment, the danger of war, and the increasing tendency on the part of the ruling class to resort to Fascist methods of government—that we should surely realise the need for utilising every available moment to complete the unity of our class and to strengthen the workers' forces with the aid of all other progressive sections of the community, to resist the common dangers which threaten to overwhelm us.

Even as I finish writing this book new struggles are opening on the question of unemployment. On 10th July, 1936, the Baldwin government published its new regulations in respect to all claimants under the Unemployment Assistance Board. Apart from some slight concessions the new scales and regulations are basically the same as those referred to in a previous chapter, which the government was compelled to withdraw in face of the working-class storm of opposition in February 1935.

The announcement of these new regulations has already produced nation-wide indignation amongst the workers. Thousands are moving into action again, particularly in South Wales. Mighty demonstrations are marching; proposals for another great national hunger march on London and for strike action to resist the new starvation scales of the government are current throughout the working-class movement.

If unity can be achieved and the struggle developed with all the strength that the present situation demands we can not only again compel the government to retreat in respect to these new regulations, but we can turn that retreat into a complete rout of the National government, and open the way for a mighty advance by the British working class against the forces of reaction towards a new era in which unemployment shall be only an evil memory of the past.

SELECTED INDEX

03954-3751
Robert.